Introduction to Couple Therapy and Counseling

A Case Study Approach

FIRST EDITION

Abbi Hattem

cognella® | ACADEMIC PUBLISHING

Bassim Hamadeh, CEO and Publisher
Kassie Graves, Director of Acquisitions and Sales
Jamie Giganti, Senior Managing Editor
Jess Estrella, Senior Graphic Designer
Kassie Graves, Director of Acquisitions
Christian Berk, Associate Production Editor
Gustavo Youngberg, Interior Designer

Printed in the United States of America.

ISBN: 978-1-5165-0969-0 (pbk) / 978-1-5165-0970-6 (br)

cognella® | ACADEMIC PUBLISHING

Introduction to Couple Therapy and Counseling

A Case Study Approach

CONTENTS

DEDICATION

This book is dedicated to the couples and students with whom I have had the privilege of working over the past 40 years. The courage of couple clients and the creativity of couple therapy students have been an inspiration.

ACKNOWLEDGEMENTS

It is customary for authors to thank their editors. Kassie Graves is very special and it's important to me that this acknowledgement not be perfunctory. Having shepherded a book I co-authored to print, Kassie was also incredibly supportive and helpful navigating this one. I very much appreciated her understanding of the changes in my life that slowed me down and her gentle prodding to set a reasonable time line despite all the distractions. The book would not have been written without her guidance during that time.

The production team at Cognella has been fabulous. I am especially grateful to Claire Benson, Jamie Giganti, Jess Estrella, Miguel Macias, Danielle Boag, Christian Berk and Dani Skeen for their wonderful work.

I am grateful to Judy Esposito for allowing me to use the case study couple from our family therapy textbook and for helping me brainstorm how Martin and Liz might have been earlier in their relationship. Judy has been there for me, as a colleague and friend, throughout the writing of this book. So often I missed our collaboration and wished we could have met to brainstorm and write together. I also want to thank Phil Miller for his very helpful feedback early in the process and Sage Publications, which published the family therapy book in which Liz and Martin got their start.

I have always been awed by the privilege of working with couples as they navigate their pain and confront destructive patterns of interaction. The couples with whom I have worked over the past 40 years have inspired me even as they have challenged me, forced me to stretch my skills and even the ethical tenets I hold dear, and broken my heart. They have stuck with me through the vicissitudes of my own stormy relationship history and through life changes including the death of both my parents, the births of my children, pregnancy loss, my nest emptying, and a sports injury. These couples are a testament to my ability to separate my own issues from my work with clients and to their own resilience when I've needed to be away from the office. I am grateful to them for the validation, for sharing their journey as well as their pain and their joy, and for teaching me to be a better couple therapist and human being.

I am also grateful to the many students I have had the privilege of teaching, supervising, and otherwise guiding to work more effectively with couples. Students who have shared their own doubts, challenges, and family stories and those who have experienced moments of insight have given me so much professional happiness. I have learned from you, even as I have "taught" you. And, looking back late in my career, I am hopeful that those of you who are still practicing are carrying on some of the approaches to couple therapy that are not always valued in the present funding climate.

Finally, I will always be indebted to my mentors, Sherrill Richarz, Carlfred Broderick, and Lawrence Allman. Their guidance, their encouragement, and their insight continue to be reflected in all my professional activities.

My friends and family have been patient and supportive when I've been consumed by writing and have been there to listen, laugh, and problem solve during the process of writing this book. I am very grateful to them all. Talking about the writing process with my journalist younger son and basking in the warmth and caring of the Hattem-Hyman clan has been supportive in ways I cannot verbalize. I would also like to thank Susan Goldstein and Bruce Hyman for their suggestions about pedagogy while I was thinking through the interactive components accompanying this book.

Most especially, I want to thank my husband, Bruce, for his patience throughout the process of writing and editing this textbook and our cats Rumpelteazer, Ashrei, and Sugar Ray for hanging out with me and helpfully sitting on the computer when it refused to write or needed a time-out. Without your love, caring, purring, and ability to listen uncritically, along with Kassie's gentle guidance and Judy's brainstorming sessions, I would never have finished.

INTRODUCTION

Several years ago, the writer collaborated with a colleague in the writing of a family therapy textbook (Esposito & Hattem, 2017). The logical next step was to codify her years of clinical experience, teaching, and studying couples in a textbook about couple therapy.

Dr. Esposito and the writer created a 17-year-old client. Christina Manning-Jones was a composite of self-revelations from our students' family reflection papers and our years of clinical experience. We then created a family around her, also based on composites of the families our students described and those of clients we had seen. Christina became what is termed the Identified Patient, or the one whose symptoms bring a family to family therapy, when she and her fictional family were referred for family therapy with a fictional family therapist. The family therapist was based upon our experience working in the field. Esposito and Hattem (2017) then used the family throughout the textbook to illustrate the theories and concepts of family therapy.

In this textbook, you will examine Christina's parents' couple therapy. Liz Manning-Jones and Martin Jones' couple therapy spanned a nine-year period beginning three months after Christina was born in 1993. One of the defining characteristics of their couple therapy was their hesitancy to remain in couple therapy long enough to address the issues that then continued to undermine their relationship.

Christina, her parents and siblings, and her extended family members were created and developed based upon the conceptual needs of the two textbooks. That none represents a specific client or student with whom either Dr. Esposito or the writer has worked cannot be overemphasized.

As you read this book, you will learn about core concepts in couple therapy. You will also learn about the theories and techniques upon which the field was founded and those that have arisen during its relatively brief history. Some of the newer, loosely termed post-modern theories of couple therapy have clear origins in the older, foundational theories.

You will also examine special issues relevant to couples who present for couple therapy and a range of services for which couple therapists refer. And you will examine the experience of the couple therapist who worked with Liz Manning-Jones and Martin Jones, as well as the ethics and statutes governing the practice of couple therapy.

This textbook is designed for those studying couple therapy on both an advanced undergraduate and beginning graduate student level. It addresses concepts, contexts, and the relationship between the field of couple therapy and a variety of other disciplines. The goal is to provide relevant background for those who will encounter couples during their work as couple therapists as well as in fields other than couple therapy, including family sociology, human development and family studies, public health, human service studies, social work, counselor education, psychology, medicine, and law.

You will be introduced to the concept of multicultural competence in working with couples. The importance of paying close attention to sociocultural contexts that affect couples and those who work professionally with them cannot be overstated. You will also explore the evolution of the concepts of coupling, marriage, and uncoupling from historical, sociological, and anthropological perspectives and the role of coupling in contemporary Western societies. By learning to view couples through a biopsychosocial lens, you will learn to recognize the intrapsychic functioning of the partners who comprise a couple, the partners' interpersonal dynamics, and the influence of societal, cultural, and temporal contexts upon couples.

The writer has chosen the term couple for a variety of reasons. The field of couple therapy continues to be referred to as marital therapy by licensing boards and professional organizations. However, it is inarguable that social changes in the last half century have led to unmarried couples presenting for couple therapy. Unmarried couples may have been denied the opportunity to marry, chosen not to marry, or consider marriage to be a future possibility. Unmarried couples who request couple therapy are as serious in their commitment, dynamics, and goals in seeking couple therapy as married couples who request couple therapy. Because using the terms marriage or marital therapy excludes and marginalizes an increasing segment of the population and diminishes unmarried partners' genuine commitments to each other, the term couple is used instead.

In the last decade or two, some professionals have referred to the field as relational therapy. The writer has chosen not to adapt the term relational because it implies a broader range of dyadic relationships. Roommates, colleagues, and friends all relate in pairs. Some of these pairings endure for many years. The term couple has the advantage of implying the emotionally and physically intimate nature of the dyadic relationship and, in many cases, the intention of permanence with or without a legal or spiritual marriage document.

The writer begins her classes about psychotherapy, whether the focus is on individuals, couples, or families, with the concepts of ambivalence and ambiguity. The human condition is fraught with both, and unless the professionals who serve human beings can tolerate their own and their clients' ambivalence, as well as the ambiguities of their situations, those professionals will become depleted and of little value to their clients.

You will be asked to begin a journal to use throughout this class and revisit during the concluding chapter of this textbook. You will be asked to include responses in your journal to the questions posed in a series of Stop and Think exercises throughout this book. You may also write your thoughts in your journal while reading other parts of the book and at any other time you find relevant.

Stop and Think:

Be sure to include your responses in your journal.

1. Begin by writing about your comfort and discomfort with ambivalence when you experience it and with ambiguity, or uncertainty about the future.
2. List your reasons for taking the class for which this book was assigned.
3. Describe your goals for yourself as a student in the class for which this book was assigned.

Schopenhauer's (1819/1969) philosophical work posited, among other things, that suffering derives from longing for that which one does not have. The reality of long-term coupling is that the romantic ideal, even if present at the inception of the relationship, changes as reality impinges. Creating and maintaining a home, employment, raising a family, managing resources, and interacting with both extended family and a larger community must be negotiated. The inevitable time demands of these, as well as each partner's individual preferences must be accommodated. Love and good will between partners ebbs and flows over a period of time. Thus, the particular moment in time during which a couple therapist works with a couple does not, in and of itself, reflect the partners' historical feelings toward one another. Much like Schröedinger's (1935) cat, the love, as well as the motivation to remain a couple, can appear to be both alive and not alive, leaving the couple therapist with the unanswered question of when and how potentially multiple shifts back and forth occur.

The ambivalence of couple intimacy often manifests in an approach-avoidance dance (Gottman & Gottman, 2008; Kantor, 2017; Kantor & Lehr, 1975; Lerner, 1990; Wile, 2013). Partners long to be emotionally intimate, yet such intimacy can be frightening for a variety of intrapsychic and interpersonal reasons. While Kantor and Lehr (1975) framed this ambivalence as one aspect of emotional distance regulation and Lerner (1990) framed it as a dance of intimacy, Luepnitz (2002) compared a couple's approach-avoidance behaviors to porcupines, who band closely together in cold weather to keep warm. When the porcupines begin to prick each other painfully with their quills, they move apart. However, as they move further away from one another, they lose the benefit of the others' body heat and move closer until once again the quills begin to cause pain. Others have described methods of distance regulation (Kantor & Lehr, 1975), including pursue-withdraw cycles in which one partner rejects the other's advances to maintain an emotionally comfortable distance between them.

Tolerating approach-avoidance and pursue-withdraw dynamics and each partner's anxiety about relinquishing these, even as they long for and fear true intimacy, is frequently the primary challenge for couple therapists. The couple therapist's goal is to guide the couple through their anxiety, any anger and sadness about the impact of their own and their partners' ambivalence upon them, and their patterns of interaction that interfere with resolving the intimacy dilemma and finding a balance that is neither so close as to ignite fear nor so distant as to trigger longing. This challenge for couples and their therapists requires tolerance both of the client couple's ambivalence and of the uncertainty, or ambiguity, about what the outcome of couple therapy will be.

The choice to become a couple therapist is both a personal and a professional one. Some students find the complexity of interpersonal dynamics fascinating, while others find the individual psyche more compelling. On a personal level, it may be safe to say that the choice of any profession is guided by an individual's sociocultural intersectional identity, experience, history, and personality. One goal of this textbook is to help you decide whether you wish to pursue a career in couple therapy or another profession that involves couple work, especially if you have not already chosen a professional goal.

This textbook is organized into three sections. Section I provides background, or a way in which to frame the couples you will see. Section II then adds theoretical models of couple therapy to your repertoire. Section III uses both to introduce the nuances of everyday practice.

Chapter 1 introduces you to the case study couple for which this book is named through the clinical perspective of their couple therapist. It includes descriptions of the details a couple therapist would need to know in order to assess and intervene most effectively with examples from Liz and Martin's couple therapy.

Chapter 2 includes a brief and necessarily cursory review of sociological, historical, and anthropological perspectives on coupling and uncoupling as a lens for viewing contemporary couples. Because its focus is the cultural and historical backdrop to the temporal period and spatial place in which you will practice, the emphasis is upon understanding the cultural context for the majority of couple clients with whom you are likely to work. The backdrop is at times focused on the dominant culture, for the simple reason that during points in history that was the only group being observed by a particular social science discipline. Salvador Minuchin, one of the founders of family therapy whose theory was adapted in the post-modern era for couple therapy, was the only foundational theorist to address cross-cultural issues. Couple and family therapy had their origins in mid-twentieth century US coastal culture, and it was likely because Minuchin himself was a Spanish-speaking immigrant that he was interested in low-income populations for whom English may not have been the first language.

In Chapter 3, you will be introduced to some of the assessment tools used in couple therapy and to the components of a therapeutic alliance with a couple. Students will become acquainted in both Chapter 1 and Chapter 3 with what couple therapists do once a couple seeking couple therapy arrives for the first appointment.

In Section II, you will read about foundational and post-modern theoretical perspectives on couples and couple therapy. Interventions grounded in the various theories will also be described, with transcripts from Liz and Martin's couple therapy used to illustrate how these interventions work in practice. Chapter 4 focuses on systems theory as applied to couples and as exemplified by Liz and Martin. The concepts and theoretical tenets of systems theory underlie all approaches to couple therapy and will provide you with the foundation you need to understand the more specific theories and their applications.

Chapter 5 describes behavioral and cognitive-behavioral couple therapy theory, while Chapter 6 focuses on three theories loosely related under the umbrella of psychodynamic theory. Though heavily experiential, the common denominator remains the interface between each partner's intrapsychic processes and the couple system. Chapter 7 discusses several post-modern theories. It also includes two family therapy foundational approaches to couple therapy that were not applied to couple therapy until after they were modified to include post-modern thought. Other approaches to facilitating positive change in couple dynamics, such as sex therapy and group couple therapy, are described in Chapter 8.

In Section III, you will be introduced to aspects of the practice of couple therapy beyond the fundamentals of assessment, theory, and intervention. Cultural competence, which is essential to the ethical practice of couple therapy, is described in Chapter 9, despite being relevant throughout the book. The writer believes that it may be easier for you to integrate the complexities of working with couples who do not fit the dominant cultural model after you have acquired knowledge of the theories, concepts, and practice that underlie couple therapy work. In addition to multicultural competence, race, gender, life cycle transitions, and various challenges couples may experience are introduced in Chapter 9.

Chapter 10 addresses the couple therapist's experience of doing couple therapy. As you may have concluded from reading about ambivalence and ambiguity, practicing couple therapy can be an intense experience. Additionally, a couple therapist brings who she or he is, his or her personal and relationship history, and her or his current situation to the work.

In Chapter 11, you will learn about legal statutes and ethics governing the practice of couple therapy. You will also read about how to manage the intensity of couple therapy using self-awareness and self-care.

Chapter 12 address professional services couple clients may need in addition to couple therapy. And finally, Chapter 13 addresses the conclusion of Liz and Martin's couple therapy and includes reflections about practicing couple therapy by student readers and the writer.

References

Esposito, J. & Hattem, A. (2017). *Introduction to family counseling. A case study approach*. Los Angeles CA: Sage Press.

Gottman, J. M. & Gottman, J. S. (2008). Gottman method couple therapy. In A. S. Gurman (Ed.). *Clinical handbook of couple therapy (4th ed.)*. New York NY: Guilford.

Kantor, D. (2017). The structural dynamics theory. Kantor Institute. Retrieved from http://www.kantorinstitute.com/fullwidth.html.

Kantor, D. & Lehr, W. (1975). *Inside the family. Toward a theory of family process*. San Francisco CA: Jossey-Bass.

Lerner, H. G. (1990). *The dance of intimacy. A woman's guide to courageous acts of change in key relationships*. New York NY: Perennial Library.

Luepnitz, D. A. (2002). *Schopenhauer's porcupines. Intimacy and its dilemmas*. New York NY: Basic Books.

Schopenhauer, A. (1819/1969). *The world as will and representation*. Translated by E. Payne. New York NY: Dover.

Schrödinger, E, (1935). Die gegenwärtige Situation in der Quantenmechanik (The present situation in quantum mechanics). *Naturwissenschaften*, 23, (48), 807–812. Bibcode:1935NW.....23..807S. doi:10.1007/BF01491891.

Wile, D. B. (2013). Opening the circle of pursuit and distance. *Family Process*, 52 (1). Retrieved from https://manhattanpsychoanalysis.com/wp-content/uploads/readings/Greenspun_COUPLES_SEMINAR%202014_15/WILE_Opening_the_circle_of_pursuit_and.pdf.

CHAPTER 1
Liz Manning-Jones and Martin Jones

COUPLE THERAPIST: What did you enjoy doing together when you were first dating?

MARTIN: [Smiling] Oh, wow. She was so beautiful.

LIZ: [Smiling] That's not what she asked.

MARTIN: I know, but you were. And smart. I'd been playing around a lot but hadn't found my intellectual equal till I met Liz.

LIZ: Yeah, your mom said that when you got the scholarship to [name of college] she knew you weren't going to meet a whole lot of black women, but then when you got the research fellowship to grad school she completely gave up.

CT: Liz, I notice you keep minimizing Martin's compliments.

LIZ: I do? Yeah, I guess I do.

CT: So, what else can you say to him?

LIZ: [Pause] I felt the same way. He was so handsome and confident. I was always attracted to competent people. I think I thought that way they wouldn't be like my father. And yes, he was smart. And not another law student.

MARTIN: [Reaches for her hand, smiles] Thank you, I guess. [To CT] We liked the same movies. And the same music.

LIZ: And he liked brunch. I've always loved brunch, and I loved going to brunch with Martin on the weekends after we'd been out with friends the night before. You know, reading the paper, talking.

Learning Objectives

1. Identify a couple's presenting problem.
2. Describe the history of the presenting problem.
3. Identify the sociocultural context of the couple.
4. Identify the components of a couple's social support network.
5. Understand the couple therapist's observations and clinical impressions.
6. Summarize the important information learned from observing and listening to the couple in a preliminary assessment.
7. Identify the importance of a theory-based conceptualization of the couple's presenting problem.

In this chapter, you will meet the case study couple, Liz Manning-Jones and Martin Jones, through the eyes of their couple therapist. In order to fully assess a couple and use that assessment as a basis for intervention, couple therapists need information about what the couple believes the problem to be, its history, and the social context in which the couple lives. While race, ethnicity, and social class will be noted here as part of the couple therapist's assessment of the potential impact of Liz and Martin's families of origin on the history of the problem, they will be addressed more fully in Chapter 9.

Couple therapists also observe couple interactions to determine how the couple's dynamics, or repetitive interaction patterns, affect the problem. These observations are included here as part of the couple therapist's clinical impressions.

Finally, you will read the couple therapist's preliminary assessment of Liz and Martin and her theoretical conceptualization. These form the basis for intervention to bring about the changes desired by the couple.

Liz, Martin, their children, and their extended family members are not real people. Rather, they are a composite of the author's four decades of practicing psychotherapy with individuals, couples, families, and groups and teaching and supervising graduate students and family medicine residents. They and their extended families were initially created in collaboration with the writer's colleague, Judy Esposito, to illustrate family therapy concepts and theories (Esposito & Hattem, 2017).

While Liz and Martin are illustrative of complex couples, no one couple can represent either the variety or the complexity of couples with whom couple therapists work. Thus, while they, their children, and their extended family provide clinical examples of the concepts and theories discussed throughout this book, readers cannot assume that either the assessment or the hypothetical sessions about which they read demonstrate a one-size-fits-all model for couples. For example, Liz and Martin are illustrative of some of the issues encountered by biracial couples and their couple therapists. However, with any sociocultural construct, such as race, there is more variance within than between categories (Diller, 2007; Lum, 2007). Liz and Martin are both highly educated professionals living close to extended family members who have accepted their relationship. They do not represent couples living with fewer resources and more isolation either because of geographic distance from family or because family members refuse to accept their relationship. In these latter situations, their couple distress would likely be exacerbated by the additional financial and social stressors.

Liz and Martin's couple therapy trajectory began in 1993, shortly after the birth of their first child. They participated in couple therapy with the same couple therapist then and three additional times over a period of nine years. Their last presentation for treatment was in June, 2002. The time line below presents an overview of their relationship and couple therapy histories, as well as of the significant events that impacted them as a couple.

As you read Section I of this textbook, you will notice that Liz and Martin's first presentation for couple therapy in 1993 is used to exemplify the concepts presented. The remaining chapters (Chapters 4–13) will rely on their 2002 couple therapy, with occasional references to sessions that occurred during the intervening years.

Liz and Martin's couple therapist's assessment would have happened primarily during their first presentation in 1993. Liz and Martin's couple therapy in 1993, 1997, and 2000 ended as soon as the symptoms that led them to seek couple therapy lessened, despite the couple therapist's increasingly vehement recommendations they remain in treatment to address the issues that continued to undermine their relationship (see Chapter 10). Because they declined her recommendation prior to 2002, much of the important work and the resolution of their couple therapy occurred during that treatment.

Time Line

FEBRUARY, 1966 — Liz Manning-Jones born, third child of Sally and Bill Manning.

JULY, 1966 — Martin Jones born, second child and only son of Samuel and Roxanne Jones.

OCTOBER, 1988 — Liz and Martin meet at a Halloween party hosted by one of Martin's pharmacy school friends and her roommate, who was one of Liz's law school friends.

DECEMBER, 1989 — Liz and Martin married in a small ceremony attended by their immediate families and closest friends.

JUNE, 1991 — Liz and Martin separated, citing irreconcilable differences.

AUGUST, 1991 — Liz met briefly with Couple Therapist in the latter's role as an individual psychotherapist.

FEBRUARY, 1992 — Liz and Martin reconciled. Liz hyphenated her last name.

APRIL, 1993 — Christina Jones born to Liz Manning-Jones and Martin Jones.

JULY, 1993 — Liz and Martin sought couple therapy with Couple Therapist and ended after symptoms abated three months later.

AUGUST, 1996 — Martin Jones Jr. born to Liz Manning-Jones and Martin Jones.

JUNE, 1997 — Liz and Martin again sought couple therapy with Couple Therapist, duration two and a half months.

MARCH, 2000 — Liz and Martin again sought couple therapy with Couple Therapist, duration six weeks.

APRIL, 2002 — Bill Manning, Liz's 66-year-old father, died of heart disease complicated by poly-substance abuse.

JUNE, 2002 — Liz and Martin again sought couple therapy with Couple Therapist and continued until they and CT agreed the process was completed.

Cast List (June, 2002)

LIZ — 36-year-old wife of Martin, mother of Christina and Martin Jr., daughter of Sally and the late Bill Manning, sister of Barbara and David, attorney

MARTIN — 35-year-old husband of Liz; father of Christina and Martin Jr.; son of Samuel and Roxanne Jones; brother of Lynette, Daisy, and Selena; research pharmacist

CHRISTINA — nine-year-old daughter of Liz and Martin, sister of Martin Jr.

MARTIN JR. (MJ) — five-year-old son of Liz and Martin, brother of Christina

SALLY — 66-year-old mother of Liz, widow of Bill, homemaker, with untreated borderline high blood pressure

BILL — died April 2002 at the age of 66 of cardiovascular disease complicated by poly-substance abuse, father of Liz, husband of Sally, retired postal service employee

BARBARA — 40-year-old sister of Liz, wife of Peter, mother of Paul and Patricia (twins), homemaker occasionally employed in her husband's dental practice

DAVID — 38-year-old brother of Liz, sporadically employed, estranged from his ex-wife Susan and son Carl, poly-substance abuser with untreated metabolic disease

ROXANNE — 60-year-old mother of Martin, wife of Samuel, homemaker, cardiovascular disease well managed

SAMUEL — 60-year-old father of Martin, husband of Roxanne, plumber

LYNNETTE — 37-year-old sister of Martin, wife of Paul, mother of Jeanette and Jeannine, nurse

DAISY — 32-year-old sister of Martin, divorced mother, administrative assistant

SELENA — 29-year-old sister of Martin, single mother, lives with her parents, mobility challenges

---

The cast list reflects the family composition in 2002, because Liz and Martin's families of procreation and of origin had changed in two significant ways during the years since they began couple therapy. Liz and Martin had given birth to a second child, and Liz's father had died. Note that both the 1997 couple therapy and the 2002 couple therapy followed quickly upon one of these two events. Liz and Martin's initial presentation for couple therapy also occurred within months of the birth of their first child.

Stop and Think:

1 What might be the significance of the birth and death of a family member for a couple? Be sure to include your responses in your journal.

Genogram in June, 2002

A genogram (McGoldrick, 2008) allows a pictorial, multi-generational map of family members, important dates, and other information a couple therapist might find useful. It is an assessment tool that will be described more fully in Chapter 3, along with an example of how Liz and Martin's was constructed during a couple therapy session.

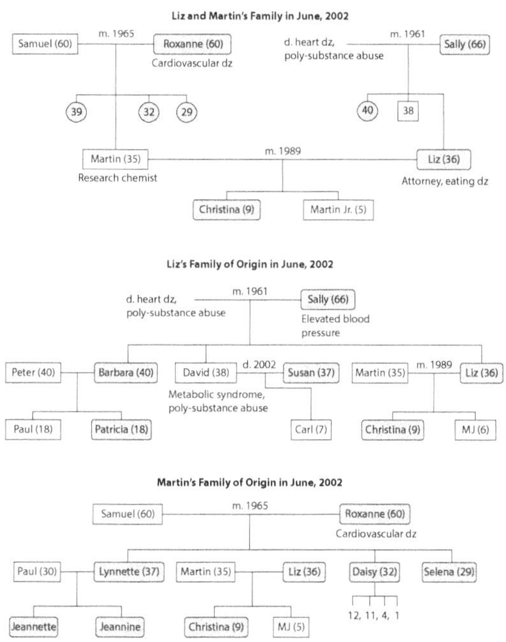

Presenting Problem

The problem that motivates a couple to seek therapy is called the presenting problem. Couple therapists, like individual and family therapists, want to know how the client couple defines the presenting problem.

As you will see, there may be differences in two partners' views of their presenting problem. Many couple therapists agree that couple consensus about goals is more important than agreement about the problem. Encouraging partners to agree on the presenting problem merely leads to unnecessary fights and possibly further damage to the relationship. Rather, their inability to agree can be conceptualized as an aspect of their problem.

The couple therapist may also discover new aspects of the presenting problem and/or issues related to it while assessing the couple and as treatment progresses. For example, the repetitive patterns of interactions between the partners, also known as couple dynamics, may be more obvious to an observer than to the two participants. Identifying a couple's dynamics occurs through observation over several sessions.

Defining the Presenting Problem

Couple therapists usually ask each partner to describe how he or she defines the problem or problems during the first session. The couple therapist's tasks include listening empathetically to each partner's view, discouraging both verbal and nonverbal interruptions by the other partner as each speaks, and refraining from taking sides. These tasks can be challenging. A partner who interrupts may react negatively to being asked to defer his or her verbal and nonverbal comments, and one or both partners may make overt and/or covert demands that the couple therapist take sides.

Couple therapists may find themselves feeling more empathetic toward one of the partners than the other. Bearing in mind that the relationship dynamics are often more complicated than they first appear may help the couple therapist resist taking sides. For example, a partner who is critical or angry may appear unsympathetic. Yet she or he may be responding to the other's passive-aggression, indifference, or broken promises. Viewed in the context of the couple's dynamics, the partner on the receiving end of the criticism or anger may appear far less sympathetic.

The couple therapist needs to both avoid becoming defensive when a partner reacts negatively and resist taking sides. These imperatives cannot be overemphasized. A couple therapist who is on the receiving end of criticism, anger, or pressure is well-advised to engage in self-soothing self-talk during sessions and to remain mindful of the ethical standards of her or his profession. Ethical practice and self-care will be addressed in Chapter 11.

Stop and Think

Be sure to include your responses in your journal.

Think about a time when you have been in the presence of two people who are in conflict with each other. The two people might be roommates, friends, siblings, cousins, your parents or grandparents, or a friend and her or his partner.

1. What were your feelings as an observer (discomfort, disgust, incredulity, sadness, frustration about being there, etc.)? Did you think one person was right or justified and the other not? Did you think they each had good points? Did you think the conflict seemed disproportionate to what they were arguing about?
2. Did they want you to take sides? Did you want to? How were you able to resist the pressure to take sides? If you were unable to resist and found yourself taking sides, what happened?
3. Did they want you to help them resolve their conflict? How did they let you know they wanted your help?
4. Did you want to help them resolve their conflict?
5. Did they resist any efforts you made to help them, such as "yes, but" statements?
6. Did either or both of them become frustrated with you? If so, what was that like for you and how did you react?

The situation you chose for the Stop and Think exercise is similar to what you might experience as a couple therapist. The only differences would be (1) the client couple will not be people who are already important to you and (2) you will have had more training and access to colleagues and mentors to help you with the challenges.

Some couples also pressure the couple therapist to solve their problem during the first session. In the writer's experience, beginning couple therapists pressure themselves to create a quick fix, even without pressure from the couple client. Like you, couple therapists want to help and as a result may pressure themselves to find a solution before fully understanding all facets of the problem. It is important to remember that one cannot solve any problem until one understands its nuances. Without a full understanding of the partners, their dynamics, and their sociocultural context, intervention is less likely to be effective. Asking about how each partner defines the problem is a necessary first step. Additional steps will be described later in this chapter.

Some couple therapists begin the process of learning about the couple and the presenting problem by addressing the partner who did not arrange the session. Alternatively, a couple therapist might suggest that whoever would like to begin speak first. The advantage of asking the partner who did not initiate treatment is the subtext that he or she is as important as the one with whom the couple therapist has interacted to arrange the session. The advantage of letting the partners decide is observing how they do so and which one takes the lead.

Some partners are able to clearly articulate their view of the presenting problem. Others sound vague, knowing a problem exists and needing the couple therapist to guide them to a clear understanding of it. Understanding the presenting problem is crucial to the partners identifying what they wish to change and the couple therapist deciding what needs to be done to facilitate their doing so.

Imagine asking for directions on iMaps, Google Maps, or any other GPS program without being able to specify both the starting and ending points. The same may be said for couple therapy, even though the analogy is imperfect. The couple therapist, like the program being used, will point the way. She or he can help couples navigate metaphorical dead ends, one-way streets, and traffic congestion, while the couple remains free to take a different route.

Liz saw their couple therapist for three sessions of individual psychotherapy in 1991 while she and Martin were separated. As with couple work, her pattern was to leave as soon as the emotional pain that drove her to therapy subsided. While relief from acute pain is an early goal of all therapy, in the writer's experience treatment beyond cessation of acute emotional distress is often necessary to prevent recurrence.

Liz knew from the friend who had suggested counseling and recommended this particular therapist that she also practiced couple therapy. Liz had trusted the therapist and found their individual sessions helpful.

She did not attribute the re-emergence of problems with Martin as a failing on the part of the therapist and therefore called her after she and Martin had reconciled, their daughter had been born, and they were again experiencing relationship difficulties.

The couple therapist agreed to see Liz and Martin together, so long as Martin was comfortable with the fact that she and Liz had already established a therapeutic relationship. The risks of having an individual therapeutic relationship with one member of a couple in addition to a couple therapeutic relationship with both, even if not simultaneously, will be discussed further in Chapter 11. Briefly, Martin might feel that the couple therapist and Liz were colluding to pressure him into being or doing what Liz wanted. This risk might be exacerbated by the fact that Liz and the couple therapist shared both gender and race with one another and neither with Martin.

Because she had previously worked with Liz and Liz had requested couple therapy, the couple therapist began by reviewing the emotional risks of couple therapy with a therapist one partner had previously seen individually and asked Martin his thoughts about working with her. She offered to provide him and Liz with three names of other couple therapists, as is customary when referring to another therapist. By making the risks overt, she attempted to avoid the possibility that Martin would tell her he was comfortable working with her so as not to offend her. As a psychotherapist attempting to practice in a culturally competent way, minimizing the possibility that Martin, a black man, would avoid expressing a preference to a white authority figure was especially important to her.

COUPLE THERAPIST: Martin, I'd like to begin with you because we've only just met. Is that alright with you, or would you prefer I started with Liz?

MARTIN: No, that's fine.

CT: Great. Because I saw Liz a couple of years ago after you two had separated, I'm concerned about the possibility that you might feel excluded from our previous bond. And I want to be sure you know I'd be happy to give you the names of three of my colleagues who do couple therapy if you have any doubts at all about working with me, for this or any other reason.

MARTIN: No, I'm fine.

CT: OK. I'm especially concerned because husbands often feel that a woman therapist is taking their wife's side or that the two of them are ganging up on him, even when they didn't previously work together.

Note: The risk of a gender coalition between the couple therapist and one of the partners is relevant only when working with heterosexual couples. Note also that she would have said "men" rather than "husbands" and "woman's" rather than "wife's" had the couple not been married. Finally, she chose to delay reference to racial differences to avoid inadvertently suggesting she did not wish to work with Martin because he was black.

MARTIN: [Smiles]

CT: And Liz and I are both white—both females, both white. I want to check out whether either is an issue.

MARTIN: No. No worries.

CT: OK. Please tell me if anything becomes an issue during our work together.

MARTIN: [Nods]

Note: The literature about ethnic and racial differences between the couple therapist and either partner will be touched upon in Chapter 9.

CT: So tell me what brings you here, and then I'll ask Liz the same question.

MARTIN: Well, Liz suggested this, but I think we can work it out.

CT: And what have you already tried to do to work it out?

MARTIN: Well, not enough. But we're smart, we can do it.

CT: OK. Since you're here, I'd like to know what you'd like to work out.

MARTIN: You want me to tell you why we're here?

CT: I'd like to know your view of why you're here, what you see as the problem or problems you and Liz need to work out.

MARTIN: Well, we have a new baby [smiles]...

CT: [smiles] ...yes, congratulations.

MARTIN: Thank you. [Pause]

CT: So the new baby...?

MARTIN: She never sleeps.

LIZ: [Rolls eyes and mumbles] Get to the point, Martin.

CT: Sleep loss is horrible. Tell me how it has become a problem for you and Liz.

MARTIN: She's always mad at me. [Looks at Liz] Like that.

CT: So Liz's anger at you is the problem?

LIZ: [Shakes head] Yep, it's all me.

CT: Liz, I hear you don't agree. And I also want to hear how you view the problem, after Martin finishes.

MARTIN: [Smiles without his eyes at Liz] And she's mad at me because I'm not "supportive" enough of her career.

CT: The air quotes mean you're not sure what she means by supportive? Or you think you are supportive? Or...?

MARTIN: I really don't know what I'm supposed to do.

CT: That must be frustrating.

MARTIN: [Frowning] Maybe a little.

Note: Many people would be more than a little frustrated. However, some people minimize feelings or are uncomfortable with anger. The couple therapist decided not to ask Martin more about his frustration, because she would be changing the topic. Couples often initiate topic changes as feelings become heated, and it is the therapist's responsibility to keep them on track.

CT: This began after the baby was born?

Note: This question is about the history of the problem. CT asked because she knew from Liz's individual therapy that Martin and Liz had had conflict about Liz's career before they separated.

MARTIN: No, we've always argued about her career. She thinks I don't want her to have a career. And she's wrong. But I can't find a way to get her to believe me when I say that.

LIZ: Seriously?!

CT: Just one more thing, and then I want to hear your take on this, Liz. Martin, you've told me a lot about Liz. What about you? What would you like?

Note: The couple therapist has skipped ahead to the question of goals. Her purpose was to shift Martin's focus from the problem being all Liz's to his own concerns. Their problem is a couple problem and not merely Liz's anger and career.

MARTIN: I'd like Liz to be less angry at me, to give me the benefit of the doubt that I love her and want her to do what makes her happy.

LIZ: [Rolls her eyes]

CT: Liz, I appreciate how difficult this is. As I mentioned on the phone, couple therapy requires the therapist to listen to both people, and it might feel like I care less about you than I did when we met alone. I hope that doesn't hurt our working relationship. And if it does, please let me know.

LIZ: [Sighs] OK. Now can I talk?

CT: Let me be sure I heard Martin accurately first. Martin, you love Liz and want her to be happy, and you'd like to convince her both are true.

MARTIN: Yes. Exactly.

CT: [Nods] Liz, I appreciate your patience, and I'd like to hear your views about why you're here.

LIZ: [Sarcastically] Thank you. The problem is, no matter what he says, he wants me to be a housewife like our mothers. I think he's threatened by my career.

MARTIN: [Softly] Threatened, Liz?

LIZ: Please, Martin. It's obvious. Something good happens at work; you don't want to hear about it. And then the sex stops.

MARTIN: [A bit louder, still very controlled although his eyebrows furrow] What?!

LIZ: Yes. That's how I know you're threatened.

CT: This sounds like an important topic to come back to. But first I want to finish hearing Liz's view of what brought you here.

Note: The couple therapist had to choose between allowing Martin and Liz to continue, which would have given her information about how they argued as well as about how their arguments played out in their sexual relationship, or returning to the topic at hand. She chose the latter in order to make it clear to the couple that she would keep them focused, even when the situation became difficult for them. She also assumed she would have other opportunities to observe them arguing and to hear about how their issues might affect their sexual relationship.

MARTIN: Sorry.

LIZ: Where was I? [Glaring at Martin] He distracted me. [Pause] Oh yes. I've been fighting to be equally important since the day we met. I told you that when we first met, remember? My career is important to me. And now with Christina...

CT: Yes?

LIZ: I want to be sure I can support her if, you know, anything happens. And I also want to be a good mother. And I don't know what that means, whether I should stay home with her or not work so much or what.

CT: And you want Martin's help with your decision and to approve of it?

LIZ: [Softly] Yes, but he doesn't support my career in the first place.

In addition to information about how each defines the presenting problem, you now have a preliminary sense of Liz and Martin's relationship dynamics. The concept of couple dynamics refers to a couple's repetitive patterns of interactions. Often, these patterns, or dynamics, are more important than the content of what a couple presents as the problem. In other words, that Liz and Martin interrupt, accuse, speak softly even when upset with each other, and have not found ways to get what each wants from the other may be at least as important as how Liz balances career and motherhood, whether Martin approves or helps her decide, and how their marriage may need to adapt to accommodate her choice.

Before discussing the above transcript from Liz and Martin's first session with the couple therapist, create a journal on your electronic device or in a notebook. This journal will allow you to track the evolution of your thinking as you learn more about Liz and Martin and the process of couple therapy. Start your journal with written answers to the following questions. Then, if time allows, your professor may ask you to discuss them in class.

Stop and Think:

Be sure to include your responses in your journal.

1. What did you learn about Martin?
2. What did you learn about Liz?
3. How would you describe the ways they interact with each other?
4. What did you learn from observing the couple therapist?
5. How would you have handled Martin and Liz's frustrations differently?
6. How would you have handled their doubt about couple therapy?

As you will learn from classes, texts, and your own supervised clinical work, no couple therapist can address everything that is said during a session, especially when the partners' emotions are high. The couple therapist learned that Martin was frustrated with Liz, apparently because he could not convince her that he wanted her to manage her career in a way that felt right to her. The couple therapist needed information about what Martin had already done to convince Liz and whether those efforts had exacerbated his frustration and/or her doubt.

We know that Liz was of multiple minds, or ambivalent, about how to balance her career and her role as a mother. She appeared to want something from Martin that had not been clearly articulated, that he had not yet given her, and that may be impossible for him to give if part of what she needed was to accept herself and the choices she has made. The couple therapist needed to inquire about the specifics of what she wanted from Martin.

The couple therapist also needed to facilitate Liz's decision making about how to balance career and motherhood. Liz talked about other people's expectations, or what she thought she "should" do. Helping her identify her own wishes might also help her to become more clear with Martin about what she wanted from him.

From her previous work with Liz, the couple therapist knew that the presenting problem was not new and had contributed to their decision to separate in 1991. She therefore speculated that becoming parents and specifically the significant sleep loss associated with infants had exacerbated a problem that already existed. She needed to seek confirmation or refutation for her hypothesis from both Liz and Martin.

Finally, we know that Martin and Liz were in the process of transitioning from being a couple to being a family, exhausted from sleep loss associated with their daughter's infancy, and angry with each other about what was currently going on between them as well as about their past. The couple therapist believed that not getting what they wanted from each other as they moved forward and their frustration about their dynamics were more important than who was correct about whether or not Martin supported Liz's career or how she resolved her dilemma regarding the balance of motherhood and career.

The couple therapist chose not to address Liz's prior and Martin's current skepticism about the effectiveness of psychotherapy for a variety of reasons, even though many psychotherapists would have. As previously mentioned, no one can address every issue that arises at the time it arises. In this case, she consistently chose to demonstrate her commitment to remaining focused, rather than allowing herself to be distracted by even an important related topic.

There were distractions and interruptions occurring between Liz and Martin as each described their view of the presenting problem. Interruptions, changes in topic, arguing about who is correct, and other distractions tend to occur when a topic or dynamic provokes anxiety (Schreiner, 2017). As you will learn in Chapter 4, distractions are what is termed a homeostatic mechanism that returns the couple to interactions and topics with which the partners feel comfortable. The couple therapist could have pursued any of several related distractions because each was also important. By taking the issues Liz and Martin raised one at a time, however, she prevented them from shifting topics rather than working to resolve a problem and thus began to demonstrate how to resolve conflict.

You were presented with a large amount of new information in this section. We will return to the salient points throughout this textbook, just as a couple therapist would return to salient issues as they become relevant.

Why Now?

The presenting problem likely did not first appear on the day the couple arrived at their couple therapist's office. So the couple therapist will want to know what happened that prompted the couple to seek therapy at a particular point in time. In other words, what changed and what feels more pressing to them now?

Sometimes couples are referred for couple therapy by another mental health professional, a physician, or an attorney. Other times, a court or social service agency will mandate couple therapy. When couples do not initiate the process themselves, they may be less engaged, more skeptical, and more resistant to the couple therapist's attempts to intervene. The why-now question, however, becomes moot.

When a couple initiates therapy or agrees with the referral source that couple therapy is a good idea, the couple therapist can assume they have attempted to solve or resolve the presenting problem and not been successful. It then becomes important to ask what the couple has already done to attempt to alleviate the distress and how it has worked. Although the answer to the latter may be "obviously not well enough", the couple therapist can avoid repeating ineffective interventions by learning the specifics of what has and has not been effective from the couple's previous efforts. Similarly, if the couple has been in therapy with someone else, learning what was helpful and not may speed the current couple therapist's work with them.

Sometimes couples come to therapy because a particular event has alerted them to the fact that they cannot continue to postpone addressing their presenting problem. An extra-relationship emotional or sexual affair when the partners have agreed to be exclusive and monogamous is an example of a single event precipitating a request for couple therapy. Other times, lack of resolution of a problem becomes an issue of its own, as unresolved fight after unresolved fight creates a sense of futility. Couples then seek therapy as a last resort before giving up on their relationship. Finally, couples may have experienced manageable levels of conflict or distress until their coping mechanisms were overwhelmed by an event, perhaps even one outside the relationship such as the illness and/or death of a parent, job loss, or a critically ill or injured child.

With minimal guidance from the couple therapist, Liz and Martin began to articulate their presenting problem. Based on the previous transcript, we might speculate about why Liz and Martin presented for couple therapy when they did. Perhaps it was the life transition of becoming parents and the impact of its attendant sleep loss, shift in roles to include parenting, and additional responsibilities of infant care that provided enough stress to overwhelm how they had managed their conflict until then. The transition to parenthood and/or some as yet undisclosed event appears to have returned them to at least one of the issues that had led them to separate. Until their couple therapist asked, however, there was no way to know.

We rejoin Liz, Martin, and the couple therapist later in the first session.

COUPLE THERAPIST: I think we've done some great work identifying what brought you here. Before we stop for today, I'd also like to hear a little about what prompted you to call me now.

LIZ: When else would we have called you?

CT: Well, it sounds as though these problems aren't new, and so I'm curious whether something happened that led you to come in now.

LIZ: I see. [Looks at Martin]

MARTIN: I'm not sure. It was Liz's idea.

LIZ: What?!

CT: Let's come back to that. What prompted you to call me?

Note: Martin inferred that he was present at the couple therapy session to please Liz. The couple therapist did not challenge his statement, in part because she wanted to establish a therapeutic alliance with him first. Additionally, she did not allow Liz's challenge to shift them away from her question.

LIZ: I guess it's what I said earlier, that I am upset with Martin for all the years he hasn't been supportive of my career. And it's worse now that I have Christina and don't know what to do.

CT: It sounds like you've wanted approval or something you don't feel you have from Martin. And now that you're uncertain about how you want to balance being a mom with your career and are concerned about what you think other people expect of you, it sounds like you need him to do it even more.

Note: The couple therapist added the words "you think" because she did not yet know who, if anyone other than Liz, had expectations for her as a mother. It became apparent that both her mother and sister were critical of Liz and pointed out that they were wonderful mothers because they did not work outside their homes.

LIZ: Yes.

CT: Martin, can you tell Liz what you just heard her say?

MARTIN: She thinks I don't support her career and now that she doesn't know what to do about it she needs me to support her even more. I still don't know what she means by support.

CT: I know, and we need to clarify that. Liz, did Martin hear what you wanted him to hear?

LIZ: [Hesitant] Yes.

CT: I don't want to put words in your mouth. You can edit what he said he heard you say to make it more accurate.

LIZ: No. It's OK.

Note: This is a helpful technique with couples. It disrupts any reaction to defend oneself and also makes certain each partner feels heard by the other. And by reflecting back what the other said, each partner validates without pressure to agree. In other words, the partners learn they can agree about what they intended to say without endorsing the content of any particular statement.

Stop and Think:

Be sure to include your responses in your journal, irrespective of whether you discuss them in class.

1. If you had been the couple therapist, how might you have reacted when Liz challenged your "why now" question?
2. Would you have allowed Martin to get away with implying he had no stake in the therapy had you been the couple therapist?
3. What other questions would you like to ask Liz and Martin, either about the presenting problem or about why they presented for couple therapy when they did?

Couple Goals

Learning all the nuances of the presenting problem may not occur in a single session. Sometimes couples are not fully aware of what the problem is, cannot articulate it, or there is insufficient time for them to describe all aspects of it. Other times, they may be embarrassed or even ashamed and withhold information until they more fully trust the therapist. And finally, they may not agree about what the problem is or even whether there is a problem.

In determining the goals for a particular couple, couple therapists combine what they have heard each partner say and what they have observed about the couple's dynamics. Couple dynamics are often outside the partners' awareness, and the couple therapist helps them recognize its relevance. Couple therapists also ask each partner directly about his or her goals for therapy.

Stop and Think:

Include your answers in your journal, irrespective of whether or not you discuss them in class.

1. What have you heard Liz and Martin say about their problem(s)?
2. What have you observed about how they interact?
3. What have you heard them say about their goals, for example, what they would like to change about their relationship?

The couple therapist heard Liz's ambivalence about balancing her roles as wife, mother, and professional. Martin expressed confusion about what Liz meant when she said he did not support her career. He also questioned her assumption that he was threatened by it. Finally, Liz brought up the temporal association between her career achievements and lack of sex in their relationship, an accusation with which Martin immediately disagreed and about which the couple therapist needs more information.

In a part of the transcript not included here, Martin and Liz agreed that they wanted to resolve their arguments about her career, as well as about who was responsible for initiating sex and earning money. Like many couples, they said they wanted to learn to communicate more effectively. The couple therapist interpreted communication to mean they needed to express their wishes more directly, resolve their arguments, and learn from their experience in couple therapy how to do both on their own. She also knew that each might have individual issues that might make these changes more difficult than they appeared.

The couple therapist observed that the argument about whose point of view was correct or valid precluded Liz and Martin remaining focused on the content of their arguments and resolving them. She also observed that their soft voice tones did not always match the emotional tone of their words. She therefore suggested they add becoming more comfortable with anger and conflict to their list of goals.

The couple therapist noted that Liz and Martin appeared to have different expectations for what good wives and mothers do. She also speculated they experienced differing pressures from extended family members and friends to organize their roles and relationship in particular and perhaps even contradictory ways. She decided to defer asking about these possibilities until she had learned about Liz and Martin's histories and their families of origin.

History of the Presenting Problem

In order to fully understand the presenting problem, it is important that the couple therapist have information about the historical and sociocultural context in which it developed.

Couple History

Learning about the history of a couple's relationship is essential to fully understanding current functioning. Many patterns of interaction, or couple dynamics, arise early in a relationship. They become part of the couple's relationship contract (Sager, 1994) and become increasingly entrenched with time. If any of these dynamics is problematic, the problems similarly compound over time. Chapter 4 includes a description of the processes by which this happens.

A couple's history provides information about how the couple has handled challenges throughout their relationship and what those challenges have been. It also provides information about a couple's strengths and vulnerabilities.

Liz and Martin met in 1988, during their first year of graduate school. Liz was in law school, and Martin was in a doctoral program in chemistry focusing on pharmacology. Although both are highly educated, Liz and Martin are in debt because their families could not afford the educations they received. Liz had been encouraged to pursue traditional female roles and went to college despite the debt she incurred because her friends were going. By contrast, Martin's interests and abilities in science and especially chemistry were identified by a high school teacher who mentored him as he applied to colleges and scholarships.

A year after they met, Liz and Martin decided to move in together. Martin, whose mother pressured him to lead a life more consistent with the family's church's values, was concerned about her reaction and so, in deference to her beliefs and values, they married prior to cohabiting and without the lengthy engagement and wedding planning Liz's mother would have preferred.

Liz and Martin separated 15 months later. They could not agree on how to prioritize their careers when opportunities were in conflict and decided they could not make their marriage work. After eight months apart, they realized they were happier together and reconciled without resolving the issue they believed had undermined their marriage. Within months, they conceived their first child.

A friend of Liz's had suggested she might benefit from "talking to someone" about the stress of her new job as an associate in a medium-sized law firm and the dissolution of her marriage. After several sessions, Liz and Martin had begun talking about reconciling and she told the therapist she no longer needed treatment. The therapist suggested she and Martin maximize the chance that their reconciliation would be successful by engaging in couple therapy to resolve the issues that had led to their separation and offered a list of referrals to Liz. Liz declined her offer.

Liz contacted the therapist again two years later, after Christina was born, requesting couple therapy. As soon as their fighting abated, Liz decided they had neither the time nor financial resources to continue. As with her individual therapy, she told the therapist of her decision at the end of a session. This time, the therapist simply noted the pattern.

Liz and Martin returned to couple therapy with the same therapist four years later, when their son, MJ, was a year old. Both acknowledged they were having the same disagreements about the same topics. Specifically, they were arguing about whether Martin supported Liz professionally, whether he disrespected her choice to adapt her career to mothering rather than hire a nanny and continue on the partner track at her law firm, and whether Martin's involvement in the life of the family was sufficient. Martin claimed her expectations of him were inconsistent with their agreement that she would take more responsibility for home and child care during work hours because she no longer worked full time. Liz suggested they meet every other week, again citing time and money as deterrents. The couple therapist recommended that they meet weekly for four to six weeks to gain momentum and then re-evaluate the frequency of sessions. Liz declined and once again ended therapy when the pain abated, saying they had not fought for more than a week and thought they could manage on their own.

Less than two years later, Liz requested an individual session with the couple therapist. She said she had "had it" with Martin. However, she wanted to keep the marriage intact for the sake of their children and wanted the therapist to help her accomplish that goal. During the session, the couple therapist pointed out that she was talking only about Martin and not about herself and again suggested couple work. Liz agreed. Martin and Liz once again decided they were alright after a few sessions and discontinued treatment. The couple therapist took the position that their history suggested they needed to remain in therapy long enough to address what underlay their conflict and strongly recommended they do so. They declined.

Sections II and III of this textbook will focus on Liz and Martin's final course of couple therapy in 2002, which began two months after Liz's father died. They requested sessions with the goal of stopping themselves from regressing into old, unproductive habits. The couple therapist said that unless they were willing to work on deeper issues she saw no point in going through the pain of "returning from the edge of a cliff" only to "rush toward it again a year or two later." Liz and Martin reluctantly agreed. The ethics of the couple therapist's decision will be discussed in Chapter 11 and the couple therapist's experience that led her to issue a virtual ultimatum will be described in Chapter 10. The outcome of this final course of couple therapy will be discussed in Chapter 13.

Stop and Think:

Be sure to include your answers in your journal.

1. How would you feel if a couple declined your help and then, when they were fighting again, asked you to help them?
2. Based on what you already know about Liz and Martin and without access to transcripts of future therapy sessions, do you think they will remain together? Explain.

Each Partner's Relationship History

Each partner brings her or his own history to the relationship. For example, someone who was abused as a child or sexually assaulted as an adult may respond to a sexual partner as though she or he is an abuser, leaving the partner feeling confused or rejected. When personal history affects a relationship, it becomes a part of the couple's therapy.

Liz was sexually assaulted by a man she considered a friend during her freshman year of college. Following the assault, Liz experimented with lesbian relationships and subsequently identified as bisexual. She did not allow herself to become emotionally involved with her female partners nor sexually involved with a man until she met Martin. Because Liz and Martin later agreed that their commitment involves monogamy, her sexuality has not been an issue in their relationship. LGBTQIA relationships will be further explored in Chapter 9.

In times of high stress, Liz experienced flash-backs during sexual encounters with Martin. She sometimes removed herself emotionally from their love making, which distressed him. People did not speak of date rape when Liz was in college, and she felt guilty and ashamed about what had happened to her.

Martin had had girlfriends in high school and throughout college. These relationships had not lasted more than an academic year because he had not considered any of the young women to be potential life partners.

Each Partner's Nuclear Family of Origin

As with individual history, family history also impacts intimate adult relationships. For example, if one partner grew up in a household where voices were often raised but nothing was ever resolved while the other was raised in a family in which conflict was avoided, neither partner would have learned how to effectively resolve conflict. However, each might have learned to deal with conflict differently and therefore each may be horrified by the other's behavior.

Liz's family of origin was of Polish descent, and they were practicing Catholics. Her father's alcohol abuse, unacceptable in the larger ethnic community, led to seemingly unprovoked rages at home. Despite his drinking, he held a steady job and went to church every Sunday.

Liz's mother functioned as peace-maker, appeasing her husband and then telling the children everything was fine. Liz, too, attempted to minimize conflict until it overwhelmed her. She then displayed more anger than one would expect given the provocation. Her mother, on the other hand, appeared to release her anger by judging others, especially her daughters.

Liz's older brother, David, had begun using drugs while in high school. His behavior became erratic and Liz, who wanted to bring what she considered a problem to her parents' attention, was discouraged from doing so by her older sister, Barbara. She often wondered whether she missed the opportunity help him by listening to her sister.

Martin grew up in a household in which both parents were engaged in parenting and in the life of their community. He remembered his parents arguing quietly in another room and never going to bed angry. He reacted to both Liz's and his own anger by speaking softly. He said he was concerned for them as a couple when they went to bed angry. He was also concerned when Liz raised her voice in the presence of their daughter.

Martin's parents were intensely religious. Martin rarely attended church, which he knew saddened his mother. Liz worried that Martin's mother blamed her for his lapse, while his mother was confused about why Liz seemed tense when they were together. Martin also worried that the gap between his own education, career, and socioeconomic status and his family's would drive a wedge between them. Liz, who had also pursued an advanced degree and a career that exceeded her father's, was puzzled by his concern.

Liz's father, Bill, expressed displeasure when she became serious about a black man. After he met Martin, his attitude softened, and he and Martin maintained a cordial relationship. Martin's parents were not surprised that he became involved with a white woman and welcomed Liz into the family.

Both Liz and Martin were raised in families in which the women assumed traditional sex roles. Her mother and sister disapproved of Liz working outside the home after becoming a mother. Martin's mother expressed concern about day care centers in general, which Liz interpreted as disapproval of her continuing to work outside the home. The couple therapist hypothesized that at least a portion of Liz's ambivalence about balancing career and motherhood resulted from these interactions.

Each Partner's Extended Family of Origin

Being part of an extended family involves sharing traditions and values across generations (Berg-Cross, 2000). These traditions and values affect family members' intimate adult relationships. An undergraduate client complained to the writer that her parents were happy she was in college but at holiday gatherings no one in her extended family understood why she would rather go to college than get married. Similarly, grandparents may be less comfortable with a young adult dating and marrying outside the family's racial, ethnic, or religious group or with LGBTQIA relationships than are her or his parents. Liz's sister and her husband were delighted with their son's choice of husbands, whereas Liz and Barbara's mother, Sally, was horrified that he married a man.

Traditions such as religiosity and stay-at-home mothers were part of both Liz and Martin's extended families of origin. Roxanne maintained close relationships with her parents, aunts, and uncles throughout their lives and with her siblings and cousins who were still living. By contrast, Samuel, Bill, and Sally had little to do with their extended families of origin, and Liz's brother had almost no contact with the family unless he needed money.

Social Context and Social Support

Sociocultural Context

It is crucial that couple therapists learn about the couple's position in their larger sociocultural context. Race, ethnicity, socioeconomic status, education level, type of employment, community involvement, social network, dwelling, sexual identity, and resultant life chances impact individual experience, choice of partner, and world view (Basirico, Cashion, & Eshleman, 2014). The specifics of this assertion will be further explored in Chapter 9.

Liz and Martin were a biracial couple. Liz's family was white, Polish, and Catholic; Martin's was black and affiliated with a Baptist church. Both families were considered middle class and owned their homes. Members of Liz and Martin's generation were the first to attend college. Both Liz and Martin's parents were in long-term, heterosexual marriages sanctioned by the state and their churches. In other words, the primary difference in their families of origin had to do with race.

The impact of race upon an individual's development and experience will be addressed in Chapter 9. Suffice it to say that, just as Liz was not confident she was making appropriate parenting choices, Martin was never certain whether his professional position was earned or was the product of a "diversity" policy. Unlike Liz, who was the only white person only when with Martin's family or at his parents' church, Martin was often the only black person at business and social events and was subject to micro-aggressions, or subtle demeaning and marginalizing, on a regular basis in every aspect of his life (Wong, Derthick, David, Saw, & Okazaki, 2014).

Like all heterosexual couples, Liz and Martin were both biologically and socially predisposed to approach one another in gender-specific ways that can be problematic in times of distress. Tannen (1990), a linguist interested in gender differences in communication, has written an accessible book for those interested in learning more about this topic. Similarly, Myers (2008) cited Brizendine's (2007) research on the biological bases of male-female differences in her very accessible writing. Liz also experienced social pressure to conform to the norms governing middle-class women who are mothers and the consequences of normative expectations for her career advancement and earning potential in a way that a man would not. Like racism, sexism impacts how people are treated, view themselves, and subsequently how they behave (Basirico et al., 2014; Lum, 2007; Wong et al., 2014).

Social Support

Social support may come from friends, extended family members, neighbors, spiritual and service groups, interest groups, work colleagues, and caretakers such as primary care physicians, home health helpers, and hospice staff. Taken together, these sources of social support form an individual, couple, or family's social network.

Each Partner's Current Social Network. Both Liz and Martin maintain frequent contact with their parents and siblings, with the exception of Liz's brother, as well as with friends from college and graduate school. Martin also has friends from childhood. They have each created friendships at work. However, their focus on career and family has precluded involvement in their community other than volunteering at Christina's day care center.

Couple's Social Network. Both Liz and Martin have brought their individual friends' partners to their network of couple friends. They have befriended neighbors and are beginning to befriend couples at Christina's day care. They are also connected as a couple to their families of origin.

Clinical Observations and Impressions

Couple therapists observe and form clinical impressions to guide their work with clients. Because new information arises over time, couple therapists cannot reliably draw conclusions after a single session with a couple.

However, their clinical observations and impressions serve to guide how they acquire more information, define goals, and begin to intervene to facilitate change.

Stop and Think:

Be sure to include your answers in your journal.

1. What are your impressions of Liz and Martin, both as individuals and as a couple?
2. What challenges do you see them facing?
3. As you read the couple therapist's observations and impressions, think about whether or not you agree with her and why.

The couple therapist viewed Liz and Martin as a couple with whom she would enjoy working. Her impression was that they cared about one another and were also somewhat reactive to one another's communications. Additionally, Liz needed something she was not getting from Martin and had not yet found a way to articulate what it was. Both Liz and Martin needed to become more comfortable with their anger and learn to express and then resolve it.

The couple therapist also viewed Liz and Martin as reasonably committed to improving their relationship. People tend to fear change, even when avoiding change is painful. And couples, like individuals and families, may perceive the potential risks of therapy to be greater than the potential benefits. Knowing these impediments, the couple therapist did not expect Liz and Martin to be enthusiastic about couple therapy.

Contrast these initial impressions with the impressions she must have had when, many years later, she insisted they commit to working on their deeper issues. She firmly believed that they would again become frustrated with couple therapy producing no long-term benefits and would eventually give up not only on the process but more importantly on their relationship. She therefore believed that another failure of couple therapy could be more detrimental to their marriage than not re-engaging in couple therapy at all.

Life Cycle Transitions

Duvall (1977) was a pioneer in applying the concept of life cycles to families, and the writer has seen no better description. Liz and Martin had recently entered what she termed the childbearing stage of the couple and family life cycle. Becoming parents involves taking on new roles and attendant expectations. Since most newborns require care during the night, becoming parents also involves chronic sleep loss, with its attendant dysphoria, grumpiness, lowered immune functioning, and health risks (Colten & Altevogt, 2006; Swain, O'Hara, Starr, & Gorman, 1997).

Expectations for behavior change whenever an individual adds a new role. Liz and Martin were both experiencing shifts in expectations for themselves as they added the role of parent, although expectations for mothers and fathers differ in our culture and differed in Liz and Martin's families of origin.

Duvall (1977) and subsequent writers posited that each individual, couple, and family progresses through a series of stages. These begin with the couple's commitment and proceed through childbearing, childrearing school-aged and then adolescent children, launching young adult children into their own lives and families, retirement, aging, and death. Individuals also progress through a series of life cycle stages, many of which parallel those of the family.

All life cycle theories are dialectical. They posit that the stages are sequential and that there is a challenge associated with each stage that must be resolved to effectively meet the challenges of subsequent stages. Viewed in this dialectical perspective, Liz and Martin's unresolved conflicts from the stage of forming a new couple relationship precluded their successful resolution of the transition to parenthood.

While the family life cycle, like other stage theories, implies that everyone passes through the same sequence of stages, individuals and couples can live happy and fulfilling lives without children despite the theories being focused on childbearing, childrearing, and child-launching. For couples who either choose or cannot have children, resolving disappointment or agreeing to not have children culminates in the resolution of the relevant stages of the life cycle.

Expectations. Liz and Martin each brought expectations to their relationship about how they and their partner would behave as a couple and as parents. Their own parents served as role models. Families also transmit expectations for parental behavior across generations. And the larger society in which a couple lives socializes its members to behave in certain predictable ways when they assume a role as clearly defined as mother or father. Martin and Liz were each influenced by all these sources of expectations.

In addition to expectations, parenting also brings new responsibilities. The added tasks of caring for an infant necessitate redistributing former responsibilities as well as the new ones in a mutually acceptable way. In the writer's personal and professional experience, there is so much to do that distribution of tasks following the birth of a couple's first child never feels fair. Additionally, no matter how clearly each partner has described how she or he wants to parent, it is impossible to anticipate everything, including one's own feelings upon becoming a parent. Thus, couples are usually in the position of negotiating change in the midst of exhaustion, elevated expectations, and feeling overwhelmed by new responsibilities. The result may be a lack of empathy for the other partner, who is also experiencing many, if not all of the same things.

Martin appeared to want Liz to set her own priorities regarding balancing motherhood and work outside the home. Whether he held an expectation that she follow their mothers' paths and only work outside the home if finances necessitated was not yet apparent to the couple therapist.

Liz was uncertain about how to balance her professional and maternal roles. On the one hand, she wanted her mother, mother-in-law, and sister's approval. On the other hand, she resisted the societal expectation that good mothers stay at home. She wanted to be a good mother and was uncertain what that meant. The couple therapist's knowledge and experience suggested that Liz and Martin needed to clarify their own expectations and accept the other's as valid but not a demand.

The couple therapist also noticed a similarity between Liz's current perception of Martin's view of her career and the one she expressed when she had met individually with the therapist during their marital separation. Liz believed Martin wanted her career to be secondary to her mothering. She had also said that he had never taken her career seriously. Liz's belief about how Martin viewed her career therefore appeared to be unchanged by their daughter's birth. The therapist concluded that how Martin viewed Liz's career and her perceptions of his view needed exploration and resolution apart from their expectations for her as a mother.

Managing Conflict. The couple therapist's second clinical impression was that Liz and Martin needed to question their assumptions about the meaning of conflict and then expand their repertoire for managing it. Both viewed conflict as a relationship failure and as a result delayed addressing anything involving conflict until they could no longer avoid it. From her observation of the argument in her office, she concluded they could benefit from learning to listen empathetically and learning to avoid distractions, such as arguing about who is correct. She also knew that not resolving conflict could itself become a source of additional conflict.

Sex. The couple therapist's third clinical impression was that Liz and Martin's conflict had spilled over into their sexual relationship. Liz had accused Martin of withholding sex. In a subsequent session, he responded that she rarely initiated sex and if she did she would know how untrue her accusation was. The couple therapist concluded that initiating and withholding sex to manage relationship distress needed further attention. She also wondered whether their struggle regarding who initiated sex reflected a more general struggle for power within their relationship.

The couple therapist was aware that every challenge with which Liz and Martin struggled, as a couple and as individuals, could not be identified in one or even two sessions. She also knew they might not be fully aware of their dynamics or the range of resulting issues. Her role was to target questions toward identifying and clarifying what existed that needed to be changed in order for Liz and Martin to accomplish their therapeutic goals.

Preliminary Assessment

The couple therapist's preliminary assessment reflected her clinical observations and impressions. Her case notes read:

Liz Manning-Jones and Martin Jones presented for couple therapy three months following the birth of their daughter and first child, Christina. They are a well-educated, professional couple who appear motivated to remain together and ambivalent about couple therapy. Their history includes meeting through mutual friends when they were in professional school and marrying 14 months later. They separated after a year and a half; Liz's perspective on the reason for their separation is in her individual record and no information about Martin's perspective is currently available. Presenting problem involves conflicts about Liz's maternal role and whether Martin "supports" it. It was observed that, in addition to resolution of the presenting problem, the couple is reactive to one another and may need additional skills for expressing anger and resolving conflict. Liz and Martin interrupted one another and changed topics as emotions became more heated. They also devolved into conflict about who was correct. The need for skills to avoid these pitfalls and increase empathy is indicated. There was minimal attention to how their issues play out in their sexual relationship; this needs to be further addressed in future sessions. At this time, it does not appear that either Liz's sexual assault history or her identified sexual preference contributes to the problem. The potential risks of couple therapy with Liz's former individual therapist were explained to both Liz and Martin, and issues of the couple therapist's gender and race were introduced.

Stop and Think:

Be sure to include your answers in your journal.

1. What are your thoughts about the couple therapist's preliminary assessment?
2. What would you add or delete, based on what you have learned about Liz and Martin as you have read this chapter?

Theoretical Conceptualization

After completing a preliminary assessment, couple therapists decide what theoretical approach best fits what they know about a particular couple, as well as their own world view of how couples resolve the challenges and conflicts they face. The preliminary assessment can be viewed as a working hypothesis and changed as further assessment and theory-based intervention yield new information. In Section II of this book, you will learn about some of the foundational and more recent theories of couple therapy, as well as how they can be used in couple therapy with Liz and Martin.

Conclusions

This chapter introduced you to Liz and Martin, the couple you will follow throughout this textbook, through the professional eyes of their couple therapist. You have learned about their presenting problem, the history of the problem, and their sociocultural context and social support. You have also read about their couple therapist's observations of their couple dynamics and read her preliminary assessment from which she will use theory to guide her interventions.

Liz and Martin are a multi-problem couple and part of a large and complex family network. Couple therapists do not need to remember every detail of what they learn about a couple. What they do need to remember are the couple's dynamics, so they can guide client couples toward changing those interaction patterns that have led to and sustained the problems the couple and the therapist have identified and that have prevented the couple from changing on their own.

Stop and Think:

Be sure to include your answers in your journal.

1. What do you know now about Liz and Martin?
2. What are your assumptions about them?
3. How might you distinguish what you know from what you assume?
4. What else might you need to know in order to understand this couple?

As you continue to follow Liz and Martin, you will learn how their dynamics illustrate couple concepts and the various schools of couple psychotherapy. You will also observe the couple therapist interacting with them. You will then learn about various sociocultural challenges Liz, Martin, and their couple therapist face. You will also learn about the couple therapist's experience of couple therapy sessions with Liz and Martin and about the ethics of her profession. Finally, you will learn about other professional services couples may require and about how to refer for those services. For now, you have an introduction to who Liz and Martin are and to their couple therapy.

References

Basirico, L. A., Cashion, B. G., & Eshleman, J. R. (2014). *Introduction to sociology (16th ed.)*. Redding CA: BVT.

Berg-Cross, L. (2000). *Basic concepts in family therapy (2nd ed.)*. New York NY: The Haworth Press.

Brizendine, L. (2007). *The female brain.* New York NY: Morgan Road Books.

Colten, H. R. & Altevogt, B. M. (Eds.). (2006). *Sleep disorders and sleep deprivation: An unmet public health problem.* Washington DC: National Academies Press. Retrieved from https://www.ncbi.nlm.nih.gov/books/NBK19961/.

Diller, J. V. (2007). *Cultural diversity. A primer for the human services* (3rd ed.). Belmont CA: Brooks/Cole.

Duvall, E. M. (1977). *Marriage and family development* (5th ed.). Philadelphia: Lippincott.

Esposito, J. & Hattem, A. (2017). *Introduction to family counseling. A cast study approach.* Los Angeles CA: Sage Publishing.

Lum, D. (2007). *Culturally competent practice. A framework for understanding diverse groups and justice issues* (3rd ed.). Belmont CA: Brooks/Cole.

McGoldrick, M. (2008). *Genograms: Assessment and intervention.* New York NY: Norton.

Myers, D. (2008). *Why women should rule the world.* New York NY: HarperCollins.

Sager, C. J. (1994). *Marriage contracts and couple therapy. Hidden forces in intimate relationships.* Northvale NJ: Jason Aronson, Inc.

Schreiner, M. (2017). Handling deflection. Retrieved from https://evolutioncounseling.com/handling-deflection/.

Swain, A. M., O'Hara, M. W., Starr, K. R., & Gorman, L. L. (1997). A prospective study of sleep, mood and cognitive function in postpartum and nonpostpartum women. *Obstetrics and Gynecology*, 90 (3), 381–386. Retrieved from http://doi.org/10.1016/S0029-7844(97)89252-6.

Tannen, D. (1990). *You just don't understand! Women and men in conversation.* New York NY: HarperCollins.

Wong, G., Derthick, A. O., David, E. J. R., Saw, A., & Okazaki, S. (2014). The what, the why, and the how. A review of race microaggressions research in psychology. *Race and Social Problems*, 6 (2), 181–200.

CHAPTER 2

Coupling and Uncoupling

Learning Objectives

1. Summarize the historical context of contemporary Western coupling, uncoupling, and marriage.
2. Identify the legal aspects of contemporary Western coupling, uncoupling, and marriage.
3. Describe four sociological perspectives on Western coupling and marriage.
4. List five anthropological concepts used to describe coupling and marriage cross-culturally.
5. Explain the importance of recognizing cultural myths and assumptions.
6. Contrast romantic love and other motives to couple and marry.
7. Describe rituals and variations in how couples create a committed relationship in twenty-first century North America.
8. Critique the choice not to marry.

This chapter will provide you with a backdrop and context for studying couple therapy. You will read about the historical context of contemporary Western marriage. You will also be introduced to legal, sociological, and anthropological perspectives on coupling, marriage, and uncoupling. Romantic love, coupling in contemporary US culture, and the choice not to couple will also be addressed. Emphasis will unavoidably be placed on dominant cultural themes because they were the focus of historians and sociologists studying western European and North American culture until relatively recently. Anthropological concepts, being grounded in cross-cultural research, will be introduced to highlight the impact of students' own cultural experience upon their views of coupling, marriage, and uncoupling.

The universal presence of a dominant cultural norm suggests that there exists a single, correct way to be a couple. However, the specifics of dominant cultural norms are not universal across cultures, and a brief examination to support this point is included.

The focus of this chapter is Western history because most readers will work with couples who have been heavily influenced by Western culture. The historical and sociological reviews emphasize white, middle-class couples because that was who the fields focused on almost exclusively until recently, when attention turned to multicultural couples. Of the early couple and family therapists, only Minuchin (1974) mentioned people of color and only because he made Spanish-speaking immigrant families a central part of his work. Lum (2007) gave a thought-provoking example of stereotyping non-white hospital patients, speaking in a language they do not understand, and then misdiagnosing them as a result of the language barrier. It is an important topic, but not one historians and sociologists paid much attention to until late in the last century. Chapter 9 provides a more detailed focus on multicultural practice.

This chapter is not intended to be an exhaustive study of the historical, sociological, and anthropological aspects of marriage. Rather, it is intended to introduce you to these perspectives as a backdrop to the study of couple therapy and the impact of Western culture upon the couples with whom you will work.

Stop and Think:

Be sure to include your answers in your journal.

1. How do you define coupling? Are commitment, permanence, and/or social recognition essential to your definition?
2. Now, define marriage. How is it similar to coupling? How is it different?
3. Examining your definitions, think about and discuss what has influenced your definitions.

Historical Context and Contemporary Western Marriage

Overview

The purpose of coupling was first survival and then accumulation of wealth and power through cooperative alliances, whether formally contracted or informally entered upon. Coupling began as a way of extending cooperative networks of people in order to ensure survival. As human societies shifted from hunter-gatherer to agrarian, the need for cooperation in order to survive continued. As the economic and political structures continued to evolve, families were able to accumulate property, wealth, and power and to develop lines of inheritance. To maintain and increase power and wealth, families expanded their social connections through cooperative agreements with other families, or marriage. The marital alliances between kinship groups served as the mechanism to achieve the goals of wealth, power, and maintaining inheritance lines. For those with higher status and more accumulated wealth, polygamy allowed for an even greater expansion of economic and political alliances and thus consolidation of wealth and power. Most Western cultures prohibit polygamy. However, polygamy has served the historical and cross-cultural function of allowing for the accumulation of even greater wealth and power (Coontz, 2005).

Viewing marriage as an alliance between kinship groups for survival, accumulation and inheritance of wealth, and expansion of power may clarify why hormone-challenged young lovers were not allowed to determine who they married. As a business transaction, marriage was not about romantic love or sexual attraction. Rather, it was about considering the family's resources, identifying other families of reasonably similar means and influence, and negotiating an economic alliance. Procreation in order to expand workers and ensure lines of inheritance, as well as family alliances to increase influence and available work force were the sole purposes of marriage. Thus, we can assume that the sexual identification and preferences of prospective partners was ignored, at least within the realm of marriage. Same-sexed coupling, a contemporary phenomenon, will be discussed in Chapter 9.

In societies that continue to arrange marriages, it can be observed that wealthier and more influential families can sometimes consider the prospective spouses' preferences of partner, if not their sexual identification and preference. For example, the writer's late grandmother-in-law was given the choice between two men her father deemed appropriate who had asked to marry her. In her stories, her late husband and the other man had approached her father independently of their own families.

Stop and Think:

Be sure to include your responses in your journal.

Think about families of similar economic and social status in your parents' community with whom they might have wanted to form an alliance. Then think about the members of these families who are similar in age to you and your siblings.

1. Imagine your father telling you he had arranged a marriage between you or one of your siblings and a member of one of those families. Note what it might have been like in your journal.
2. The bride usually went to live with the groom's family, isolating her from her family and friends, and her father paid his father a dowry toward her support. Imagine how it would feel if your fathers exchanged money to essentially buy you a husband or wife. Imagine how it would feel if your father sent you away to live with your spouse's family, where it was impossible to maintain contact with family and friends.
3. Note how your experience in your current cultural and historical context may influence how you think about the historical realities of marriage.

Monogamous marriage based on romantic love between the two partners is thus a relatively recent and limited phenomenon. It was not until the late eighteenth century, a mere 150 years ago, and only in North America and western Europe that young adults were empowered to oppose their parents' choices and marry based upon their own wishes. The cultural sentimentalization of the nineteenth century and the sexualization of the twentieth century further ensconced these changes (Coontz, 2005).

Economic prosperity for the middle and upper classes in the 1950s and 1960s allowed for the rise of single-income, neolocal, nuclear families created through marriages of choice. Those decades are the first evidence historians and anthropologists have found of such social organization. Along with this change in marriage came the presumption that marriage would lead to self-fulfillment. Continuing affluence and demands for self-fulfillment late in the last century led to greater valuation and expression of women's capabilities beginning in the late 1960s and 1970s. These capabilities and their expression allowed a woman to be independent of her husband's role as financial provider and both to dissolve relationships that were not personally fulfilling. In other words, the same factors that allowed for what the dominant culture in the United States now considers traditional marriage also contributed to the soaring rate of uncoupling, or dissolution of marriages, that began in the 1970s (Coontz, 2005). However, it must be noted that white women's earnings continue to lag behind white men's, and people of color earn less than either.

The remainder of this section about the historical context of contemporary Western marriage delves further into five aspects of coupling: contracts between families, dowries, arranged marriages, coupling rituals, and a brief overview of uncoupling. It is important to note that the emotional and clinical aspects of uncoupling through divorce and uncoupling through the death of a partner are very distinct. These distinctions will be addressed in Chapter 9, while the historical context for Western uncoupling is addressed in this chapter.

A Contract between Two Families

As previously noted, the purposes of marriage throughout much of recorded history were to expand influence and consolidate wealth and power. Additionally, marriage provides comfort and care for spouses and allows for a socially sanctioned context for bearing and raising children.

Until the late 1800s, parents in Western societies were considered the authority on what individual and family characteristics were desirable in a mate for their child, and family considerations were prioritized over individual preferences. In some cultures at some periods in time, love between spouses was even discouraged because of its potential to be disruptive of the social order. If couples were to marry for love, then the needs of the kinship group for survival, consolidation of whatever wealth or power was available to them, and passing occupations and/or material resources to their heirs might not be met. By these standards, parents who allowed a prospective bride and groom to have a say in their union despite social conventions would be viewed as subversive.

In Western society, romantic love was viewed as a phenomenon that occurred outside of marriage. The story of Antony and Cleopatra typifies the use of marriage to increase power, despite the subsequent romanticizations of the couple's feelings for each other (Coontz, 2005). Characters of oral and written traditions, such as Lancelot and Guinevere in the story of Camelot, knew that their love was distinct from the institution of marriage. Disaster followed when attempts were made to combine love and marriage, as in Shakespeare's Romeo and Juliet. The couple's scheme to marry despite their parents' wishes ultimately resulted in disaster for everyone, illustrating the point to theater-goers that romantic love could not and should not form the basis of marriage.

Legal statutes pertaining to marriage reflect the reality that romantic love is a relatively recent component. Despite the romantic wording of marriage vows, marriage laws focus on who is allowed to marry, the legal contract between partners, and the rights and responsibilities a marriage contract entails. Contemporary marriage laws do not address romantic love between partners at all. Even where statutes pertaining to what is called alienation of affection exist, the presumption is that the spouse has violated her or his contractual relationship and that the fault lies with the person with whom that spouse has had an extramarital relationship. It also underscores the notion that the wife is the husband's property. Many states repealed their alienation of affection laws after codifying no-fault divorce laws. Where they remain, they are rarely enforced.

Similarly, romantic love is not included in traditional religious literature pertaining to marriage. These texts refer to marriage as a spiritual contract between the couple and the divine witnessed by the religious community. While contemporary clergy and lay officiants may refer to romantic love and passion in the wedding ceremonies they perform, such references are not essential to solemnizing and legalizing marriage within either spiritual, religious, or secular traditions.

Dowry and Brideprice

One aspect of marital contracts between families was the dowry. A dowry is the amount of money or property a bride's family pays the groom's family. Dowries were especially relevant in patrilocal societies, including Europe, where wives lived with their husbands' families. Cultural mythology held that dowries at least symbolically offset the cost of caring for the bride for the remainder of her life. However, Coontz (2005) pointed out that a bride, her subsequent children, and sometimes additional members of her extended family increased the labor pool and size of her husband's family, thus offsetting the cost of her living with them.

The resources a prospective bride's family was able to contribute to her dowry delimited the pool of prospective husbands available to her. If her family was poor, then only a poor man's family would be willing to accept her dowry, unless she brought nonmaterial assets to the union such as a powerful family connection. By contrast, if the prospective bride's family had many resources, her father would be more likely to insist she marry someone of means. Thus, a dowry was used to seal a financial alliance between two families, and the subsequent marriage was based upon a mutually beneficial financial contract between them.

In some cultures, the groom's family paid the bride's family to acquire her. This is called brideprice and is another form of sealing a marital contract. Brideprice also delimits the pool of eligible mates and treats both partners as a commodity to be exchanged for money or property to enrich and expand their families.

Stop and Think:

Be sure to include your answers in your journal.

1. Have you ever felt like a commodity?
2. If yes, what was it like?
3. If not, imagine what it would be like to be treated as though someone and especially someone about whom you cared was more concerned with your economic value than with who you are as a human being.

Poor families often sent some of their daughters out to work, being unable to garner dowries for all their female children. Most people reading this book have seen or are aware of the television series *Downton Abbey*. The program covered an historical period when dowries no longer existed in Europe. However, the female servants were sent into "service" because their families could not afford to support them until they found a mate who could, whereas the males became servants because their families' income source, such as a farm, was too small to sustain another worker. Servants had no hope of upward mobility from a marriage.

Twentieth century feminists have argued that the concept of a dowry is grounded in the belief that women are extraneous property to be unloaded. If Coontz (2005) is correct in her assessment, both the bride and groom were treated as assets to be invested in order to increase the family's labor pool, wealth, and/or power. Additionally, the feminist view of dowries does not account for societies that used a brideprice.

Arranged Marriages

Throughout most of Western history, marriages were arranged between two families, rather than between the prospective bride and groom. Arranged marriage is consistent with marriage being a contract between two families, with a dowry or brideprice to legitimize it. The musical *Fiddler on the Roof* exemplified the practice of using a match-maker to facilitate the process.

Arranged marriages continue today in some parts of the world. An arranged marriage, like marriage laws in the United States, focuses on the contractual nature of marriage. Romantic love is not a consideration. While taking romantic love out of the decision to marry may sound antiquated and perhaps repugnant to you, consider the impact romantic love may have on the partners' relationship.

Stop and Think:

Be sure to include your answers in your journal.

1. What besides romantic love is important to you in a life partner? Be specific.
2. Think about marrying someone your parents want you to marry and with whom you are not in love. What are your expectations for that person and your feelings about her or him?
3. What characteristics do you associate with love? What about being "in love"? Are they the same phenomenon? If not, what are the similarities and differences between love and "in love"?

4 Think about the last time you or one of your close friends was "in love." What was positive about the experience? What was painful or disruptive?

5 Based on what you have read, what you already know, and what you think, what might the advantages of separating the contractual aspect of marriage from romantic love be? What might the disadvantages be?

Imagine an economic partnership in which you share responsibility for earning and spending money, establishing and maintaining a home, raising children, interacting with friends and family, and participating in the life of your community without asking yourself whether or not you love your partner. Such imagination requires you to step back from your own cultural, or ethnocentric perspective, which includes your experiences and/or observations and the beliefs and expectations that arose from them.

Partners' expectations for each other may be very different in arranged marriages than in marriages of choice. In any marriage, partners expect to work together to build a shared life, home, and family, as described in the previous paragraph. In arranged marriages, they do not also expect to find romantic love and self-fulfillment with their spouse, although they might hope to enjoy their spouse's company and to be treated well by him or her. When marriage is based on romantic love, the expectations that partners will always be entranced, passionate, and fulfilled by one another is added to the already lengthy list of expectations for their partnership.

As previously noted, the writer's late grandmother-in-law was in an arranged marriage in the 1920s when she was 18 years old. She believed she was fortunate because her father asked for her input in deciding between two suitors. She grew to love her husband, despite a generation's difference in their ages. Apropos of this discussion, she said her marriage had been easier than marriages she had observed since living in this country because their expectations had not been as high.

When couples first fall in love, their feelings for each other may be based on fantasies about who the other appears to be and who each needs the other to be, rather than who the other person really is. Gus Napier (Aponte, 2009; Napier, 1988; Napier & Whitaker, 1978) wrote that couples initially come together expecting the other to heal the emotional wounds from their relationships with their parents and previous partners and then become disenchanted as they learn that their partners cannot do these things for them. In truth, no one other than oneself can heal wounds from one's previous relationships. You will learn more about Napier and other psychodynamic and experiential couple therapists in Chapter 6.

Coupling Rituals

Rituals often punctuate progression from one stage of the individual, couple, and family life cycle to the next. Coupling in general and marriage in particular usually involve rituals of some sort. In sociological terms, these rituals include dating, courting, engagement, and weddings or commitment ceremonies, each entailing an increased level of commitment to the relationship.

Coupling rituals have changed over time. Coontz (2005) cited anthropological data indicating that in one early culture sharing a meal was sufficient. In more recent Western history, posting the banns and community celebrations became more common. Today in the United States, wedding ceremonies vary from a civil officiant or clergy person's office to a destination event with multiple celebrations over the course of several days.

When individuals choose their partners, the process is termed mate selection. The choice of a life partner is, to some extent, socially determined, despite the inclusion of romantic love as a variable in mate selection. This fact horrifies some students, and you will have an opportunity to address it in a Stop and Think in the sociological perspectives section of this chapter.

Courtship is defined across species as the process by which the male of the species entices a female to be his partner, as when a male peacock displays his legendary feathers. Courting and the less committed dating in contemporary Western societies have variously involved a couple with a chaperone, a couple without a chaperone, and paired groups of friends. Until the past few decades, the male was expected to initiate dating and courtship, and the custom of men approaching women has persisted for some beyond the third wave of feminism. The television programs *Downton Abbey* and *Happy Days* and films such as *American Graffiti* demonstrate male-initiated dating and courtship from the early nineteenth through the mid-twentieth centuries.

Stop and Think:

Be sure to include your answers in your journal.

1 Identify two of your favorite contemporary films or programs involving some illustration of coupling.
2 How did the initiations of the relationships differ from those depicted in the older programs and films cited above? How were they similar?

Dating and courting usually entail increased emotional and physical intimacy over time. While the man was primarily responsible for moving the relationship forward, the woman had been tasked with controlling and preventing more sexual intimacy than was socially appropriate until feminism re-emerged in western Europe and the United States in the late 1960s. In recent decades, dating has become a more mutual process, with women able to initiate both emotional and sexual intimacy. Historically, a woman has had the right to decline a man's advances unless commanded to accept them by her parents, and nonconsensual sex outside of marriage, though underreported, has been regulated by criminal statutes (10 US Code 920).

At some point, a dating couple loses interest, encounters an insurmountable barrier, or moves their relationship to a higher level of commitment. While a woman can encourage and then wait passively for a man to suggest greater commitment, in recent decades women can also initiate it. When commitment includes the presumption of permanence and becomes public, a couple begins transitioning to the next stage of the individual, couple, and family life cycle. When this commitment also includes marriage, the process of transitioning to marriage begins.

Some form of ritual is associated with the transition to marriage in both civil and spiritual traditions, although this has not always been true. Over the centuries, the rituals involved in coupling and marriage have included eating or sleeping together in the presence of the community, posting the banns, meeting in the town square in community celebration of a union, elopement, and the elaborate weddings and commitment ceremonies that have become part of Western culture in the past 100 years. These will be discussed in subsequent subsections of this chapter.

Uncoupling: Widowhood and Marital Dissolution

While there is a presumption of permanence when two people commit to marriage, all relationships end. This does not mean that all couples dissolve their relationships or that all marriages end in divorce. It does mean that everyone dies, and it is far more common for one spouse to be widowed than for both to die simultaneously. The emotional and clinical differences between these ways in which relationships end will be addressed in Chapter 9, while the historical and sociocultural aspects will be addressed here.

Relationships less frequently end in divorce or dissolution than in the death of one of the partners. Current statistics indicate that half of all marriages end in divorce. However, these statistics are based on a comparison of the number of marriages that take place in a given year with the number of divorces occurring in that same year. They do not reflect an examination of new marriages over time to determine what percentage of them end in divorce. Additionally, divorce only pertains to legally married couples. The outcomes of domestic partnerships, civil unions, and committed relationships not governed by legal statutes regulating their creation and dissolution are difficult, if not impossible, to track.

As with marriage, the rights and responsibilities of each partner during a divorce have changed over time. In the patrilineal and patrilocal societies of historical Western culture, wives had no financial or sometimes even custody rights upon dissolution of the marriage or death of the husband. In some Western cultures, a wife would also no longer be desirable as a prospective partner were she divorced.

In the twenty-first century, women are able to leave marriages with full rights to jointly owned assets and to custody of children from the marriage. This means assets (the exceptions being inheritance kept separately and in some states assets acquired prior to the marriage) and custody are usually divided equally and contentious divorces establishing fault, or blame, are less likely to occur. When there is disparity between what each partner earns, spousal support or alimony and child support may be available. And, unless one partner is proven to be incompetent to raise children, former spouses are encouraged to share both legal and residential custody whenever possible. When children have been born into a relationship that is not legally codified, one partner's rights to custody and visitation and the other's right to child support may be limited. Like many laws, these vary among states.

Western women who were widowed did not historically have rights to inherit from their deceased husbands. The popular television program, *Downton Abbey*, portrayed the vulnerability of women as recently as the beginning of the last century. The husband's property could not be inherited by his wife or daughters; as a result they faced the possibility of being dependent upon someone, like the distant male cousin in Downton Abbey that no one had met, upon the husband's death.

In Biblical times, a widowed woman was expected to marry her husband's brother. This custom continues to be practiced in some cultures. Alternatively, a widowed woman might have remained as an unpaid servant in her husband's family's house or return to her own family, and the latter might require leaving the children with her late husband's family. Presently, in Europe and North America, women have full rights to inheritance from their deceased husbands, as do men from their late wives. Couples who marry with children from previous relationships may create a legal document that specifies the children, rather than the current spouse, as beneficiaries of each one's estate. This can be problematic if, for example, the couple has been living in a home owned by the deceased or if the survivor's income is insufficient to cover the cost of remaining in the home they lived in jointly.

Until recently, the high rate of maternal mortality during and immediately following childbirth left a significant number of men widowed fathers with infants. Unlike widowed mothers, widowed men were expected and even encouraged to remarry, irrespective of whether or not the infant survived.

The decision to end a marriage, domestic partnership, or other committed couple relationship is never an easy one. Our culture denigrates divorce, and cultural mythology implies that it only happens to irresponsible people who casually decide for no apparent reason that they do not want to be married anymore. Personally and professionally, the writer has never encountered anyone who did not struggle with the decision to dissolve a committed relationship and suffer both during and after dissolving the relationship. The professional literature also fails to support the cultural myth that people casually dissolve marriages and other commitments they assumed to be permanent.

The loss of a life partner, whether through death or dissolution of the relationship, is a painful and difficult process. Even when a relationship has deteriorated over time and been distressed, people who are divorced or widowed suffer emotionally from losing an intimate partner, their life together, the status of being part of a couple, and their hopes for the future together. At the same time, widows and divorcees may be forced to relocate their homes and reinvent their lives. Divorce requires at least one of the former spouses to move, and both divorce and widowhood may create disruptive emotional and financial circumstances.

For widows and widowers, the sudden death of a partner involves the added difficulty of not having been able to say good-bye or resolve any ill will that may have existed between the partners at the time one of them died. Prolonged illnesses, while allowing time to say good-bye, may lead to physical and emotional exhaustion for the care-giving partner. Additionally, the process of watching a life partner suffer and die can be emotionally traumatic. Whether the partners were legally married in addition to being emotionally committed to one another does not alter any of these impacts. However, access to the dying partner when hospitalized and control over many important decisions (e.g., what to do if the dying partner becomes incompetent; funeral decisions; estate planning; the custody of minor children, if any) may not be available to the surviving partner in a domestic partnership or civil union, further complicating the loss.

Divorce involves the death of a relationship without the death of the partner as the precipitating event. Watching a relationship die and finding that every effort to save it is futile may result in feelings of failure and hopelessness, the former of which is generally supported by the dominant cultural attitude toward divorce. Lowered self-esteem and lack of the social support available to widows and widowers following a death can prolong the process of adjustment and feelings of hopelessness about the future. Without the protections of marriage, divorced partners, like their widowed counterparts, may find their lives disrupted by financial change and lack of access to minor children, if any. You will learn more about the clinical aspects of death and divorce in Chapter 9.

Stop and Think:

Be sure to include your answers in your journal.

1 What are your beliefs about divorce and people who get divorced? How do these influence your thoughts about the legal rights of former spouses?

2 How do you view people who live together without marriage? How does your view influence your thoughts about the legal rights of cohabiting partners?
3 Has anyone you know been widowed? Has anyone you know been divorced? How have they reacted? How have they been treated? What are the similarities and differences you have noticed in how they are treated?

Legal Aspects of Contemporary Western Marriage

Contemporary Western legal definitions of marriage specify the rights, obligations, and mutual protections afforded married couples. Legal statutes in every state specify these rights and obligations as they pertain to sexuality, gender roles, relationships with in-laws, and children's legitimacy. For example, married couples in the United States have next-of-kin rights when one is hospitalized, whereas cohabiting couples and couples in domestic partnerships usually do not.

Legal statutes pertaining to marriage in the United States also delineate who can marry. In 1967, the Supreme Court ruled that denying the right to marry to biracial couples was a violation of their constitutional rights (Loving v Virginia, 1967). Yet, the last state to repeal laws banning and even criminalizing biracial marriage was Alabama in 2000. Similarly, it was not until 2015 that the Supreme Court ruled that denying same-sexed couples the right to marry similarly violated rights guaranteed by the Constitution, yet some states continue to make it difficult if not impossible for same-sexed couples to marry and continue to discriminate in myriad ways against transgendered and same-sexed couples. Issues of race and gender in couple therapy will be discussed in Chapter 9.

Most states do not allow people under the age of eighteen to marry, although people 16 and older can marry in some states with parental consent. Most states also do not allow close relatives to marry. When close relatives have been allowed to marry, the purpose has been to consolidate wealth and power and to insure inheritance within a small group.

The incest taboo precluding sexual relationships and therefore marriage between parents and children is universal. In many cultures, this taboo also precludes sexual relationships and therefore marriage between siblings. Step-siblings, however, are related by the marriage of their parents, rather than by blood, and therefore are exempt from the taboo on sexual relationships and marriage among family members. Sexual relationships between step-siblings, if they develop, may be emotionally confusing for step-siblings who grew up in the same household. While they can legally marry, this right does not preclude charges of sexual abuse of minors if one partner was less than 18 years old when the sexual relationship began. As you know from studying European history, marriages between first cousins was a way of consolidating wealth and power among the ruling classes. However, in many but not all US jurisdictions, first cousins cannot marry.

Additionally, legal statutes have prevented anyone who is already married from marrying in most states in the United States. US culture values monogamy and views on exceptions tend to be emotionally loaded. Polygamy, or multiple spouses, has historically been more common than not across cultures and remains a feature of contemporary marriage in some non-Western cultures.

Spiritual Marriage

Spiritual and legal marriages are often conflated. Although religious practices and legal statutes may appear identical, they are not. The former are subject to the precepts and practices of the organized religion in which a couple wishes to marry, whereas the latter are governed by the laws of the civic jurisdiction in which the couple wishes to marry. The US Constitution includes an establishment clause forbidding a state religion. States allow clergy to perform marriage ceremonies. However, the marriage is not legal until a license issued by the county of the state in which the couple wishes to marry has been signed and filed by the clergy or civil officiant.

According to Coontz (2005), spiritually sanctioned marriage is a relatively recent phenomenon. Religious marriage practices are designed to maintain the integrity of the spiritual community. Unlike biracial and same-sexed couples who were legally prohibited from marrying, members of a spiritual community who choose to marry outside the faith can be legally married in a civil ceremony even if they cannot in a spiritual ceremony sanctioned by the religious community.

Divorce

Historically, marriages were easily dispensed with when alliances failed to produce the anticipated results. One of our Western cultural myths is that divorce is a recent phenomenon, but in fact it is only more prevalent than it had been in the mid-twentieth century. Prehistoric evidence suggests that alliances were formed and dissolved as circumstances dictated. Historical data suggests the same, based on failure to produce heirs and on shifting political alliances among extended families joined by marriage. It was not until the nineteenth and twentieth centuries that social, political, and cultural changes in the West allowed individuals to choose their life partners. And it was only in the late-nineteenth century and only in North America and Europe that these factors coalesced to create marriages of choice with the husband as provider and the wife as nurturer (Coontz, 2005).

Prior to no-fault divorce and community property being introduced into law in the second half of the last century, the wife's rights were subservient to her husband's and also severely limited. Between the twelfth century in England and the late 1700s in the United States, Western women were not allowed to own or inherit property (McGee & Moore, 2014). In the United States, women did not have equal access to their husband's assets nor were they allowed to have credit in their own names until the 1970s. Estranged husbands charged with physical or emotional abuse or with engaging in extramarital sexual relationships were sometimes directed to provide financial assets in compensation. Unfortunately, such charges needed to be proven in a court of law, precipitating increased contentiousness between divorcing spouses and increased legal fees. As a result, the concept of no-fault divorce was introduced into law during the 1970s and 1980s, as were community property laws.

Women's Rights

Women's rights to property and credit have varied by state and increased only incrementally between the 1770s and 1970s in the United States (McGee & Moore, 2014). Women also did not have rights to their bodies during that time period. The concepts of spousal rape and intimate partner violence did not emerge until the late twentieth and early twenty-first centuries. Wives in the United States traditionally did not have the power to determine where or how the couple lived, how many children she bore, or (unless granted by her husband) the power to refuse his sexual advances. Intimate partner violence, which includes marital rape, will be discussed in Chapter 9.

Sociological Perspectives on Coupling and Marriage

Coupling and marriage have been studied by a variety of scholars outside the field of couple therapy, as well as by experts within the field. Like historians, sociologists and social psychologists are among those who have examined coupling from a non-clinical perspective.

Mate Selection

Sociologists refer to the process of identifying an appropriate life partner as mate selection (Basirico, Cashion, & Eshleman, 2014). The purpose of including the topic of mate selection in this chapter is to underscore that our and our couple clients' choices of partner are not entirely individual preference. They are also governed by societal norms for behavior and by social circumstances, even if we would prefer to think otherwise.

Mate selection is regulated by the rules of exogamy, endogamy, and propinquity. These limit who one can select as a mate.

Exogamy refers to a proscription against choosing a mate who is closely related. Different societies define the limits of exogamy differently, as does the same society over time. Exogamy defines the boundaries of incestuous relationships and allows for the expansion of the kinship group. In the United States, one must marry outside one's biological nuclear family, and in most states first cousins are also precluded from forming a legal marriage. Liz could not marry her brother, David, and Martin could not marry any of his sisters. Step-siblings are not related by blood, and there is no state that prohibits step-siblings from marrying; however, half-sibling relationships fall into the category of incestuous and are thus both a violation of the norms of exogamy and of legal statutes in all states.

Endogamy refers to the phenomenon that people also choose a partner from within a sociocultural group that shares certain characteristics. People usually do not choose a partner from whom they diverge dramatically on demographic factors including age, income, education, ethnicity, religion, race, socioeconomic status, and nationality. The operative word in the previous sentence is usually and, as you will see in Chapter 9, biracial marriages have increased dramatically in the United States in recent decades (Killian, 2013).

The norms of endogamy are no longer codified, as they were when statutes prohibited biracial marriage. However, social pressures and learned preferences continue to lead most people to partner with someone who has reasonably similar life experiences. Liz's father reacted negatively to her violation of one of the norms of endogamy. Martin's parents were more resigned to the possibility but nevertheless would have preferred him marrying a black woman.

Propinquity refers to choosing a partner who lives within a certain geographic distance. Prior to the wide-spread use of social media and internet dating, it was virtually impossible to meet anyone who did not live nearby or with whom an individual or his or her friends, family, co-workers, or members of a spiritual or interest community did not interact. Now people are able to meet and form romantic connections with people they would not otherwise have encountered. Nevertheless, partners who meet through internet dating sites and other social media more often than not already live reasonably close to each other.

Martin and Liz were born within months of each other to unrelated sets of parents. They grew up in similar socioeconomic circumstances. Both families identified as Christian, although each affiliated with a different denomination; in both cases, the parents were more devout than the children. Both families were middle class, and both Liz and Martin incurred debt as they pursued their higher education. They grew up in the same geographic area. As a result of these similar life experiences, they shared values and life goals.

Liz and Martin were both intelligent, highly educated, and therefore able to pursue professional careers. They met through friends while they were in graduate school at the same university.

Liz and Martin's significant demographic difference involved race. While race is a significant sociological and experiential factor impacting their everyday life outside their marriage, they appeared to have adapted within their relationship. In Chapter 9 you will learn in more detail how partners adapt to differing life experiences based on race.

Stop and Think:

Be sure to include your answers in your journal.

1 What was your first thought when you read that falling in love and choosing one's own mate are influenced by social factors outside one's control?

2 Look back at the list you made of what you are looking for in a life partner in addition to love. Which factors fit the definition of exogamy? Which fit the definition of endogamy? Which fit the definition of propinquity?
3 How did you meet or do you anticipate meeting your life partner? Does propinquity matter to you?
4 Do you know anyone who is in or anticipates being in an arranged marriage? Does that person's partner or potential partner fit similar characteristics of exogamy, endogamy, and/or propinquity to those you have selected for yourself?

Marriage

Sociological theory examines concepts such as the function of marriage in the structure of society and the impact of marriage on various groups within the society. Sociologists also study the social factors that support and undermine committed intimate relationships.

All societies create some form of kinship structure. In other words, families and the marriages of which they are comprised are universal phenomena. The mutual impact of kinship and the larger society upon one another is therefore an important area of study for sociologists and anthropologists alike (Basirico et al., 2014).

Within the field of sociology, the proponents of structure-functional theory examine the structure, or organization, of marriage and its functions within the larger society. These functions are to teach children how to behave in socially approved ways, to provide partners and their children with emotional support and affection, to prevent sexual relationships from deviating from societal norms, to provide a legally regulated environment for bearing and raising children, and to determine the roles and statuses family members can occupy (Basirico et al., 2014, pp. 372–374). The latter function means that a couple's socioeconomic status determines the options that are available not only to them but also to their children, and this determination occurs through the mechanism termed life chances. For example, because both Liz and Martin's families were middle class, they were exposed to educational opportunities and teacher attitudes that allowed them to consider college, even though neither set of parents could afford college for them and Liz's parents did not consider college beneficial for young women.

An example of how a couple's socioeconomic status affects their children's life chances involves school funding in the United States. Schools rely on local property taxes for a significant portion of their funding. Liz and Martin's income allowed them to live in the catchment area for a local school district that was well funded. Their children would therefore attend schools with more resources, including higher teacher expectations for students, to prepare and encourage them to achieve academically than children whose parents earned less money. Teachers in poorer schools are more likely to share persistent stereotypes about low socioeconomic status students. In this way, schools contribute to differences in life chances. Our for-profit health care system, food insecurity, lack of affordable child care for low-wage earning parents, and poverty-level wages requiring parents to work more than one job without benefits (e.g., employer-based health insurance, sick leave, parental leave, vacation days) also contribute to differing life chances based on the socioeconomic status of a child's family. Children whose families cannot afford health care are more likely to be more ill more often, and nutrition has been associated with academic achievement. Parental stress from all these factors diminishes parents' ability to attend to the physical, emotional, and cognitive needs of their children, further diminishing the children's potential to compete with children from more affluent families.

Sociologists who subscribe to the theory that all social phenomena have a purpose in maintaining the society have been criticized for implicitly supporting and maintaining the status quo, despite its negative impact on low-income families and irrespective of whether it works for most people or arguably even for the larger society. These sociologists would argue that the social structure requires laborers as well as professionals and that stratified schools allow for the training of less educated workers. These arguments ignore the question of whether underfunded schools where failure is expected contribute to negative outcomes for children as well as the larger society that far exceed how the children subsequently earn a living in adulthood. Additionally, these theorists suggest that all but the most evolutionary change threatens the social structure.

A second widely recognized sociological approach to marriage arises from conflict theory. Sociologists who subscribe to this theory believe that social change allows a society to remain flexible, adaptable, and vibrant, while lack of change creates entropy, or deterioration. Equalizing funding for public schools, creating a minimum wage adapted to the current costs of living, and universal health care to equalize the playing field for low-income couples and their children are not frightening concepts to these sociologists.

Sociologists subscribing to conflict theory have posited that traditional marriage as it is practiced in Europe and North America disempowers, subjugates, and controls the sexuality of women. For conflict theorists, excluding couples from the benefits of marriage if they do not conform to dominant cultural norms is another form of subjugation. Until same-sexed marriage was legalized, the sexuality and sexual identification of a substantial number of men and women were also controlled and their status subjugated to that of heterosexual, cis-gendered men and women. In sum, conflict theorists hold that questioning the need to subjugate groups within the society is crucial to the social order, rather than harmful or threatening.

The distribution of power between husbands and wives as evidenced by their decision-making process provides an example of the contrast between these two schools of sociological thought. Because the dominant culture has promoted the husband as sole earner for over a century, a power differential between husbands and wives arose. The writer's memory of sociological research from that time is that wives were shown to have less power than husbands in couple and family decision making, unless the husband delegated a certain decision to his wife; unfortunately, she has been unable to locate a reference to a study. These studies were likely limited to white, middle-class, married couples.

Feminist and conflict theorists challenged such disempowerment of women, while more traditional structure-functionalist sociologists held that power differentials were essential to harmonious marital and societal functioning. Similar arguments and positions arose around socioeconomic stratification as the civil rights movement and President Johnson's Great Society initiatives of the 1960s brought greater awareness of the extent and impact of both poverty and racism in the United States. Structure-functionalist sociologists believed that stratification by economic status served a purpose and more or less ignored racism, while conflict sociologists held that society would be better for everyone if the playing field was even.

There are two other sociological theories that can be applied to marriage. These are social exchange theory and symbolic interaction theory.

Social exchange theorists believe that mate selection is based on an assessment of one's own and one's prospective partner's assets and liabilities. Some sociologists have referred to this as the "marriage market" (Davis, 1986). Assets and liabilities include nonmaterial resources such as attractiveness, age, medical history, intelligence, level of education, prestige of career, social status, and shared values as well as financial resources. Individuals then attempt to find a partner who is of higher status, their success being determined by what they are able to offer in exchange. While finding a mate of higher status might seem impossible, the higher-status partner may place special value on a resource the lower-status partner brings to their relationship.

When your grandparents met, women most often brought physical and personality trait attractiveness to the marriage market, while men most often brought earning potential and other forms of social status. Today, you and your partner may be looking for very different assets in one another.

Symbolic interaction theorists hold that our social institutions and our behaviors within them developed and are maintained by socially agreed-upon conventions. Language is an example of such conventions. The letters c, a, and t in sequence have no meaning other than that attributed to them by our socially agreed-upon convention that "cat" is the verbal symbol representing a particular species of mammal. Similarly, race is a socially agreed-upon construct arising from a heightened social emphasis upon perceived differences, rather than anything biological (Basirico et al., 2014; Gannon, 2016).

For symbolic interactionists, there exists no structure independent of mutually created social meanings. Social meanings are not unique to a specific individual or couple, but rather are accepted throughout the larger social group. Dominant social constructs are those agreed upon by people in power. Thus, marriage can be understood in terms of its meaning to the dominant social group within a particular society at any given point in time, and this meaning changes as the society changes. Egalitarian marriages like Liz and Martin had agreed upon could be variously conceptualized as a threat to the social structure because it changes the function of marriage (structure-functionalist theory), a move away from marriage's subjugation of women and attendant lack of access to wealth and power (conflict theory), an exchange of egalitarian rather than complementary roles (social exchange theory), or a shift in the socially agreed-upon meaning of marriage (symbolic interactionist theory).

Stop and Think:

Be sure to include your answers in your journal.

1. Which theoretical approach to marriage best fits your world view? Explain your answer.
2. Do you believe we are more threatened as a society by change or by the maintenance of the status quo?
3. When you read the term "marriage market", what was your first reaction? What does your reaction tell you about your view of marriage?

Cross-Cultural Perspective on Coupling and Marriage

Anthropologists study coupling both within and across cultures. Below is a description of five anthropological concepts pertaining to couples. These are: conjugal families, marital status, monogamy/polygamy and related concepts, norms of residence, and norms of descent and inheritance.

As you read this section, bear in mind that your perspective is heavily influenced by your own experience. We will return to the issue of the impact of your unique cultural perspective on your cross-cultural work with couples in Chapter 9.

Conjugal families are the family unit of the couple only. Conjugal families are the smallest unit of the family and of any society, as well as the one most relevant to this book. Conjugal families, like nuclear and extended families, vary cross-culturally based on marital status, number of spouses, where partners live, rules of inheritance, rules about power, and rules governing mate selection. You have been introduced to each of these concepts in terms of the dominant culture in the United States. The purpose of this section of the chapter is to provide you with an anthropological perspective on your work with couples who are not members of the dominant culture.

Marital status is defined as whether or not someone is married in accordance with the social norms of the time. Statuses include single, married, separated, widowed, divorced, and monastic. The social status of those occupying a particular marital status varies across cultures, genders, and history. During most of the last two centuries, Western women who chose to remain single were labeled derogatorily as spinsters and presumed to be undesirable partners. Some women wanted to pursue careers at a time when married women were not allowed to work. Others were unwilling to submit to the will of a husband. Still others were not attracted to men. These motivations to remain single were not even recognized as legitimate, much less valued. In recent years, our society has begun to recognize and support the choice to remain unmarried for both women and men (see Chapter 9).

The United States is a monogamous society, despite the frequency of extramarital sexual relationships and remarriage following divorce. Polygamy, or multiple marriages simultaneously, is prohibited in all 50 states as of this writing.

Monogamy is not the norm cross-culturally, however. The most common form of polygamy is polygyny, or multiple wives. Polyandry, or multiple husbands, is less common. Because of the expense involved, most people in polygynous societies are unable to afford more than one wife and thus are monogamous by default. Multiple wives, like other possessions, indicate higher social status.

Open marriage and polyamory have been experimented with in the United States. Other societies that also prohibit polygamy, such as those of western Europe, presume that couples will not be monogamous for decades and view extramarital relationships as less threatening and titillating than many residents of the United States do.

In norms of residence, US society is neolocal. This means that couples are allowed to live independently of either one's parents and extended family, although they can choose to live with or in close proximity to them. Many cultures are or were patrilocal. In these cultures, couples live with the husband's family or nearby within the same community. Fewer cultures are or were matrilocal.

Even in neolocal societies, couples may be much closer emotionally or geographically to one partner's side of the family than the other's. With access to cell phones, Skype, FaceTime, and other forms of electronic communication and social networking, place of residence is not the sole determinant of the amount and quality of interactions between a couple and each partner's parents and extended family members.

Descent and inheritance refer to who gets what when parents are unable to work and when they die. The most common form of descent and inheritance is patrilineal. Titles, occupations, and material inheritance in patrilineal societies are passed from father to sons, with the oldest son generally being the greatest beneficiary. In the less common matrilineal societies, the mother's extended family members play important roles in the life of the couple and their children. The United States currently relies on bilateral lineage, which means both male and female offspring can inherit from both parents. Descent in contemporary European monarchies is complex, as evidenced by how Queen Elizabeth acquired the throne and to whom it will descend when she relinquishes it. Family farms and businesses currently pass to the most interested and competent adult child or are sold upon retirement or death of the parents.

These anthropological concepts arose from cross-cultural research and pertain to married couples, irrespective of the formality of the mechanism that joins the partners. Most contemporary societies do not recognize unmarried couples and thus less information about them exists. In recent decades, domestic partnerships and civil unions have conferred legal status in some jurisdictions in North America and western Europe and have thus become alternatives to marriage. Couples in state-sanctioned domestic partnerships are able to obtain some, though not all, of the rights and statuses of married couples without marrying. These include employer-based health insurance, hospital rights, and custody rights.

Romantic Love and Other Motivations for Coupling and Marrying

Stop and Think:

Be sure to include your answers in your journal.

1. For you personally, what are the benefits and drawbacks of legal marriage? Spiritual marriage?
2. What has been your experience of loving couples who cohabit without marrying? What are your beliefs about their choice?
3. What would motivate you to couple and/or marry besides romantic love?

There are many reasons one might choose to couple and marry, and romantic love is only one of them. Security, status, protection, and social pressure are among the other reasons. As you continue to learn about couples and how to practice couple therapy, refer back to this list and those you made while doing the Stop and Think exercise as you expand upon them.

Romantic love has been studied by evolutionary and neurobiologists. In an interesting cross-species study, Fisher, Aron, and Brown (2006) found a basis for romantic love underlying mate selection, sexual attraction, and remaining together a sufficient length of time to bear and raise offspring. Their work and the work of others suggests the biological basis of romantic love may not be enduring. As it ebbs, motivators other than romantic love must arise in order for the relationship to endure.

Stop and Think:

What might motivate a couple to remain together once the newness of sexual attraction and the hormonal euphoria of romantic love abate? Be sure to include your answers in your journal.

A partnership based upon falling in love, without consideration of what else each partner needs or may need throughout his or her life, entails risks to long-term compatibility and thus stability. Sometimes couples remain happily loving for decades. Other times, each partner begins to wonder what she or he saw in the other as the romantic blush diminishes. In his book *Love's Executioner and Other Tales of Psychotherapy*, Irvin Yalom (1989) eloquently noted that people who are in love are not only unreceptive to potential problems with their choice of partner being pointed out to them but also may respond with hostility. His point, well taken, is that they make horrible therapy clients. The writer cannot imagine a distressed couple that has been together several years reacting in the same manner.

Having worked with distressed couples for 40 years, the writer has observed that couples remain together for many reasons, some unfathomable. Years ago, the writer was working with two couples simultaneously, one of which appeared very well suited. They were kind and gentle with each other, shared values and interests, and were often chatting and laughing companionably when the writer entered the waiting room to greet them. The other couple was the exact opposite. They came through the door fighting, and it required vigilance to keep them from devolving into new arguments during sessions, especially when progress toward resolving the argument in which they were engaged appeared possible. They were careless of one another's feelings, lacked empathy for one another, and had been treating each other in the same way for many years. Yet, the first couple separated while the second remained together. Perhaps the two couples differed in terms of partners' expectations for themselves and each other, reasons and motivation to couple and remain coupled, fear of the consequences of dissolving their relationship, or hopelessness about each other.

Coupling in Twenty-First Century Western Culture

We will now turn our attention to the time and place in which you live and in which you are most likely to begin practicing couple therapy. Many of the topics included in this section have been addressed earlier in the chapter and so will be handled only briefly here.

Marriage

The US Census Bureau, as well as news outlets such as CNN, *The Dallas Morning News*, and *The Huffington Post*, have reported that the rate at which people marry has fallen in recent years. Marriage and divorce rates have often been associated with economic upticks and downturns and with a couple's socioeconomic status. People can afford to take on the expense of marriage, the cost of a wedding, and the cost of maintaining two households upon separation when they are financially secure. The economic environment faced by millennials has not been secure and this factor may account for at least some of the increase in the number of young adults choosing to defer marriage or not marry at all.

On the other hand, following the 2015 Supreme Court decision regarding marriage equality, the number of people allowed to marry has increased. Some same-sexed couples had chosen commitment ceremonies or civil unions where available prior to 2015, and ceremonies and events marking these alternatives to marriage can be as complex as a wedding. On the other hand, many same-sexed couples lived in states where they could not marry or create domestic partnerships or civil unions, chose to cohabit, and then decided to marry when it became an option. As of this writing, data on marriage rates in 2015 and beyond are not yet available.

Weddings

A wedding is the event that marks the transition from single to married status for the partners. It is the legal inception of a marriage. A wedding is a single, relatively brief event. Marriage is a legal and emotional state of living for the couple that extends from the time of the wedding until one partner dies or the marriage dissolves. It is important to distinguish a wedding from a marriage, at least in part because the latter is far more enduring in the life of the partners than the former. Ideally, being married is the goal, whereas the wedding is the means of accomplishing that goal and a celebration of the couple. Couples sometimes lose sight of this distinction during the stressful process of planning a contemporary wedding.

Any person who has been deemed a qualified officiant by the jurisdiction in which the wedding takes place can perform a wedding ceremony. Officiants are usually either public employees, such as magistrates or judges, or members of the clergy. Both civil and clerical officiants can sign the legal papers certifying that the couple is married. Members of the clergy can add ceremonies that legitimize the marriage within the couple's religious tradition.

Weddings became major life transition events in US culture between 1920 and 1950 (Davis, 1986). Prior to that, marriage as a status was the focus while the wedding as a marker of the inception of that status was minimized. The community assembled to witness the ceremony, with a brief celebration following. Contemporary weddings vary from two people going to a magistrate with the required number of witnesses and then out for a small celebratory meal to weekend-long destination events costing more than $100,000. Celebrity weddings are sometimes even more elaborate. Alternatively, couples may choose to elope and marry without a formal wedding and reception, sometimes with the encouragement of their parents.

All states require prospective spouses to apply for a license to marry. Both need to demonstrate that they are who they claim to be, of legal age, and not married to anyone else. Some states also require blood tests to screen for sexually transmitted infections. The application for a license to marry must occur prior to the wedding, with different jurisdictions requiring different wait times. For example, a perusal of state websites indicates that in 2016 Illinois required a 24-hour waiting period between applying for the license and the wedding, while Pennsylvania required a 72-hour waiting period.

Tracking the costs of contemporary weddings is difficult. The wedding industry involves multiple vendors, such as clothiers, florists, caterers, photographers, stationers (invitations, save-the-dates, programs), hair and make-up specialists, manicure and pedicurists, venues, officiants, wedding consultants, accommodations and transportation for out-of-town visitors, favors for wedding guests, gifts for members of the wedding party, and a similar array of vendors for related events such as bachelor and bachelorette parties, rehearsal dinners, bridesmaids' luncheons, and day-after brunches. Not every wedding involves all of these. Some people prefer a smaller, less elaborate wedding. Others cannot afford yet feel pressured to conform to the wedding norms of their social group.

The costs of wedding vendors also vary from place to place, and statistics about costs are difficult to obtain. However, national cost of living comparisons, such as the cost of living index, indicate geographic variations and it follows logically that the cost of a wedding also varies geographically.

The cost of a wedding may be especially problematic when a couple and/or their parents experience psychological or social pressure to plan a larger and more elaborate wedding than they can comfortably afford. Going into debt for a wedding is very different than going into debt for a home, a vehicle needed to get to work, or an education to further one's career and earning potential. Even when resources are available, prioritizing how to use them may call into question the wisdom of spending tens of thousands of dollars on an event.

Beyond costs, weddings involve a great deal of detailed planning far in advance of the event, anxiety about all aspects of the process, and frustration among everyone involved as expectations clash, deadlines loom, and costs exceed expectations. Excitement about the event and about getting married also comes into play. The term "bridezilla" suggests how planning a wedding affects people. However, the term is derogatory and singles out brides as the ones whose behavior is problematic during wedding planning. It overlooks the impact of a wedding on the bride's prospective spouse, the two of them as a couple, their parents, their friends, and the children either may have had with a previous partner. When partners have unequal resources and/or if either or both have children from a previous relationship, they may also need to negotiate a prenuptial agreement with the help of separate attorneys, a process that can become another source of contention.

Perhaps most importantly for the purposes of this textbook, the impact of planning a wedding may entail an emotional cost for each partner and for the couple's relationship. Partners may have differing expectations for the wedding itself and for the other partner as a participant in planning it. One partner might then conclude that the other partner is less interested in the marriage. This is one important reason for couples and their couple therapists to distinguish between weddings and marriages. Contrary to sex-role stereotyping, the writer's son became interested in wedding attire long before her daughter-in-law did, yet they were equally excited about being married and it would have been a potentially deleterious mistake for either to presume that differing interest in attire early in wedding planning reflected differing attitudes about being married.

When a prenuptial agreement is necessary, even more challenges arise. A prenuptial agreement is a legal contract concerning how resources will be handled when the marriage ends. While the marital laws of all 50 states address this issue, couples with unequal resources and/or children from previous relationships may wish to override at least some of these laws. Imagine marrying someone you love, with shared hopes and plans for your future together, and having to also negotiate what will happen when one of you dies or your marriage dissolves to protect one or both of you and your separate children. Negotiating a prenuptial agreement forces the couple to anticipate a contentious divorce or a contested will at a happy and hopeful time. The difficulty is inherent in the process. Consulting competent and responsive attorneys minimizes, but does not obliterate, the challenges of prenuptial agreements.

You will learn about premarital counseling in Chapter 8. Couples who seek premarital counseling create with their counselor a place to address the stresses, pressures, and emotions surrounding a wedding and, when necessary, the stresses and emotions surrounding the process of negotiating a prenuptial agreement in addition to negotiating what might become differences after they are married. Many clergy require premarital counseling. However, unless trained and licensed in pastoral counseling with couples and families, members of the clergy may not be able to observe and consider a couple's unique dynamics.

Cohabitation

Cohabitation, also referred to as domestic partnership, has become an acceptable alternative to marriage for many US couples. The number of women who cohabited with their first partner rose from 30 percent to 48 percent in the decade following the millennium. Additionally, a significant number of couples cohabit prior to marriage (Morris, 2013).

Domestic partnerships are legally recognized in some jurisdictions. When domestic partnerships are recognized, partners share some of the protections of being married, such as coverage of one partner by the other's employer-based health insurance policy (Equality Maine).

Laws governing cohabitation vary from state to state. Family law precedent suggests that there are six criteria essential to establish cohabitation: partners are members of the same household; partners are engaged in a stable relationship; partners provide financial support to one another; partners are engaged in a sexually intimate relationship with one another; partners share at least one child; and there exists public acknowledgement of the relationship (Morris, 2013). Because a significant number of couples cohabit prior to, rather than instead of, marrying and some couples are either unable or choose not to procreate, one might question the fifth criterion.

Civil Unions

Civil unions are legalized alternatives to marriage. Civil unions provide more protections than domestic partnerships but not all of the protections afforded married couples (Equality Maine). Civil unions are not available in most US states. They are, however, a legally recognized form of coupledom in Canada and many western European countries. Prior to the 2015 Supreme Court decision granting marriage equality to same-sexed couples, civil unions, where available, provided an alternative for at least some of the protections of marriage for same-sexed couples. Commitment ceremonies, a public statement of both partners' commitment to one another, were another alternative. However, commitment ceremonies do not provide any legal protections to partners and, as previously noted, neither domestic partnerships nor civil unions afford the same protections as marriage in the United States.

Open Relationships and Polyamory

Couple therapists began recognizing open marriages in the 1970s. More recently, some couples have identified their relationship as open or polyamorous. Partners in both open and polyamorous relationships reject the concept of monogamy without rejecting the concept of marriage.

Couples in open marriages may agree that relationships with other partners be limited to sexual intimacy only. The risk, of course, is that repeated sex with a single partner will lead to deeper feelings. Couples in open marriages may also agree to more emotionally intimate partnerships with people outside the marriage.

By contrast, couples in polyamorous relationships consider one another primary partners while other paramours remain in a secondary role. Polyamory is similar to polygyny, in that there is a first, or primary wife. The differences between polygamous societies and polyamorous relationships include the mutual agreement that both partners will engage in secondary relationships and the illegality of other partners becoming spouses in polyamorous marriages. Polygynous and polyamorous relationships share the preclusion of secondary partners from replacing the primary partner.

At least in theory, polyamorous relationships and open marriages equate the status of both partners in the decision to create and participate in extramarital relationships.

Because US society views itself as monogamous, many people are either horrified or titillated by the ideas of open marriage and polyamory. Thus, couples who choose these options may discover similar social obstacles that all couples who do not conform to cultural norms experience. The difference, however, is that open marriage and polyamory are choices a couple consciously makes and agrees upon, whereas other so-called deviations from social norms, such as sexual orientation, race, and socioeconomic status, are not choices. As a result, open marriage and polyamory can be hidden without attendant denial of who one is, whereas sexual orientation, race, and socioeconomic status cannot be.

The Choice Not to Couple

As previously noted, the number of people choosing not to couple is on the rise (Morris, 2013), and the state of the economy may be part of the reason. Additionally, while remaining uncoupled has always been an option for both men and women, it has only been in recent years that being single has not been socially sanctioned. Prior to that, remaining uncoupled had often been a way of hiding one's sexuality and, for women, also enabling them to continue to work. While tolerated in men, who could remain bachelors and still be considered desirable, remaining uncoupled was usually treated with derision in women, who were labeled undesirable spinsters, and thus inferior to women who married.

With increased social acceptance, those who choose not to couple have experienced increased social support. As the number of people who choose not to couple or re-couple following a death or divorce increases, it has become easier to form groups of friends who fulfill the supportive roles previously occupied by partners and families. Similarly, as more people choose to remain single, more people become available for dating and sexual relationships without the expectation or pressure of cohabitation and permanence. Additionally, employers, obstetricians, and adoption agencies may be less likely to discriminate against un-partnered employees, patients, and applicants, respectively, as they encounter an ever-increasing number of single people. And finally, individuals may receive less pressure to couple from family and friends as remaining single becomes an increasingly normative choice (Lewis & Kreider, 2015; Morris, 2013).

Because this is a textbook about couple therapy, the topic of choosing not to be part of a couple will not be revisited. If you are interested in learning about and working with people who choose not to couple, you are encouraged to pursue the topic in either an individual (never married) or family (single parenting, grief and divorce counseling) therapy context.

Conclusions

This chapter provided a backdrop and context for studying couple therapy. You read about the historical context of contemporary Western marriage. You were also introduced to legal, sociological, and anthropological perspectives on coupling, marriage, and uncoupling. Romantic love, coupling in contemporary US culture, and the choice not to couple were also addressed. Emphasis was placed on dominant cultural themes because of how historians and sociologists especially have studied couples. Anthropological concepts, being grounded in cross-cultural research, were introduced to highlight the impact of students' own cultural experience upon their views of coupling, marriage, and uncoupling.

The remainder of this book will be devoted to topics directly related to counseling and psychotherapy with couples. You will begin with an exploration of assessment when couples present for therapy in the next chapter.

References

Aponte, R. (2009). Augustus Napier on experiential family therapy. Psychotherapy.net. Retrieved from http://www.psychotherapy.net/interview/augustus-napier#section-experiential-family-therapy.

Basirico, L. A., Cashion, B. G., & Eshleman, J. R. (2014). *Introduction to sociology (16th ed.)*. Redding CA: BVT.

Coontz, S. (2005). *Marriage, a history. How love conquered marriage*. New York NY: Penguin Books Ltd.

Davis, K. (1986). *Contemporary marriage*. New York NY: The Russell Sage Foundation.

Equality Maine. http://equalitymaine.org/marriage-civil-unions-and-domestic-partnerships-comparison.

Fisher, H. E., Aron, A., & Brown, L. L. (2006). Romantic love: A mammalian brain system for mate choice. *Philosophical Transactions of the Royal Society B: Biological Sciences*, 361 (1476), 2173–2186. Retrieved from https://www.ncbi.nlm.nih.gov/pmc/articles/PMC1764845/.

Flanders, J. (2014). *The making of home. The 500-year story of how our houses became our homes*. New York NY: St. Martin's Press.

Gannon, M. (2016). Race is a social construct, scientists argue. *Scientific American*. Retrieved from https://www.scientificamerican.com/article/race-is-a-social-construct-scientists-argue/.

Killian, K. (2013). *Interracial couples, intimacy, and therapy: Crossing racial borders*. New York NY: Columbia University Press.

Lewis, J. M. & Kreider, R. M. (2015). Remarriage in the US. American community survey reports. Washington DC: US Census. https://www.census.gov/content/dam/Census/library/publications/2015/acs/acs-30.pdf.

Loving v Virginia. (1967). Retrieved from http://caselaw.findlaw.com/us-supreme-court/388/1.html.

Lum, D. (2007). Culturally competent practice. A framework for understanding diverse groupss and justice issues (3rd ed.). Belmont CA: Brooks/Cole.

McGee, S. & Moore, H. (2014). Women's rights and their money: A timeline from Cleopatra to Lilly Ledbetter. *The Guardian*. Retrieved from https://www.theguardian.com/money/us-money-blog/2014/aug/11/women-rights-money-timeline-history.

Minuchin S. (1974). *Families and family therapy*. Cambridge MA: Harvard University Press.

Morris, G. (2013). The cohabitation conundrum. *New Law Journal*. Retrieved from http://www.newlawjournal.co.uk/nlj/content/cohabitation-conundrum.

Napier, A. Y. (1988). *The fragile bond. In search of an equal, intimate and enduring marriage*. New York NY: Harper Collins.

Napier, A. Y. & Whitaker, C. A. (1978). *The family crucible*. New York NY: Harper and Row.

National Survey of Family Growth. http://www.cdc.gov/nchs/nsfg/key_statistics/d.htm.

10 US Code 920. Retrieved from https://www.law.cornell.edu/uscode/text/10/920.

Yalom, I. D. (1989). *Love's executioner and other tales of psychotherapy*. New York NY: Basic Books.

CHAPTER 3

Assessing Couples and Creating a Therapeutic Alliance

Learning Objectives

1. Describe the importance of creating a therapeutic alliance.
2. Summarize the challenges of triadic relationships.
3. Identify the 11 aspects of a clinical interview.
4. List four types of assessment tools.
5. Evaluate whether a couple therapist needs to know the partners' and couple's histories in order to fully assess the presenting problem.
6. Describe the difference between a working hypothesis and a fixed diagnosis.
7. Discuss the importance of determining the best theoretical approach to a problem.
8. Explain the importance of determining whether a couple therapist can help a given couple or whether another form of therapy is better suited to their situation.

In this chapter you will learn how couple therapists bond with and assess couples. You will learn about the challenges of triadic, or three-person, relationships that are by definition a part of couple therapy and about building alliances based on trust with both partners.

Although a variety of formal assessment tools are available, clinical interviews provide essential information that cannot be obtained any other way. In the writer's experience, beginning with a clinical interview—during which the psychotherapist begins to assess observable couple dynamics, responds empathetically and reflectively, and experiments with potentially helpful active listening—facilitates development of the therapeutic alliance without which clients have little motivation to return for further sessions. Secondarily, such interviews allow the client couple the relief that accrues from sharing their story with a sensitive and active listener, information on which to build trust, and hope that the couple therapist might be of help. Adding pencil-and-paper assessment tools prior to or as homework after the first session does not diminish these advantages.

As part of any assessment, couple therapists locate the couple in their individual, couple, and family life cycles, identify their strengths and challenges, and obtain relationship and family-of-origin histories for each individual as well as for the couple. These need not all be obtained in the first session. The therapist also begins to observe the couple's interactions, how they become problematic, and the functions they serve including how they impede change.

The characteristics of a therapeutic alliance and of the therapist-client fit will be addressed in this chapter. Additionally, the question of whether the couple therapist will recommend individual therapy, couple therapy, family therapy, group therapy, or some combination of these will be discussed.

Therapeutic Alliance: Challenges of the Triadic Clinical Relationship

Individual psychotherapy involves two people, the psychotherapist and the client. While the relationship between the psychotherapist and client may reflect aspects of the client's other relationships, the psychotherapist only monitors the one with her or him.

Goodness of fit, or the connection between the two parties to the therapeutic relationship, has consistently been shown to be the best predictor in outcome studies of counseling and psychotherapy (Howgego, Yellowlees, Owen, Meldrum, & Dark, 2003; Miller, Hubble, & Duncan, 2014; Siegel, 2013). As a result, most theories of psychotherapy and counseling address the therapeutic relationship as part of the client's healing.

Couple therapy adds a layer of complexity to the client-psychotherapist relationship. The triadic relationship inherent in couple therapy involves three individuals and therefore four interpersonal relationships: each partner with the couple therapist and with each other and the couple therapist with the couple system. The couple therapist engages in an interpersonal relationship with each partner, and the partners maintain their relationship with each other irrespective of whether it changes during treatment. The fourth relationship is between the therapist and the couple. As you will learn in Chapter 4, the couple exists in addition to and apart from either partner individually. All four relationships occur simultaneously and are sometimes in conflict with one another. The couple as a system is far stronger than either partner's relationship with the couple therapist and therefore less amenable to change.

Transcripts from Liz and Martin's first session with the couple therapist demonstrate several aspects of the complexity of working with couples. First, couple therapists need to create relationships with each partner individually. As noted in Chapter 1, many couple therapists assume they have begun a relationship with the partner who initiated treatment, even if that relationship has been limited to the business of scheduling the first session. These therapists therefore begin the first session by addressing the other partner in order to begin establishing a relationship with her or him.

In addition to Liz initiating couple therapy, the couple therapist had previously worked with her. This fact lent additional pressure to create a therapeutic alliance with Martin as soon as possible. To refresh your memory, the couple therapist started the first session with Liz and Martin by saying:

COUPLE THERAPIST: Martin, I'd like to begin with you because we've only just met. Is that alright with you, or would you prefer I started with Liz?

MARTIN: No, that's fine.

Stop and Think:

Be sure to include your answers in your journal.

1. If your goal was to begin to build a therapeutic relationship with Martin, would you have given him a choice about whether he wanted to speak first? Explain your answer.
2. What else might you have done? Why?

Although the couple therapist's work with Liz and Martin together created ethical challenges and is therefore not usually recommended, sometimes it is the best option. In Chapter 11, you will read about the ethical reasons to refer former clients and their partners to another couple therapist and this couple therapist's decision-making process when Liz declined to accept a referral.

When couple therapists consent to engage in couple therapy with an individual client and her or his partner, establishing a relationship with the partner becomes even more challenging because that partner needs to become an equal in a pre-existing relationship between the other partner and the psychotherapist.

Additionally, couple work changes the relationship between the couple therapist and the partner he or she had seen individually. For example, the couple therapist must validate both partners' experience, which can be seen as disloyalty from the perspective of a former individual client. The couple therapist addressed these added complexities directly, in order to practice ethically, to facilitate the establishment of a therapeutic alliance with Martin and the maintenance of one with Liz, and to again offer to refer them to another couple therapist.

CT: Because I saw Liz a couple of years ago, after you two had separated, I'm concerned you might feel excluded. So I want to be sure you know I'd be happy to give you the names of three of my colleagues who do couple therapy if you have any doubts at all about working with me, for this or any other reason.

MARTIN: No, I'm fine.

CT: OK. I'm especially concerned because husbands often feel that a woman therapist is taking their wife's side or that the two of them are ganging up on him, even when she didn't previously work with his wife.

The need for couple therapists to build and maintain individual relationships with each partner may be complicated by each partner's individual needs and their couple dynamics. Some people perceive attention to their partner as an invalidation of their own importance to the couple therapist, irrespective of whether or not the client previously worked as an individual with the same couple therapist. The client might interrupt, start an argument with her or his partner, challenge the couple therapist, or withdraw as a result.

Liz interrupted the conversation between the couple therapist and Martin several times during this first couple therapy session (Chapter 1). She did so verbally, as well as nonverbally by sighing and rolling her eyes. One of the ways she interrupted was arguing with what Martin had said.

CT: So the new baby...?

MARTIN: She never sleeps...

LIZ: [Rolls eyes and mumbles] Get to the point, Martin.

CT: [Ignoring Liz] ... So tell me how that is a problem for you and Liz.

MARTIN: She's always mad at me. Like that.

CT: So Liz's anger at you is the problem?

LIZ: As always, it's my fault. He has no responsibility.

CT: Liz, I hear that's an issue for you. And I also want to hear how you view the problem after Martin finishes.

Note: This time, the couple therapist addressed Liz's indirect request to be part of the conversation. Additionally, when she turned to Liz a few minutes later, the couple therapist began by addressing the complexity of moving from individual psychotherapy to couple therapy.

CT: Liz, I appreciate how difficult this session is. As I mentioned on the phone, doing couple therapy requires me to listen to both of you and that can feel like I care less about you than I did when we met alone. Because I want you and Martin to have the best possible experience and benefit from couple therapy, please let me know if you'd be more comfortable working with someone new.

Note: The first sentence of the couple therapist's last statement must involve nonverbal communication consistent with the words, or genuineness. If the couple therapist does not feel empathy for Liz's reaction to the shift in their relationship, the sentence must not be said at all. Without her nonverbal communications matching the words, or genuineness, those words would sound contrived and thus diminish, rather than increase, trust.

Whether or not either partner had previously worked with the couple therapist in a different context, a partner who feels that the couple therapist's attention to the other partner is an invalidation of their own perspective and/or importance may react angrily, by challenging the couple therapist.

> LIZ: I don't know what I expected, but I didn't expect you to [air quotes] gang up on me with him.

> CT: Tell me what I did that left you feeling ganged up on? I'd like to avoid repeating it, if possible.

Stop and Think:

Be sure to include your answers in your journal.

1. How do you suppose the couple therapist felt after hearing Liz's last statement?
2. Describe what she would need to do so that her response reflected her feelings?
3. If you had been the couple therapist, what would you have said in response to Liz? Include your reasoning.

Partners protect each other by interfering when the couple therapist's intervention is perceived to threaten the stability of their relationship dynamics, for example, by changing the subject or challenging the couple therapist. The transcript resumes during a subsequent session.

> CT: Liz, what would it take to believe Martin when he says he's behind whatever decision you make about your career?

LIZ: I can't believe you still buy that [expletive]. [Shrug] But he doesn't say the stuff he says at home here, so I guess you don't hear it.

CT: What's said at home that isn't said here?

LIZ: He tells me to just make up my mind.

CT: He sounds impatient?

LIZ: Yes, I guess so. But he's also saying he's already decided what I should do.

CT: How does he tell you that?

LIZ: I don't know. He just does.

MARTIN: I do get frustrated with her, but it's because I think she'll be happier once she decides what she wants. It doesn't mean I don't want her to keep working. [To Liz] My older sister works, and she has kids.

LIZ: She's a nurse! She works when she wants to, and she never brings work home.

MARTIN: It's a professional job, Liz.

CT: I'm still missing the link between you being frustrated that she hasn't decided what she wants to do, Martin, and you hearing that he wants you to make a certain decision, Liz.

Note: Liz and Martin successfully changed the topic to an argument about Martin's sister's job. It was the couple therapist's job to bring them back to how Martin's frustration and Liz's reaction to it prevented her from believing his words.

In order to build and maintain individual relationships with each partner, couple therapists must simultaneously attend to the one who is speaking and to the other partner's verbal and nonverbal reactions. Thus, in addition to observing the speaker's verbal and nonverbal messages, a couple therapist must also attend to how the other partner is reacting to the speaker. She or he must observe what these messages say about the partners' relationship with each other and each partner's relationship with the couple therapist. The couple therapist must then integrate this information into her or his working hypotheses about what is going on with the couple and what they need. Finally, she or he must make a decision about where and how to intervene as the session unfolds.

These already complex tasks are further complicated in situations like Liz and Martin's, when one partner has worked individually with the couple therapist. When working as an individual psychotherapist, one is able to focus solely on the client who is in the room. That focus usually leaves the client feeling that she or he is important to the psychotherapist and that the psychotherapist understands him or her and is his or her advocate. When an individual client subsequently works with the same psychotherapist in couple therapy, the client must share the focus, understanding, and advocacy with her or his partner. Especially when the client's relationship with her or his partner is distressed, as can be assumed when a couple has sought couple therapy, sharing the therapist's focus, understanding, and advocacy may elicit feelings of discomfort, loss, abandonment, and anger. Whenever an indication of such feelings emerges, it is incumbent upon the couple therapist to address it.

Couple therapists' efforts to manage partners interrupting each other and deflecting the conversation away from a difficult topic are not only ways to bring about change but are also designed to preserve the couple therapist's relationship with each partner. In the previous excerpt, Liz and Martin were unable to remain on topic and shifted to arguing about his sister's work. By bringing them back to the difficult task of communicating about Liz's career, the couple therapist demonstrated that they could trust her to be less anxious than they were about their conflict. While they might react angrily to the couple therapist's redirection, they would likely welcome the relationship message that the couple therapist was committed to interrupting the dynamics that prevented them from resolving their conflicts.

Finally, couples come to couple therapy with a relationship that, however distressed, is far stronger than the relationship that develops between the couple and the couple therapist. This phenomenon will be elaborated upon in Chapter 4. Liz and Martin's history of leaving and returning to couple therapy exemplified this phenomenon. When their immediate emotional pain and anxiety about their marriage was alleviated and the difficult work of changing to prevent future crises in their relationship resumed, they agreed, either overtly or covertly, to cease treatment. While their stated reasons were money and time constraints, the therapist knew that they had employer-based health insurance through Martin's job that covered mental health care reasonably well, relatively high incomes, and access to child care. She also knew from experience that when clients are motivated to continue, they negotiate with their therapist to find a workable time and an affordable fee.

Clinical Interview and Observation

One of the best ways to learn about a couple is to observe them. Clinical interviews provide a mechanism for observing a couple, experiencing what it is like to be with them as a reflection of what it is like for the partners to be with each other, and obtaining information about them using questions that prompt them to talk about themselves and then using follow-up questions about what they have said. Follow-up questions have the additional benefit of promoting the therapeutic relationship because they indicate the therapist has been listening carefully to what has been communicated both verbally and nonverbally.

Some couple therapists prefer to use a structured interview that targets an array of pre-determined questions applicable to most couples. Others recommend beginning with paper-and-pencil assessment tools, some of which will be described later in this chapter. Couple therapists who use unstructured interviewing as an assessment tool also think about what they need to know about a couple. While they may not use a written check-list, their mental list is likely to include most if not all of the topics included in Chapter 1. To review, these include but are not limited to the following:

1. How do you each view the presenting problem?
2. What prompted you to seek couple therapy now?
3. Have you been in couple therapy in the past? If so, what was and wasn't helpful? If not, what are your concerns and hesitations about it now?
4. What are your goals? What would you like to be different between you? What will happen if you don't make these changes?
5. What is your history as a couple?
6. Tell me about you as a family. Do you have children? If yes, what are their names and ages? Do they live at home? Are any of them step-children for either of you? If yes, tell me about how you blended your families. Does anyone else live with you?
7. Tell me about each of your relationship histories. Tell me about your families of origin.
8. Tell me about your extended families.

9. Who can you rely on? Friends? Family? Colleagues? Neighbors? Spiritual and social groups? Professionals and spiritual leaders? Other community groups?
10. What else is going on in either of your lives that might affect your relationship?
11. What would you like the outcome of couple therapy to be?

Following up on the couple's answers, rather than immediately continuing to the next question, facilitates couple therapy in two important ways. First, as previously noted, each partner is more likely to feel heard and understood and therefore to trust the couple therapist. Second, the couple is more likely to believe the couple therapist can help them. Both increase the likelihood the couple will remain in treatment long enough for the couple therapist to be of help. Unless the couple remains in treatment, assessment is useless.

Active listening with follow-up questions is a lengthier process than a structured interview. The couple therapist is unlikely to ask questions in the particular order in which they are listed. In the writer's experience, the pace and order in which questions are asked and information obtained is irrelevant by comparison to the quality of information obtained through active listening and follow-up questions.

To exemplify these different approaches, you will first read a transcript in which the couple therapist asked the interview questions in order, with minimal follow-up, and then one in which the couple therapist used active listening and follow-up questions.

Transcript 1:

COUPLE THERAPIST: [Looks down at check-list and then addresses her questions to both Liz and Martin] How do you view your problem?

LIZ: Problem? I'm not comfortable problematizing our situation. We need your help with making our relationship better.

CT: [Writes "wife declined to answer, husband sat quietly"] Uh huh. And what prompted you to seek couple therapy now?

LIZ: Well, as I've told you, we have been arguing more and I don't feel respected.

CT: [Writes "fighting, lack of respect"] Uh huh. Have you been in couple therapy before?

LIZ: [Exasperated] You know we haven't.

MARTIN: Liz, go easy. She has to ask these questions.

LIZ: She's wasting our time.

MARTIN: We don't know that.

LIZ: [Sighs and turns to CT] Could you explain to us why you are asking questions you already know the answer to?

CT: Yes, part of an assessment is an interview. I'll use this information to help you change what is bothering you.

MARTIN: See, Liz?

LIZ: Sometimes you are so passive!

CT: [Writes "wife declined to answer, some tension between the couple about husband's passivity"] What are your goals?

Stop and Think:

Be sure to include your answers in your journal.

1. What were your thoughts as you read this excerpt?
2. If you were Liz and Martin, would you have felt that Couple Therapist was listening to you? That she could help you? Would you have wanted to schedule another session? Explain the reasons for your answers.
3. What, if anything, would you have done differently if you were the couple therapist?

Transcript 2:

COUPLE THERAPIST: I'd like to hear from each of you what brought you here today. Who would like to begin?

LIZ: Martin?

MARTIN: Well, we've been arguing again, same stuff as before we separated. And Liz thought coming to you might help.

CT: Uh huh. And what are your thoughts about whether it might help?

MARTIN: I don't know. I've never done this before, so I'll defer to Liz.

CT: Liz, did Martin characterize your reason for being here the way you see it?

LIZ: Yep.

CT: Anything you'd like to add or clarify?

LIZ: I think that's about it.

CT: OK. You asked Martin to tell me why you're here and you agree you've been arguing more about some of the same things you argued about before your separation. Perhaps you can talk a little about what prompted you to call now.

LIZ: You mean instead of last week or last month?

CT: [Nods] Uh huh.

LIZ: I don't really know. Except I'm sick of feeling disrespected and not being supported. Yes, that's what I want to add. He doesn't see it, but he doesn't support me in what I want to do.

CT: There's a lot there I'd like to hear more about: how sick you are of what's happening; being sure Martin knows what you mean by support; and being clear yourself about what you want to do all sound important.

Stop and Think:

Be sure to include your answers in your journal.

1. What was different about the second excerpt? What are your thoughts about those differences?
2. Compare and contrast Liz and Martin's reactions to both styles of questioning.
3. Compare and contrast your own reactions to both styles of questioning.
4. If you were Liz and Martin, would you have felt that the couple therapist was listening to you in this transcript? That she could help you? Would you have wanted to schedule another session? Explain the reasons for your answers.
5. How are your answers different than your answers to the Stop and Think about Transcript 1?

Notice that although the transcripts were of similar length, the couple therapist did not progress as far into her list of questions in Transcript 2. On the other hand, she obtained more information, was able to comment on how Liz and Martin interacted around who would answer the first question, and identified three issues requiring intervention, two of which had not been mentioned by either and might be outside their awareness. All of these may have created trust and motivation to return, whereas the frustration Liz displayed in Transcript 1 might have decreased both.

Notice also that the couple therapist did not take notes or read from a structured questionnaire during Transcript 2. Some couple therapists, like some individual and family therapists, take notes during sessions; others do not. The rationale for taking notes is that notes provide information that the couple therapist may not recall and that needs to be reviewed prior to future sessions. The rationale for not taking notes is that the couple therapist can more fully attend to the couple, the couple will be more likely to believe she or he empathizes with them, and memory as well as what happens in future sessions will provide enough information about what is important for both case notes and future sessions.

One of the writer's clinical supervisors in graduate school suggested an exercise that may shed light on the note-taking controversy. He instructed clinical interns to write down everything they remembered immediately following a session and again a week later without looking at the previous notes. The point was that what was on the second list and not the first list provided important information to the couple therapist. For example, the couple therapist might not remember Liz challenging her immediately following the session but remember it a week later. This difference would provide information about her reaction to Liz's challenges and perhaps facilitate her empathy and understanding of both Liz and Martin.

Determining whether the partners agree, disagree, or are unsure about whether they want to remain together is a less formal but equally important part of any assessment. If either partner is finished with the relationship, the couple may best be served by acknowledging the reality, rather than wasting time and money on couple therapy that is already doomed to fail. Occasionally, the reality of ending a relationship is a motivator to work toward change. If either or both is unsure, it is important to return to that uncertainty periodically to ensure both partners remain invested in the relationship or, if necessary, accept its dissolution. Couple therapists can ask directly what the couple would like the outcome of couple therapy to be.

COUPLE THERAPIST: Tell me what you'd like the outcome of couple therapy to be?

LIZ: That he respects and supports me.

MARTIN: That we get along better.

CT: It sounds like you both want to be together, and our work will be about making being together better for both of you.

Regardless of how a couple is assessed, it is important that the couple therapist remain alert to the possibility that partners may withhold important information pending the development of trust. Additionally, new information often emerges when the couple therapist intervenes to facilitate change as couple therapy proceeds.

Assessment Tools for Couples

There are a number of self-report, paper-and-pencil assessment tools available for couples. These are completed either at home or in the waiting room prior to the first couple therapy session. The couple therapist is therefore unable to observe any interactions between the partners that occur while they are answering questions.

Some couple assessment questionnaires are completed by each partner individually and then compiled. Other questionnaires are completed by both partners together and then given to the couple therapist.

Some assessment questionnaires provide general information about a couple (Hoskins, 1988) and may include the kinds of questions listed earlier in this chapter. Others assess factors relevant to well functioning relationships, such as communication, cohesion, and flexibility (Olson, 2000), dyadic adjustment (Spanier, 2001), marital satisfaction (Snyder, 1997), and sexual functioning (Derogatis, 1996). Other questionnaires assess dysfunction, such as conflict and violence (Straus, Hamby, & Warren, 2003).

A couple therapist might assume that any couple who presents for couple therapy is dissatisfied with their relationship. Similarly, a couple therapist might assume a couple would bring sexual dysfunction, substance abuse, or intimate partner violence to his or her attention in order to obtain help. However, neither assumption is universally true. Some couples who love each other deeply and are content with their relationship present for couple therapy because they are concerned that a current stressor, trauma, or new phase of their life cycle will undermine their stability. Sexual issues, substance abuse, and intimate partner violence may engender feelings of shame in one or both partners, leaving the couple reluctant to reveal these problems until trust is well established. Sexual issues will be addressed in Chapter 8, while substance abuse and intimate partner violence will be addressed in Chapter 9.

A couple therapist using unstructured interviews without paper-and-pencil tools would need to add 3 topics to the list of 11 assessment questions earlier in this chapter. The couple therapist would need to ask direct questions about whether fights have ever led to physical or verbal violence or manipulation. He or she would also ask about substance use as indicated by partners' references to their own or the other's use. Finally, she or he would also ask questions about the couple's sexual history, with emphases on whether it was initially satisfactory and how it had changed over time. Couple therapists might ask less targeted questions about how the partners felt about one another, what they enjoyed doing together early in their relationship, how they initially got along, and how their relationship has changed over time. He or she would observe how the couple communicated around conflict, how cohesive as a couple they appeared to be, and ask questions aimed at flexibility of roles and willingness to help each other when necessary.

Additional assessment tools exist for individuals, children and adolescents, and families. These cover topics such as depression, substance abuse, autism, behavior problems, and family functioning along many of the same dimensions as pertain to couples.

An alternative tool for assessing couples is a genogram. Genograms were first developed for use with multi-generational family therapy (Bowen, 1978). They were further elaborated upon by a student of Bowen's, Monica McGoldrick (McGoldrick, 2008; McGoldrick & Gerson, 1985). Unlike the assessment tools already discussed, a genogram is not a pencil-and-paper questionnaire or a structured interview.

A genogram is a tool for depicting multi-generational patterns affecting individuals, couples, and families. It is similar to a family tree, with the addition of information about occupations, marital statuses, and biomedical and psychosocial diagnoses in order to identify intergenerational patterns. A genogram is a cross-section in that it is created at a particular point in time and thus may change. For example, Liz's father, Bill, was alive when Martin and Liz first presented for couple therapy in 1993. However, he died two months prior to their presentation in 2002, and the couple therapist hypothesized that there was a connection between his death and their return to couple therapy. In 2010, when Martin and Liz's daughter, Christina, was 17, her physician recommended family therapy. At that point, Liz's mother, Sally, had remarried, and she and her second husband were struggling with his Alzheimer's disease (Esposito and Hattem, 2017). These changes altered Liz and Martin's genogram.

Liz and Martin's 2002 genogram was included in Chapter 1 and can serve as an example of the use of genograms in couple therapy. As an assessment tool, a genogram is more useful if completed earlier in couple therapy, either by the couple therapist for his or her reference or collaboratively with the couple as part of assessment and/or intervention. However, because of its complexity, constructing a genogram at the beginning of couple therapy risks leaving the couple with the impression that the couple therapist is more interested in assessment than in addressing their more pressing concerns.

Liz and Martin's couple therapist constructed a genogram collaboratively with them in 1993 after the tension between them had subsided. However, because the genogram included in Chapter 1 reflects their extended family in 2002, dates and circumstances described in the following transcript appear as though the genogram was constructed then, instead of at an earlier time.

As you read the following transcript, note that the couple therapist linked construction of the genogram to assessing the impact of their families of origin upon their relationship and not as an unrelated tool.

COUPLE THERAPIST: Martin, let's talk about the family you grew up in. First, tell me about your parents.

MARTIN: They're wonderful people, very loving and caring. And devoted to their family.

CT: How old are they?

MARTIN: Let's see. My parents are the same age, both 60.

CT: Uh huh. Are they both working outside the home?

MARTIN: No. My dad's a plumber. Mom has worked off and on but was home with us most of the time while we were growing up and only works when she absolutely has to.

LIZ: [Snorts]

MARTIN: Outside the home, I should say.

CT: How's their health?

MARTIN: Fine. Mom's doctor keeps telling her to take better care of herself, that her blood pressure's a little high and she needs to lose some weight. I try not to worry about her.

CT: I imagine that's difficult.

MARTIN: [Nods]

CT: Do you have brothers and sisters?

MARTIN: Yes, three sisters.

CT: Whew! Are they all grown?

MARTIN: Yes. My big sister's married and is a nurse. One of my little sisters is a single mom who works but isn't a professional. The other one has never been quite right, can't really function on her own. She has a kid and lives with my parents.

CT: What about your grandparents?

MARTIN: My dad never talks about his family. He went in the service and never looked back. Mom is one of five kids, and we see her family all the time. My grandma on that side's still alive.

CT: But not your grandfather?

MARTIN: No.

While this may sound very similar to a structured interview, the couple therapist had told Liz and Martin she was going to construct a genogram with them and explained that genograms help identify multi-generational patterns in families. Once Liz and Martin had decided they were curious about the results, they were forthcoming with information.

The excerpt reveals what is called a cut-off within Martin's family. His father has no contact with his parents and siblings, and Martin knows nothing about them. There is undoubtedly an interesting story there, but since Liz and Martin's relationship with his family appears reasonably good the couple therapist decided it was not relevant to the assessment.

Three patterns that may be relevant to Liz and Martin's issues emerged after similar questions were asked of Liz. First, a significant multi-generational history of substance abuse existed in Liz's family of origin. Liz's maternal grandparents, two of her mother's siblings, her father, and her brother all exhibited symptoms of substance abuse. Like Martin, little was known about her father's family. However, that her father abused both alcohol and prescription medications suggested the possibility other members of his family of origin also had abused substances. This pattern in Liz's family of origin would alert the couple therapist to ask about both Liz and Martin's use of alcohol, prescription medications, and recreational drugs.

Second, the women in previous generations of Liz's family, as well as her older sister, were all identified as housewives and stay-at-home mothers. Absent missing information, Liz was the first woman to pursue a professional career outside the home. Martin's older sister, Lynette, was also a professional. However, as a nurse, Lynette had more control over how many hours she worked, the ability to take significant time off when her children were young and then return to her career, and, as Liz mentioned earlier in this chapter, whether or not to bring work home. Liz referred to this family-of-origin history in describing the pressure she felt to relinquish a professional career outside the home. She was already aware of the pattern of mothers not pursuing careers, although she may have more fully grasped its extent when she saw it depicted in the genogram.

A third phenomenon involved the absence of divorce in both Liz and Martin's families of origin. With the exception of Liz's older brother and one of Martin's younger sisters, no one in either family had divorced as far as Liz and Martin knew. Her brother's divorce appeared to be part of his debilitation from drug and alcohol abuse and Martin's sister Daisy had been briefly married to a man who became violent after their children were born and currently cohabited with another partner. Both divorces could be explained by the presence of abuse, leaving Liz and Martin the first couple to have separated without being able to point to a specific and easily comprehensible explanation. Observing this relative absence of divorce in the genogram suggested the possibility that at least one motivation for Liz and Martin to reconcile and resolve their marital issues could be to avoid being the first and only couple to divorce without a significant deal-breaker occurring.

Stop and Think:

Be sure to include your answers in your journal.

1. Looking back at Liz and Martin's genogram in Chapter 1, what other patterns can you identify?
2. How might these patterns be relevant to couple therapy with Liz and Martin?

Does History Matter?

Not all couple therapists agree that individual, couple, and family histories are relevant to couple therapy. Some theories of couple therapy focus on the present to the exclusion of the past, while others include the past as a contributor to the present. A particular couple therapist's view will likely be influenced by how she or he views the world and his or her choice of theory.

Additionally, there are situations in which disrupting destructive patterns, such as intimate partner violence, must take priority over obtaining the historical information a couple therapist might otherwise consider necessary to effectively alter the dynamics associated with the violence. In such situations, couple therapists sometimes cease couple therapy and, even when treating the violence within the context of couple therapy, do not return to assessment until after the violence has ceased.

All couple therapy theories derive from family systems theory (Chapter 4). Some, including structural/strategic and emotionally focused couple therapies, arose directly from the precepts of family systems theory. Others, such as psychodynamic and behavioral couple therapies used systems concepts to expand upon existing theories of individual psychotherapy see Section II).

Systems theory as applied to couple therapy examines repetitive patterns of interactions, or dynamics, between and among humans in intimate relationships. Additionally, and importantly for the purpose of this discussion, systems theory also focuses on the context in which these patterns of interaction, or dynamics, occur. Context includes, though it is not limited to, the historical context in which these patterns of interaction developed.

Consider Liz and Martin, with a slight twist on their history of therapy. In this hypothetical situation, Liz had not found the couple therapist helpful during her individual psychotherapy and as a result asked her primary care physician for a referral to a different couple therapist for herself and Martin. The new couple therapist subscribed to a theoretical approach that focused on the here-and-now to the exclusion of the past and as a result did not ask about individual and relationship history. He therefore did not know three things we know from Chapter 1: (1) Liz was sexually assaulted in college, suffered symptoms of PTSD (post-traumatic stress disorder), and identified as bisexual; (2) Liz and Martin were separated for eight months less than two years after they married; and (3) Liz experienced pressure from their extended families to conform to a pattern of stay-at-home mothering since before Christina's birth.

Now consider the potentially important information obtained from the portion of the assessment interview with Liz and Martin that focused on their relationship history.

CT: Tell me a little bit about your relationship early on.

LIZ: Martin?

MARTIN: We met at a Halloween party our first year in grad school.

LIZ: She already knew that.

Stop and Think:

1 Be sure to include your answers in your journal. Liz had, in fact, told the couple therapist how she and Martin met during one of their individual psychotherapy sessions. Do you think she was entrapping Martin by asking him to answer the question in the couple therapy session, rather than reminding the couple therapist she had already answered that question?
2 How might the couple therapist have responded without appearing to scold Martin along with Liz?

CT: I'm also curious about what attracted you to one another, what you enjoyed doing together. I'd like to hear from both of you about this time at the beginning of your relationship.

MARTIN: [Smiling] I think we bonded about graduate school. We were both first years, in different programs, but it was so much more intense than undergrad had been, so different. We both liked to run, it helps us with stress, so we started running together early on. I like to stay in shape, and Liz worries a lot about her weight, even though I don't think she has to [smiles at Liz].

LIZ: [Smiles] That's why I don't have to, because I watch it.

CT: So the stress of grad school affected you both?

MARTIN: Yeah, but I think it affected me a bit differently. I was the only black kid in my program. My parents always said I was a representative of all black people in situations like that. A lot of pressure. And it seemed like the faculty and most of the other students were uncomfortable with me. Like we were all wondering, did they let me in because I'm black, or did everyone just think that. To be perfectly honest, it pissed me off, no offense.

CT: None taken. I think I'd be pissed off, too.

MARTIN: Yeah, well anger can get out of control real fast. Not good. Running and working out helped me deal with it.

CT: Tell me about your anger getting out of control.

MARTIN: Well, it never has, but that's because I'm very careful.

CT: I see. Like Liz's weight. What about now?

MARTIN: Well, that's the thing. With the baby, we can't run at the same time. Liz gets up early to run, and I stay home in case the baby wakes up.

CT: And what about you? When do you have time to exercise?

LIZ: Oh for heaven's sake! He has the whole day! He can leave as soon as I get home—he never watches the baby while I get dressed anyway. He can go to the gym then or at lunch time or after work.

CT: Martin?

MARTIN: [To Liz] I really can't be late for work or take long lunch hours, especially with the responsibility of supporting this family. And you seem more than ready for me to be home when I walk in the door. [To therapist] I go to the gym on weekends, which makes her mad, but I have to.

Three historical clinical impressions that were relevant to the present couple therapy emerged in this excerpt. The first was further evidence of Liz's control. She attempted during this part of the assessment interview to control who answered which questions. She and Martin also agreed that she worked hard to control her weight. Incidentally, she had also revealed during an individual session that her mother, Sally, was very conscious of weight and critical when she believed Liz or her sister Barbara were not being careful about theirs.

The second impression entailed Martin's anxiety about being angry. He was remarkably open early on in couple therapy, perhaps in part because his wife had trusted the couple therapist even before he met her. The source of his anger in graduate school was racism and particularly the fact that his white peers had the privilege of assuming they were admitted based on their merits whereas he did not. Liz could observe what was happening to him and its impact upon him, but as a white woman in professional school at a time when women's numbers were already significant, she did not experience it. Clinically, Martin's fear of losing control when angry required further exploration, particularly because his anxiety appeared to be disproportionate to his prior experience (i.e., he had never lost control). The extent of his anger at Liz remained unclear in this excerpt.

The third clinical impression was that Liz and Martin needed a mechanism to handle racial issues and the impact of institutionalized racism within their marriage. Biracial marriages can be challenged by partners' different experiences of race, as well as pressures from family, friends, and the larger society. We will return to the topic of biracial couples in Chapter 9.

The couple therapist added all three of these clinical impressions to the list she created in Chapter 1. She also included questions about them in her working hypothesis, which will be detailed later in this chapter.

Stop and Think:

Be sure to include your answers in your journal.

1. From what you have read, do you think history matters when working with couples who are distressed in the present? Be specific.
2. How might the three pieces of historical information in the preceding excerpt be helpful to a couple therapist working with Liz and Martin?
3. How might the three impressions arising from the preceding excerpt be helpful to Liz and Martin's couple therapist?
4. Role play a couple therapist working with Liz and Martin in groups of three. Begin by role playing the couple therapist who does not know their history and does not ask; the two students playing Liz and Martin need to avoid talking about their history, and the couple therapist's questions need to avoid the subject of their history. Then switch roles and allow the couple therapist to ask about history.
5. What were the similarities and differences between each mock session?

Finally, the couple therapist began to ponder the similarities and differences between Liz's fear of being assaulted and its potential to have exacerbated her wish to control both her weight and people she allowed to be close to her and Martin's reaction to the micro-aggressions he experienced as a person of color. Racism, like sexism, entails emotional assaults as well as the threat and/or reality of physical assault. While women and people of color adapt to how they are treated, such adaptation takes an emotional toll. While Liz's skin color gave her privileges that Martin did not have (such as assuming she was admitted to graduate school and employed on the basis of her merits), her life experience suggested to her that she was more physically vulnerable than he was. Neither had control over these external realities. The couple therapist wondered about the impact of Martin's experience of racism and Liz's experience of sexual assault on their relationship, especially as it played out in their efforts to control what they could, which appeared to her to be themselves and each other.

Additional Aspects of the Couple Therapist's Assessment

Once a couple therapist has identified a couple's presenting problem, observed their dynamics, and learned the histories of both partners as well as the two of them as a couple, she or he then faces five additional assessment tasks: (1) developing a working hypothesis; (2) using assessment and the working hypothesis to guide intervention; (3) determining the appropriate theoretical approach to use with a particular couple; (4) considering the need for other psychotherapy services; and (5) asking herself or himself whether he or she is trained to work with the couple's issues.

Developing a Working Hypothesis

Diagnoses, as codified in the *Diagnostic and Statistical Manual of Mental Disorders* (DSM) and the *International Classification of Diseases* (ICD), are currently viewed as objective descriptions that can be agreed upon by an array of experts about an individual, couple, or family client's mental illness. Since 1981, when the third edition of the DSM was published, the demands of the for-profit insurance industry have required clinicians to use diagnosis to justify the need for psychotherapy. However, not all diagnoses included in the DSM are considered to be "medically necessary" and thus not all diagnoses are eligible for reimbursement. Diagnoses of couples and families have been largely discounted by the insurance industry.

There are several risks of viewing clients solely through the lens of their diagnoses. First, this view has shifted the focus of mental health treatment from facilitating mental health to justifying the need for treatment based on a client's mental illness. Psychotherapy has become increasingly medicalized and problematized in response to these funding demands, and medicine as it is currently practiced in the United States similarly focuses on diagnosing and treating illness rather than maintaining and enhancing health. The result for both biomedical and psychosocial health care is that practitioners tend to view patients and clients as sick and to focus on the pathology. Practicing strength-based psychotherapy with individuals, couples, and families may be an attempt to circumvent this approach. However, no theoretical approach circumvents the need for diagnosis if third-party payments are involved.

A second and related risk of viewing clients through the lens of their diagnoses is a shift away from attention to the nuances of clients' challenges. Liz was sexually assaulted in college, and she connects the assault to those times when she responds negatively to Martin's sexual advances. With additional assessment, the couple therapist could likely diagnose her with PTSD, treat the PTSD in the context of her relationship with Martin, and receive reimbursement from Liz's insurer. However, as is clear, Liz and Martin's sexual challenges extend beyond her PTSD into couple dynamics that are not included in the current versions of the DSM or ICD.

Diagnostic codification thus shifts a clinician's perspective away from a holistic view of the client or patient. Clients become a symptom picture, rather than complex, unpredictable people, and their relationships become problematic, rather than complex, evolving systems. In other words, complexities are easily discounted in favor of a treatment plan aimed at a particular symptom.

Finally, despite the therapeutic relationship, or goodness of fit between client(s) and therapist being the single best predictor of outcome, as previously noted, the therapist's interactions with and experience of individuals and systems is not considered in the diagnostic codes. As a result, clinicians risk viewing clients as their diagnoses rather than as human beings and viewing themselves as technicians rather than as healers. Yalom (2003) and Siegel (2013) have elaborated upon these risks.

In sum, then, the lens of diagnosing pathology focuses clinicians on the need to problematize challenges and coping mechanisms, simplifies the clients and the challenges they face, overlooks indicators of mental health, and discounts the potential for growth and change in favor of treatments that quickly reduce symptoms. When a diagnosis is presumed to be a full description of a couple and the partners who comprise it, it risks limiting the therapist's view of each partner as a whole and evolving person and of the couple as a dynamic and changing entity. It dehumanizes all the participants, including the couple therapist, who becomes a technician hired to fix, as stated in the treatment plan, the problem, as stated in the diagnostic code.

Alternatively, viewing diagnosis as a working hypothesis that changes over time as new information arises allows individual, couple, and family therapists to avoid these risks. Shifting one's perspective from diagnosing to developing a working hypothesis allows for a nuanced perspective, acknowledgement of client couples' strengths and their potential for change, and recognition that all parties to the therapeutic relationship are complex human beings engaged in a number of evolving relationships with one another.

The concept of a working hypothesis does not preclude diagnosis, but rather expands upon it. An individual is not depressed; rather, she or he is displaying depressive symptoms that meet the diagnostic criteria for a particular form of depression in the presence of a variety of internal and external challenges and with whatever experiences and coping skills he or she brings to the situation. Similarly, a client couple is not dysfunctional, but rather the couple's efforts to improve their relationship have not brought about the changes they desire and may have instead resulted in increasing distress and disillusionment.

After completing her assessment of Liz and Martin, the couple therapist developed her working hypothesis. She believed that Liz and Martin's dynamic involved control. Liz strove to be in control of their lives, apparently fearing she was not, while Martin avoided conflict because he feared he would lose control of his anger. Liz also wanted to please others and feel valued by Martin for who she was. These dynamics played out in their attempts to negotiate the tasks of transitioning first to marriage and then to parenthood. Both transitions left Liz feeling out of control and Martin more stressed and angry, thus exacerbating their dysfunctional couple dynamics around control. She hypothesized that pressures from family members regarding Liz's career and weight and micro-aggressions from colleagues and supervisors regarding Martin's race further inflamed the situation. Additionally, triggers from Liz's sexual trauma, as well as the couple's relationship dynamic around control and anger appeared to manifest in their sexual relationship. Finally, their shared mechanism for reducing stress was no longer as accessible to them as it had been prior to the birth of their daughter, and they had not replaced it.

Stop and Think:

Be sure to include your answers in your journal.

1. What else have you noticed about Liz and Martin that might be helpful to include in the couple therapist's working hypothesis?
2. Describe how your observations would be included in the couple therapist's working hypothesis.

A couple therapist's working hypothesis, like any other hypothesis, must be tested. The most effective way to test a clinical hypothesis is to begin therapeutic interventions, also referred to as treatment, based upon it. Observing how the couple reacts to these interventions helps couple therapists modify the working hypothesis to better fit the particular client couple.

Additionally, new information tends to emerge in the course of treatment. Thus, couple therapists can expect to learn more about the couple even after the assessment phase of couple therapy is completed. Through continuing assessment and feedback from interventions, the couple therapist finds support, refutation, and modification of her or his working hypothesis.

Theory is a crucial underpinning of clinical intervention. In Section II of this textbook, you will read examples of how theoretically based interventions provided new information the couple therapist then used to modify her working hypothesis and inform her subsequent interventions. For example, in Chapter 1 the couple therapist intervened in Liz's interruptions of Martin. Stopping partners from interrupting one another is a technique recommended by several theoretical models of couple therapy. Liz's reaction alerted the couple therapist that the control inherent in interrupting one's partner would not be easy for Liz to relinquish. In other words, the intervention yielded information that supported the couple therapist's working hypothesis.

Using Assessment and the Working Hypothesis to Define Intervention

It cannot be overemphasized that couple therapists, like individual and family therapists, use assessment and a working hypothesis, along with a theoretical perspective (Section II) to guide their interventions with couple clients. The importance of a full assessment prior to developing a working hypothesis is equally critical to effective intervention.

The couple therapist used her working hypothesis to guide her interventions. At the beginning, she focused on Liz and Martin's power dynamics, interrupting interruptions, modeling empathy for the other's perspective, and suggesting alternatives for managing conflict. She used the feedback from their reactions and the effectiveness of her interventions to refine her working hypothesis and guide further interventions. The specifics of how she did this will become more apparent as you read the transcripts of sessions included in Section II of this textbook.

Students frequently ask whether clients need to know their individual, couple, or family therapist's assessment of them. Some clinicians are trained to always share their assessment so that it becomes part of a list of goals of treatment agreed upon by both therapist and client. Legally, clients are the owners of their personal health information (PHI) under the federal Health Insurance Portability and Accountability Act of 1996 (HIPAA). However, this right does not force a clinician to reveal information that, in her or his judgment, would not be helpful to a client or to the therapeutic relationship unless the client requests her or his PHI. Additionally, the law does not prevent a psychotherapist from recommending that clients who want to read their medical records do so with the clinician present to answer questions and concerns as they arise. Such recommendations are especially important when an individual's ego is fragile, when partners might use the information as an emotional or legal weapon against one another, and when domestic violence is a risk.

When considering whether to share one's assessment when clients have not invoked their HIPAA rights, a clinician might find it helpful to ask herself or himself whether sharing her or his assessment would likely be helpful to the client as an intervention in and of itself. Additionally, it is at least equally important, given the risks, that the clinician ask himself or herself whether, in his or her clinical judgment, sharing the assessment is contraindicated, for example by any of the conditions listed in the previous paragraph.

Stop and Think:

Be sure to include your answers in your journal.

1. How do you think Liz would react if the couple therapist shared her hypothesis that Liz's efforts to control Martin were affecting her marriage? How might Martin react?
2. How do you think Martin would react if the couple therapist shared with him her hypothesis that he was not acknowledging the extent of his anger and therefore its role in his marriage? How might Liz react?
3. How could the couple therapist phrase her assessment of the roles played by Liz's trauma, Martin's anger, and their control dynamics in their sexual relationship? How do you think Liz would react? How do you think Martin would react?

After considering the questions posed in the Stop and Think, the couple therapist decided not to share her full assessment upon its completion. She was concerned that both Liz and Martin would become defensive and that such defensiveness would be counterproductive to their work.

The couple therapist also believed that her assessment and working hypothesis would become apparent, both implicitly and explicitly, in the context of her on-going couple therapy with Liz and Martin. She further believed that experiencing change was a more effective tool than a discussion about what needed to be changed. Her approach arose from her training in experiential individual, couple, and family therapies (see Chapter 6) and from her experience practicing individual, couple, and family therapy.

From the couple therapist's perspective, interrupting Liz's interruptions of Martin was a technique for changing her efforts at control, allowing her to experience exerting less control during a couple therapy session when both the empathy and guidance of the couple therapist were available to her. Similarly, the couple therapist intended to suggest the possibility that Martin was angry as situations in which he shut down or otherwise avoided anger arose, again knowing she would be available to empathize and facilitate change during the session. Third, she could suggest the possible role of her trauma history to Liz when Liz and Martin were already talking about their sexual relationship, rather than bringing it up out of context when Liz might feel she was being blamed and Martin absolved from responsibility for their distress. And finally, she would be able to monitor and direct the listening partner's distress and to disrupt couple dynamics that could undermine change.

Determining the Theoretical Approach to Guide Intervention

Section II of this textbook is about theoretical approaches to couple therapy. While it is not an exhaustive review, it will introduce you to a range of theoretical possibilities to guide couple therapy interventions.

Following assessment and the development of a working hypothesis, a couple therapist next decides what theoretical model or models to use as the foundation for her or his interventions. As previously mentioned, the tasks of assessment, developing a working hypothesis, and intervention are neither linear nor distinct from one another. Some intervention occurs during assessment, some assessment occurs during intervention as new information emerges, and a working hypothesis is, by definition, a work in progress and therefore changes over time.

Learning theoretical approaches to couple therapy is part of every couple therapist's training, and the writer believes it would be impossible for a couple therapist to work with couples without a theoretical framework to organize her or his approach to the couple. Additionally, the assessment process, while in many ways similar across theories, would be chaotic without a framework for organizing information. Theory provides such a framework. Thus, theory enters the couple therapy process before the couple therapist has assessed the couple sufficiently to develop a working hypothesis. It guides assessment and development of the working hypothesis, as well as intervention, and is thus relevant to this chapter.

Theory provides a way for the couple therapist to organize information obtained during assessment and intervention in a way that is useful to her or him (Gehart, 2013). It is the link between assessment and treatment, informing both. Theory is not a technique, but rather a conceptualization that suggests techniques for intervention. For example, cognitive-behavioral (Chapter 5), experiential (Chapter 6), and structural/strategic couple therapies (Chapter 7) share reframing as a technique for intervention. Theorists from each of the three perspectives might explain the use of reframing differently and even alter it to fit a different therapeutic context, but the technique itself appears remarkably similar across these very divergent theoretical approaches.

Corey and Corey (2011) pointed out that theory is for the benefit of the therapist and need not be discussed or shared with the client. Theory helps the couple therapist organize the myriad information she or he receives from each couple and provides the basis and sometimes the tools for intervention. Some clients may ask, in which case it is alright to brief them about one's theoretical perspective and even provide an example of how it might play out in couple therapy.

The theory of couple therapy with which a particular couple therapist is most aligned often reflects his or her world view. World view encompasses how an individual conceptualizes experience and then uses that conceptualization to define his or her philosophy of life and expectations for self and others. If a couple's world view was that therapy is only for crazy people, they probably would avoid it. If a couple therapist's world view was that she or he had the answers for every couple, she or he would choose a theory that defined the couple therapist as expert and/or teacher. If a couple therapist believed mental health is the absence of emotional pain, he or she might gravitate toward the theories underlying symptom-focused treatments. If a couple therapist believed that mental health involves developing resiliency to stress, effective ways of coping, and the ability to self-soothe and empathize with oneself and others during difficult periods, she or he would likely choose a theory that reflects that perspective. And if a couple therapist believed that people function independently and sometimes touch one another's lives, then he or she might discount systems theory, with its focus on the impact of interpersonal dynamics, and discourage interdependence between partners.

The following two Stop and Think exercises focus on your own world view as a starting place for your theoretical approach to couple therapy.

Stop and Think:

Be sure to include your responses in your journal.

1. How does the world work (predictable, random, pre-determined, or...)?
2. Are choices dichotomous?
3. What roles do fairness and order play in how the world works?
4. Are you most comfortable with people who are rational, intuitive, emotive, or...?
5. How do you resolve contradictions and conflict (win/lose, accommodate, compromise, collaborate, problem solve, ignore, or...)?
6. What is mental health (balance, absence of symptoms, or...)?
7. What is mental illness?
8. How do people best learn?
9. Do you trust your intuitive responses?
10. Do you trust other people?
11. How much responsibility do individuals have for their lives?
12. How much control do individuals have over their lives?
13. How do you negotiate relationships?

A final theoretical consideration involves whether a couple therapist's preferred theory of couple therapy is a good fit for a particular client couple. For example, feminist couple therapy might not be a good fit for an unassimilated traditional couple of Middle Eastern descent with a cultural valuation of traditional women's roles. Similarly, a couple may have already tried and been frustrated with the results of couple therapy based on a particular theory and may present seeking an alternative approach. Presumably, the couple therapist's training, experience, and flexibility would allow him or her to adapt to the client's needs in both situations. Additionally, as couple therapy progresses, the couple therapist's theoretical conceptualization, like his or her working hypothesis, may require adaptations to fit the couple's reality, as well as the addition of techniques from other theoretical perspectives. The goal is always to maximize the couple therapist's effectiveness on behalf of the client couple, not theoretical purity. If one wishes to study the effectiveness of various theories, one can do so in the context of professional research with appropriate regulation by a research institution and informed consent from client couples.

Stop and Think

Be sure to include your answers in your journal.

1. What do you know about how the world works and how do you know it?
2. What do you believe about human nature?
3. What do you believe about how relationships work?
4. How do you define a successful outcome of couple therapy?
5. How do you define couple health?
6. How do your experiences, including your culture, race, and gender, affect your world view?
7. Summarize your world view based on your answers to the six preceding questions.

Individual, Couple, or Family Counseling?

The couple therapist must decide, while assessing the couple and developing a working hypothesis, whether anything he or she has learned about the couple suggests the need for either individual or family therapy, instead of or in addition to couple therapy. In Chapter 12, you will be introduced to an array of services, including individual and family therapy, to which couple therapists may need to refer.

Sometimes an individual presents for psychotherapy and frames her or his presenting problem as almost entirely about her or his partner. In this case, an ethical psychotherapist would recommend couple, rather than individual therapy, unless domestic violence were occurring. A client may tell his or her therapist that his or her partner would not come to a couple therapy session. In the writer's experience, the partner is often quite motivated to participate, as illustrated by Liz and Martin during their first couple therapy session (Chapter 1). Below is a hypothetical transcript of Liz scheduling an individual session without agreeing to Martin joining her.

COUPLE THERAPIST: Liz, a lot of what we've talked about today has involved Martin, and I think it might be helpful if he came to a session.

LIZ: I can already tell you he won't.

CT: Perhaps not. But I'm concerned that we're overlooking the potential to make positive change in your relationship by excluding him.

LIZ: Well, maybe. I guess I could bring it up with him. He'll probably say no, though.

CT: And then what would happen?

LIZ: I don't know. Maybe he'd think about it. But I don't think he'd say yes.

CT: He could surprise you. Or he could say no. You can tell him I'd like to hear what he has to say, if you think that would help.

LIZ: Should I let you know before next time if he's going to be here?

CT: If you'd like. It's also alright to surprise me.

In some situations, one or both partners exhibit symptoms of depression, bipolar disorder, anxiety, a personality disorder, substance abuse, dissociative disorder, or some other individual mental health challenge that negatively impacts not only the affected individual but also the couple's relationship. When these symptoms suggest the need for individual psychotherapy and the disorder is one that the couple therapist is trained and experienced to treat, the couple therapist must then decide whether to refer for individual psychotherapy or treat it within the context of couple therapy, in other words with both partners present. On the other hand, if the symptoms are disruptive of couple work, the couple therapist may suggest concurrent individual therapy. You will read about the contraindications of the couple therapist seeing each partner separately as well as together in Chapter 11; the writer recommends that if individual psychotherapy is indicated, the couple therapist provide a referral list of three colleagues.

Finally, some couples may be more concerned about a child's struggles and parenting than about their relationship as a couple. The ethical couple therapist would suggest family therapy. If she or he is trained and experienced in the practice of family therapy, she or he can see the couple with their children and/or for parenting issues and then resume couple therapy, if needed, at a later time.

Can This Couple Therapist Help This Couple?

Every couple therapist must ask himself or herself whether he or she can help a particular couple. The answer involves not only what the couple needs and the couple therapist's training and experience, but also the couple therapist's reactions to the couple's issue and to the partners themselves. For example, Liz and Martin needed a culturally competent couple therapist because they were a biracial couple. But even a culturally competent couple therapist might be experiencing unresolved issues that would preclude her effectiveness with Liz and Martin. He or she may have recently ended a relationship with a partner with control issues and find it difficult to distinguish how Liz enacts her ambivalence about her roles as mother and professional from the ex-partner's behavior for which, at the moment, the couple therapist has little empathy. Alternatively and not relevant to Liz and Martin, a couple therapist with a trauma history might choose not to work with perpetrators of intimate partner violence.

When a couple is best served by seeking couple therapy from a different therapist, it is up to the couple therapist with whom they first met to provide the names and contact information for at least three other couple therapists and to take full responsibility for being unable to work with the couple. It would be an ethical violation to in any way imply that the couple's presenting problem is the issue. We will return to the couple therapist's experience in Chapter 10 and to ethical considerations in Chapter 11.

Conclusions

This chapter acquainted you with the process of and tools for assessing couples and arriving at a working hypothesis. These included clinical interviews, observation, and assessment tools used by couple therapists. The definition and utility of working hypotheses as distinct from diagnoses were also addressed.

Several related topics were explored. These include building a therapeutic alliance, a process that occurs simultaneously with assessment. A discussion of the couple's history and the potential need for other therapeutic modalities or professionals was also presented.

Prior to being introduced to specific theories of couple therapy in Section II, the importance of a theoretical underpinning for assessment and treatment was explored. It was suggested that without theory, the amount of information and possible ways to intervene would be too great to manage effectively.

References

American Psychiatric Association. (2013). *Diagnostic and statistical manual of mental disorders* (5th ed.). Washington DC: American Psychiatric Publishing.

Bowen, M. (1978). *Family therapy in clinical practice*. New York NY: Jason Aronson.

Corey, M. S. & Corey, G. (2011). *Becoming a helper* (6th ed.). Belmont CA: Brooks/Cole.

Derogatis, L. R. (1996). *Derogatis interview for sexual functioning*. Baltimore MD: Clinical Psychometric Research.

Esposito, J. & Hattem, A. (2017). *Introduction to family counseling. A case study approach*. Los Angeles CA: Sage Publishing.

Gehart, D. R. (2013). *Mastering competencies in family therapy. A practical approach to theory and clinical case documentation* (2nd ed.). Belmont CA: Brooks/Cole.

Hoskins, C. N. (1988). *Partner relationship inventory*. Palo Alto CA: Consulting Psychologists Press.

Howgego, I. M., Yellowlees, P., Owen, C., Meldrum, L., & Dark, F. (2003). The therapeutic alliance. The key to effective patient outcome? A descriptive review of the evidence in community mental health case management. *Australia New Zealand Journal of Psychiatry*, 37 (2), 169–183. Retrieved from https://www.ncbi.nlm.nih.gov/pubmed/12656956.

McGoldrick, M. (2008). *Genograms: Assessment and intervention*. New York NY: W. W. Norton & Co.

McGoldrick, M. & Gerson, R. (1985). *Genograms in family assessment*. New York NY: W. W. Norton & Co.

Miller, S., Hubble, M., & Duncan, B. (2014). Supershrinks. What's the secret of their success? *Psychotherapy Networker*. Retrieved from https://www.psychotherapynetworker.org/blog/details/393/supershrinks.

Olson, D. H. (2000). *Clinical rating scale (CRS) for the circumplex model of marital and family systems*. Minneapolis MN: Life Innovations.

Siegel, R. (2013). Wisdom in psychotherapy. *Psychotherapy Networker*, 37 (2), 18–25.

Snyder, D. K. (1997). *Marital satisfaction inventory, revised* (MSI-R). Los Angeles CA: Western Psychological Services.

Spanier, G. B. (2001). *Dyadic adjustment scale* (DAS). North Tonawanda NY: MHS.

Straus, M. S., Hamby, S. L., & Warren, W. L. (2003). *Conflict tactics scales handbook*. Los Angeles CA: Western Psychological Services.

Yalom, I. (2003). *The gift of therapy: An open letter to a new generation of therapists and their patients*. New York NY: Harper.

CHAPTER 4
Couples as Systems

Learning Objectives

1. Evaluate the idea that a couple is more than the two individuals who comprise it.
2. Identify the ways their couple dynamics appeared in Liz and Martin's discussions about her career.
3. Define circular causation.
4. Discuss the role of feedback loops and homeostatic mechanisms in a couple's equilibrium.
5. Distinguish first- and second-order change.
6. Compare and contrast the concept of distance regulation with the concept of approach-withdraw cycles.
7. List the components of couple resilience.
8. Describe the concept of couple contracts.

A knowledge of the tenets of family systems theory provides the foundation for understanding other theories of couple therapy. Through repetitive interaction patterns, a couple becomes more than the two individuals who comprise it, and as a result systems theorists hold that a system is greater than the sum of its parts. These repetitive interaction patterns, or couple dynamics, are a focus of couple therapy. While the content of a couple's issues is important, enduring change only occurs when the processes by which partners interact, or the couple's dynamics, change.

Consider a person who is responsible at work, charming and helpful to neighbors and friends, intelligent, interesting, and unable to remember events that are important to his or her partner. This partner is similarly respected at work, caring to friends and colleagues, intelligent, and interesting. This partner is also nasty and derisive toward his or her partner.

Stop and Think:

Be sure to include your answers in your journal.

1. Is their couple dynamic a reflection of one or both partner's individual psychopathology?
2. Does the forgetful partner's behavior account for the nasty partner's nasty, derisive behavior?
3. Does the nasty, derisive partner's behavior account for the forgetful partner's behavior?
4. Without yet understanding systems theory, where would you intervene to change this couple's dynamics?

Your answers to the questions in the Stop and Think illustrate how couple therapy differs from individual psychotherapy with two clients. The questions suggest that a psychotherapist could examine each partner's problem or label one of the partners as the problem. A third alternative, the one subscribed to by couple therapists, examines the dynamics that are part of being a couple.

Three overarching ideas underlie systems theory as it applies to couple therapy. First, partners co-create their repetitive patterns of interaction. Thus, couple dynamics are never about one partner or his or her pathology. Rather, couple therapists hold the view that, like the couple described above, two well functioning individuals can inadvertently co-create dynamics that change who they are with one another and then find themselves stuck in patterns of interacting they cannot easily link to their unhappiness with one another. It is easier to view the forgetful partner as passive-aggressive and the nasty, dismissive partner as not very nice than to identify how their dynamics impact their unhappiness. Couple therapists, rather than viewing either partner at fault, address the dynamics that undermine their relationship.

A second overarching idea of systems theory is attention to what happens in the context of the couple therapy itself. While the influence of history upon the present is deemed important, the focus of intervention is on what is happening in any given session.

Finally, as previously noted, systems theory focuses more on process, or couple dynamics, than on the content of the information a couple presents and a couple therapist uses as illustrative. Neither Liz, Martin, nor any couple therapist can change Liz's assault history or the familial and sociocultural pressures about women's roles that impact her. Nor can any of them change Martin's daily experience of being a black man at this moment in time in this country. The factors that are susceptible to change are the ways Liz and Martin relate to themselves and one another around these external facts, or content.

This chapter begins with a review of the relatively brief history of couple therapy. Terminology has changed from the founding of the field in the middle of the last century, and wording will continue to change throughout your careers. Theorists alter the wording of the writings in order to fit their unique ways of conceptualizing couple systems. For example, Kantor and Lehr (1975) wrote about the concept of distance regulation. Lerner (1990), writing about ambivalence in the dance of intimacy, mirrored the idea that balancing distance and closeness in couple relationships is critical to avoiding partners feeling either submerged in or disconnected from each other. More recently, Gottman and Gottman's (2008) writings about the approach-withdraw cycle in couple relationships also addresses balancing closeness and distance.

Stop and Think:

Be sure to include your answers in your journal.

1. How much closeness are you comfortable with in a relationship? What components—emotional, physical, intellectual, etc.—contribute to your sense of closeness?
2. How much time do you need for yourself and to socialize with friends independently of a partner?

3. Imagine that your partner is similar to you in his or her needs for closeness and separateness. How realistic do you think it is that your needs will be in sync? For example, you may want to be alone or with friends at times your partner would like to see you, and the reverse may also occur, leading you to feel that you were either smothered or not together often enough.
4. Imagine that you and your partner were different in terms of your needs for closeness and distance. How might that play out as a dance or as an approach-withdraw cycle?

This chapter also introduces the reader to ten systems theory concepts as they apply to couples: couple systems and dynamics, subsystems, circular causation and feedback loops, homeostasis and equilibrium, rules, first- and second-order change, second-order cybernetics, function of the presenting problem, distance regulation, and couple resilience. Additionally, because couple contracts arise from couple dynamics (Sager, 1977), they will be included in a separate section within this chapter.

In Chapters 5 and 6, you will learn about some of the classical theoretical approaches to couple therapy, while in Chapter 7 you will learn about more recent theories of couple therapy. While there are theoretical approaches to couple therapy that are not included, many, if not most of these can be subsumed within these two broad categories, and an exhaustive review of the couple therapy literature is beyond the scope of an introductory textbook.

Transcripts and examples will be taken from later couple therapy sessions with Liz and Martin. When they presented in 2002 for their final segment of couple therapy, Christina was nine years old and Martin Jr. (MJ) was six. The Manning-Jones family had thus moved to a more stable period in its family life cycle than when Liz and Martin had first requested couple therapy when their daughter was an infant and their son not yet conceived. However, their couple dynamics had not changed to the extent that they were able to maintain these changes in the face of external pressures including the protracted illness and death of Liz's father and her being passed over for partner in her law firm.

Origins of Couple Therapy

Couple therapy, also referred to historically as marital therapy and currently as relational therapy, is a twentieth century phenomenon. Although it may best be described as intimate partner relationship therapy, that description is cumbersome and so it will continue to be referred to as couple therapy throughout this book. The distinction between intimate partner relationship therapy, or couple therapy, and relational therapy is based on the assumptions iterated in the introduction. These include that, for our purposes, a couple is a physically and emotionally intimate dyad, each partner is the other's either sole or primary partner, there exists the intention of permanence or sufficient duration to warrant couple therapy, the partners are identified as a couple within their social networks, and some degree of economic interdependence is present. The term relational therapy without the qualifier of intimate implies the potential to include those relationships that exclude the intention of sufficient duration to warrant therapy, those without any form of public commitment however informal, and those that preclude sexual intimacy. While it is important for couple therapists to extend their competency to include dyads comprising two people who are dating, couples who choose celibacy, siblings caring for an elderly parent, colleagues who must work together and cannot, and friends who are important enough to each other to want to work out a crisis in their friendship, this textbook will not focus on applying the tenants of therapy to these dyadic relationships.

Although it arose concurrently with family therapy, couple therapy's origins were different. Specifically, Gurman and Fraenkel (2002) noted in their millennial review of the first 40 years of couple therapy that couple therapy arose from the observation by individual psychotherapists that many of their clients presented with relationship issues. Family therapy, on the other hand, arose out of work at the Mental Research Institute in California and the Ackerman Institute in New York. The pioneers of the application of systems theory to human groups and most especially to family therapy included Nathan Ackerman (1970), Gregory Bateson (1972), Murray Bowen (1978), Jay Haley (1963), Ervin Laszlo (1972), Salvador Minuchin (1974), Peggy Papp (1997), Virginia Satir (Satir, Stachowiak, & Taschman, 1975), Paul Watzlawick and John Weakland (Watzlawick, Weakland, & Fisch, 1974), and Carl Whitaker (Napier & Whitaker, 1978).

Early couple therapy involved the application of individual theories of intervention, especially psychoanalytic therapy, to each partner within the couple. Couple therapists viewed each partner as an individual whose pathology complemented his or her partner's. Thus, early couple therapists treated each one's individual psychopathology, assuming individual change would benefit the couple (Gurman & Fraenkel, 2002).

This was followed by a period during which systems theory was extended to include couples by family therapists who were seeing couples for parenting issues or as subsystems within the families they treated. During this stage of the development of couple therapy, couple therapy was subsumed under family therapy and did not exist as an independent field. The partners as individuals were ignored in the belief that changing the family system would benefit the couple's relationship as well as all of the individuals in the family (Gurman & Fraenkel, 2002).

During the past 30 years, couple therapists have utilized a combination of individual and systems theories to focus their attention simultaneously on the partners as individuals and on the couple system they co-create together. Any psychopathology is seen as unique to the individual, although it can originate within the system and inevitably becomes a part of the functioning of any system of which the individual is a part (Gurman & Fraenkel, 2002; Nichols, 1987). With this history in mind, you will now learn about ten systems theory concepts as they apply to couple therapy.

Systems Theory Concepts Applied to Couples

We tend to think of a couple as two individuals and to view their interactions as linear in time. Adding a specific example to the hypothetical couple noted in the introduction to this chapter in individual and linear terms, Partner 1 arrives home from work an hour late on the couple's date night without any communication with Partner 2, Partner 2 expresses anger, and Partner 1 becomes defensive. Depending on where an observer entered this scenario, he or she might view Partner 1 as either incapable of empathy or defensive and Partner 2 as angry. Neither addresses what is occurring between them as partners in a couple.

While a couple therapist might attend to individual psychopathology because individual issues do impact a couple's relationship, she or he would find it imperative to examine systemic and circular phenomena. In what context did the observed individual behaviors arise? How does each partner's response impact what happens next? If one partner is tasked with initiating a date night and the other with rejecting or undermining it, what might their pattern tell you about how the couple regulates distance, handles intimacy, and exhibits approach-withdrawal in their relationship? In other words, the couple therapist is interested in sequences of behaviors that create patterns of interaction that result in similar outcomes despite different content.

This section of this chapter will address ten systems theory concepts as they pertain to couples: couple systems and dynamics, subsystems, circular causation and feedback loops, homeostasis and equilibrium, rules, first- and second-order change, second-order cybernetics, function of the presenting problem, distance regulation, and couple resilience. These concepts reappear as relevant throughout the remainder of this textbook in the examination of specific theories of intervention and the topics covered in Section III.

The descriptions of these concepts derive from the work of the early systems theorists and therapists noted in the previous section of this chapter. While many have been relabeled and altered slightly over the years to fit the perspective of subsequent generations of writers in the field, the principles remain. Understanding these foundational concepts will help readers evaluate both the original and more contemporary iterations.

Please note that these concepts are extremely complex and often contradictory to linear, cause-and-effect Western thought. As a result, they may not be easily understood and remembered from this first reading. Rather than attempting to memorize them, attend to the dialogue that exemplifies them to further elucidate their meaning.

Couple Systems and Dynamics

A system is a group of interacting and interdependent, as opposed to independent or dependent, parts. For human systems such as couples, each part is an individual person. The interactions between people, as distinguished from the individuals themselves, create phenomena that are distinct from the people themselves. Thus, couple therapists adhere to the systems theory concept that the system as a whole is greater than the sum of its parts. For example, your pet is more than its ears, eyes, tail, fur, whiskers, and bark or purr. Applied to couples, it means the couple as a system is distinct from, though not independent of, the two partners who comprise it.

What is it about human groups in general and couples in particular that makes a couple more than the two partners as individuals? It is the couple's dynamics, defined as repetitive patterns of verbal and nonverbal interactions between the partners. A system's dynamics are more easily observable by someone who is not part of the couple system, for example, by a couple therapist. Partners become embroiled in the content of their interactions, which can obscure their ability to see their dynamics, or repetitive patterns of interaction.

Liz and Martin argued about several different topics in their first sessions, including her career, his support for her career, whether he is competitive with her professionally and if so whether that manifests in their sexual relationship. The way these arguments unfolded was strikingly similar irrespective of their content, because Liz and Martin's patterns of interaction were repeated. In other words, their dynamics remained unchanged, irrespective of the topic about which they were arguing.

An excerpt from the couple therapist's preliminary assessment (Chapter 1) illustrates this point: "Liz and Martin interrupt one another and change topics as emotions become more heated. They also devolve into conflict about who is correct." Several times, the couple therapist asked a question to both Liz and Martin and Liz asked Martin to respond to it, then interrupted him in order to edit what he was saying. She also interrupted him when he was responding to a question the couple therapist had directed to him. Martin did not challenge Liz's interruptions. These observations held, no matter which topic was the argument's focus.

When the couple therapist brought this dynamic to Liz and Martin's awareness, Martin pounced on it.

COUPLE THERAPIST: I'm curious that when one of you is talking and the other interrupts, it doesn't appear to bother either of you. Am I observing correctly?

MARTIN: No. It bothers me, quite a lot actually. But the best thing is to let Liz have her say.

CT: What would happen if you didn't let her have her say?

MARTIN: She'd get more upset.

CT: And what about when Martin interrupts you, Liz?

LIZ: He never interrupts me. He's the most passive human being I've ever met, and to tell you the truth it totally infuriates me.

CT: So you'd prefer Martin said something when you interrupt him and interrupted you when he has something to say?

LIZ: It's not the interrupting—that sounds really awful, and I don't like to think of myself as someone who interrupts. It's the not saying when he's upset, so I have to guess.

CT: And that's when you think he disapproves? Like of your career choice or parenting?

LIZ: Exactly. But also, when I interrupt him, I wish he'd tell me to let him finish.

CT: Martin?

MARTIN: Really? You want me to tell you to let me finish? You wouldn't get angrier at me?

LIZ: (Laughing) Oh probably, but I'd also feel like you were with me in the conversation.

Stop and Think:

Be sure to include your answers in your journal.

1. What did you learn about Liz from this excerpt?
2. What did you learn about Martin?
3. What did you learn about their relationship dynamics?
4. How does what you learned about their dynamics differ from what you already thought you knew about each of them?
5. How does your answer to Question 4 illustrate how the couple system is greater than the sum of its parts?

Shifting topics as the emotional intensity of an interaction increases is a dynamic utilized by many couples to prevent conflict from escalating. The partners are usually unaware of what they are doing, although they may acknowledge this dynamic when a couple therapist comments upon it. We will explore this dynamic further in the subsection on homeostasis.

Subsystems

Systems are comprised of interlocking subsystems. Imagine peeling the layers of an onion. Each layer you remove is sufficient on its own, although the whole onion, especially when it is alive and growing, requires each layer to be present. Like the layers of an onion, each subsystem is a system in and of itself. Whether a particular subsystem, such as a couple, is referred to as a system or a subsystem depends upon where the observer focuses her or his lens. In this subsection, we will examine couples as subsystems of larger familial and social groups.

In addition to being a discrete system, a couple is also a subsystem of each partner's family of origin and of the family the couple creates through procreating, adopting, or blending of their children from previous relationships. The couple subsystem interacts with various other subsystems within each partner's extended family, such as parents and parents-in-law, siblings and their families, grandparents, aunts, uncles, and cousins. How the couple is viewed and treated by other subsystems impacts how it functions within the family as a whole. Like individuals in a system, a couple's interactions with their children and their extended families involve dynamics unique to the family that might not be present when the couple is on its own.

Consider the issue of appearance in Liz's family of origin and how it affects both Liz and her couple dynamics with Martin. As an aside, it will also one day affect her daughter, Christina (Esposito & Hattem, 2017). Liz's mother, Sally, had always been concerned about her own and her daughters' appearance and especially about their weight. Sally would routinely comment on what Liz and her sister, Barbara, ate and their weight. In adolescence, they occasionally fought back.

LIZ: One of us would say, "Mom, really, this isn't helping" and she'd be all hurt and upset and we'd end up comforting her, and then the next time one of us accepted dessert at a family birthday celebration or put potatoes on our plate at Thanksgiving she'd start in again.

COUPLE THERAPIST: And then what happened?

LIZ: Same thing. But after my dad died, we stopped saying anything to her. We just listen quietly and continue doing whatever we're doing.

CT: Including what you're eating?

LIZ: Yes, but then she gets all hurt about aren't we listening to her when she's only trying to help us. Sometimes we don't eat whatever it is.

CT: What's it like for you when that happens?

Note: The couple therapist intentionally left the question vague, leaving Liz to decide which of several possible reactions to address.

LIZ: I don't know. I guess the message sinks in, but that's nothing new. Martin thinks that's why I watch my weight so carefully and exercise so much even when I'm exhausted, like right after the children were born. But he exercises, too.

MARTIN: Not as much as you do.

CT: And what do you think, Liz?

LIZ: [Rolling her eyes] I guess he might be right.

Note: Liz described a repetitive pattern of interactions in her family of origin that shifted some when her father died but remained unchanged in its impact.

Within Liz and Martin's couple subsystem, Liz's concern about her appearance was also apparent. Liz had informed Martin that if she did not have time to exercise every day she would become anxious and depressed and fat. When Martin pointed out that he also needed time away from family responsibilities to exercise, Liz responded that he had time during his workday. Liz and Martin, like Liz, her sister, and their mother, had co-created dynamics regarding her appearance, even though the dynamics were different in their couple subsystem than in her family of origin.

MARTIN: [To Couple Therapist] Liz worries too much about being fat. Of course she's gained a few pounds and her body has changed since the kids were born. But she looks great, at least to me. I don't have any complaints.

CT: What do you want Liz to hear in what you just said?

MARTIN: That I think she looks great.

LIZ: [To CT] That's because I work hard on it. [To Martin] And I wouldn't look great if I didn't. You don't get that.

MARTIN: [To CT] See, she never believes me.

CT: There are a couple of things on the table here: your disagreement about how Liz looks and your disagreement about whether she has to work so hard to maintain her appearance. I don't hear that either of you questions the value of her appearance or whether one of you cares more than the other about it.

LIZ: What are you talking about?

MARTIN: I love Liz the way she is, and I'd love her if she was heavier and less in shape. She doesn't believe that, but it's true.

CT: Tell her that.

MARTIN: OK. [To Liz] You look great, Hon. And I love you for who you are, not what you look like.

LIZ: Oh bulls..., Martin!

Stop and Think:

Be sure to include your answers in your journal.

1. What do you think the couple therapist was attempting to accomplish when she talked about multiple issues "on the table"?
2. How would you describe Liz and Martin's dynamic around the issue of weight?
3. Compare and contrast Liz and Martin's dynamic about weight with Liz and her mother's dynamic about it.

Now that they have children, Liz and Martin must function as a parental subsystem as well as an intimate partner subsystem. A parental subsystem discusses the children's needs, schedules, discipline, or limit-setting and the consequences of violating rules, and how to manage each of these. The couple subsystem must also work to maintain their intimate partner relationship and make decisions about the life of the family. Some couples have more success as a parental subsystem than as an intimate partner subsystem, while for others the reverse is true. Liz and Martin experienced difficulties in both, although their intimate partner subsystem appeared more distressed than their parental subsystem.

MARTIN: I think we do pretty well as parents. We fight some about who is responsible for what, but we basically agree about childrearing.

COUPLE THERAPIST: Liz?

LIZ: Yes. Of course, our children are pretty easy and these are pretty easy ages. Who knows what will happen when they're teenagers.

CT: So it's great that you're working on your relationship now, before your parenting is challenged by having teenagers.

Stop and Think:

What were your reactions to the couple therapist's praise? Be sure to include your answer in your journal.

To summarize, a couple system is a distinct subsystem within the family the partners create. If there are children, the couple functions as a parental subsystem in addition to being an intimate partner subsystem. The dynamics between the parental subsystem and the sibling subsystem may be different than the dynamics within either subsystem or than those between individual members of each subsystem. For example, siblings may keep each other's secrets from parents, while one of the siblings might reveal more about herself or himself to one parent than to the other or than other siblings do. And the way all members of the family interact as a family may differ from the interactions within and among the various subsystems.

Circular Causation and Feedback Loops

By definition, dynamics are circular. Liz asked Martin to answer a question, Martin began to answer, she interrupted him, he responded to the content of her interruption while ignoring the fact that she had interrupted him, and this cycle continued until one of them got so frustrated or furious that the conversation ended. The circularity is that every effect circles back to become the cause of a subsequent effect.

We tend to think of causation as linear. For example, a child refusing to do homework is deprived of her or his electronic devices until the homework is finished. If the child tantrums and the parents continue to enforce the consequence, eventually the child will stop tantruming, whether or not he or she does homework. Alternatively, if the parents relent and return the electronics, the child has been reinforced for tantruming. A systems therapist would interpret this seemingly linear causation as circular by suggesting the existence of a repetitive pattern of escalation between the parents and the child, irrespective of the subject, or content, of the conflict.

Returning to Liz interrupting Martin, one could hypothesize that Martin reinforced Liz's interruptions by not challenging them. A systemic therapist would also hypothesize that although Martin may be reinforcing Liz's interruptions, a more salient aspect is the circular causation evidenced by Liz and Martin working together to change the subject and as a result failing to resolve whatever issue they discuss.

Circular causation allows a couple therapist to intervene at any point in the circle. This allows flexibility to address what is happening in the moment in the therapy session.

Feedback loops involve repetitive patterns of circular causation. In the earlier example, when the parents enforced a limit and the child began to tantrum, a feedback loop was set in motion during which the parents' subsequent interaction with the child would either escalate the conflict (positive feedback loop) or defuse it (negative feedback loop). Attempting to control the tantrum set in motion a positive feedback loop of escalating conflict. Had the parents not relented in response to the tantrum, the conflict would not have continued to escalate. In that case the pattern would have been child refusing to do homework followed by a parent enforcing a consequence followed by child tantruming followed by the parent continuing to enforce the consequence until the conflict de-escalated. This negative circular causation might happen spontaneously or be initiated by a child, couple, or family therapist to whom the parents turned for help. When Liz interrupted Martin and he allowed the subject to change, a positive feedback loop of escalating interruptions and subject changes was set in motion.

The use of the adjectives positive and negative with respect to feedback loops is not an evaluation. Rather, a positive feedback loop of conflict would likely lead to negative feelings between partners, whereas a negative feedback loop might allow them to resolve their conflict and feel better about each other. The use of the terms positive and negative in this regard are counterintuitive unless viewed from a systemic perspective.

Martin and Liz's dynamic included a positive feedback loop of circular causation around not only interruptions but also whether or not he supported her choice about how to balance career with motherhood.

LIZ: I've been asking you to give me a little credit for taking care of our home and the kids and still working 20 or 30 hours a week.

MARTIN: Come on, Liz. I help you with the kids.

LIZ: When you're home. You tell me you're stressed about money as though I should be making more, and I can't do that unless you do more with the kids, which you say you don't have time to do.

MARTIN: If you wanted to work full time again...

LIZ: I don't want to work full time again. And we agreed after Christina was born that we would make it work for me to be part time.

MARTIN: Then what's the problem?

LIZ: You've never supported me in that choice!

MARTIN: I don't know what you want me to do.

LIZ: Support me!

MARTIN: What does that mean?

LIZ: If you can't figure it out...

MARTIN: Seriously, Liz? I give up. Nothing I do makes you happy.

Note how each statement affected the other partner's next statement in an escalating cycle, or positive feedback loop, of circular causation. Martin's last statement leads to the next subsection of this chapter.

Homeostasis and Equilibrium

In systems theory, equilibrium refers to a system in balance. Homeostasis, on the other hand, entails the process by which a system achieves and maintains balance. Homeostasis and equilibrium are similar to the heating or cooling system in your home. If you set the heat to 68 degrees Fahrenheit, the temperature will, in fact, not remain at 68 degrees. Rather, your home will begin to cool, and as the temperature drops to 67 degrees the thermostat will turn on the heater. Then, as the heater runs and the temperature climbs to 69 degrees, the thermostat will turn off the heater. The thermostat functions as a homeostatic mechanism to interrupt the positive feedback loops of increasing and decreasing temperatures and thus keeps the climate in your home in equilibrium around, although not always exactly, 68 degrees Fahrenheit.

Homeostasis and equilibrium function identically in couple systems. As the anger in the previous excerpt heated, Liz and Martin first attempted to change the subject to caring for their children and then Martin said, "I give up," effectively ending the argument. Shifting topics and refusing to continue an argument, either verbally as Martin did or through physically exiting the couple space, are homeostatic mechanisms partners use to maintain equilibrium. The homeostatic mechanism involved interrupting the positive feedback loop of escalating distress to return the couple system to a more familiar and therefore more comfortable equilibrium.

The purpose of a homeostatic mechanism is to prevent a positive feedback loop from destroying the system. The couple therapist assumed that the prospect of resolving their conflict was perceived to be more destabilizing to Liz and Martin's couple system than returning to an unsatisfactory but familiar state of equilibrium.

Unfortunately, distressed couples like Liz and Martin tend to initiate a homeostatic mechanism before they have resolved an argument. It may appear that the couple fears that if the argument continued it would permanently disrupt their couple bond. Some couple therapists guide a couple toward resolution while simultaneously encouraging them to remain focused on both the content of their argument and the process by which they argue until their argument is resolved, assuming this circumvents the homeostatic mechanism long enough to achieve a new equilibrium. Other couple therapists intentionally disrupt the couple's homeostatic mechanism and then guide them toward resolution of both the content and process of their argument. Whichever theoretically based intervention route a couple therapist chooses, the point is to change the dynamic that leads a couple to invoke a homeostatic mechanism that then impedes the couple's ability to resolve conflict.

Rules

Couple rules arise from repetitive patterns of interaction as these govern the couple's expectations for each other, their interactions with each other, and the couple's interactions with their family and community systems. Like all aspects of a couple's dynamics, rules appear to become fixed early in a couple's relationship.

Rules include expectations guiding role behaviors and the meaning of being a good partner. When a couple marries, a set of social and familial role expectations for husbands and/or wives also enters their relationship. When they become parents, similar expectations about mothers and/or fathers are added.

Liz and Martin said they married when they did because his mother's values precluded cohabitation without marriage. Thus, her expectations entered their relationship when they decided to cohabit. Additionally, both had expectations for being a husband or wife gleaned from being socialized in their families of origin and in the larger sociocultural context in which they were born and raised.

Stop and Think:

Be sure to include your answers in your journal.

1. How does each of your parents view being a partner in an intimate domestic relationship? Note that they have a viewpoint irrespective of whether they are currently partnered.
2. How do your friends view being a partner in an intimate domestic relationship?
3. What have you learned from the culture in which you were raised about being a partner in an intimate domestic relationship? Culture includes but is not limited to music, movies, television programs, and your professional, social, and spiritual or religious communities.

Liz described pressure she felt from her mother and sister, as well as from her mother-in-law, to stop working outside the home after Christina was born. What follows is an excerpt from a 1997 couple session.

LIZ: They make me feel like a bad mother, like I'm selfish for wanting to keep my career afloat. But I'm not sure it's bad for the kids to learn to trust other adults and to be around other children.

COUPLE THERAPIST: Right now, talking to me, it sounds like you're totally confident you're doing the right thing. What changes when you talk to your mother and sister that shakes that confidence?

LIZ: My mother's always made me doubt myself. Do I really want potatoes on Thanksgiving? Do I really want a Christmas cookie? Do I really want to go to grad school and be a lawyer—you know what people think of lawyers—oh, don't I think an M.R.S. degree would be a better idea! I don't know, there's something about how she says these things.

CT: Does Barbara [Liz's sister] say it the same way?

LIZ: Yes. They sound like they're reading the same script. Which surprises me, because Barbara also doubts herself when Mom gets going on her.

CT: Maybe that's what's leading you to doubt continuing your career?

LIZ: Oh. [Pause] Yeah, I guess. But Martin agrees.

MARTIN: Oh for heaven's sake, Liz.

LIZ: Well, your mother does.

MARTIN: She's never said anything about it.

LIZ: But we both know what she thinks.

MARTIN: And anyway, what she thinks and what I think are not the same thing.

LIZ: Yeah, right.

MARTIN: What have I ever said to try to influence your decision one way or the other?

LIZ: It's not what you say, it's what you're thinking...

MARTIN: Oh, and you know exactly what I'm thinking.

LIZ: It's not rocket science. The minute I went back to work, sex went out the window.

MARTIN: Yeah, because you've been too tired.

LIZ: How do you know? You never ask!

MARTIN: Being blamed for everything isn't exactly a turn-on.

Note: A couple therapist would have intervened to facilitate Liz and Martin remaining focused on one topic and using new skills for communicating about it, unless this had happened during the first session and he or she wanted to see how their arguments developed. To illustrate systems theory concepts, the couple therapist did not intervene.

Stop and Think:

Be sure to include your answers in your journal.

1. Identify the positive feedback loop(s) in this transcript.
2. Identify the homeostatic mechanisms Liz and Martin employed to interrupt the positive feedback loop(s).
3. Identify the relationship rules revealed in this excerpt.
4. Were you the couple therapist, where in transcript would you have intervened? Why? In systemic terms, what would you have hoped to accomplish?

First- and Second-Order Change

Systems theory, as applied to human groups, posits that most individuals, couples, and families attempt to remedy their distress by either doing more of the same, on the assumption that more is better, or doing the opposite of what has failed to work. These attempts at first-order change reflect a dichotomous way of thinking. Doing more of the same or doing the opposite suggests one's options for change are limited to only these two possibilities.

Consider Liz's relationships with her mother, sister, and mother-in-law in terms of her decision about whether to return to work after Christina's birth. It appeared that her mother had been pressuring her daughters to conform to her view of how a woman, wife, and mother should be and appear for many years. In terms of her appearance, Liz's approach had been to do more of the same, in this case exercise more and eat less. With respect to her career, however, she had done the opposite of what her mother wanted her to do. Instead of focusing on getting married and raising a family, as her sister Barbara had done, she not only pursued a professional career but also one that her mother viewed as unpopular and therefore undesirable even for a man much less for a woman. In neither instance did Liz formulate an approach to her life that was her own. Thus, the birth of Christina left her with only two options: being an even better wife, mother, and homemaker than her mother Sally (i.e., more of the same) or returning to work full time and resuming her climb up the corporate ladder (i.e., the opposite).

By contrast, second-order change involves changing the rules in order to increase options for change. Second-order change requires the individual, couple, or family to break free from the dichotomous choices that reference the problem and that have impeded change. And while some individuals, couples, and families find their way to second-order change on their own, it underlies all theories of therapeutic intervention.

For Liz, second-order change entailed an approach to balancing career and parenting that worked for her, Martin, and their children. Rather than adhering to or rejecting her mother's dated model of women's roles, Liz and Martin needed to create couple rules that allowed them each to make choices about balancing professional and parenting roles within the realistic constraints of their family's needs.

COUPLE THERAPIST: I wonder what your lives would be like if you took a year's leave of absence from your firm, Liz.

LIZ: Why aren't you asking Martin that question?

CT: I didn't think we were talking about the possibility of Martin not working.

MARTIN: [Vehemently] No. We weren't.

LIZ: You could stay home and parent as well as I could.

MARTIN: But I don't want to. And if you don't want to either, the kids are fine at day care.

LIZ: That's really unfair.

MARTIN: It's how it is.

CT: And how it is is very difficult. I don't see your dilemma as being about who should stay home because you've both made it clear that your children are fine with two working parents. It's about what you want to do,

Liz, and the answer is clearly not a simple one. I guess it'd feel more fair if Martin was vying with you to stay home with the kids, but it would also be more complicated. For the two of you, it seems totally appropriate for you to ask Martin to have your back with both of your mothers, as well as with the complications of two professional parents balancing careers and parenting, whatever you decide.

LIZ: OK, you're saying I'm trying to make this Martin's problem.

CT: That isn't exactly what I was saying but, yeah, it's not for him to decide, though he can help you think it through. And it sounds as though your mother is pretty traditional, that even if Martin wanted to be a stay-at-home dad she'd think the parent at home should be you and not hesitate to tell you about it.

LIZ: Yes, absolutely. It's my mother, not Martin, in my head about staying home. [To Martin] I guess it always has been?

MARTIN: [Gently] I'm not Sally, Liz. I don't think like she does, and I'm on your side.

LIZ: If we thought someone should stay home, would you talk about which of us it should be?

MARTIN: Is that really what you want? Because it's fine with me if you make changes, but I don't want to and I think the kids are fine.

LIZ: No. I don't want you to stay home. I just meant am I the one who is supposed to?

MARTIN: I don't think so, and I don't really think you think so.

CT: Maybe talking about the options and how they would work for you as a couple and a family would help you decide what sounds good to you and is also doable.

The couple therapist opened this excerpt by suggesting a third option, thereby questioning the assumptions underlying first-order change and substituting the idea that a range of possibilities exists. She also asked Liz to begin focusing on her own agency in creating her life, which would involve a second-order change from the assumption that she must either do what her mother wanted or the opposite. Finally, as part of second-order change, she pointed Liz and Martin toward a couple perspective, resulting in greater empathy between them as well as the option of forward momentum.

In the writer's experience, second-order change involves the psychotherapist questioning clients' assumptions. Later in couple therapy, Liz, who was working part time and had taken on daytime responsibility for their two children, criticized Martin for not being more involved. Questioning revealed that Liz assumed both parents should be equally involved in childrearing. To support her assumption, she cited the husband of a neighbor, who she had seen playing with their children outside and picking them up at school. This husband, however, was an emergency room nurse whose full-time work entailed three 12-hour shifts each week and was otherwise at home. The couple therapist questioned Liz's assumption that all fathers who worked full time outside the home needed to be as involved in parenting as Liz and Martin's neighbor was. Second-order change arose from her shift in perspective to the idea that neither she nor her husband needed to conform to an imagined ideal. Liz was then able to listen to and empathize with Martin's desire to be involved with their children as much as possible given the realistic constraints of his career.

As second-order change shifted Liz and Martin's perspective on their respective parenting roles, their fight about what he truly thought of her decision to work part time resolved. It developed that Liz had assumed that Martin was expressing his displeasure about her career choice by thwarting her desire for him to be more involved with the children or portraying himself as more important than she. Her ideas about how Martin viewed her and was demeaning her likely arose from her habitual response to her mother's criticisms, as well as the dominant culture's demeaning of traditional women's roles. This time, however, instead of the first-order change argument about how involved he should be, Liz and Martin, with the help of their couple therapist, instigated a second-order change that helped resolve their conflict.

Despite Liz's mother's attitudes, the impact of the dominant culture on Liz and Martin's dilemma cannot be ignored. Women who can afford to stay at home with children face a first-order dilemma: become a stay-at-home mother or return to full career involvement quickly. Without extended parental leaves such as those available in western European countries and reasonable options to balance a career and parenting without forfeiting career advancement and future earning potential, even second-order change, such as Liz and Martin's, entails sacrifice. Liz was passed over for partner, with attendant caps on her earning potential. While these are clearly problems for couples affluent enough to have choices, constraints on women in couples with fewer resources are also enormous. Earning sufficiently to contribute to the support of the family while finding time to parent and child care that is both safe and affordable are virtually insurmountable challenges in the twenty-first century United States. Because of their education opportunities and even with Liz's reduced earning potential, Liz and Martin were able to go to work without worry about their children's safety and welfare.

Second-Order Cybernetics

Second-order change and second-order cybernetics sound synonymous but are, in fact, very different. Second-order cybernetics refers to the mutual impact of the couple system and the couple therapist upon each other. It is a helpful concept in that it directs a couple therapist's attention to how her or his interactions with the couple lead to him or her becoming a part of the couple system. Second-order cybernetics allow the couple therapist to experience some of what each partner experiences as part of the couple and gives her or him legitimacy for interventions from inside. Second-order cybernetics simultaneously carries the risk of the couple therapist becoming sufficiently engaged in the couple system's dynamics to be blinded to them and their repercussions, in much the same way the couple is. Finding a balance of legitimate system membership without losing a more objective perspective allows the couple therapist greater effectiveness.

What happens as a couple therapist is inducted into a couple system? Like all members of a system, the couple therapist adds her or his unique perspective; the risk of membership is that this perspective may be obscured by the rules of interaction within the system. As an outsider, the couple therapist can observe the couple's dynamics and note the rules; from inside, these tasks become more challenging. If one loses the capacity to observe a system objectively, one's awareness of dysfunctional dynamics and their impact also becomes obscured. As a result, a couple therapist who is not vigilant about maintaining an extra-system perspective may inadvertently become a homeostatic mechanism that sustains the problem.

As previously noted, anxiety that a positive feedback loop will spin out of control and undermine the stability of the couple system may trigger deployment of a homeostatic mechanism, such as changing the topic of an argument, to stop the escalating feedback loop and bring the system into a familiar equilibrium. A couple therapist's job is to encourage the partners to tolerate their anxiety and allow the feedback loop to continue until a new and, with the couple therapist's guidance, more functional equilibrium is attained. A couple therapist who has become a member of the couple system risks failure to notice when a homeostatic mechanism is engaged. Thus, if the couple therapist cannot maintain a balance between system membership and objective observer, her or his ability to encourage the couple to tolerate increasing discomfort and remain on topic long enough to facilitate resolution may be compromised and opportunities for positive change and a new equilibrium lost.

Stop and Think:

What might couple therapists do to prevent themselves from being inducted into the couple system to the extent they lose their ability to intervene? Be sure to include your answers in your journal.

Couple therapists, like individual and family therapists, use various techniques to minimize the risks associated with being inducted into a couple, or individual or family, system. These include, but need not be limited to, self-awareness, peer supervision, and consultation. If you thought of additional ways couple therapists can protect themselves, and thus their clients, be sure to make note of them for future reference.

Self-awareness is often the key to practicing effectively as well as ethically. Self-awareness involves attending to one's own process at the same time one is interacting with clients. As the couple therapist observed Liz and Martin during the session from which the excerpt in the previous subsection was taken, the first thing she noted was her reaction to Liz's opening challenge. When Liz asked, "Why aren't you asking Martin that question?", the couple therapist experienced hostility from Liz and noticed her own desire to react defensively. Reacting defensively would be a different manifestation of Martin's reaction when challenged and thus a sign that the couple therapist had become too embedded in the couple system. Rather than reacting defensively, the couple therapist used self-awareness to step back and then highlight a homeostatic mechanism in Liz and Martin's relationship: shifting from the positive feedback loop to the familiar challenge-react equilibrium.

COUPLE THERAPIST: I could guess what upset you about my question, but I would rather hear it from you.

LIZ: It's a sexist question.

CT: I agree. I also found myself wanting to react defensively when you asked me why I hadn't asked Martin the question. I wonder if that's one way your arguments veer away from resolution at home?

Stop and Think:

Be sure to include your answers in your journal.

1. What were your intellectual and emotional reactions to the couple therapist's intervention?
2. What else might she have said?

In summary, second-order cybernetics holds that the couple therapist inevitably becomes a part of the couple system. She or he must maintain a balance between membership in the couple system and remaining outside the couple system enough to intervene effectively. Using self-awareness, peer supervision, and consultation to maintain this balance, as well as to maintain other aspects of ethical practice, will be discussed in more detail in Chapter 11.

Function of the Presenting Problem

Systems theory posits that symptoms serve a function for the couple system. In other words, the dynamics manifested in the presenting problem function as a homeostatic mechanism to keep the couple system in balance. However, because this homeostatic mechanism contributes to the expressed difficulties in a couple's relationship, neither it nor the equilibrium in which it keeps the couple system is functional for the couple.

Hafner (1986) illustrated this point in a book entitled *Marriage and Mental Illness*. One of the homeostatic mechanisms he noted was a see-saw of mental health symptoms. While one partner appears emotionally distressed, the other appears fine. However, as the symptomatic partner's symptoms resolve, the second partner becomes symptomatic. In response, the first partner assumes the role of healthier presence in the relationship until they begin to see-saw again. The identical couple dynamic of one sick and one well partner remains in place irrespective of which partner assumes which role.

Stop and Think:

What might the function(s) of Liz and Martin's presenting problem(s) be? Be sure to include your answer in your journal.

Liz and Martin's couple therapist hypothesized that the possible functions of their presenting problem included avoidance of anger and anxiety that their issues of long duration could not be resolved and would lead to the dissolution of their marriage if fully addressed. Their on-going distress also may have functioned to maintain a comfortable balance of closeness and distance in their relationship and thus may have masked ambivalence about emotional and/or physical intimacy.

Distance Regulation

The term distance regulation refers to the process by which couples maintain an acceptable physical and emotional distance, or space, between partners. Physical distance is an easier concept to conceptualize. Everyone has known someone who stands too close for comfort when conversing. As one moves to create more physical distance from this person, he or she moves closer. This dance maintains a physical distance that is comfortable for neither, one person feeling his or her space has been violated and the other feeling too far away to have the conversation.

Couples also regulate physical distance, though the mechanisms by which they do so vary among couples. In some cases, one partner initiates more physical affection than the other. Other couples experience a discrepancy in how frequently each partner wishes to engage in sexual interactions and who is comfortable initiating sexual contact. Partners with differing preferences regarding physical distance from each other can negotiate what is comfortable for both. When such negotiations have been ineffective or avoided, couples may develop dynamics around regulating distance that leave both partners feeling unhappy. The partner who wants to cuddle or be told he or she is loved may ask flirtatiously for these or give them her or himself with the expectation of reciprocity. That partner may then become disappointed, frustrated, and angry at the lack of her or his partner's response.

Liz preferred cuddling to sex, while Martin preferred sex to cuddling. Initially, he had taken responsibility for initiating sex and she for initiating cuddling. Increasingly frustrated with one another, both had given up their tasks and were waiting for the other to initiate. Both became increasingly hurt, frustrated, and hopeless that the other would.

Emotional distance regulation is also important for couples. The transcripts of Liz and Martin's couple therapy indicate that she wanted to have emotionally intimate conversations about her feelings about working outside the home while mothering. Martin, by contrast, indicated a preference for Liz making her decision with the knowledge that he wanted her to do what was best for her.

The concept of distance regulation suggests that implicitly, if not explicitly, both partners have agreed to the distance. For example, only one partner initiating sex or cuddling may indicate that both partners have agreed to the physical and emotional distance that mechanism maintains. However, the mechanism for regulating this distance may become problematic, in that the roles of initiator and accepter/decliner have become fixed, leaving the partners stuck in maintaining homeostasis in their relationship in a way they no longer prefer. If Liz had suddenly consented to sex whenever Martin initiated, they would have presumably been faced with more physical intimacy than either wanted. And when Martin gave up and stopped initiating, they then engaged in sex with each other less than either preferred. Martin, locked in role, would not say, "I'd love it if you initiated" or even, "I'm not in the mood myself." Similarly, Liz would not initiate because of the risk of disrupting their balance of sexual distance and closeness.

LIZ: Something good happens to me at work, and you don't want to hear about it. And then the sex stops.

MARTIN: That is such b.s., Liz. [To Couple Therapist] Excuse me...

CT: Not a problem...

MARTIN: [To Liz] I don't know how you can even say that.

LIZ: Oh really! When was the last time you suggested we go out to celebrate a case I won or when Jerry told me if I came back full time he was sure I'd make partner?

MARTIN: And when was the last time you initiated sex, Liz? Huh? If you ever did, you'd know the last thing in the world I'd do is cut us both off from something we used to love. Or I thought we used to love.

CT: What happens when you initiate, Martin?

MARTIN: About 99 percent of the time she says no.

LIZ: What do you expect? We have children. And don't tell me you're not tired all the time because if you're not you should be getting up more with them.

CT: So Martin initiates and Liz says no. What happened before Christina and MJ were born?

MARTIN: Same thing.

LIZ: [Simultaneously] He initiated more. Seems like all he cares about is hurting me now.

CT: So throughout your relationship it's been Martin's job to initiate?

MARTIN: Yes.

LIZ: [Simultaneously] Not entirely.

MARTIN: [Mumbling] Entirely my job.

CT: I'm unclear what you would like now.

LIZ: I want to be closer to Martin, to feel closer to him.

MARTIN: Well, sex is one way to feel close.

LIZ: [Laughing] Touché.

CT: I think it might be helpful to begin by focusing on what is a comfortable amount of sex for each of you and then negotiate who initiates in a way that works for you as a couple, recognizing that you can always increase the frequency as the children get older and you're less tired. What do you think about sharing which of you initiates and then both having the right to say no?

Stop & Think

What other topic(s) in this excerpt could the couple therapist have focused Liz and Martin's attention upon? Be sure to include your response in your journal.

Emotional distance is regulated in similar ways. Berg-Cross (2009) identified six aspects of space couples presumably regulate. These include contact time, personal space, emotional space, informational space, conversation space, and decision space (pp. 43–44). For example, if only one partner initiates time together, the other may be tasked with regulating their emotional space by declining often enough to ensure they do not spend so much time together that they, as a couple, become uncomfortable. As with sex, once roles become fixed it is likely neither partner will be happy. So while the manner in which a couple regulates distance may appear to keep the couple in equilibrium, it may also lead to so little time together that their emotional connection weakens. In other words, as with the example of physical intimacy, the very mechanism designed to maintain emotional intimacy in the relationship undermines that intimacy.

MARTIN: I would really like her, I mean you, Liz, to not be all over me when I get home 15 or 20 minutes later than you expected.

LIZ: [To Couple Therapist] I don't know what to say to that.

CT: What are your thoughts?

LIZ: That if I say, oh sure, fine, he'll hear it as it's OK with me for him to come home whenever he feels like it.

CT: What about telling him that?

LIZ: Really?

CT: Uh-huh.

LIZ: Martin, I don't want you to think that if I don't get upset about a few minutes it means I'm OK with you coming home whenever you want. I can't be. Someone's got to pick the kids up before day care closes on the days I work, and it's too much if it's always me. Plus, I can't just go off and leave them alone if I feel like working later or going for a run.

MARTIN: We bought a double running stroller for them. You could use it.

CT: Martin, what did you hear Liz say?

MARTIN: That it's not fair if I come home later because she can't and that she feels trapped.

CT: Liz, is that what you wanted him to hear?

LIZ: Of course not.

CT: Can you rephrase what you said?

LIZ: This is ridiculous. The point is, he doesn't care about family time, about pulling his weight parenting. He's happier working and going to the gym.

CT: I hear how frustrated you are, but I don't think the two of you can negotiate how to manage your work and children or how much time you spend as a family until you each hear accurately what the other is saying.

LIZ: It doesn't matter. He'll just do whatever he pleases anyway.

MARTIN: Oh right, Liz. I don't care at all about my children or my wife. What kind of fantasy land are you living in?

CT: I'd like you each to think about how much time you'd like to be together as a family. It will change as your children get older and right now a lot of it is baby and child care, but it'll be easier for you to adapt as the kids change if you're on the same page about family time and if how you negotiate works for you as a couple. And to do that, I think it's going to be important to listen to each other and not simply to the anger you've each been feeling.

Note that the couple therapist began by using fairly standard communication training with Liz and Martin in this excerpt. However, after learning that the content involved distance regulation with respect to family time, she shifted the focus of her intervention and then doubled back to point out the importance of communication.

While all couples regulate the physical and emotional space between them, they vary in terms not only of the amount of space but also of how they regulate it. Some couples, like Liz and Martin, regulate it with habitual conflict. Others regulate it with empathy and honed conflict negotiation skills. Still others regulate it with acting out, such as extra-relationship affairs when the presumption is a monogamous relationship, or acting in with symptomatology. By viewing the couple from a systems theory perspective, the couple therapist is able to avoid labeling one of the partners as bad or sick and instead focus her or his attention on those aspects of the couple's dynamics that are dysfunctional for each partner and their relationship, maintaining the view that any "bad" behavior is a way of alerting the couple to problematic dynamics, and then exploring and practicing ways to change those dynamics.

Couple Resilience

Resilience can be defined as the balance between challenges a couple faces, their perceptions of the severity of those challenges, and their resources for coping with the challenges they face. The challenge itself, unless within the couple's control, cannot be changed by couple therapy.

How a couple perceives the seriousness of the challenge affects its impact upon them. For example, most couples would likely view one partner losing a job as stressful in terms of its potential impact on their finances, lifestyle, and the partner's sense of well-being. Some couples would expand these concerns to include their future well-being, as though the partner will never be employed again. For these couples, the job loss would be even more stressful. Still other couples might view the situation as an opportunity to either make a long-desired job change or, if affordable, retire earlier than anticipated. For these couples, the job loss would be stressful, although less so than for the others.

Apart from the seriousness of the challenge, both in fact and in perception, couples need resources for managing it. In the above example, a couple with more financial resources and social support will have more options for managing one partner's job loss.

If the company Martin worked for merged with another drug company that took over research and development as part of the merger, Liz could resume her career full time and Martin could use his training and experience to search for a new job. Some couples, however, do not have the financial and educational resources available to Liz and Martin and would need to make major lifestyle adjustments. For a couple living at a poverty level, even the slightest economic set-back, such as a minor illness, can be far more financially devastating than a job loss would be for Liz and Martin.

Financial resources are beyond a couple therapist's ability to change, although he or she can refer a couple for social services available in the community. Couple therapists can also help more financially secure couples negotiate changes necessary to adapt to a temporary or even permanent decrease in income.

Other resources for managing challenges include a strong social network, flexibility to adapt to change, flexibility of roles needed to maintain the couple and their children if any, and a way of managing the inevitable feelings that arise as the result of any challenge. A couple that can call on friends, extended family, neighbors, and/or members of community groups with which they are involved; that is able to make even unwanted changes without feeling debilitated by them; that is not locked into gender-specific or other expectation-driven roles within their relationship; and who can share their sense of sadness, anxiety, and feelings of being overwhelmed with one another and/or trusted friends is more likely to weather the challenge.

A couple that defines the challenge as something the partners will find a way to manage and who has sufficient resources to manage it is considered a resilient couple. Note that some couples may be less resilient than others through no fault of their own. As Basirico, Cashion, and Eshleman (2014) pointed out, the family and sociocultural context into which a child is born determines her or his life chances. Thus, poverty, migration, family size, illnesses and accidents that decrease family size, inherited biomedical or mental illness, and other similar factors are often beyond partners' control to change. While couple therapists can facilitate increased resilience in aspects over which partners have control, no one can change the circumstances of clients' history and attendant life chances.

Couple Contracts

In his classic book on couple contracts, Clifford Sager (1977) posited that couples implicitly agree to contracts governing their relationship early in the time they are together. These implicit contracts involve partners' expectations for one another and for being a couple, as well as the couple system's rules of relating that circularly inform and result from their dynamics. Couples also develop more explicit contracts around topics they discuss, such as increased commitment, whether they want children, and who is responsible for what.

Both partners are aware of the explicit contracts, or agreements with one another. Thus, explicit contracts can be clarified, adapted to changing circumstances, and renegotiated when necessary. By contrast, implicit couple contracts are generally agreed upon and enacted outside partners' awareness. Thus, these contracts are difficult if not impossible to clarify, alter, or renegotiate. As a result, when change to an implicit contract occurs, one or both partners may be confused, resistant, and/or angry.

Liz viewed herself as an independent woman capable of earning a living, living alone, and managing her life. However, she often became passive in her interpersonal relationships. She would tell friends and dates that she did not care what they did when they got together and then find herself in a restaurant or at a movie she did not especially like. Thus, the implicit relationship contracts she developed with both friends and ultimately with Martin included a clause that the other person would make decisions about their time together.

More importantly, given their presenting problem, Liz and Martin's implicit and explicit relationship contracts both included clauses regarding Liz as a professional career woman. She had worked hard as a law student and then as a professional and had been committed to becoming a partner in her law firm. Both she and Martin fully expected her to continue on this career path when they became parents.

After Christina was born, however, Liz discovered she wanted to be at home with her daughter more of the time than her career track would allow. The work change she subsequently initiated also involved a change in her explicit and implicit couple contracts with Martin. He appeared amenable to the logistics and finances of her career change and to its impact on their division of responsibilities, although conflict remained about the latter. In light of Liz and Martin's relationship dynamics and the function of their presenting problem, the possibility that Martin would not have been so agreeable to these changes in their explicit contract if Liz had been less ambivalent about them than she was cannot be ruled out. Liz's expectation that Martin assist her in resolving her ambivalence was part of their implicit contract. Unsurprisingly, they experienced difficulty communicating about this implicit expectation.

Early in her career, the writer worked with a number of couples whose children were launched into their adult lives and who were in what is often referred to as the empty nest period of the family life cycle. Most of these couples had had children before the third wave of feminism emerged in the United States and were sufficiently traditional and middle class that the wives had not worked outside the home. These women found themselves retired from the job of mothering children who lived at home and many of them wished to return to the labor force. Their husbands were confused by this development, not understanding why their wives wished to work when finances did not require them to and at a time when the husbands were moving into late career and contemplating their own retirement. Additionally, these husbands were used to their lives outside of work running smoothly without their involvement and were concerned about the impact of their wives working outside the home on the lifestyle to which they had become accustomed. One even told his wife that he thought maybe it would be alright for her to get a job, as long as she was home in time to have dinner on the table at the usual time. The wives naturally felt devalued and taken for granted, and those of us who came of age after the third wave of feminism would likely agree that their husbands needed to adapt. Irrespective of one's views on feminism, this is an excellent example of the impact upon a couple when one partner wishes to change an implicit relationship contract.

Couple therapists are alert to the presence of implicit contracts that may help explain the intractability of presenting problems. While systems concepts provide significant explanation, clients are more likely to understand the notion of unspoken agreements between them than the more esoteric concepts of systems theory.

Systemic Assessment of Liz Manning-Jones and Martin Jones

In Chapter 1, you read a preliminary assessment of Liz and Martin. Although most couple therapists do not write assessments based on all of the aspects of systems theory covered in this chapter, for illustrative purposes you will now read a systemic assessment of their relationship.

Liz and Martin are a couple system, as well as couple and parental subsystems within their families of origin, family of procreation, extended families, and community. Circular causation and feedback loops occur as a result of repetitive patterns of interactions both within their couple system and between their couple subsystem and the other systems and subsystems with which they interact. Within their couple system, feedback loops requiring intervention result from escalating tension around Liz's career. These feedback loops are then derailed using several homeostatic mechanisms to restore the couple's former equilibrium, before the conflict can be resolved. System rules support this process. Repeatedly engaging in the same conflicts suggests attempts at first-order change by doing more of the same. Distance is regulated by conflicts about their sexual relationship and family time, as well as about Liz's career. This couple appears resilient in terms of financial resources, social support, and role flexibility. However, there is evidence they define the impact of becoming parents upon Liz's roles as mother and professional as potentially disruptive of their relationship.

Conclusions

In this chapter, you read a brief history of couple therapy. You were then introduced to ten system theory concepts as they apply to couples: couple systems and dynamics, subsystems, circular causation and feedback loops, homeostasis and equilibrium, rules, first- and second-order change, second-order cybernetics, function of the presenting problem, distance regulation, and couple resilience. Examples from Liz and Martin's couple therapy work were included to illustrate these complex concepts. Further examples will appear, as relevant, throughout this book. Finally, you were introduced to the concept of couple contracts and its contribution to couple therapy.

The next three chapters will elucidate the application of systems theory to couple therapy theory and practice. Theories of couple therapy all utilize systems concepts, and so a grounding in systems theory as applied to couples was essential to your understanding of the more specific treatment theories and intervention techniques.

References

Ackerman, N. W. (1970). *Family process*. New York NY: Basic Books.

Basirico, L. A., Cashion, B. G., & Eshleman, J. R. (2014). *Introduction to sociology (16th ed.)*. Redding CA: BVT.

Bateson, G. (1972). Steps to an ecology of mind. A revolutionary approach to man's understanding of himself. New York NY: Ballantine Books.

Berg-Cross, L. (2009). Basic concepts in family therapy. An introductory text. New York NY: Routledge.

Bowen, M. (1978). *Family therapy in clinical practice*. New York NY: Jason Aronson.

Esposito, J. & Hattem, A. (2017). *Introduction to family counseling. A case study approach*. Los Angeles CA: Sage Press.

Gottman, J. M. & Gottman, J. S. (2008). Gottman method couple therapy. In A. S. Gurman (Ed.). *Clinical handbook of couple therapy (4th ed.)*. New York NY: Guilford.

Gurman, A. S. & Fraenkel, P. (2002). The history of couple therapy. A millennial review. *Family Process*, 41 (2), 199–260.

Hafner, R. J. (1986). *Marriage and mental illness: A sex roles perspective*. New York NY: The Guilford Press.

Haley, J. (1963). *Strategies of psychotherapy*. New York NY: Grune & Stratton.

Kantor, D. & Lehr, W. (1975). *Inside the family. Toward a theory of family process*. San Francisco CA: Jossey-Bass.

Laszlo, E. (1972). The systems view of the world. The nature and philosophy of the new developments in the sciences. New York NY: George Barziller.

Lerner, H. G. (1990). The dance of intimacy. A woman's guide to courageous acts of change in key relationships. New York NY: Perennial Library.

Minuchin, S. (1974). *Families and family therapy*. Cambridge MA: Harvard University Press.

Napier, A. Y. & Whitaker, C. A. (1978). *The family crucible*. New York NY: Harper and Row, Publishers.

Nichols, M. P. (1987). The self in the system. Expanding the limits of family therapy. New York NY: Brunner/Mazel.

Papp, P. (1997). Listening to the system. *Family Therapy Networker*, 21, pp. 52–58.

Sager, C. J. (1977). Marriage contracts and couple therapy. Hidden forces in intimate relationships. New York NY: Routledge.

Satir, V., Stachowiak, J., & Taschman, H. A. (1975). *Helping families to change*. New York NY: Jason Aronson.

Watzlawick, P., Weakland, J., & Fisch, R. (1974). *Change. Principles of problem formation and problem resolution*. New York NY: W. W. Norton & Company, Inc.

CHAPTER 5

Foundational Couple Therapy Theory: Behavioral Couple Therapy

Learning Objectives

1. Illustrate the concept of schemata.
2. Illustrate the concept of automatic thoughts.
3. Illustrate the concept of cognitive distortions.
4. Describe cognitive restructuring as an intervention in couple behavioral therapy.
5. Describe enactment as an intervention in couple behavioral therapy.
6. Critique the role of the couple therapist in couple behavioral therapy.
7. Critique the advantages of integrative behavioral therapy.

You will first read a brief history of behavioral couple therapy. You will then learn about specific behavioral couple therapy concepts in order to understand the practice of behavioral couple therapy. A description of the practice of behavioral couple therapy follows. Integrative behavioral couple therapy is included in a separate section because, while cognitive-behavioral couple therapy (CBCT) was an expansion of behavioral couple therapy to make it better fit clinicians and researchers' observations, integrative behavioral couple therapy (IBCT) is a distinct form of behavioral couple therapy. Finally, you will learn how the behavioral couple therapy concepts and their application to practice can be used by a behavioral couple therapist working with Liz and Martin.

History of Behavioral Couple Therapy

Behavioral couple therapy, originally known as behavioral marital therapy, has been a mainstay of couple therapy since its inception. Behavioral marital therapy initially combined the operant conditioning model of behavioral theory with the sequential tenets of social learning theory. Behavioral marital therapists tracked sequences of communication to determine reinforcers and then used from individual behavioral therapy techniques to alter them for each partner with the other in the room (Jacobson & Margolin, 1979). When individual behavioral therapy added cognitive components and their emotional sequelae as mediators of the relationship between stimulus and response, behavioral marital therapy also added these components , becoming cognitive-behavioral couple therapy (Baucom, Epstein, LaTaillade, & Kirby, 2008).

Social learning theory, as applied to behavioral marital therapy, posited that partners positively reinforce behaviors they appreciate in the other and ignore or punish those behaviors they dislike. Similarly, they also exhibit more positive behaviors in response to positive behavior from the other and more negative behaviors in response to negative behavior from the other. In other words, each partner reinforces, extinguishes, and thus learns from the other's positive and negative behaviors toward her or him. Research has indicated that distressed couples exchange fewer positive and more negative behaviors than non-distressed couples, and that the ratio of positive to negative responses can be used to predict both satisfaction and stability (Jacobson & Holzworth-Munroe, 1986).

As the larger society changed (see Chapter 2) and alternatives to what had been considered traditional marriage during the middle of the last century in the United States became more socially acceptable, clinicians found the term "marital" in behavioral marital therapy to be dated. Current usage, behavioral couple therapy or behavioral relational therapy, reflects the broad range of possible relationships a couple therapist encounters. These include but are not limited to LGBTQIA relationships, domestic partnerships, polyamorous relationships, and monogamous heterosexual couples cohabiting either before or instead of marriage.

During the 1980s and 1990s, behavioral therapy was expanded upon to include cognitions, emotions, and the person of the therapist. Humans think, their thoughts trigger emotions, and both influence subsequent behavior toward thc partner. Intervening at the level of thoughts is believed to alter subsequent emotions and the behavior that results from both thoughts and feelings that follow them.

Gottman, one of the founders of behavioral marital therapy, found that physiological arousal in men during a conflictual conversation with their wives led to immediate withdrawal and lower satisfaction. This finding held on follow-up three years later (Gottman, 1991). He also found that lack of eye contact between partners and a woman's facial expression of disgust correlated with couple dissolution four years following observation. Clinically, he observed that when women's facial expressions progressed from anger through disgust to indifference, the relationship was likely irreparable. Gottman's couple therapy developed techniques aimed at disrupting the escalation of reciprocal, negative emotions (Gottman & Gottman, 2015).

In more recent years, integrative behavioral couple therapy (IBCT) emerged. IBCT theorists noted that traditional behavioral couple therapy was more effective for younger, less distressed couples who did not display either individual psychopathology or adhere to traditional roles. They then suggested that inevitable differences between partners can trigger emotional vulnerabilities, that these vulnerabilities can be exacerbated by stressors external to the couple's relationship, and that the resulting distress can erode positive feelings between partners. The focus of IBCT is on enhancing partners' emotional adaptation to one another (Christensen, Dimidjian, & Martell, 2015; Jacobson & Christensen, 1998).

Behavioral Couple Therapy Concepts

In this section, you will learn about five behavioral couple therapy concepts: schemata, automatic thoughts, cognitive distortions, cognitive restructuring, enactment. In addition, five forms of cognitive distortions will be described: attribution, dichotomous thinking, overgeneralization, magnification and minimization, and personalization. As you will learn, cognitive distortions influence schemata and automatic thoughts. You will also learn about behavioral contracts and homework, two concepts that translate to specific techniques used in behavioral couple therapy.

Schemata, Automatic Thoughts, and Cognitive Distortions

Schemata are beliefs about self, others, social interactions, and how the world works. As such, they comprise one's world view. While they are susceptible of change, day-to-day experience has little impact upon them.

Schemata inform emotions and subsequent behaviors. One of Liz's schemata is that her family does not support her career. Her emotional response is anger, and her subsequent argumentative and accusatory behavior around the topic reflects both her belief, or schema, and her emotional reaction to it. Viewing her behavior in this light allows a behavioral couple therapist to both empathize and intervene to bring about behavioral change through changing the schema and thus its attendant emotions and behavior.

Stop and Think:

Be sure to include your responses in your journal.

1. List and describe five schemata of your own. Think about how you view yourself, others, and your interactions with other people, the sociocultural beliefs with which you were raised, and/or refer to what you previously wrote about various aspects of your world view.
2. Describe a time someone has suggested you alter one of these schema. Note especially your memory of how you reacted and your relationship with the person who suggested change.

Automatic thoughts are a subset of schemata. Like schemata, they inform subsequent emotions and behaviors. Unlike schemata, automatic thoughts are ideas or beliefs about one's current, rather than general, situation. Automatic thoughts arise directly from schemata. However, they are more easily observed by therapists and more accessible to clients than are the more general schemata. They are therefore more amenable to change and can be used in interventions aimed at changing schemata.

When the couple therapist asked Liz about her career, her automatic thoughts may have been triggered by a specific comment her mother Sally or her sister Barbara made. For Liz, these automatic thoughts fit her schema that no one in her family supported her career.

Stop and Think:

Be sure to include your response in your journal.

1. Think of something that has happened in the past week or two that prompted a strong reaction in you.
2. What were your thoughts about that particular situation?
3. How might those thoughts have influenced your reaction?

The concept of cognitive distortion is closely related to that of automatic thoughts. As one attaches meaning to his or her own and to other people's behavior, that meaning changes, or distorts her or his automatic thoughts. Through automatic thoughts, meaning also informs and distorts one's underlying schemata.

The meaning Liz attached to Martin's statement that he wanted her to do what she believed was best for her was distorted by her automatic thoughts about what her mother and sister had said. Thus, the meaning she attached to his statement was identical to those she attached to what her mother and sister said. This distortion of Martin's intended meaning lent support to Liz's schema that no one in her family wanted her to work outside the home after she became a mother. Note that it was the distortion with respect to Martin's statement that caused Liz distress and conflict between Liz and Martin.

Dattilio and Bevilacqua (2006) described 10 forms of cognitive distortion: attribution, selective abstractions, overgeneralization, magnification and minimization, personalization, dichotomous thinking, labeling and mislabeling, tunnel vision, biased explanations, and mind reading. Many of these terms are self-explanatory based on vernacular usage in the English language. While all of these are important thought distortions, five deserve further attention in an introductory textbook.

Attribution. You may have read about attribution theory in a psychology class. Attributions are characteristics we ascribe to another person based on our observations, our own perceptual and emotional filters, our relationship with that person, and how the conclusions we draw from these sources fit our previous experiences. For example, referring to a family member who cries when she is teased as "overly sensitive" is an attribution. It may be being used to control her behavior so that other family members may hurt her feelings without consequences. More importantly, because attributions are not based solely on objective observations, they may be inaccurate, thus qualifying as a cognitive distortion.

One way people develop a sense of self is through others' perceptions. Cooley (1902) coined the term "looking glass self" to convey the concept that how one sees oneself is a reflection of how one perceives being seen by others. Social constructivist theorists within the field of social psychology continue to study the impact of others on one'se sense of self (Starks, 2007). Thus, attributions as reflections of how others view one may become self-fulfilling prophecies. As part of one's sense of self, attributions influence one's generalized schemata and attendant automatic thoughts and feelings, which then impact behavior. The resulting behavior then becomes a trigger for others to continue to ascribe the attribution, setting in motion a positive feedback loop in which the attribution becomes an entrenched part of one's sense of self, behavior, interactions with others, automatic thoughts, and schemata. In other words, the attribution, however inaccurate it may be, becomes a part of one's schemata and resulting automatic thoughts about oneself, no matter how the attribution itself may have distorted them. The family member labeled as "overly sensitive" may come to hide her feelings or cry more easily as a result of attempting to hide painful feelings. And she or he may devalue her or his own emotional response to others. Thus, when someone is verbally abusive to her or him in the future, she or he might assume responsibility for having been abused, doubting any impulse to protect herself or himself as evidence of her or his "over-sensitivity". In intimate partner and parent-child relationships, attributions are more impactful than in other contexts due to the importance of the relationships.

Liz's mother, Sally, had attributed to Liz insufficient concern for her appearance and especially her weight. Whether this was a result of Sally's anxiety about her own weight might not be of interest to a behavioral couple therapist, because the act of attribution said more about Sally than Liz. On the other hand, the behavioral couple therapist might use this observation about the nature of attributions in order to correct Liz's cognitive distortion about her weight and the resulting automatic thoughts and schemata associated with it. In other words, whether or not one is interested in Sally's intrapsychic processes, the impact of her attribution on Liz is important to Liz and Martin's couple therapy. Specifically, Sally's attribution had influenced Liz's view of herself, and she therefore behaved as though she saw herself as either fat or at least at imminent risk of becoming so. Martin did not share Sally's attribution and so Liz and Martin argued over the validity of her concern about her weight, without taking into account that Liz's entrenched view of herself, or schemata, arose from years of attributions by one of the most important people in her life.

Stop and Think:

Be sure to include your responses in your journal.

1. How might Liz's mother telling her she was fat or at risk of becoming fat over a period of years have affected her interactions with friends, colleagues, and new people with whom she comes in contact?
2. Think of an attribution that someone has ascribed to you. It could be a label or a statement about you.
3. Who has ascribed the attribution to you?
4. How might this attribution have affected your interactions with friends, colleagues, and new people you meet?

Dichotomous Thinking. Dichotomous thinking involves simplifying people, interactions, situations, and cognitions along with their attendant feelings into two categories. Since all of these are usually more complex, dichotomous thinking is a cognitive distortion of reality that risks overlooking additional alternatives that may be helpful.

The pitfalls of dichotomous thinking were discussed in relation to the systemic concepts of first- and second-order change in Chapter 4. By obscuring alternatives other than two (often polar opposite) categories, dichotomous thinking may impede, rather than facilitate, change. While it is equally important to avoid dichotomous thinking in the practice of both behavioral and systemic couple therapies, these two theories explain the phenomenon quite differently. In behavioral theory, dichotomous thinking is considered a form of cognitive distortion, whereas in systems theory dichotomous thinking specifically limits partners to first-order changes that may not be effective while blinding them to other, second-order options for change.

Returning to the example of Liz's career, dichotomous thinking as a cognitive distortion involved Liz's assumption that people either encouraged or disparaged her only two options for balancing her career and mothering responsibilities. Based on that assumption, not only were there no third options for balancing career and mothering, but also the possibility that Martin supported and encouraged Liz irrespective of her choice was omitted. What Martin communicated did not fit the dichotomous thinking that informed her automatic thoughts, and therefore her automatic thoughts generated feelings and behaviors that did not fit what Martin intended to communicate. Martin's schemata about the role of her career for Liz and for them as a couple was therefore obscured in their interactions, which further frustrated him and increased conflict between them.

Stop and Think:

Over the next week, listen to yourself and record in your journal how many times you frame choices in terms of either-or dichotomous thinking.

Overgeneralization. Humans tend to generalize their experience. You may have found over time that you enjoy eating cookies and then continue to believe that generalization even when you burn a batch of cookies and they do not taste very good, attributing their bad taste to overcooking rather than a possible loss of appeal of cookies in general.

When people overgeneralize, the cognitive conclusions they draw from their experience become distorted. Overgeneralization is seen in statements such as, "He never helps with the kids" and "She always criticizes me when I interact with the kids." While each may be true much of the time, they are unlikely to be the all-or-nothing dichotomies each partner presented to their couple therapist.

The question as to how overgeneralization distorts cognition may be answered by considering a dog. If it rushes across the room when its person enters their home, greets the person by jumping up to be petted, and then runs to get a toy, the person will likely generalize the dog's behavior to the automatic thought, "my dog is happy to see me" and the underlying schema that "my dog loves me." Overgeneralization might lead to the misinterpretation that the dog's failure to greet means it no longer loves its person when in fact it is unwell or becoming deaf and didn't hear the door. The person's overgeneralization might even include the conclusion that the dog, like everyone else, discovered that he or she is unlovable. Clearly, these over-generalizations are cognitive distortions that may result in the dog's infirmity being overlooked.

For Liz and Martin, overgeneralization might have begun the first time Liz wanted to talk about her dilemma about whether to continue working outside the home after Christina was born. Martin had been exhausted and preoccupied with a problem at work. If she overgeneralized his lack of responsiveness from "he doesn't want to talk tonight" to "he never wants to talk about my career" or even "this means he doesn't support my career," then her overgeneralization would become part of the distorted automatic thoughts that led to her anger during their conflicts around her career and further entrenched her schema regarding lack of family support to work outside the home.

Stop and Think:

Be sure to write your responses in your journal.

1. What circumstances might prompt someone to overgeneralize?
2. Think of a time you or a friend overgeneralized. What were the circumstances and about whom were you or your friend talking or thinking?

Magnification and Minimization. Partners' thoughts about their interactions are also distorted by magnification and minimization. As these two terms imply, magnification overemphasizes a negative aspect while minimization largely overlooks a positive aspect of a distressed couple's interactions. Instead of remembering a romantic evening that happened the previous week, distressed couples' distorted cognitions lead them to remember a fight that happened the previous month.

Liz might have magnified Martin's distraction and exhaustion on the evening in question into the distorted cognition and resultant automatic thought that he did not care about her career dilemma. This would directly contradict Martin's claim to want what was best for her and at least partially explain her refusal to believe him. By contrast, if after Christina had gone to sleep he had offered to talk, Liz might have minimized his offer by assuming that if he really wanted to talk about her dilemma he would have offered earlier in the evening when she was not as exhausted or he would have been more responsive when she had asked him to listen.

Personalization. When partners personalize, they attribute external events to themselves. This type of distortion involves those situations in which events have little or nothing to do with the partner who is personalizing them.

Liz was personalizing when she attributed Martin's unresponsiveness to her desire to talk about her career dilemma to his feelings about what she was asking of him, rather than to his exhaustion and preoccupation with work. His exhaustion and preoccupation had nothing to do with Liz or how Martin felt about her career choices. Had she not personalized Martin's behavior, their exchange would not have confirmed her schema that he agreed with her mother.

Some cognitive distortions involve multiple types of distortion. For example, when a partner overgeneralizes and personalizes, the result can be devastating. Imagine Liz saying, "He never wants to talk when I want to, so it's obvious he doesn't love me anymore."

Cognitive Restructuring

Cognitive restructuring involves the process of identifying, monitoring, questioning, and altering each partner's cognitive distortions about the other and about their relationship. Cognitive restructuring is foundational to behavioral and thus relationship change, and you will learn more about this concept in the next two sections of this chapter.

Enactment

Enactment plays a role in all couple therapy that attends to the here-and-now, or what is happening during couple sessions. Rather than simply talking about what happened at home, couple therapists using enactment focus on what occurs in the moment during couple therapy sessions.

Used in behavioral couple therapy, enactment allows a behavioral couple therapist to intervene to direct change as the couple is interacting. The behavioral couple therapist might question automatic thoughts or coach partners in a more effective way to address the topic at hand. Similarly, behavioral couple therapists direct couples to practice effective communication and problem-solving techniques in the office, so that the behavioral couple therapist can intervene to decrease distortions and increase the ratio of positive to negative interactions. As with cognitive restructuring, you will learn more about enactments in the next section of this chapter.

Behavioral Contracts and Homework

Behavioral contracts are agreements between both partners specifying desired behavior changes and what each one will do to bring about these behavioral goals. Homework assignments are directives for partners to practice agreed-upon behavior changes between sessions. Lack of compliance with homework assignments informs the couple therapist that further intervention is needed. For example, when a couple has not completed a homework assignment, there may be a plausible explanation, such as a surprise visit from a parent or one of the children being ill. More often, noncompliance warrants further intervention, as when, for example, an assignment is too difficult, the couple is hesitant to enact agreed-upon changes, or the couple's motivation to change is less than one or both is willing to admit.

Contracts and homework were a formalized part of early behavioral marital therapy. While they remain integral to the current practice of behavioral couple therapy, they are less likely to be written and signed by each partner than they were.

Behavioral Couple Therapy Practice

Behavioral therapy and behavioral marital therapy both rely on the tenets of operant conditioning. One partner emits a behavior, and the other reacts by behaving in a way that positively reinforces (rewards), ignores (extinguishes), or negatively reinforces (punishes) that behavior. Thoughts, or cognitions, and emotions were viewed as irrelevant. If an individual or couple therapist could change the reinforcers of behavior, it was presumed that he or she could change the individual or couple.

Behavioral couple therapists first identify and then reinforce successive approximations to desirable behaviors. They assign homework to encourage couples to practice new behaviors. Homework assignments include agreements that partners will positively reinforce one another and ignore, rather than fight about, each other's learning curve. Behavioral couple therapists taught and encouraged the practice of new, more functional ways for couples to relate to one another in order to increase their ratio of positive to negative responses, and to negotiate their differences.

Cognitive-behavioral couple therapists added cognitions and their attendant emotions, as described in the previous section, to the mix in order to more fully understand and more successfully intervene to facilitate change. In this section, you will read about the fundamentals of behavioral couple therapy as based in their cognitive-behavioral theoretical underpinnings.

Treatment Goals

The goal of behavioral and cognitive-behavioral couple therapy is to increase positive and decrease negative interactions between partners. Positive and negative are evaluative words. It is therefore important to note that in behavioral couple therapy both are defined according to a client couple's descriptions of their couple conflict and their goals for change. The behavioral couple therapist may identify additional behaviors and cognitions unrecognized by the partners and nevertheless contributing to the couple's distress. She or he may also identify behaviors and cognitions that might increase the couple's good will toward one another and seek agreement from the couple to include these additional behaviors in the treatment goals.

It is unrealistic to assume a couple will never engage in conflict. Individuals are unique, and living intimately with another person in a high-stakes relationship is bound to create conflict and even antipathy from time to time. The goal of behavioral couple therapies, like all couple therapy, is to diminish the negative impact of these phenomena and to help couples learn to manage them without the couple therapist's intervention.

Accomplishing the goals of behavioral couple therapy also involves changing the unrealistic expectations and faulty cognitions each partner holds for and about the other. As noted in Chapter 2, the current pairing of romantic love and marriage in Western Europe and North America sets the stage for unrealistic expectations for marriage and for one's spouse. The author would argue that any couple, irrespective of marital status, would be vulnerable to the same unrealistic expectations arising from the pairing of romantic love with the business of creating and maintaining a life together with the expectation of permanence.

Behavioral, cognitive-behavioral, and integrative behavioral theories all predict that verbal and nonverbal negative behavior from one partner increases the probability of a negative behavioral response from the other. Whether one posits that couples learn to interact with one another in negative ways (social learning theory), inadvertently reinforce each other's negative behaviors by responding to rather than ignoring them (behavioral theory), distort cognitions about the negative behavior that then affect how they feel about each other and together these cognitions and emotions interact to produce negative behaviors (cognitive-behavioral and integrative behavioral theories), or instigate a positive feedback loop of negative dynamics through the processes described by couple behavioral theorists (systems theory); one arrives at the same conclusion.

In order to accomplish the overarching goals of reducing the number of negative interactions between partners, increasing the number of positive interactions, and teaching couples to work independently of the couple therapist, behavioral couple therapies prescribe a specific treatment process. You will examine this process, the techniques of treatment, and the role of the couple therapist in behavioral couple therapy in the next two sections of this chapter. The distinctions between the traditional behavioral couple therapies and integrative behavioral couple therapy will be noted in a separate section of this chapter.

Assessment

Assessment is a distinct phase of behavioral couple therapy and does not overlap with intervention, or the treatment phase of couple therapy. Many other theoretical approaches view assessment as on-going and thus intervention as a process that occurs simultaneously with assessment. In these approaches, the couple therapist begins facilitating change knowing that how the couple responds to her or his intervention efforts provides more information for assessment.

The behavioral couple therapy assessment process begins with a clinical interview at which both partners and the couple therapist are present. During the interview, the couple therapist asks questions and follows up on answers with the goal of learning at least three things about the couple: each partner's thoughts about their conflict, their relationship history as a couple, and their interactions. The first two are assessed through interviewing, while the third is accomplished through observation.

During the assessment phase, behavioral couple therapists listen to each partner's thoughts about the presenting problem, however discrepant they are from the other's and irrespective of whether the couple's framing of the presenting problem appears to involve cognitive distortions. Additionally, not all couples describe their presenting problem as conflict, and it is up to the couple therapist to reflect wording to which the partners will be responsive rather than defensive.

The relationship history involves learning about how the couple met, the path toward commitment their relationship took, what attracted each to the other, and what they enjoyed doing together early in their relationship. Talking about a presumably happier time may increase warm feelings, trigger positive cognitions, and result in positive behaviors, at least during the course of the interview. Behavioral couple therapists also want to know when and under what circumstances the presenting problem arose, what the couple has already attempted to do to address it, and the outcome of their efforts. While their presentation for couple therapy suggests their efforts were not successful, it is important to know what these efforts were and how they may have increased the conflict between the partners.

Behavioral couple therapists ask very specific questions about sequences of behavior in order to identify patterns of how each partner may be promoting negative behavior and discouraging positive behavior in the other. These may include what happened during a fight, what happens in the course of day-to-day interactions, and what happens in the session as partners describe the history of their relationship and their conflict.

Throughout the interview process, the behavioral couple therapist observes interactions between the partners. This technique is more or less universal to couple therapy. What the couple therapist observes will be included as notes throughout transcripts of couple therapy sessions to illustrate the types of observations a particular theory emphasizes and how couple therapists with different theoretical perspectives use their observations.

Following the assessment interview, each partner is given a battery of pencil-and-paper questionnaires to complete independently of each other. Some of these questionnaires were described in Chapter 3.

Finally, after reviewing the pencil-and-paper questionnaires, behavioral couple therapists schedule separate sessions with each partner to review her or his questionnaires and obtain additional information about her or his individual history. The behavioral couple therapist is then in a position to develop a treatment plan for the couple.

Whether to schedule individual sessions with one or both partners has been a controversial subject in the field of couple therapy. Systems theory, with its emphasis on process, requires the presence of the system, rather than its individual components, and many systemic couple therapists would refuse to see partners separately. Other couple therapists have suggested that some issues, such as Liz's sexual assault, may be more easily spoken of without the partner there. Individual appointments can be used to explore these issues and the couple therapist can then encourage the individual to bring what may be relevant to the relationship to his or her partner in a conjoint couple therapy session. Still other couple therapists have suggested that information can be obtained from one partner that would not be shared with the other one present, for example, one partner being a sexual abuse survivor and feeling too ashamed to tell the other partner.

Many couple therapists, including those practicing from a behavioral theoretical orientation and some more psychodynamically oriented couple therapists (see Chapter 6), have successfully used individual sessions. Couple therapists who opt to see partners separately, either as part of the assessment or at a partner's request, must remain alert to the risk that a secret with potentially significant impact on the relationship might be shared with the couple therapist (e.g., an on-going and current extra-relationship emotional or sexual affair when the couple had agreed their relationship would be monogamous).

The writer's experience has led her to conclude that there exists disagreement in the field of couple therapy about what to do about secrets. Even when a couple therapist has informed a couple that nothing said during an individual session can be considered confidential from the other, legal, ethical, and treatment risks occur should the couple therapist reveal a secret. As a result, couple therapists refrain from divulging secrets told to them by one of the partners. However, couple therapists can encourage or, when necessary, even insist the partner reveal the secret when she or he believes knowledge about it might impact the partner's commitment to couple therapy and/or the relationship.

If the secret holder declines to reveal the secret to her or his partner, the couple therapist is essentially colluding with the secret holder to hide important information from the partner. The couple therapist cannot reveal the secret without violating the secret holder's confidentiality, yet her or his effectiveness as a couple therapist is inevitably undermined by maintaining secrecy.

The couple therapist in this situation has effectively become part of a coalition, or fixed triangle, with one partner against the other. Should the secret later be revealed, the partner from whom it had been withheld would then find himself or herself unable to trust either his or her partner or their couple therapist.

Stop and Think:

Be sure to include your responses in your journal.

1. How might a client respond if he or she learned that his or her partner, with whom he or she presumed a monogamous relationship existed, was having an extra-relationship affair?
2. What might you as their couple therapist say or do that might be helpful? Explain how you think what you have identified might help?
3. Now imagine that the partner also revealed that you as the couple therapist had known about the extra-relationship affair for some time. How might that knowledge complicate the betrayed partner's feelings? What could you as their couple therapist say or do that might be helpful? Explain your answers.

Treatment

Dattilio (2010; Dattilio & Bevilacqua, 2006) identified nine components of the process of behavioral couple therapy treatment: educating couple clients about behavioral couple therapy; identifying the automatic thoughts that trigger negative emotions and behaviors for each client; restructuring each partner's schemata (cognitive restructuring); enacting change; attending to roadblocks and resistance to change; addressing the potential for relapse (regression into previous negative behaviors); addressing hopelessness and anxiety about change; addressing differing agendas between partners; facilitating the partners' relinquishment of power and their perception of control in their relationship; and facilitating each taking responsibility for change. You will read about these nine components of behavioral couple therapy treatment throughout the remainder of this subsection.

Three overarching techniques are used by behavioral couple therapists: psychoeducation, reframing, and rehearsing. Psychoeducation refers to the process of teaching clients about behavioral couple therapy and the various tools available to them to improve their relationship, such as those involved in effective communication and problem solving. Reframing entails the couple therapist suggesting an alternative view of an event, behavior, or characteristic of the partner, in order to challenge distorted cognitions, automatic thoughts, and resulting schemata. And finally, rehearsing involves practicing with an eye to future possibilities. These techniques will be described in more detail as they become relevant to interventions.

There are six more specific techniques that are part of every behavioral couple therapist's repertoire: communication training; problem-solving training; behavioral contracts; cognitive restructuring; enactment, reframing, and rehearsal; and homework. Each of these is described below.

Communication Training. Experience suggests that many couples believe their distress is caused by ineffective communication and that most couples benefit from learning about and rehearsing effective communication in the here-and-now of couple therapy sessions and then follow-up practice, with adaptations when necessary, at home.

In the writer's experience, many couples also need to learn empathy for one another's viewpoints. Empathy involves recognizing one's partner's perspective as valid, even if different from one's own; accepting that two people will not view the world in identical ways no matter how much they love one another; and imagining what it would be like to view the world as one's partner does. Empathy involves an ability to understand and validate the partner. Empathy does not require one to agree or to change oneself. Rather, empathy results in one's partner feeling heard and appreciated for herself or himself and separates disagreements between partners from questions of whether they care, understand, and are there for one another.

Children learn empathy during their preschool years by observing their parents' empathetic behaviors, or modeling. "I know you're angry, and I can't let you hit your brother" is one way parents convey empathy while setting limits. The message is very different than, "Bad girl" or "Good girls don't hit their brothers". Although all three examples label hitting behavior itself as inappropriate, only the first communicates empathy for the child's urge to hit.

Children also learn by observing parental empathy toward others. For example, "Honey, I'm sorry it was a rough day. I'll take your turn doing dishes tonight" is very different than, "I don't care what kind of day you've had, mine hasn't been perfect either and this house is your responsibility, too."

Anyone whose parents lacked empathy is unlikely to learn it as a young child. However, adults can learn empathy in couple therapy by observing the couple therapist's empathetic responses, understanding the importance of empathy, learning the behaviors associated with empathy, practicing these behaviors, and tolerating the feelings associated with empathizing while disagreeing.

Communication between partners is a complex emotional and behavioral process, informed by thoughts, attributions, and emotions. Communication itself involves: one partner having a thought with its attendant emotions; expressing that thought in words and the feelings in nonverbal ways such as voice tone and body language; the partner receiving both the verbal and nonverbal messages; and the receiving partner interpreting the verbal and nonverbal messages. It is only then that the second partner begins a similar process of responding.

Behavioral couple therapists teach partners to identify the most important point each wants the other to hear in a particular communication, express it clearly and constructively without accusations or other messages that would likely trigger a defensive response, recognize his or her own discrepant verbal and nonverbal messages and alter them to be consistent, obtain feedback from the partner about what he or she heard, address and revise any misunderstanding of the speaker's intent without recrimination, obtain feedback about what the partner heard in the revised message, and then continue this process until what was intended was also heard. Couple therapists coach partners through this process before the listening partner responds to the message. The couple therapist then repeats the process with the couple as the partner responds. Couples are encouraged to rehearse these techniques in the couple therapist's office and then to practice them at home as part of their homework contract.

Stop and Think:

Be sure to include your responses in your journal.

1 Choose a neutral topic and, with a classmate, friend, or partner, enact the process of feedback about what the listener heard and revisions by the speaker until the two match. How many times did the speaker need to revise what she or he said? Did either of you find yourself frustrated by the process?

2 Imagine using this couple communication technique with a couple in which one or both partners interrupt one another, as you have read about Liz and Martin doing. What roadblocks might arise and how would you address each?

Other factors important to communication include timing, location, and requesting a time-out. Partners need to talk about important and potentially conflictual topics when both can fully engage in the process. Finding a time that both partners are alert and not preoccupied by other demands or concerns can be challenging when partners are busy with jobs, family, and community responsibilities. Additionally, the conversation would best take place in a comfortable space where both partners are either seated or walking together, neither is in a one-down position, and the risk of interruption is as minimal as possible. And finally, either partner must be allowed to request a time-out, with the condition that the partner asking for the time-out be specific about when he or she will be ready to resume. This allows partners to avoid being flooded by feelings that could undermine their communication without avoiding the conversation or being perceived as avoiding it.

A relationship message is part of any couple communication, and partners sometimes respond to that message, rather than the intended one. A relationship message involves a subtle statement about the relationship, usually conveyed nonverbally. For example, when only one partner interrupts the other, the interrupter may be communicating a relationship message that he or she is empowered to decide who speaks and when. The suggested readings at the end of this chapter include more information about communication training for couples.

One additional communication concept deserves recognition: metacommunication. Metacommunication addresses how people communicate, as opposed to the content of the communication itself. It involves communicating about communication. An example of metacommunication with Liz and Martin would be the couple therapist noting that when Liz asked Martin to answer one of the couple therapist's questions she then critiqued his response. Talking about how a couple communicates, or metacommunication, is a powerful tool for addressing the dynamics which transcend any particular topic.

Problem-Solving Techniques. Effective problem solving is a multi-stage process. It involves identifying a problem, determining several possible solutions to the problem, deciding which solution both partners agree might be most effective for them, implementing that solution, evaluating whether the outcome was satisfactory to both partners or requires adjustment, and then continuing to repeat implementation and evaluation until the adjustments lead to an acceptable outcome. If the potential solution simply did not work, partners can then continue to the next solution previously identified. Couple therapists monitor the couple's communications through the problem-solving process, helping them make any adjustments to their cognitions about the problem and to their methods of communicating about it.

Experience suggests that many couples become frustrated during the problem-solving process, and their frustration reminds them of previous anger and hurt about other problems. Liz and Martin exemplified this behavior, and you read it as an example of a homeostatic mechanism (Chapter 4). Behavioral couple therapists engaging in problem-solving training also stop couples when they shift topics and refocus them on the problem and solution at hand.

Behavioral Contracts. As previously noted, behavioral contracts are agreements by both partners to increase positive behaviors and decrease negative behaviors, with the goal of increasing relationship satisfaction and stability. The specific behaviors are identified and agreed upon by the partners and rehearsed during couple therapy sessions. Earlier in the history of behavioral couple therapy, contracts were formal, often written and signed by both partners and the couple therapist. As behavioral couple therapy evolved, contracts, like homework assignments, have become less formalized.

Cognitive Restructuring. Cognitive restructuring involves the process whereby cognitive behavioral couple therapists facilitate change in automatic thoughts and the schemata they represent in order to change behavior. The first step in cognitive restructuring is identifying each partner's automatic thoughts about their distress or problem and the cognitive distortions underlying them. A cognitive behavioral couple therapist identifies automatic thoughts by monitoring partners' behavioral responses to each other, on the assumption that behavior reflects automatic thoughts. Cognitive behavioral couple therapists also look for themes in couple behavior that suggest each partner's schemata. They then use logic to test the validity of automatic thoughts and the cognitive distortions that underlie them.

Cognitive restructuring is crucial to behavior change. The cognitive behavioral couple therapist must be directive, instructional, and logical throughout the process. These roles for the couple therapist will be addressed in the following subsection of this chapter.

Reframing, Enactment, and Rehearsal. As previously noted, reframing is the process by which a couple therapist suggests an alternative conceptualization of a partner's behavior. It is a technique by which cognitive behavioral couple therapists alter automatic thoughts and their correlates of overgeneralization, magnification and minimization, personalization, labeling and mislabeling, biased explanations, and mind reading.

Enactment involves creating an example that reflects what happens outside of couple therapy and then portraying that example in the here-and-now of the couple therapy session. Sometimes an enactment arises organically from the content of a particular couple therapy session. Other times, the behavioral couple therapist asks a couple to enact, rather than describe, something that occurred outside of couple therapy during the session.

Enactment and reframing are tools used in several theoretical approaches to working with couples, as well as with families and groups. Rehearsal, by contrast, is more focused on a particular technique than on a sequence of events requiring change at multiple points.

Homework. Homework, like contracts, is less formalized than it was several decades ago. Cognitive behavioral couple therapists assign couples the tasks of observing their automatic thoughts and experimenting with new behaviors between sessions. In creating a homework assignment, the behavioral couple therapist must be attentive to the couple's current level of functioning and tailor homework assignments to avoid creating more couple distress or a sense of inadequacy.

Couple therapists follow up on homework assignments during the next couple therapy session. When couples do not do their homework, the couple therapist views this noncompliance as evidence that the homework assignment needs to be adjusted. Noncompliance may reflect anxiety about or lack of motivation to change. From a systemic perspective, noncompliance may be a homeostatic mechanism to avoid a positive feedback loop the couple fears would undermine their relationship.

Behavioral couple therapists are not punitive about noncompliance. Rather, they work with couples to identify whatever precluded compliance and adjust the next homework assignment to accommodate the couple's needs. Couple input during this process is helpful. However, the couple therapist avoids allowing partners to accuse the other of noncompliance while not taking responsibility for their own role in this couple phenomenon.

Role of the Couple Therapist

The role of a behavioral couple therapist is varied. He or she is a psychoeducator, an expert, the director of sessions, and a deductive reasoner who adheres to cognitive logic while recognizing its emotional sequelae.

The process of behavioral couple therapy is highly structured, and the behavioral couple therapist takes full responsibility for adhering to its structure. At the same time, he or she works collaboratively with the couple to identify what works best for them as a couple and what impedes achieving their goals.

A highly structured approach to couple therapy is very attractive to couple therapists in training. It assures new couple therapists that they have tools to manage the sometimes intense anger couples bring to them.

The structure of behavioral couple therapy also makes it relatively easy to study. Additionally, the duration of treatment is contained. As a result, behavioral couple therapy is more attractive to the for-profit insurance industry than less structured couple therapies.

Empathy, genuineness, and positive regard for the person of the client are central concepts of humanistic approaches to individual, couple, family, and group therapies. As such, they have also become foundational for many psychodynamic and post-modern couple therapies. Although behavioral couple therapists describe their importance anecdotally, the literature about behavioral couple therapy largely ignores these factors. Dattilio and Bevilacqua (2006) stated, "While it is desirable that the therapist maintain a somewhat humanistic posture of providing warmth, empathy, and positive regard for the spouses... (p. 141)." In other words, these fundamental counseling and psychotherapy concepts are treated as a means to an end, rather than as essential characteristics of the counselor or psychotherapist, in behavioral couple therapy.

Stop and Think:

Be sure to include your answers in your journal.

1. What are the potential risks of a couple therapist not feeling warmth, empathy, or positive regard for her or his clients?
2. What are the possible benefits of dispensing with these person-of-the-therapist characteristics?

Finally, as noted earlier in this text, the single best predictor of therapy outcome is the fit between the therapist and the client(s). Thus, the person of the therapist became a component of behavioral couple therapy, whether with individuals or couples, and whether or not it is emphasized in the clinical literature. As couple therapy expanded to include the tenets of systems theory, the general tenets of systems theory as well as the specific impact of the therapist on the couple's functioning (second-order cybernetics) became components of behavioral marital therapy. Some would argue that a couple therapist's empathy is not only fundamental to creating a therapeutic alliance, but also a tool from which partners can learn by modeling the couple therapist, thus enhancing the effectiveness of behavioral marital therapy.

Integrative Behavioral Couple Therapy

Integrative behavioral couple therapy (IBCT) changed the focus of behavioral couple therapy in several important ways. First, its founders argued, it shifted intervention to natural contingency behaviors. Instead of directing partners about how to positively reinforce one another based on a set of behaviorally defined rules, IBCT elaborated upon the couple's own contingencies (Christensen et al., 2015).

Second, the focus of IBCT is on managing differences in a way that leads to acceptance. This involves empathy, or the ability to respect one's partner even when one does not like the partner's perspective. To accomplish this goal, clinicians using the IBCT approach focus on four interrelated aspects of the couple's relationship: identifying differences and the dynamics that result from them; anticipating those events or behaviors that may trigger conflict; evaluating recent examples of events or behaviors that triggered conflict; and evaluating recent events or behaviors with positive outcomes. Assessment involves answering questions related to each of the four aspects of the relationship.

Finally, the therapist's role in IBCT is very different than in other behavioral couple therapies. The therapist does not begin sessions with a structured agenda, but rather responds to the partners' agenda. Additionally, IBCT therapists accept the partners and demonstrate this acceptance through empathetic connection. They then use their own empathy to demonstrate increased tolerance between partners, while remaining detached from the couple's dynamics.

Behavioral Couple Therapy with Liz and Martin

Liz and Martin agreed that their most frequent arguments centered around whether Martin supported Liz's career choice and the impact of this choice on her mother-professional role balance and on their marriage. The couple therapist had listened for themes, or repetitions, in their prior descriptions of the problem while at the same time observing their interactions.

COUPLE THERAPIST: Liz, when Martin says he supports whatever career-mothering balance works for you, I've noticed you doubt he means what he says.

LIZ: Well, you should hear what he says at home.

MARTIN: I don't say anything different than what I say here.

LIZ: Seriously, Martin?

CT: I suspect both of you are thinking something along the lines of, that's not true.

Note: While tracking sequences of interaction is a social learning approach to working with couples, CT elected to remain focused upon Liz and Martin's automatic thoughts.

LIZ: I'm not calling him a liar!

CT: I know. I'm talking about your automatic thought.

LIZ: OK. Say it again.

CT: You appear to be thinking, that's not true or he's not telling you the whole story.

LIZ: Well, he's not.

CT: And when you think Martin's not being forthcoming, it angers you.

LIZ: I wouldn't say anger.

Note: Because clients may be unaware or ashamed of what they are feeling, telling them, however empathetically, may elicit a defensive response. On the other hand, pointing out feelings moves their impact from implicit to explicit.

CT: I'd like to hear in your own words what you feel when you think Martin is not being forthcoming.

LIZ: I don't know. Frustrated, I guess.

CT: Because you don't think he's telling me what he really says at home?

LIZ: Look, I've heard him talk often enough to know what he's thinking.

MARTIN: So it doesn't matter what I actually said, you know what I think?

CT: So Liz, your automatic thought is, he's not saying what he's thinking, and that frustrates you.

LIZ: [Glaring at Martin] Yes!

CT: Liz, I suspect you have additional thoughts, perhaps, he's not telling her everything because...

LIZ: [Pause] ...because he wants to look like a supportive husband.

CT: So he wants to look like a supportive husband when he's really not?

LIZ: Yes.

MARTIN: Oh for... . What am I supposed to do about that?

CT: Martin, that's an important question and one we'll return to. Liz, why do you think an unsupportive husband would want me to think he's supportive?

LIZ: To look good.

CT: So he values my good opinion of him so much he's willing to lie about how he treats you at home, undermining our work here in order to protect his image from me seeing the truth?

Note: CT is logically deconstructing Liz's statement so that she will question her automatic thoughts.

MARTIN: Wait a minute.

LIZ: That sounds awful.

CT: We're talking about automatic thoughts. I know this may be difficult to hear, but they precede what you say, Liz, and what you hear, Martin.

MARTIN: OK. [To Liz] But Liz, really?

LIZ: No. Yes. I don't know.

CT: Tell me about other ways he misrepresents himself to look good.

MARTIN: [Snorts]

LIZ: No. No, he doesn't, he's not that way.

CT: So your thought that he's trying to look like he supports your career when he really doesn't seems illogical?

LIZ: Yes.

CT: And then it makes you angry, or frustrated, that he's being deceptive in order to look good, and your frustration is very clear in the way you respond.

LIZ: Yes.

CT: So Martin, tell me the first thought that pops into your mind when Liz says, "That isn't how he is at home."

MARTIN: Confusion?

CT: Confusion arises from thoughts that don't fit together well. I'd like to hear your specific thoughts that don't fit together well.

Note: CT decided not to share her observations before asking Martin for his because of the issue of Liz's mind reading that arose earlier. Here she was able to demonstrate an alternative.

MARTIN: That she's always angry at me.

LIZ: No, I'm not.

CT: We're talking about Martin's automatic thoughts.

LIZ: But they're not accurate.

CT: That's exactly why we're examining them, as we did yours, to determine whether or not they are logical.

LIZ: [Giggling] You sound like Dr. Spock!

CT: [Smiling] I do, don't I? So, Martin, anything in addition to, "She's always angry at me"?

MARTIN: That it's unfair because I am doing everything I can to be a good husband. And I can't seem to get it right.

CT: Let's take those thoughts one at a time. First, "She's always angry at me." That also says she's never not angry at you. Can you think of any time she's not angry?

Note: The term "always" suggests the cognitive distortion of magnification.

MARTIN: Of course.

CT: Yes. You two are often talking and laughing when I come to the waiting room. I imagine you talk and laugh without anger elsewhere, too.

MARTIN: Yes. And you're going to tell me it's not logical to conclude she's always angry at me.

CT: Yes, that's what I was going to say next. And even though we agree the thought is illogical, I imagine you feel something when you think her anger is constant, just like when it feels unfair or unjustified.

MARTIN: Absolutely. But I don't let it get the better of me.

CT: That's fine, but it influences your response anyway, especially your nonverbal response.

MARTIN: I guess.

CT: How would you describe the feeling?

MARTIN: Frustration, I guess.

CT: Or anger?

MARTIN: No.

LIZ: [Sarcastically] He doesn't get angry. Just ask him. He gets vindictive, passive-aggressive, but not angry.

CT: And how you both express frustration and avoid anger is important. But for the moment, we're examining the feelings that go with Martin's automatic thoughts when you've challenged his support for your career choice. Martin, you feel frustrated when you think she's always angry at you and it's unfair she doesn't believe what you say.

MARTIN: Yes.

Note: Again, CT refocused Liz and Martin back to the topic at hand. She chose to defer attention to how they managed feelings in order to continue to work toward changing their automatic thoughts and their impact on emotions and behaviors.

CT: What about your feelings when you think nothing you do in terms of supporting her career-mother balance is sufficient?

MARTIN: I try not to let it get me down.

CT: I hear that that's what you do, or try to do. I would also imagine you feel something or you wouldn't need to work to avoid it getting you down. Frustrated, perhaps? Hopeless about Liz believing you support her?

MARTIN: Yeah, probably.

CT: Rephrase it, please, in your own words.

MARTIN: No, that's pretty accurate.

CT: OK, so when you respond to Liz, you're thinking she's always angry at me, her anger's unjustified and unfair, and nothing I say or do will change anything. And you're feeling frustrated and even a little hopeless, perhaps also feeling some anger that you're making an effort not to feel.

MARTIN: Except for the part that she's always angry at me, it all sounds pretty logical.

CT: I understand that trying to guess what anyone might want can lead to a lot of frustrating wrong turns and dead ends. I'm not sure not having guessed it means there's no solution.

MARTIN: Fair enough. Tell me what I should do, Doc.

CT: I wonder if perhaps Liz could tell you what she would like you to say or do so that she'd feel supported by you. She's the expert on that, not me.

MARTIN: And you think I should ask her.

CT: I do. But first I want to finish your automatic thoughts. I think the sense of unfairness comes from you knowing that you want to support her. I also imagine that, over time, the automatic thoughts and feelings you both have have gotten in the way of Liz hearing your intent.

MARTIN: [Hesitant] OK.

CT: At some point we need to discuss how you both deal with anger. In a nutshell, I think you both think it's bad or scary and that thought then complicates the angry feeling you're already having. We can talk about strategies for managing the frustration and anger that arise when you're solving a problem in your relationship. For the moment, I want to hear how Liz would feel supported by you, Martin, and then talk a little about what you can do at home between now and our next session. Liz?

LIZ: That's a complicated question. I think I'd know if he were being supportive.

CT: I suspect you would. But that leaves Martin guessing and both of you more and more frustrated when his guesses don't fit what you want. Can you be specific about what that is?

LIZ: OK. Well...

MARTIN: I've told you whatever you want to do is fine with me.

LIZ: That's what you say, Martin.

CT: And your automatic thought is, he doesn't mean it?

LIZ: No. [Pause] Yes, I guess so.

CT: What does, "I support you in whatever you want to do" leave out for you?

LIZ: I don't know. It sounds fine when you say it, but not when he does.

CT: What isn't he telling you that you need to hear?

LIZ: What he wants. Yes. That's it. That's what's missing.

CT: You want to know what Martin wants you to do.

LIZ: Yes.

MARTIN: I don't want it to be my decision. It's Liz's choice, and there's no reason like finances or anything that she can't choose whatever she wants.

CT: Martin, it sounds like your automatic thought was, she wants me to make the decision for her. And you don't want to. So you respond to your thought instead of what she's asked. Liz, can you ask him a more specific question about what you want from him?

LIZ: What you said a minute ago. What was it? I want to know what you think. Not just what you think I should do, but what you think about my options.

CT: Sounds like his input would help you decide?

LIZ: Yes.

MARTIN: But it has to be her decision. I don't want to influence it.

LIZ: But it affects you, too. And our children.

CT: So the problem here is that Liz's decision does impact the entire family, she wants your input, Martin, and you want to be sure your input won't influence her decision.

MARTIN: How can it not?

CT: Liz?

LIZ: [Pause] I guess there's no way it won't. But I'm not such a wimp that I'd let him make the decision for me.

MARTIN: I don't want to make the decision for you. I want you to do what makes you happy.

LIZ: You keep saying that. It would make me happy to know what you really think.

CT: How would you use what he tells you he thinks?

LIZ: To know which options he thinks have merits. And difficulties.

CT: Martin?

MARTIN: Can I think about it first?

CT: Liz?

LIZ: Sure.

CT: We can begin there next time, if you haven't talked at home before then. What I'd like you to do before we meet again is observe and make notes about your automatic thoughts and the feelings that follow. Pick any conversation, it doesn't have to be an argument. The purpose is for you to notice your automatic thoughts, so that if you are in conflict you can begin to question their logic rather than letting them direct your responses.

The couple therapist followed up on the assignment at the following session. Due to space considerations, we will rejoin Liz and Martin as they learn problem-solving strategies to manage the frustration and the anger they both fear.

> CT: We've spoken several times about anger, how you dislike it, and what you do when you're angry and don't want to show it. You've each described anger as bad for very different reasons. Since those thoughts make it even harder to deal with a feeling you don't like, I think it would be helpful to talk about the thoughts you have about anger, as well as strategies for managing the frustration and anger that may arise while you're problem solving about your relationship.
>
> LIZ: So let me understand something. You think anger is a good thing?
>
> CT: I think anger is a feeling that simply is. It's what's called a primary feeling, which means people can't control whether they feel it, though we can control how we behave when we're angry. You've already seen that with your children. They show anger in different ways as they get older and you've helped them learn to manage it.
>
> LIZ: OK. I follow you but I'm not sure I agree.
>
> CT: OK, let's examine what each of you thinks when you begin to feel frustrated with the other anyway. Liz, do you want to begin?

In this excerpt, the behavioral couple therapist engaged in psychoeducation about anger, presenting a detailed rationale for addressing how Liz and Martin manage anger and linking it to their problem-solving skills. She also addressed Liz's skepticism about anger as a primary emotion. Her choice was based on her role of psychoeducator.

Martin's automatic thoughts when he felt frustrated or angry had to do with anxiety that his anger would result in actions he would later regret. He thought, "I have to squelch this feeling so I don't become physically or verbally violent." When asked whether he had ever become either, both he and Liz agreed he had not. They attributed this to his success at squelching his anger. The behavioral couple therapist speculated that he had and/or could learn ways to express his anger other than violence and could experiment with feeling his anger and then utilizing these other mechanisms to stop himself from becoming violent. Other mechanisms included his strong motivation to avoid violence, his well-developed verbal skills, his ability to walk away from an argument, and learning self-soothing self-talk around the notion that he can feel anger and then stop himself from acting violently. The emotion that attended his automatic thought was anxiety about feeling of anger.

Liz's automatic thoughts when she felt anger involved her tendency to turn subsequent angry behavior inward upon herself. Rather than lashing out violently, as Martin feared, Liz thought about how fat she was, the mistake she made marrying Martin, that her mother was right that her career and partner choices had ruined her life, and that she must exercise more, tolerate hunger better, and never allow anyone to see who she really is. The emotions that followed these automatic thoughts included anxiety, sadness, and self-loathing. The behavioral couple therapist reframed Liz's anger as a message to herself that something was not alright and suggested Liz respond to that message by identifying and addressing what was wrong while soothing herself with self-talk around the idea that feeling anger did not make her a bad person.

At the end of the session during which these automatic thoughts and alternatives were explored and suggested, the behavioral couple therapist assigned homework to Martin and Liz to again observe their automatic thoughts and feelings when they became frustrated or angry with each other, with their children, or at work. She also suggested that, if they were unable to practice new ways of thinking in the moment, they remind themselves of their alternatives as soon as possible afterward. Because you have already read a transcript detailing how behavioral couple therapists identify and question the logic of automatic thoughts, the transcript will resume as they problem solve about managing anger.

CT: Let's begin by brainstorming your options for handling a situation when one or both of you is frustrated or angry at the other.

LIZ: Get rid of it?

CT: [Smiling] As I recall, that wasn't working so well for you. What else?

MARTIN: We want to find something besides yelling at each other.

CT: [Writing the list as she speaks] OK, you could squelch your anger or yell at each other, but the first doesn't work and you don't like the second. I'd like you to brainstorm options first and then evaluate them.

LIZ: We could tell each other we're angry.

CT: Great. What else?

MARTIN: We could say what we'd like the other to do.

CT: Great. What else?

LIZ: I like that.

CT: These are all keepers. I'd like you to identify at least one more option before we rank them.

MARTIN: Hmm. I'm stumped.

LIZ: I don't know, maybe say, "We need to talk about this, and I'm too angry right now."

CT: Great. We have five options: squelch it, yell, tell each other about it, tell each other what you'd like instead, and take a time-out. For the last one, I'd like you to add "schedule a time to talk about it later" so you have the time you need to self-soothe, think, and finish what you might already be doing. Now we need to rank these five options beginning with the one you think might be most helpful.

MARTIN: Saying what we'd like the other to do?

CT: Liz?

LIZ: Yes, unless we're too angry to talk about it.

CT: OK, first option is to check with the other whether now is a good time for both of you to talk about it and if not, when? Is that OK with you, Martin?

MARTIN: Yes.

CT: And second is telling each other what you'd like the other to do?

MARTIN: Yes.

LIZ: Do we need to tell each other why we're angry?

CT: Martin?

MARTIN: I suppose.

CT: OK, ask if it's a good time to talk and schedule another time if not, tell each other what you're angry about, and then tell each other what you'd like.

LIZ: Yes.

MARTIN: Yes.

CT: Sometimes options are in the order of preference, how effective you think each will be. You've jumped ahead to talk about the order of your problem-solving session. When you're problem solving about other issues at home, remember the options don't have to be linked.

LIZ: OK.

MARTIN: We're so precocious!

CT: [Smiles] And what happens if one of you yells?

LIZ: I don't know.

CT: Or one of you attempts to squelch your anger?

MARTIN: It's a habit.

CT: I know. And practicing paying attention to your automatic thoughts, like anger is bad, may help you avoid falling back into old habits like squelching anger. But you're right that they're hard to break. So when you do react habitually, treat it as a learning opportunity.

LIZ: Learning opportunity?

CT: Yes. If nothing else, that old habits are harder to break than you'd hoped and it's going to take even more hard work to change. That's important to know.

LIZ: I see.

CT: We have time to practice today. You could talk about how Liz is going to make her career decision, what that means for each of you, or how to handle sleep loss.

LIZ: How I'm going to decide.

CT: Martin?

MARTIN: Sure.

CT: Great. We may not get to a decision today, though we can practice problem solving about it. Liz, why don't you start.

LIZ: OK. Martin, I want your support.

MARTIN: I never know what you mean by "support."

LIZ: How can you not know?

MARTIN: [To CT] What do I do now?

CT: Liz, I want to answer Martin's question before you continue, so please remember your frustration that he doesn't know how you want to be supported. [To Martin] Notice your automatic thoughts and feelings following her question, and then tell Liz what you want from her.

MARTIN: [Pause] Liz, I think you want me to read your mind, but I can't. I think you want me to say whatever decision you make is OK with me, and it is. But that frustrates you, and I don't know what to do.

CT: What do you want from Liz?

MARTIN: To tell me what she means by support.

LIZ: How can you not know?

CT: Liz, tell Martin you're frustrated that he doesn't know.

LIZ: I am so frustrated that after all this time you don't know what support is.

CT: You two are in quite a dilemma. Martin, you're frustrated by not knowing what Liz means by support, while Liz, you're frustrated that he doesn't know, really the other side of the same coin. How can you use problem-solving strategies to get beyond your frustration?

LIZ: I don't know. How?

CT: I can think of two options off the top of my head, but I'd like you to also think about it. Mine are either you tell Martin specifically what support means to you and/or Martin tells you what else he needs to know in order to give you the support you want.

MARTIN: Either is fine with me.

LIZ: Martin, you go.

MARTIN: Please be more specific about what you mean by support. I want to give it to you but I'm not sure what will make you feel supported.

LIZ: I am still frustrated you don't know.

CT: And it's helpful that you said so. I think this may be an example of mind reading, that you expect Martin to know what you mean and he expects you to know he wants to be supportive even though he is, and therefore sounds, frustrated because he doesn't know what to do. Can you remind yourself that telling him does not mean he doesn't care about you?

LIZ: I can try. OK, Martin, I want you to...

MARTIN: Tell me.

LIZ: I'm not sure how to say it.

CT: Say what comes to mind, and then you can adjust it.

LIZ: I can't think how to be more specific.

CT: I wonder whether that's part of why you're both so frustrated. I would like you each to make a list of at least three things you think Martin could do that would be supportive while you make your career decision. We'll begin with your lists next time.

In the next session, Martin and Liz shared their lists, agreed about what Martin could do, and continued to practice the problem-solving skills begun in the previous session. The behavioral couple therapist continued to teach and direct the development of their problem-solving skills around the specific issue of Liz's career decision.

Stop and Think:

Be sure to include your answers in your journal.

1. What do you think of the behavioral couple therapist's interventions during this session? Be specific.
2. Were you comfortable with how she directed the session?
3. Were you comfortable with the amount of psychoeducation she provided?
4. If you had been the client, how might you have felt about your experience with her?

Conclusions

In this chapter, you were introduced to the concepts and practices of one of the foundational theories of couple therapy: behavioral couple therapy and its later iterations, cognitive-behavioral couple therapy (CBCT) and integrative behavioral couple therapy (IBCT). After reviewing the history of behavioral couple therapy, specific concepts in its current practice as CBCT were described. These included the premises that emotions and behaviors follow from thoughts and that individuals formulate schemata, or beliefs about themselves and others, that inform their automatic thoughts in response to specific experiences. The ways in which these thoughts can be distorted and restructured were discussed.

Aspects of behavioral couple therapy practice were also included in this chapter. Behavioral couple therapists use here-and-now events during couple therapy sessions to enact, reframe, and rehearse cognitive and resultant behavioral changes. Behavioral couple therapists also utilize psychoeducational explanations and training in communication and problem solving to enact change. As became evident, the role of the behavioral couple therapist is as an expert who directs couple therapy sessions.

At this point, you have an introductory familiarity with the tenets and practices of one of the foundational theories of couple therapy. The following exercise will give you an appreciation for the difficulty of what may at first appear to be a straight-forward set of techniques. Such an appreciation is a reminder that learning to do couple therapy requires supervision and experience.

Stop and Think:

Be sure to include your responses in your journal.

1. In groups of three or four, do a mock couple therapy session using what you have learned and one of the issues Liz and Martin have brought to their couple therapy or another of your choice (avoid one that reflects your own relationship). If your group has four, one will be an observer who provides feedback following the mock session. If time allows, take turns being the behavioral couple therapist.
2. Discuss your observations and experiences during the role play. What stood out for you about it? How was playing the role of behavioral couple therapist similar to and different from what you expected after reading the chapter?

References

Baucom, D. H., Epstein, N., LaTaillade, J. J., & Kirby, J. S. (2008). Cognitive-behavioral couple therapy. In A. S. Gurman (Ed.). *Clinical handbook of couple therapy* (4th *ed.*). New York NY: Guilford Press.

Christensen, A., Dimidjian S., & Martell, C. R. (2015). Integrative behavioral couple therapy. In A. S. Gurman, J. L. Lebow, & D. K. Snyder (Eds.). *Clinical handbook of couple therapy* (5th *ed.*). New York NY: Guilford Press.

Jacobson, N. S. & Christensen, A. (1998). *Acceptance and change in couple therapy. A therapist's guide to transforming relationships*. New York NY: Norton.

Dattilio, F. M. (2010). *Cognitive-behavioral therapy with couples and families. A comprehensive guide for clinicians*. New York NY: The Guilford Press.

Dattilio, F. M. & Bevilacqua, L. J. (2006). A cognitive behavioral approach. In L. J. Bevilacqua & F. M. Dattilio. (2007). *Relationship dysfunction: A practitioner's guide to comparative treatments*. New York NY: Springer Publishing Co.

Gottman, J. M. (1991). Predicting the longitudinal course of marriages. *Journal of Marriage and Family Therapy*, 17, 3–7.

Gottman, J. M. & Gottman, J. S. (2015). Gottman couple therapy. In A. S. Gurman, J. L. Lebow, & D. K. Snyder (Eds.). *Clinical handbook of couple therapy (5th ed.)*. New York NY: Guilford Press.

Jacobson, N. S. & Holzworth-Munroe, A. (1986). Marital therapy. A social learning-cognitive perspective. In N. S. Jacobson & A. S. Gurman (Eds.). *Clinical handbook of marital therapy*. New York NY: The Guilford Press.

Jacobson, N. S. & Margolin, G. (1979). *Marital therapy. Strategies based on social learning theory and behavioral exchange principles*. New York NY: Brunner/Mazel.

Starks, R. (2007). *Sociology (10th ed.)*. Belmont CA: Thomson Wadsworth.

For Further Study

Fichten, C. S. & Wright, J. (1983). Problem-solving skills in happy and distressed couples. Effects of videotape and verbal feedback. *Journal of Clinical Psychology*, 39, 340–352.

Wiley, A. R. (2007). Connecting as a couple: Communication skills for healthy relationships. *The Forum for Family and Consumer Issues*, 12 (1). Retrieved from http://ncsu.edu/ffci/publications/2007/v12-n1-2007-spring/index-v12-n1-may-2007.php.

CHAPTER 6

Foundational Couple Therapy Theory: Psychodynamic Couple Therapy

Learning Objectives

1. Differentiate psychodynamic couple therapy from psychoanalysis.
2. Describe the use of here-and-now in psychodynamic couple therapy.
3. Evaluate the use of self of the couple therapist in psychodynamic couple therapies.
4. Describe the processes of transference and countertransference.
5. Describe how the concept of projected introjects is used in object relations couple therapy.
6. Illustrate the role of self-talk in couple communication as described in ego-analytic couple therapy.
7. Explain the similarities and differences between projected introjects and negative self-talk.
8. Evaluate the primary focus of experiential couple therapy.

Psychodynamic couple therapies, like behavioral couple therapies (Chapter 5), originated in theories of individual psychology and have retained many aspects of their origins. In the United States, both psychodynamic couple therapy and behavioral couple therapy were initially practiced as individual psychotherapies with the partner present. Only later did practitioners integrate systems theory concepts when using these theories in couple therapy (Gurman & Fraenkel, 2002). In Great Britain, however, couple therapists have utilized the Tavistock Institute of Marital Studies model combining psychodynamic and systems theories for work with couples from its founding in the 1970s (Clulow, 1990; Dulwich Centre, 2015).

In contradistinction to behavioral therapy, which focused exclusively on observable behavior, psychoanalytic theory, from which psychodynamic theories later emerged, focused exclusively on the unseen, often unconscious processes occurring within an individual's psyche, or intrapsychic processes. In this sense, the two theories could not have been more different.

To avoid confusion, the distinction between psychoanalytic and psychodynamic theories must also be addressed. Psychodynamic theories of individual therapy grew from a shared foundation in Freud's psychoanalytic theory. Many of Freud's students became disillusioned with him and founded alternative schools of therapy.

Psychoanalytic theory focuses on intrapsychic conflicts, in other words conflicts that occur, unseen, within an individual, and analyzes their emergence in the client's relationship with the psychoanalyst. According to the theory, individuals repress unwanted thoughts and feelings which then become inaccessible to awareness. As a result, conflict arises between conscious and these now unconscious phenomena, as well as between thoughts and feelings. Because conflicts are outside awareness and invisible to others, Freud believed they could only be inferred through the techniques of psychoanalysis (Brill, 1995). Psychoanalytic theory applied to couple work therefore involved individual psychoanalysis in the presence of the partner (Scharff, 1995; Scharff & Scharff, 2014).

By contrast, psychodynamic theory "captures the dynamic relationships between parts of the self and other" (Scharff, 1995, p. 164). Unconscious conflicts are conceptualized as arising from interpersonal experiences in childhood and then replaying themselves in interpersonal relationships until resolved. Psychodynamic theory addresses both the intrapsychic processes within individuals and how these are played out between individuals, and therefore it is more easily adapted to couple therapy. In psychodynamic couple therapy, these dynamics are visible between partners and between each partner and the psychodynamic couple therapist. Systems theory adds the view that the couple is a subsystem within the couple-couple therapist system. Psychodynamic theories are thus compatible with and directly applicable to couple therapy in a way that psychoanalytic theory is not.

Scharff and Scharff (2014) noted that many of the early systems theorists were psychoanalytically and psychodynamically trained. The various psychodynamic approaches to both couple and family therapy evolved from these psychiatrists' observations and conceptualizations of individual functioning within their couple or family systems.

Psychodynamic couple therapists share several commonalities. First, psychodynamic couple therapists are non-directive. Second, psychodynamic couple therapists follow the couple's agenda, rather than one derived from their theoretical model (see Chapter 5). Whitaker, an experiential couple and family therapist, wrote that the couple therapist must win what he termed the "battle for structure" of the couple therapy, while the couple must win the "battle for content" of the sessions. Structure includes the time, the frequency, the location, and the cost of couple therapy sessions. Content refers to what is discussed, although the couple therapist reserves the right to insert her or his professional thoughts, opinions, and conclusions (Napier & Whitaker, 1978). Third, psychodynamic couple therapists use themselves as therapeutic tools by remaining aware of and sharing as appropriate their own reactions, or countertransference (Yalom, 1999, 2003).

The psychodynamic approach to couple therapy has been criticized for a number of reasons. First, psychodynamic couple therapy can be more lengthy than its behavioral counterpart. Second, it is also more difficult to quantify and thus to study using relatively inexpensive paper-and-pencil measures. And third, some clinicians have criticized it for being too complex for students to understand. On the other hand, psychodynamic couple therapists argue that the work is deeper, going beyond symptoms to changing their causes. They argue that psychodynamic couple therapy is thus preventive of future problems, as well as curative of the current presenting problem. Further, they argue that the psychodynamic model can and has been studied using observational methodology, which is admittedly more expensive. With regard to student comprehension, the writer's experience has been that most students are able to understand the psychodynamic approach to individual, couple, and family therapy and appreciate aspects of it irrespective of whether it is the theory with which they most resonate.

An additional criticism of psychodynamic approaches to couple therapy is that they tend to problematize the client couple. Experience suggests that couples do not expose themselves to the emotionally painful, time-consuming, and expensive process of couple therapy unless at least one partner perceives a problem of some magnitude exists. Wide-spread use of the term presenting problem indicates her experience is shared by other couple therapists. And the medicalization of psychotherapy, as codified in the DSM (American Psychiatric Association, 2013), further supports the observation that problematizing what couple clients bring to couple therapy is not unique to psychodynamic couple therapists. Whether a clinician views clients' problems as pathological likely arises more from the clinician's world view than from the particular theory to which he or she subscribes.

Stop and Think:

Answer the following questions from your own perspective today. While your perspective may have been influenced by what you have learned in classes and readings, you are encouraged to answer honestly from your own perspective, rather than from that of your professor(s) or author(s) you have read. Be sure to include your responses in your journal.

1. Define couple health from your own perspective.
2. Define couple pathology (ill health) from your own perspective.
3. What do you think accounts for couple problems?
4. How do you think couples with problems differ from those without?

In this chapter, you will examine three theories within the broad category of psychodynamic couple therapy: object relations couple therapy, ego-analytic couple therapy, and experiential couple therapy.

Object Relations Couple Therapy

Object relations theory expanded upon the psychoanalytic view of internal conflict by addressing the ways in which interpersonal relationships both influence and are impacted by intrapsychic conflicts. In so doing, object relations theory was easily adaptable to couple therapy.

The language of object relations theory is complex. For purposes of this chapter, it is important that you understand how the basic concepts are operationalized in the practice of object relations couple therapy. If you find the theory compelling, suggested readings are included at the end of this chapter. Additionally, clinical supervisors with an object relations orientation may be available.

Object Relations Couple Therapy Concepts

Perhaps the most central tenet of object relations couple therapies is that the partners' individual issues undermine their efforts to resolve their couple problems. All psychodynamic schools of couple therapy hypothesize that individual issues influence choice of partner, or mate selection, as well as the emergence and maintenance of a couple's dynamics. Belsey (1990) described intervention around empathizing with each partner, thereby validating their differing experiences and viewpoints, and coaching them toward responsibility for their own contributions to the relationship difficulties. Before exploring the object relations approach to couple therapy, there are several key concepts to understand.

Projected Introjects. An object in object relations theory is one's image of a significant other. Based on interactions with the significant other, such images are internalized, or introjected. Couples identify with one another's introjected objects on an unconscious level and then project this identification onto one another in their communication. In other words, intrapsychic phenomena are observable in interpersonal interactions.

Object relations theory posits that the inevitable frustrations an infant experiences lead to a negative view of the caretaker as the source of frustration. For example, when an infant wakes up hungry, he or she cries and the caretaker makes his or her way to the infant's crib. Waiting creates distress and possibly fear that the infant's helpless self has been abandoned by the caretaker. As a result, the infant introjects, or absorbs into his or her psyche, the caretaker as an unsatisfactory object. Due to the infant's dependence upon the caretaker, this introject is a threat to the infant's well-being and thereby elicits rage and sadness, both of which are intolerable to the infant dependent on that caretaker. Because they are intolerable, the unsatisfactory aspects of the introjected caretaker object are split off into the infant's unconscious, and only the introject of the good aspects of the caretaker object remain accessible on a conscious level. The good caretaker object elicits feelings of adoration and idealization, while the anger and sadness resulting from the perceived threat inherent in an infant's frustration are repressed along with the introject of the caretaker object as the source of these intolerable feelings. These introjections—rage, sadness, fear of abandonment—are then projected onto others to whom a person is close, creating a continuous cycle in which introjections of the intolerable aspects of the caretaker are then projected onto others for whom they may not be relevant. Without treatment, this dynamic continues into adult life and appears in couples' relationship dynamics (Scharff & Scharff, 2014).

Unless the introject is altered, the individual will continue to experience frustration as a personal threat and react to it by projecting his or her unconscious sadness and rage onto whomever elicits her or his frustration. An intimate couple relationship embellishes the process because of its inherent importance. It is distinct from the caretaker-child relationship only in the sense that adults are not dependent upon one another for survival. Nevertheless, partners sometimes believe and/or behave as though they cannot survive without the other.

For some couples, an argument about whose turn it is to do the dishes may feel like rejection or devaluation to one or both partners, eliciting what may appear to an uninformed observer to be a disproportionate reaction to such a seemingly trivial negotiation. For others, one partner's desire to socialize with friends or engage in a community activity on her or his own may feel like abandonment and similarly result in what appears to be an incomprehensible level of anger and/or sadness.

The projection of unconscious introjected objects and their emotional sequelae are communicated both verbally and nonverbally. Nonverbal expressions of rage in body language, facial expression, and voice tone may be inconsistent with the projecting partner's verbal messages. An object relations couple therapist would view such incongruity as a clue that an intrapsychic process had been triggered. He or she would then assume that this process reflected the projective identification (Dicks, 1993; Klein, 1946) of an unconscious introject from childhood onto the partner.

Note that underlying emotions and the objects to which they are attached in object relations couple therapy and automatic thoughts and the schemata to which they are generalized in cognitive-behavioral couple therapy are similarly inferred by observing behavior.

Note also that what is experienced by the client and observed by her or his partner and the couple therapist is an emotional reaction rather than an intellectual reaction. Experience suggests that clients are usually very responsive to the differentiation of emotional from intellectual logic.

Transference and Countertransference. Because similar dynamics are in play between partners and each partner and the couple therapist, transference and countertransference are key components of all psychodynamic couple therapies. Object relations couple therapists view transference as the process by which a client projects an introjected object and associated emotions onto the couple therapist. Such projections are assumed to be unconscious. Yet they impact the couple therapist. The couple therapist's reaction is called countertransference, which can be influenced by his or her own introjects. By recognizing and addressing countertransference, object relations couple therapists are able to use themselves as both a clue to inferring the clients' introjects and a tool for addressing change while avoiding projecting their own introjects onto clients.

Countertransference may be uncomfortable for the object relations couple therapist. To avoid acting out, or reacting in such a way as to recreate the infant-caretaker cycle and its on-going repetition previously described, the object relations couple therapist must constantly monitor her or his reactions to clients. He or she then identifies these reactions and instead of acting on them interprets what has occurred within the partner-couple therapist relationship.

Containment, Empathy, and Interpretation. An object relations couple therapist creates a safe space in which each partner can explore his or her introjects, as well as how partners project them onto one another. This safe space allows the couple therapist to contain or hold the client's strong and sometimes intolerable emotions attached to the introjects that are being projected onto the partner. At times, these introjects and their accompanying emotions are also projected onto the couple therapist. Containment involves empathy and an ability to experience the partners' emotions with them, without reacting in the way the source of an introject or the partner would. By contrast, an object relations couple therapist remains neutral and retains her or his ability to analyze what occurs during the session. Containment, or holding, allows the partners to view their intolerably strong emotions from a different perspective, because there is no adverse reaction to them, and in this way allows for the possibility of acceptance of these feelings. Once contained and accepted, the object relations couple therapist can then begin to interpret projected introjects in an effort to alter their impact on the couple. Gottman and Gottman (2015) also addressed the issue of how to manage partners' escalating negative emotions, although from a behavioral perspective rather than an object relations perspective.

Liz challenging the couple therapist provides an example of projected introjects, countertransference, and containment. An object relations couple therapist would observe her own inclination to react defensively and instead provide containment for the emotions underlying Liz's challenging behavior, empathize with them, and interpret them as a projection of her introjected mother object, as well as her own angry feelings about feeling challenged or criticized by Sally.

Object Relations Couple Therapy Practice

Like all psychodynamic couple therapies and in contrast to behavioral couple therapies, object relations couple therapy is unstructured. Object relations couple therapists create a safe space and follow the couple's agenda in terms of the content of couple therapy sessions and the pace at which a couple progresses.

Object relations couple therapists begin with assessment. "The goals of the assessment process are to create a safe space in which to contain the affect associated with repressed introjects and to facilitate [the couple's] entry into treatment" (Scharff, 1995, p. 173). Creating a safe space allows the couple to develop a sense of what it would be like to work with the couple therapist so that they can make an informed decision about engaging in couple therapy. At the same time, the object relations couple therapist develops a sense of how the partners project their introjects both within the dynamic of their couple relationship and upon the couple therapist. Object relations couple therapists do not use pencil-and-paper questionnaires or structured interviews.

In more general terms, object relations couple therapists create therapeutic alliances while observing couple dynamics. Because assessment is aimed at observing projected introjects and their impact on the couple's dynamics, creating an alliance and assessing couple dynamics happen concurrently.

Object relations couple therapists assess by listening to each partner's unconscious, as manifested in partners' communications with each other and with the couple therapist. They follow each partner's expressions of emotion, as indicators of unconscious introjects, and thus allow meaning to emerge. They view observing, inferring, and understanding the partners' projected introjects as more important than the content of the discussion. Object relations couple therapists also listen for themes during this process.

Contrary to popular myths about psychodynamic therapies being focused on childhood, object relations couple therapists attend to the here-and-now. They ask about each partner's experience of the mutual projected introjects and include their own experiences and observations in the here-and-now in both assessment and intervention.

Liz's anger at Martin when he told her he did not understand what she meant when she asked for support is of interest because the extent of her anger reflected an unconscious introject that must be interpreted, or brought to consciousness, to be changed to lessen her angry responses. Without interference from the introject's anger, an object relations couple therapist would presume that Liz and Martin could resolve their conflict around Liz's desire for Martin's support and his comprehension of what she wanted by themselves. Object relations theory would posit, and observation of Liz and Martin supported the hypothesis, that the introject with which her anger was associated was projected onto Martin in any situation in which she felt frustrated with him. In other words, the existence, rather than the content, of her frustration was important.

Object relations couple therapists also use countertransference in both assessment and treatment. They assume their own feelings in response to each partner and to the couple's dynamics reflect how the partners feel about themselves and about one another. Object relations couple therapists analyze their own reactions, as well as their clients' expressed emotions when describing their families of origin and relating to one another. If the couple therapist was frustrated by Liz's inability to clearly define support, she or he could infer that Martin was similarly frustrated. Fantasies, images, and metaphors that emerge during sessions also indicate countertransference to clients' unconscious processes.

Specific techniques of object relations couple therapy fall into two broad categories: exploring each partner's history and exploring, understanding, and adapting to what is happening in the here-and-now. Object relations couple therapists request family-of-origin histories when emotions are intense, in order to understand the present iteration of historical relations with significant objects. They may also learn about how introjected objects have been projected onto other significant adults by asking about each partner's relationship history.

In the here-and-now, object relations couple therapists track expressed emotions and themes that emerge and then infer the unconscious content of these emotions and themes with respect to repressed aspects of significant objects. They also observe interactions between partners as well as each partner's interactions with themselves, again inferring unconscious content associated with repressed objects. They experiment with interpretations of their observations and inferences, in order to further assess and for use as interventions. Interpretation facilitates client recognition of his or her projected introjects and adaptation to them. Object relations couple therapists contain and interpret anxiety and other strong emotions while facilitating clients' ability to do both for themselves.

The goals of treatment remain open-ended, based on the assumption that they, like the couple therapist's working hypothesis, will change over time. In other words, as new information emerges, both the assessment and the goals shift to accommodate it.

The object relations couple therapist's role requires a firm and consistent approach, a tolerance for client anxiety and other strong emotions, an ability to stand back while themes emerge rather than directing sessions, and an ability to remain neutral by monitoring countertransference. Object relations couple therapists also must be comfortable revealing aspects of their own countertransference and observations as part of their interpretations.

It should be noted that object relations couple therapy requires clients to have relatively sophisticated cognitive and verbal skills and a willingness to invest time and financial resources into the process of growth. Third-party payments for lengthier treatment, as compared to behavioral couple therapy, may be more difficult to obtain.

Stop and Think:

Be sure to include your responses in your journal.

1. Describe your reactions as you read about the concept of projected introjects and its use in couple therapy. What does this information add to your knowledge about working with couples? If you found it unhelpful, describe how you reached your conclusion.
2. Describe your reactions as you read about the use of containment in couple therapy to create a new experience for one or both partners. What does this information add to your knowledge about working with couples? If you found it unhelpful, describe how you reached your conclusion.
3. Did the here-and-now orientation of psychodynamic couple therapy surprise you? Explain your response.

Object Relations Couple Therapy with Liz and Martin

What follows is a transcript from a 1997 couple therapy session with Liz and Martin approached from an object relations perspective.

COUPLE THERAPIST: Liz, when you are angry at Martin right now, what are your associations?

LIZ: I'm not sure what you're asking. I'm not even sure I'm that angry.

CT: Whatever comes to mind. Any stray thoughts or images or feelings. About now or when you've felt like this before? Maybe even before Martin?

Note: The couple therapist was suggesting the duration of Liz's feelings, rather than exploring their history.

LIZ: Oh. [Pause] I pretty much feel this way whenever my mother gets going about my weight.

CT: Say more about when your mother gets going about your weight.

LIZ: I feel like I've done something wrong. Like she knows something I haven't yet figured out.

CT: And what does Martin know you've done wrong that you haven't yet figured out?

LIZ: [Pause] Maybe that I'm a bad mother?

MARTIN: You're not.

CT: How so?

LIZ: That I don't want to stay home with the kids? That I want to keep practicing law when I should be wanting to be with Christina and MJ all the time?

Note: An experiential couple therapist would have asked about the answer being phrased as a question, while an object relations couple therapist remained focused on the projected introject.

CT: So you think you should want to be with your children all the time.

LIZ: Yes. No. I don't know. Everyone thinks I should want to stop working. What's wrong with me? But I mean, lots of women work outside the home, and they don't all have to. You know, like for financial reasons. Some of them feel better about themselves, they have an identity besides being somebody's mom and somebody else's wife. They're energized by their work. And no one thinks they're bad mothers. But everyone in my life thinks I'm a bad mother.

CT: Do you think you're a bad mother?

LIZ: No. Yes. Martin?

MARTIN: You're not a bad mother, Liz.

LIZ: That's what you say here. [To CT] He's very critical and dismissive at home.

MARTIN: What are you talking about, Liz?

CT: Before we go there, Martin, I want to talk about what Liz just said. I think what's happening here may be that when your mother criticized you long ago, you were justifiably outraged. But you also needed to see her as a loving mother, not as critical or judgmental. So you concluded there was something the matter with you, and when you couldn't figure out what because there was, in fact, nothing the matter with you, you also concluded she, a very important person in your life, knew something about you that you didn't know about yourself. And the part of you that was confused and hurt and maybe even angry, because, after all, wanting ice cream or a cookie when you're four isn't really so awful, that part of you went underground. Perhaps you even stopped listening to what you wanted.

LIZ: Mmhm.

CT: And now when Martin, who is also a very important person in your life, says he wants you to do what makes you happy, you assume he knows something bad about you that you don't know, just like your mother did. And then that confused and sad and angry part of you comes out and it's almost as though you're talking to your mother instead of to Martin.

Stop and Think:

Be sure to include you answers in your journal

1. What are the differences between how the behavioral couple therapist and the object relations couple therapist addressed Liz and Martin's distress?
2. What are the similarities?
3. Evaluate the two outcomes within the transcript and your thoughts about them.

In this transcript, the object relations couple therapist observed and then inferred that Liz had introjected her mother as an object who knew things about her that others did not; split her negative image and feelings of confusion, anger, and sadness from her conscious good and loving mother introject; relegated the negative object and attendant emotions to her unconscious; and then, when Martin withheld his opinion, projected this repressed mother introject onto him, along with feelings of anger and sadness, in this case about their marriage, that mirrored her feelings of sadness and anger when her mother criticized her about her weight.

Note that the object relations couple therapist reframed Liz's experiences as normal. She noted that Liz's wishes regarding food had been age appropriate when they were first criticized and she began to question herself as a result. Although object relations theory does not use the term reframe, she suggested that Liz think of wanting a sweet at the age of four as normal rather than indicating something bad about herself.

Ego-Analytic Couple Therapy

Both object relations couple therapy and ego-analytic couple therapy had their origins in psychoanalytic theory. And both are more applicable to couple therapy than is psychoanalytic theory. Ego-analytic couple therapy, however, differs from object relations couple therapy in its focus and how the role of the couple therapist is envisioned. Ego-analytic couple therapy combines elements of cognitive-behavioral (Chapter 5) and narrative (Chapter 8) theories and requires the couple therapist to remain sensitive to how her or his communications, however well intentioned, may feed each partner's negative self-images and negative self-talk (Wile, 1995).

Ego-Analytic Couple Therapy Concepts

Ego-analytic couple therapy is a psychodynamic approach that, like object relations and experiential couple therapies, holds that each partner's prior experiences with significant people impacts the couple's dynamics and thus the emergence and maintenance of the presenting problem and its correlates. Like other psychodynamic theories, ego-analytic couple therapy also takes into account the dynamics in the partners' relationship with the couple therapist. The clearest description of the application of ego-analytic theory to couple therapy was presented by Wile (1995).

Stop and Think:

Be sure to include your responses in your journal.

1. As you read about the concepts of ego-analytic couple therapy, notice and log in your journal how similar concepts use differing terminology in this and the two other theories you have already studied.
2. Notice also and log in your journal the subtle differences among similar concepts in the different theoretical models.

Ego-analytic couple therapy postulates that conflict arises from partners' inability to communicate their thoughts, feelings, and wishes clearly and as intended. While teaching effective communication skills is an important aspect of ego-analytic couple therapy, ego-analytic couple therapists also examine the deleterious impact of each partner's individual issues upon their ability to communicate clearly and accurately.

Stop and Think:

Be sure to include your responses in your journal.

1. How might an individual's issues, including negative schemata about herself or himself, detract from her or his ability to communicate clearly?
2. Think of a time you were trying to talk to someone important to you about an emotional topic. What was difficult about expressing yourself? Thinking back, how did you feel about yourself going into and during the conversation (for example, confident, anxious, idiotic)?

The concept of self-reproach, or negative self-talk, is central to ego-analytic couple therapy. The theory holds that children reproach themselves in response to critical, controlling, or impaired parenting. When parents are unable to nurture or to allow their developing child age-appropriate independence without anxiety or criticism; are unable to be present because of their own biomedical, emotional, or substance use impairment; or are distracted by the competing demands of other children, aging parents, financial stressors, or a distressed relationship with one another, then children internalize their experience as a reflection of their own worth. They conclude that they do not deserve the parenting they crave and that their feelings and wishes lack validity. Some children even conclude they are bad because they want emotional care-taking the parent is unable to provide.

As a result, the child becomes self-critical and pejorative toward himself or herself. Ego-analytic theory frames these feelings as self-reproach, and any feeling pertaining to or arising from self-reproach is termed a leading edge feeling. When, as an adult, one's partner displays behavior that could be interpreted as critical, controlling, abandoning, or distracted, he or she inadvertently triggers leading edge feelings of self-reproach. Leading edge feelings then direct the individual's response to her or his partner, and the ensuing feedback loop becomes a part of the couple's dynamics.

Stop and Think:

Be sure to include your responses in your journal.

1. How is the concept of leading edge feelings similar to that of emotions connected to projected introjects? How are they different?
2. How is the concept of leading edge feelings similar to that of feelings generated by the emotional sequelae of schemata and resulting automatic thoughts? How are they different?

The behavior orchestrated by leading edge feelings often appears disproportional to what triggered it. As a result, one partner acting on leading edge feelings may trigger the other partner's own leading edge feelings and instigate a positive feedback loop of escalating distress for the couple. By contrast, the couple therapist, who monitors her or his countertransference and then uses it to guide intervention, avoids being triggered by leading edge feelings and thus avoids contributing to the positive feedback loop.

In the ego-analytic conceptualization, the goal of couple therapy is to restore each partner's belief that she or he is entitled to his or her thoughts, feelings, and wishes as the first step to expressing them effectively. Embracing, rather than devaluing, one's thoughts, feelings, and wishes breaks the cycle of responding to one's partner as though he or she is the critical, controlling, or disengaged parent of a child who does not have a right to her or his thoughts, feelings, and wishes. Ego-analytic couple therapists create a platform, or safe space, in which each partner can embrace and express her or his thoughts, feelings, and wishes in order to break the cycle of responding to one another from a place of self-reproach. The couple therapist in this model must be sensitive to the potential impact of her or his own communications and consider the possibility they may be received by either or both partners as reproach.

Stop and Think:

1. What can you do to minimize the risk that a communication will sound like reproach to someone else?
2. What can you do if someone responds to you as though you have reproached or been critical of them when you did not intend to be?
3. Describe a time someone reacted to you as though you said something negative about them.
4. Describe a time you felt someone had rebuked or criticized you and what about their communication led you to conclude that? What about you led you to conclude that?

Ego-analytic couple therapists identify two presenting problems: the obvious problem and the hidden problem. The former is within the couple's awareness. The latter, however, involves partners' intolerance of the presenting problem and the anxiety that therefore arises about it. This hidden problem disrupts the partners' ability to embrace their feelings about the obvious presenting problem, distorts their feelings about one another, and undermines their ability to resolve their differences. By addressing and changing the hidden problem, the ego-analytic couple therapist paves the way for the partners to resolve their obvious problem.

Finally, ego-analytic couple therapists create what is called a joint platform. A joint platform is a safe space in which both partners are guided toward identifying their leading edge feelings in response to unclear communications from one another, reframing those feelings so that they cease to create the reactivity that impedes communication, and learning to communicate thoughts, feelings, and wishes clearly with one another.

Ego-Analytic Couple Therapy Practice

The goal of ego-analytic couple therapy is to enhance each partner's ability to track his or her leading edge feelings and to create a joint platform in which to safely and clearly express thoughts, feelings, and especially wishes. Phases of ego-analytic couple therapy include creating the safe space, identifying leading edge feelings, and teaching couples to communicate more clearly. Couples practice engaging in this process on their own before completing ego-analytic couple therapy. "The goal of any given session is to provide partners with a joint platform or safe setting in which to talk. The goal of the therapy is to enable partners to create for themselves a joint platform or safe setting" (Wile, 1995, p. 113).

Ego-analytic couple therapy utilizes five principles, or guidelines to assess and treat couples, rather than an array of techniques. These involve being entitled to one's own feelings, seeking what is appropriate, attending to clues embedded in the inappropriate, reframing negative experiences, and understanding the universality of human emotions.

The first principle involves the postulate that human experience is shared. Such human experience becomes distorted when one is taught that he or she is not entitled to his or her thoughts, feelings, and wishes. This distortion then precludes clear communication. For example, when Liz felt she was not entitled to want to work outside the home, she became confused and thus found it extremely difficult to communicate to herself or Martin what she wanted. The ego-analytic couple therapist advocating for a partner's right to her or his thoughts, feelings, and wishes then becomes the key to that partner expressing them clearly.

A second guideline is to identify and address what is appropriate, or logical, in what otherwise appears to be inappropriate or illogical client behavior. Ego-analytic theory assumes that what may seem inappropriate or illogical is, from the client's perspective, entirely rational. This view allows the ego-analytic couple therapist to both empathize and question the client's self-reproach. Martin's self-reproach for feeling angry during a frustrating communication with Liz appeared illogical and his concern about his anger disproportional to the situation. One can assume anger was denied validity in his experience, perhaps because other people discounted his anger, although some people observe anger that becomes destructive behavior and then conclude that all anger inevitably leads to a bad outcome. In other words, they overgeneralize (see Chapter 5). The appropriateness of denying his anger and thus the path to questioning such denial lay in the context in which the initial reproach, whatever it was, and ensuing distortion occurred.

Third, ego-analytic couple therapists assess relationships through clues provided by inappropriate behavior based on distorted emotions. They observe how intrapsychic distortions are displayed in the partners' relationship with one another and with the couple therapist. They then use this information to enhance each partner's awareness and to facilitate differentiation of childhood from current experience. This process is similar to the cognitive restructuring of behavioral couple therapy.

Fourth, ego-analytic couple therapists reframe the impact of negative childhood experiences as experiences that enhance each partner's ability to recognize when she or he has been provoked. This is very similar to the reframing of behavioral couple therapy.

Finally, ego-analytic couple therapists help clients shift focus away from self-reproach by recognizing that their thoughts, feelings, and wishes are an intensified version of universal human emotions and do not merit recrimination. The intensity derives from the on-going self-devaluation learned in childhood and not from the thoughts, feelings, and wishes themselves. Presenting the universality of experience diverges from both behavioral and object relations couple therapies.

Clearly, ego-analytic couple therapists borrow several techniques from behavioral couple therapy: communication training, cognitive restructuring, and reframing. However, the differing theoretical underpinnings result in the content and emphasis of these therapeutic devices being different. While a behavioral couple therapist would not link cognitions and affect to history, an ego-analytic couple therapist would. And a behavioral couple therapist would restructure cognitions to change behavior, while an ego-analytic couple therapist would only address cognitions associated with self-reproach, denying oneself the right to one's thoughts, feelings, and wishes, and resulting distortions.

Because an ego-analytic couple therapist's interventions may be received as critical by either or both partners, he or she is careful to use wording that avoids pejorative interpretations of intent. For example, an ego-analytic couple therapist might be concerned that interpreting more intense anger as an expression of repressed anger attached to a rejecting parent would be received as critical of the repressor. The ego-analytic couple therapist might instead say, "In that situation, I'd be angry, too. I'm wondering what else you felt and what you wanted." By substituting recognition of the universality of human experience and the validity of the client's feelings, ego-analytic couple therapists believe they reduce the likelihood of triggering resistance.

The role of the couple therapist in ego-analytic couple therapy revolves around the personal qualities he or she brings to the work of ego-analytic couple therapy. An ego-analytic couple therapist must be aware of her or his own feelings and wishes at all times. She or he must remember that each partner's perspective is unique and valid, in other words, deserving of the empathy essential to all humanistic approaches.

Ego-analytic couple therapists function as advocates for each partner until each partner's devaluation of his or her own experience and attendant self-reproach diminishes to the extent that he or she can advocate for herself or himself.

The three imperatives of ego-analytic couple therapy—to view clients' feelings and wishes as distortions of universal human experience, to validate those feelings and wishes that the client tends to distort, and to present interventions in such a way as to avoid triggering further self-reproach—combine to create a context in which ego-analytic couple therapists reveal more about themselves as human beings than either behavioral or object relations couple therapists do. Rather than stating one's interpretations of logical inferences as the conclusions of an expert and therefore implying that they are more valid than the client's view, ego-analytic couple therapists phrase interventions in a more self-revealing and tentative way as part of their efforts to avoid triggering client self-reproach and thus maintain a more collaborative stance.

Because psychodynamic couple therapies examine the impact of each partner's past on their present behavior and thus relationship dynamics, both object relations and ego-analytic couple therapies have been criticized for lack of attention to the present. However, examination of the impact of the past occurs only in the service of understanding and changing what is happening in the here-and-now of the couple's adult relationship with each other in both theoretical approaches. The transcripts of ego-analytic couple therapy with Liz and Martin in the next subsection illustrate this point.

Ego-Analytic Couple Therapy with Liz and Martin

What follows is a transcript from the same 1997 couple therapy session as in the object relations section of this chapter, this time with an ego-analytic couple therapist.

COUPLE THERAPIST: Most people would be confused about what they want if their mother and sister were telling them what they should want. When you think about what you want apart from them, what happens?

LIZ: I want to talk it through with Martin.

CT: Tell me what talking it through with Martin would tell you about what you want.

LIZ: I'd like him to tell me what he'd like me to do.

CT: OK. And will hearing what Martin wants help you know what you want?

LIZ: [Pause] It probably won't. But it would help me decide if he weighed in.

CT: Any feelings attached to wanting him to weigh in?

LIZ: I don't know. I just want him to.

CT: Sounds [from your voice tone] like you feel internal pressure to know what he wants.

LIZ: Yes.

CT: I'm sensing there's some risk of you saying what you want. What might that be?

LIZ: Well, I could be wrong, make the wrong decision.

CT: You're worried you'll make the "wrong" decision. Who gets to decide what's right or wrong for you, besides you?

LIZ: Well, believe me, if I make the wrong decision I'll hear about it from my mother. And Barbara will be right behind her.

CT: So if your mother doesn't like your decision, she and your sister will gang up on you?

LIZ: That sounds horrible. I think she wants me to do the right thing.

CT: And you don't believe you will?

LIZ: Well, what I want may not be the right thing.

CT: And she's more of an expert on what's right for you than you are?

LIZ: No. But she knows what's the right thing for a mother to do. [Pause] Or she thinks she does.

CT: It sounds as though your mother thinks that for some reason she knows better than you do what's right for you and your children. That you're not entitled to your own wishes or to what you know about your family.

LIZ: She loves me. She worries about me. And my kids if I make the wrong decision.

CT: So she's worried your decision isn't right for her?

LIZ: No, for me. Or the kids.

CT: When else has your mother worried that what you're doing wouldn't be the right decision for her?

LIZ: You really think it's about her? I think you're wrong.

CT: Well, when we start talking about what you want, you start talking about what she wants.

Stop and Think:

Be sure to include your responses in your journal.

1. What was your response to this segment of the transcript?
2. Were you comfortable with the couple therapist's persistence? Why or why not?
3. If you had been Liz, would you have felt defensive? Why or why not?

CT: When else has her worry about herself sounded like worry about you?

LIZ: My mother has always worried about my weight. She was always telling Barbara and me what we should eat. And she worries about her weight, too. [Pause] Maybe it was always what she thought she should eat.

CT: Yes. And how did she let you know when she thought you were eating the "wrong" things?

LIZ: I don't know. She just did.

CT: Did she say, "Don't eat that"? Or did she say it less directly?

LIZ: Sometimes she told us. Always she'd get a look on her face.

CT: What was the look?

LIZ: Disapproving.

CT: So the look told you she thought you were bad for eating what you wanted to eat, and now you tell yourself you are bad for wanting what you want about work. Sometimes even before you let yourself know what it is you want. I suspect you may be waiting to hear whether Martin thinks you're wrong, too.

LIZ: I guess so.

CT: What would it be if you knew?

LIZ: [Pause] Yes. You know, I'm confident at work. And with the kids.

CT: But not about yourself or with Martin about your decisions. When she told you not to eat something you wanted in words, what did she say?

LIZ: Oh, she'd say, "You don't want that, it'll make you fat and ugly."

CT: "You don't want that"? "Fat and ugly"?

LIZ: Yes. And fat.

CT: Sounds like fat is ugly to her.

LIZ: Isn't it to everyone?

CT: Were any of you ever fat?

LIZ: No!

CT: Then it doesn't sound like a problem. More importantly, I find myself wanting to rush to your defense, to say to her, "Of course she wants it, that's what kids do, even if you won't let her have it. And if you let her want it, then she'll learn to trust herself and make her own decisions when she grows up."

LIZ: Hm.

CT: What I hear is that she thinks she knows better than you do what you want, when you are the world's expert on you. And then she threatens you with becoming repulsive if you want something you have a right to want. I think most people would either be furious or want to hide if someone important who had power over them told them that. I'm furious, and I wonder whether on some level you were and are, too.

LIZ: I wanted to hide my ugliness.

CT: You thought you were ugly just by wanting to eat something?

LIZ: Yes. Like wanting it would make me go out of control.

CT: And now when she tells you you don't want something you want because it'll make you a bad mother, you want to hide behind Martin.

Note: Some clients might hear "bad mother" or "you want to hide" and assume the therapist is either accusing or rebuking them. "And now you feel like hiding when your mother reproaches you about your mothering" might have circumvented that risk.

LIZ: What?

CT: If he decides for you.

LIZ: Oh. I guess you could look at it that way.

CT: Martin, when Liz's mother is criticizing her, what are your [leading edge] feelings?

MARTIN: Honestly? I'd like to tell her to back off, but I was raised to respect adults. I'm an adult, but she's the older generation, you know?

CT: Yes. It's as though you become a child who knows his parents would be angry to learn he talked back to a grown-up.

MARTIN: I hadn't thought of it quite that way.

CT: How did you feel when your parents were upset with you for doing something you probably knew would upset them?

MARTIN: Oh, man, like nothing.

CT: You told yourself you were nothing?

MARTIN: Pretty much. Like, what was I thinking? Why did I do that?

CT: So you didn't understand yourself. And you didn't think maybe there was a reasonably good explanation, like with Liz, that a four year old wanting a cookie before dinner isn't a bad thing, it's a four-year-old thing. And for you, wanting to tell a grown-up who was out of line to back off seems like a reasonable wish, even though you were a child.

MARTIN: Yeah...

CT: I wonder whether you have the same feelings when Liz asks you to stand up for her to herself about how good a mother she is right now, working outside the home.

MARTIN: You mean, when she asks me what I think she should do?

CT: Yes.

MARTIN: I honestly don't know. Could be.

CT: I'd like you to notice what you're feeling next time she asks. Because you're not a child anymore, and it's OK to stand up for yourself and the people you love.

MARTIN: Yeah, I guess I know that.

Stop and Think:

Be sure to include your answers in your journal.

1. What were the similarities and differences between the transcripts of the object relations and ego-analytic couple therapy sessions?
2. Review the ego-analytic couple therapy transcript and note when the couple therapist may have inadvertently communicated reproach of Liz or Martin. How could she have phrased what she said differently to avoid any hint of reproach?

Irv Yalom (1989, 2003), another psychoanalytically trained psychotherapist who worked with both individuals and couples throughout his illustrious career, used countertransference in an even more self-revealing way than ego-analytic couple therapists do, although with the same humanistic, here-and-now perspective. He also added the element of existentialism, especially around universal issues of being with which people struggle individually and in relationship to others.

Experiential Couple Therapy

In the final section of this chapter about psychodynamic couple therapies, you will learn about experiential couple therapy. Experiential couple therapy is psychodynamic, in that it emphasizes the here-and-now relationship dynamics between partners and with the experiential couple therapist while accounting for the impact of each partner's history and intrapsychic processes upon those here-and-now relationship experiences. Experiential couple therapy differs from both object relations and ego-analytic couple therapies in how countertransference issues are handled.

Coontz (2005, p. 9) pointed out that the experience of marriage is not the same as the social functions of marriage. In other words, what goes on inside a couple's relationship is experienced intrapsychically by each partner and interpersonally by the couple in a very different way than the larger society views their formalized commitment as a couple. It is these intrapsychic and interpersonal experiences of being a member of a committed couple that are the focus of experiential couple therapy.

Most prominent among experiential couple therapists was Carl Whitaker, and this chapter will emphasize his work (Napier & Whitaker, 1978; Neill & Kniskern, 1982; Whitaker, 1989; Whitaker & Bumberry, 1988). In an interview with Rebecca Aponte (2009), Whitaker's protégé, colleague, and co-author Augustus Napier termed his approach experiential symbolic therapy. In this context, symbolic refers to the experience of couple therapy as symbolic of the clients' larger reality (Aponte, 2009; Whitaker & Bumberry, 1988). Although Virginia Satir has also been included in the literature on experiential couple therapy (Satir, 2013, 2011, 2009, 1985; Satir, Stachowiak, & Taschman, 1975), her gentleness appeared more similar to an ego-analytic couple therapist's approach than to the other experiential couple therapists included in this section. Gestalt therapy, which relies heavily on here-and-now experiences, has also included attention to couples (Yontef, 2011).

Experiential Couple Therapy Concepts

Experiential couple therapy targets the emotional layer of behavior and cognition. The theory conceptualizes emotions as normal human events. An individual has responsibility for how she or he acts upon her or his emotions, but not for whether or not she or he feels them. By recognizing, embracing, and owning one's feelings, partners are then able to exert control over whether, when, and how they choose to express them to one another.

The focus of experiential couple therapy is on the individuals, the couple system they create, and the experiential couple therapist's experience being with them. While experiential couple therapists intervene to change the couple system, they do not assume they are simultaneously treating individual psychopathology (Esposito & Hattem, 2017).

Emotional logic is an important concept in experiential couple therapy. If the couple therapist can experience the couple in the way each partner does, the emotional logic of the situation will become clear. Experiential couple therapists then use the meaning partners attach to their interactions and its accompanying emotions to question assumptions and explore alternative meanings and behaviors.

As the name implies, experiential couple therapy relies heavily on the therapist's experience of the couple during the here-and-now of couple therapy sessions. Conceptually, this is similar to the precept that countertransference is a guide to interventions. This use of countertransference is universal to all psychodynamic couple therapies.

Experiential couple therapy theory holds that one's choice of partner is an attempt to fix what has not been resolved between an individual and his or her parents. Napier postulated that the supposed spike in divorce after seven years of marriage resulted from partners giving up on each other's ability to heal their own parent-child wounds (Napier & Whitaker, 1978).

Experiential couple therapy is far more attuned to system dynamics than are either of the other two psychodynamic theories reviewed in this chapter. The theory views system health, or couple therapy goals, as creating a permeable boundary between partners and a clear boundary around them. In other words, partners are emotionally intimate with one another and view themselves as distinct from the other social systems with which they interact. To illustrate, consider a situation in which couple distress is high and one partner begins to rely on a child, sibling, friend, or parent for his or her instrumental, or task-oriented, and emotional needs. This third person then becomes part of a triangle in which there is a coalition between this partner and the third person against the other partner. In such situations, couple cohesion and satisfaction diminish, and the third person may display symptoms of distress, especially if she or he is a child of the partners. Minuchin conducted a study in which it was observed that when parents argued while a diabetic child observed them through a one-way mirror, the child's blood sugar became less stable (Minuchin, Rosman, & Baker, 1978).

Couple and family health are also characterized by role flexibility, flexible alliances within and outside the couple system, clear generational boundaries, and partners' awareness of themselves as individuals in relationship with one another. Role flexibility involves the ability to take over one another's instrumental and emotional roles when the situation demands, for example if one partner is ill, traveling for business, or caring for a sick child or parent.

Flexible alliances, by contrast to coalitions, involve one partner joining with individuals or subsystems outside the couple for a specific purpose that is usually time-limited. For example, Martin worked secretly with one of Liz's closest friends to give her a surprise 30th birthday party.

Clear generational boundaries are important to the mental health of both partners. Examples of clear generational boundaries are manifested when the couple's parents do not micromanage the couple's lives and their children view them as a team.

Finally, relationship health involves partners maintaining their individual identities while remaining aware of their partnership and sensitive to the impact of each upon the other. They display empathy for one another and respect who the other is in addition to being "my partner."

Experiential Couple Therapy Practice

The primary technique of experiential couple therapy involves the experiential couple therapist using a balance of warmth and confrontation to perturb, or disrupt, positive feedback loops in the system, always in a compassionate way. Experiential couple therapists use warmth, empathy, and themselves as fellow human beings to create connections with each partner and with them as a couple. Experiential couple therapy appears playful, and humor is liberally sprinkled throughout sessions. This humor is not laughing at the client couple. Rather, it underscores the absurdity of what feels logical but is, in fact, unnecessary and unhelpful to the couple.

To effectively practice experiential couple therapy, a couple therapist must continually practice self-awareness and be comfortable using whatever emerges in his or her mind as part of the therapeutic intervention. These include symbolic images, fantasies, emotional reactions, and behavioral impulses. In fact, in order to gently perturb a system, some experiential couple therapists embellish upon these reactions.

Consider and contrast the following two examples:

COUPLE THERAPIST 1: I'd be angry if a friend said that to me about my partner, no matter how upset I was with him.

CLIENT: Oh, no, I don't like to be angry at my friends.

COUPLE THERAPIST 2: I'd want to slap her if she said that to me.

Note: Before using this intervention, a couple therapist would determine that the client does not have a history of violence and is not an abuse perpetrator.

CLIENT: [Giggles uncomfortably] Well, maybe not slap.

Notice that the client acknowledged his or her anger without endorsing a violent expression of it in response to Couple Therapist 2, whereas the client denied he or she was angry in response to Couple Therapist 1.

Stop and Think:

Be sure to include your answers in your journal.

1 How comfortable are you with using confrontation in your work with couples? What attracts you to the use of gentle confrontation? What are your hesitations?
2 How comfortable are you with using humor in your work with couples? What attracts you to the use of humor? What are your hesitations?
3 How comfortable are you with using whatever comes to mind in your work with couples? What attracts you to the use of yourself? What are your hesitations?

Experiential couple therapists use these overarching techniques to assess and intervene. They also borrow specific techniques from other schools of couple therapy. For example, an experiential couple therapist would use humor and confrontation, rather than the logic used by a behavioral couple therapist, with the same goal of questioning the assumptions that impede change.

COUPLE THERAPIST: OK, so if you allow yourself to get angry with him you'll go completely out of control, demolish the house, beat him up, say outrageously mean things.

LIZ: Me? No. But I might say something I'd regret.

CT: Like what? What might you say?

LIZ: I don't know. Maybe, "Just tell me what you think"? But I'd yell it.

CT: And if you yelled, the house would fall down around your ears and Martin would curl up in a corner and die.

LIZ: [Giggles] No. But he might get mad at me for yelling.

CT: And then what would happen to you?

LIZ: I don't know.

CT: Maybe you'd be the one to curl up in a corner and die.

LIZ: What? If he were mad at me?

CT: Sounds like you think you're both too fragile to withstand one another's anger. But I think you've withstood a lot in your life, including real out of control rage when your father was drinking, and Martin being angry at you would be easy by comparison. And Martin, you didn't see enough anger at home growing up, so you're scared of it, too. Maybe Liz could help you get angry if she yells enough.

LIZ: Hasn't worked so far.

MARTIN: [Smiles]

CT: And it sounds like you both believe that anger is synonymous with being out of control, even though neither of you has ever lost control. You are so nice to each other that you let this bubbling cauldron of upset eat away at the floor under your marriage. And I think we need to change that, we need to figure out a way for you to be less frightened by your angry feelings. So, Martin, let's talk about your anger.

Stop and Think:

Be sure to note your responses in your journal.

1. Experience suggests that most students have strong reactions to experiential couple therapy. Write down your immediate reactions to CT's interventions.
2. Now compare and contrast how the goal of questioning the couple's assumptions is addressed by behavioral couple therapists, ego-analytic couple therapists, and experiential couple therapists.

Note that the experiential couple therapist was both empathetic and confrontative. Additionally, in her last statement, she differentiated angry feelings from angry behaviors. Throughout, she questioned the assumption that anger leads to violence when, in fact, anger is a primary emotion that, once acknowledged, can be acted upon in a variety of ways over which an individual has choices. Awareness and acceptance of one's feelings, whether one likes them or not, is essential to finding options for expressing them beyond the dichotomy of repressing or allowing them free reign (Polster & Polster, 1973).

Being fully present with clients constitutes the foundation of the couple therapist's role in experiential couple therapy. Several experiential couple theorists have addressed the importance of being genuinely oneself with clients, experiencing their pain and distress through empathy, and then using that experience to guide assessments and interventions. They caution that a focus on theory and technique undermines the couple therapist's role (Nichols, 1984; Siegel, 2013; Yalom, 2003). Nichols wrote that Whitaker

"...says that therapists who base their work on theory are likely to substitute observation for caring.... Instead of having the courage to just 'be' with the [couple] and help them grapple with their problems..." (Nichols, 1984, p. 264).

Similarly, Richard Siegel (2013) noted that wisdom accrues from introspection and being in the world in connection with others and has virtually nothing to do with theory and technique, unless they arise from it. Irving Yalom (2003) approached this notion from a slightly different perspective, pointing out that theory and technique distract a therapist from seeing and experiencing clients as full human beings. If theory is viewed as a way for therapists to organize their thoughts (Gehart, 2010), then it may be relevant to experiential couple therapy as a framework for experience, rather than a prescription for assessment and intervention.

Stop and Think:

Be sure to include your answers in your journal.

1. Do you agree or disagree that using one's experience of being with a couple is undermined by attention to theory and technique? Explain your answer.
2. Think about something that happened in the past week or two in a relationship that is important to you. What was it like for you as a participant?
3. Now think about something that happened to someone you know in a relationship that is important to her or him. What was it like for you as an observer?
4. Now notice yourself as you interact with the important people in your life over the next week. Simply notice, no need to do anything other than write your observations.

Experiential Couple Therapy with Liz and Martin

We will once again revisit the 1997 couple therapy session described in the previous two sections of this chapter so that you can further explore the differences among these three psychodynamic approaches. Following is a very long transcript that covers more than one subject. The uninterrupted length will give you the opportunity to observe the flow of an experiential couple therapy session, to experience it in a way a brief excerpt would not allow.

COUPLE THERAPIST: So your mom and sister think they know you and what you want better than you do?

LIZ: I never thought about it that way.

CT: How do they know?

LIZ: Well, they've both raised kids, and they think their way is right. It's worked out pretty well for them, I guess, although my brother's a mess. But Mom and Barb are happy.

CT: So because they're happy with the way they've done things, you're supposed to disregard yourself? I still don't understand how they became better experts on you and what's good for your children than you are?

LIZ: As I said, they're more experienced.

CT: Not with what goes on in your head or your family.

LIZ: Well, maybe, but they always act like they are.

CT: So you believe them. And what does that do to you?

LIZ: Shuts me right up. I just nod.

CT: How old are you?

LIZ: 31.

CT: No, when you shut up and nod.

LIZ: Eight.

CT: And what do you look like? What are you wearing?

LIZ: I'm wearing a dress of Barbie's [notice the name change with age], and the sleeves hang below my wrists but it's tight in the middle. I look awful.

CT: So when your mother and Barbara tell you what you want, you turn into a chubby little girl whose mommy makes her wear a dress that doesn't fit and then blames her for looking awful?

LIZ: If I hadn't eaten that cookie at my friend's, maybe the dress would fit better.

CT: And did you want the cookie?

LIZ: Oh yes, but look what it did to me.

CT: Made your sister's dress tight on you?

LIZ: [Tearful, shakes head] Made me ugly.

CT: What do you want from your mom right now?

LIZ: To be loved.

CT: And your grown-up, 31-year-old self would say to your 8-year-old self?

LIZ: I don't know.

CT: If a dress was too tight on Christina, what would you tell her?

LIZ: That she's...that she's beautiful anyway, and I love her.

CT: Anyway? Imagine her sitting right here [indicates an extra chair]. Tell her.

LIZ: You're beautiful, and I love you. It's OK that the dress is too tight, it means you're growing up. Let's find another dress to put on.

CT: Yes. You are a good mother who wouldn't do anything to make her feel badly about herself.

LIZ: Absolutely not.

CT: Now tell eight-year-old Liz you love her and she's beautiful even when someone else's dress doesn't fit perfectly.

LIZ: [Softly] I, you're beautiful even though Barbie's dress is tight on you.

CT: You don't sound like you mean it. Remember you deserve the same things you would do for Christina.

LIZ: [Louder] You're beautiful. It's OK that Barbie's dress is tight on you. Let's find you another dress.

CT: You're a good mother, to Christina and to yourself.

LIZ: I guess.

CT: I'd like to hear you say it.

LIZ: I'm a good mother. Yes, I am a good mother. It's harder to be a good mother to myself, but I am a good mother to Christina. And to MJ.

CT: Now tell Martin.

LIZ: I wouldn't do anything to hurt Christina or MJ because I love them, and I don't want Christina to ever feel bad about herself the way I do.

MARTIN: I know, Liz. You're a good mother.

LIZ: I am? [Pause] I am.

CT: Martin, what was it like for you listening to Liz?

MARTIN: I've never liked how Sally and Barbara think they know everything and treat Liz like she doesn't know anything. And I don't like that she's always so critical about how she looks.

LIZ: Mom and Barbara only want what's best for me, for us.

MARTIN: But she's [indicating CT] right, Liz, we know what's best for us and for our kids.

CT: I suspect Sally and Barbara can take care of themselves, that they don't need defending, though it's a good daughter and sister thing to do. Liz, what would you like Martin to do or say when your mom or sister starts telling you what to do and how to look?

LIZ: I'm afraid he'll say something to them, like "back off" or "our family is ours to raise."

CT: And what would you prefer he did?

LIZ: I guess what he just said to me, that I'm a good mother. [To Martin] Yes. I'd like you to tell them I'm a good mother. [Smiles]

MARTIN: [Smiles] I can do that.

CT: You can also remind yourself that you're a good mother, even when your mother doesn't think you're being a compliant little girl.

LIZ: [Angry] I am so sick of being a good girl. What b.s.!

MARTIN: Whoa, Liz.

CT: Martin, what just happened?

MARTIN: She doesn't need to swear here.

CT: I'm curious what happened for you when she got angry and swore.

MARTIN: What I just said.

CT: It's OK to be angry and swear here. I'm wondering what happened inside you.

MARTIN: Oh, well, it's uncomfortable. [Pause] And I wanted her to stop.

CT: Before...?

MARTIN: Before she got out of control?

CT: She? Or you?

MARTIN: Me?

CT: Yes. I get the sense something happened inside, and I suspect whatever it was affects what happens between you and Liz.

MARTIN: Oh, I see.

CT: Don't think about it. Ask yourself, what is happening inside me and then let your mind be open to whatever your self tells you.

MARTIN: [Pause] I don't know.

CT: You looked angry, too, when Liz got angry and swore. Can you remember how your face and body felt?

MARTIN: Yes. Clenched.

CT: Clench your face and body now.

MARTIN: [Clenches face and fists] That feels awful.

CT: Say more.

MARTIN: I want to punch her. Not Liz, Sally. And Barbara.

CT: [Tosses a cushion to Martin] Punch the pillow.

MARTIN: [Puts it in his lap] No, I can't.

CT: Throw the pillow at the floor between us then. Hard.

MARTIN: [Tosses the pillow] This is why I run. And work out.

CT: I think you're more scared of your anger than I am. Liz, what about you? When he tossed the pillow, were you scared?

LIZ: I was OK. I know he wouldn't hurt me. Or you.

CT: So here we are, Liz feeling like a fat little girl when she asks herself what she wants and Martin feeling like an out of control monster when they both got angry. I have an image of the monster frightening the little girl and her trying to be even more good so it stops, and then her adult self feeling angry for being intimidated. I don't know what Sally looks like, but I wonder if sometimes Martin's monster has Sally's face.

LIZ: Oh probably.

CT: And then what happens?

LIZ: Well, if it's Martin and we're alone, I can talk back.

CT: Talk for the fat little girl who wants to be loved.

LIZ: Now?

CT: Yes.

LIZ: Leave me alone, monster. Go away. I hate you. And I am so sick and tired of trying to be good and getting absolutely no credit for it.

CT: I bet you are. Martin?

MARTIN: [Puts hands up, palms out] I just leave her alone.

CT: I'd like you to tell your monster self that nothing bad happened just now. Liz got angry, and you didn't punch her, you didn't lose control, even when you felt angry. I think you can soothe yourself knowing that.

MARTIN: OK.

CT: Say it.

MARTIN: I didn't lose control when I got angry.

CT: No, you didn't. And when you soothe your monster self that nothing bad is happening, can you tell Liz it's OK, she isn't a bad girl for wanting something different than her mother wants?

MARTIN: That's the easy part.

CT: I know. You're going to need to pay attention to the first sign of your monster coming out, your anger, so that you can soothe yourself that it's OK, it's not going to get out of control. What's the first sign?

MARTIN: I don't know.

CT: Whatever it was emerged when Liz got angry and swore. I'd like you to watch for first signs during the week. My guess is when you find yourself trying to control yourself you know you've felt a twinge and you can ask yourself what just happened.

MARTIN: OK.

Notice how the experiential couple therapist took the session back and forth from each partner's experience to the couple system. Note also that, to the extent possible, she kept the focus in the here-and-now of the session and the dynamics among the three participants in the couple therapy system. She also used her own experience of Liz and Martin and the dynamics of their exchanges with her as grist for the couple therapy mill.

Conclusions

Before comparing and contrasting the three psychodynamic couple therapy theories about which you have read in this chapter, stop and think about your own thoughts and feelings about them.

Stop and Think:

Be sure to include your answers in your journal.

1. Which of the three psychodynamic couple therapy theories (object relations, ego-analytic, and experiential) best fits your world view? Be specific about how you resonated with the concepts and practice of your preferred theory.
2. With which theoretical approach were you most comfortable? Explain.
3. What, if anything, discomforted you about one or more of these psychodynamic approaches?
4. What makes psychodynamic theories of couple therapy more attractive to you than behavioral couple therapy? What makes them less so?

Psychodynamic couple therapies share an emphasis on transference, whether framed as a projected introject, leading edge emotion, or as an attempt to heal emotional pain of long duration. They also devote significant attention to countertransference, and especially the use of the couple therapist's response to the couple client as a guide for intervention. They also share the assumptions that individual issues are played out in couple dynamics and that healing the individual partners will change the couple's dynamics.

One important aspect of couple therapy that is frequently overlooked and is implied in the concept of transference is the potential for one or both partners to view the couple therapist as an ideal partner. Clients do not see their therapists in their own lives, and thus their view may be distorted by the professional persona of calmness, empathy, acceptance, and wisdom. The risk is that the couple therapist might become, in object relations terminology, the idealized partner split off from her or his faults and missteps while the real partner, who is seen in everyday life, becomes the devalued one. When clients view their couple therapist as an ideal partner, then the therapeutic relationship has an unintended and deleterious impact on the couple's relationship. By focusing the couple therapist's attention on transference and countertransference, psychodynamic couple therapists are in a position to notice and address any idealization of themselves and its subsequent impact on the couple's relationship. While each of the three theories would manage idealization differently, couple therapists adhering to any psychodynamic approach would remain sensitive to it.

The importance of empathy between partners is an implicit, if not explicit, component of all psychodynamic couple therapies. Teaching empathy through modeling empathetic behavior is not incompatible with behavioral couple therapy. Experience suggests that the partners' ability to empathize with one another is fundamental to any successful couple intervention.

Having introduced the foundational theories of couple therapy in Chapters 4, 5, and 6, you will next read about the more contemporary approaches to couple therapy in Chapters 7 and 8. While these chapters are not exhaustive, they provide an introduction to the range of options available to couple therapists.

References

American Psychiatric Association. (2013). *Diagnostic and statistical manual of mental disorders (5th ed.).* Washington DC: American Psychiatric Publishing.

Aponte, R. (2009). Augustus Napier on experiential family therapy. Retrieved from http://www.psychotherapy.net/interview/augustus-napier#section-experiential-family-therapy.

Belsey, P. (1990). Couples therapy. Integrating the psychoanalytic and systems viewpoints. *Clinical Social Work Journal, 18* (2), 167–171.

Brill, A. A. (Ed.). (1995). *The basic writings of Sigmund Freud.* New York NY: Random House, Inc.

Clulow, C. F. (1990). *Marriage. Dissolution and hope. Papers celebrating forty years of the Tavistock Institute of Marital Studies.* New York NY: Brunner/Mazel.

Coontz, S. (2005). *Marriage, a history. How love conquered marriage.* New York NY: Penguin Books Ltd.

Dicks, H. V. (1993). *Marital tensions. Clinical studies towards a psychological theory of interaction.* London: Karnac Books.

Dulwich Centre. (2015). *What is narrative therapy?* Dulwich Centre Publications Pty Ltd & Dulwich Centre Foundation, Inc. Retrieved from http://www.dulwichcentre.com.au/what-is-narrative-therapy.

Esposito, J. & Hattem, A. (2017). *Introduction to family counseling. A case study approach.* Los Angeles CA: Sage Press.

Gehart, D. (2010). *Mastering competencies in family therapy. A practical approach to theories and clinical documentation.* Belmont CA: Brooks/Cole.

Gurman, A. S. & Fraenkel, P. (2002). The history of couple therapy. A millennial review. *Family Process,* 41 (2), 199–260.

Gurman, A. S., Lebow, J. L., & Snyder, D. K. (2015). *Clinical handbook of couple therapy (5th ed.).* New York NY: Guilford Press.

Kernberg, O. (2004). *Contemporary controversies in psychoanalytic theory, techniques, and their application.* New Haven CT: Yale University Press.Koch, A. & Ingram, T. (1985). The treatment of borderline personality disorder within a distressed relationship. *Journal of Marriage and Family Therapy,* 11 (4), 373–380.

Lanman, M., Grier, F., & Evans, C. (2003). Objectivity in psychoanalytic assessment of couple relationships. *The British Journal of Psychiatry,* 182 (3), 255–260.

Minuchin, S., Rosman, B. L., & Baker, L. (1978). *Psychosomatic families. Anorexia nervosa in context.* Cambridge MA: Harvard University Press.

Napier, A. Y. (1988). *The fragile bond. In search of an equal, intimate and enduring marriage.* New York NY: Harper Collins.

Napier, A. Y. & Whitaker, C. A. (1978). *The family crucible.* New York NY: Harper and Row, Publishers.

Neill, J. R. & Kniskern, D. P. (1982). *From psyche to system. The evolving therapy of Carol Whitaker.* New York NY: The Guilford Press.

Nichols, M. (1984). *Family therapy. Concepts and methods.* New York NY: Gardner Press.

Polster, E. & Polster, M. (1973). *Gestalt therapy integrated.* New York NY: Brunner/Mazel.

Satir, V. (2013). The therapist's story. In M. Baldwin (Ed.). *Use of the self in therapy (2nd ed.).* Binghamton NY: Howarth Press, Inc. DOI: 10.1300/J287v03n01_04.

Satir, V. (2011). *Making contact.* Madison WI: Virginia Satir Global Network.

Satir, V. (2009). *Your many faces: The first step to being loved (3rd ed.)*. Berkeley CA: Celestial Arts.

Satir, V. (1985). Forward. In E. McCann (Ed.). *The two-step: The dance toward intimacy*. New York NY: Grove Press.

Satir, V., Stachowiak, J., & Taschman, H. A. (1975). *Helping families to change*. New York NY: Jason Aronson.

Scharff, J. S. (1995). Psychoanalytic marital therapy. In A. S. Gurman (Ed.). *Clinical handbook of couple therapy (4th ed.)*. New York NY: Guilford Press.

Scharff, D. E. & Scharff, J. S. (2014). An overview of psychodynamic couple therapy. In D. E. Scharff & J. S. Scharff (Eds.). *Psychoanalytic couple therapy: Foundations of theory and practice*. London: Karnac.

Siegel, R. (2013). Wisdom in psychotherapy. *Psychotherapy Networker, 37* (2), 18–25.

Whitaker, C. (1989). *Midnight musings of a family therapist*. New York NY: W. W. Norton & Company.

Whitaker C. & Bumberry, W. M. (1988). *Dancing with the family. A symbolic-experiential approach*. New York NY: Brunner/Mazel.

Wile, D. B. (1995). The ego-analytic approach to couple therapy. In N. S. Jacobson & A. S. Gurman (Eds.). *Clinical handbook of marital therapy (2nd ed.)*. New York NY: Guilford Press.

Yalom, I. D. (1989). *Love's executioner and other tales of psychotherapy*. New York NY: Basic Books.

Yalom, I. D. (1999). *Momma and the meaning of life. Tales of psychotherapy*. New York NY: Perennial.

Yalom, I. D. (2003). *The gift of therapy. An open letter to a new generation of therapists and their patients*. New York NY: Harper Perennial.

Yontef, G. (2011). The four relationships of Gestalt therapy couples work. Retrieved from http://www.gestalttherapybrisbane.qld.edu.au/wp-content/uploads/2012/12/The-four-relationships-of-Gestalt-therapy-couples-work.pdf.

For Further Study

Kohut, H. (1977). *The restoration of self*. Chicago IL: University of Chicago Press.

Napier, A. Y. (1988). *The fragile bond. In search of an equal, intimate and enduring marriage*. New York NY: Harper Collins.

CHAPTER 7

Post-Modern Couple Therapy Theories

Learning Objectives

1. Describe the impact of post-modern thought on couple therapy.
2. Describe the concept of narratives and their use by narrative couple therapists.
3. Discuss the role of gender inequality as a barrier to couple change.
4. Illustrate the use of the "miracle solution" in solution-focused couple therapy.
5. Explain the purpose of enactments in structural couple therapy.
6. Define ironic process and illustrate its role in brief strategic couple therapy.
7. Describe the underpinnings of a secure attachment.
8. Explain the links between emotionally focused couple therapy and psychodynamic, cognitive-behavioral, systemic, and post-modern theories.

Following its origins in behavioral, psychodynamic, and family systems therapies, couple therapy continued to evolve as a new generation of couple therapists replaced its founders. This second generation of couple therapists was influenced by post-modern theory, as well as by mentors from among the founders of couple therapy. The second generation couple therapies they developed reflect post-modern thinking.

Each of the six theories of couple therapy included in this chapter were influenced by post-modern thought. The three that identify as uniquely post-modern are narrative couple therapy, feminist couple therapy, and solution-focused couple therapy. The first two of these theoretical perspectives provide overarching conceptual frameworks from which to view couple therapy while, like experiential family therapy, not promoting specific techniques.

Solution-focused couple therapy is also a post-modern theory and is closely related to narrative theory. Solution-focused couple therapy could not have arisen until meaning could be detached, or deconstructed, from human experience.

By contrast, structural couple therapy, brief strategic couple therapy, and emotionally focused couple therapy imposed a post-modern conceptual framework on a previous foundational theory of couple or family therapy. Structural couple therapy and brief strategic couple therapy both derived from family systems theory and were initially described only with respect to families, as strategic and structural family therapies (Haley, 1963; Minuchin, 1974). Although used by clinicians working with couples, their theoretical application to couple therapy was not formally conceptualized until after the advent of post-modern thought and was therefore heavily influenced by it.

Emotionally focused couple therapy (EFT) first identified as a spin-off of psychodynamic theory and later as a combination of experiential and systemic couple therapy (Greenberg & Johnson, 1988; Johnson, 2015). EFT went on to include elements of narrative theory in its approach (Johnson, 2004). EFT was developed collaboratively by a member of the founding generation of couple therapy, Leslie Greenberg, and his mentee, Susan Johnson, who was influenced by post-modern thought and continued his work from that perspective. Thus, in its present iteration, EFT emphasizes meaning and narrative, while de-emphasizing intrapsychic processes (Johnson, 2015).

Post-Modern Theories of Couple Therapy

Post-modern theory arose in the second half of the last century in the various fields within the humanities and social sciences. It is a rejection of the positivism and objectivity that had dominated Western thought. Post-modern theory replaced objectivity with an emphasis on experience, the meaning attached to it, and the social context in which individuals, couples, and families function.

Writings about post-modern theory are often complex and difficult to understand. The four fundamental premises are (1) meaning is constructed, or derived, from experience; (2) experience can be interpreted in many ways and thus meanings vary; (3) how one interprets one's experience as an individual in relationship to others affects the meaning one ascribes to it; and (4) both interpretations of and the meaning ascribed to experience are influenced by the sociocultural context, including interpersonal interactions, in which an individual or couple finds herself, himself, or themselves. In other words, objective reality, which would lead multiple observers to the same conclusions, does not exist. Instead, multiple observers experience and interpret the same events differently and thus arrive at multiple conclusions. This perspective explains how two partners can view a particular incident and/or their relationship from two entirely different perspectives.

Post-modern theories rely on shared meaning as an explanation of social and cultural behavior and in this way are related to the social constructionist school of sociology (Chapter 2). Shared meaning is a socially agreed-upon construct that becomes meaningless outside that social agreement. Thus, couples are faced with the task of finding shared meanings despite their differing interpretations of their experiences. In this way, post-modern theory has been more applicable than previous theories to work with biracial and bicultural couples.

Stop and Think:

Be sure to include your responses in your journal.

1. Behavioral couple therapy arose from experience with mostly white, middle-class, heterosexual couples. Given what you have learned about it, how might it be applied to couples who do not fit this dominant cultural model?
2. Psychodynamic couple therapies also arose from work with couples within the dominant cultural norm. Given what you have learned about psychodynamic couple therapies, how might they be applied to couples outside this dominant cultural model?

Additionally, the context in which any given culture and its members find themselves at any given point in time heavily influences meanings, both individual and those that are socially agreed upon. For example, the meaning of marriage would have been very different in seventeenth century western Europe, before it was paired with romantic love, than it is today. The meaning of marriage also differs across cultures, the specifics of which are beyond the scope of this textbook. Meanings may differ across families, even in similar sociocultural groups. And finally, individual temperament and experience filter larger sociocultural meanings and individualize them. Thus, partners must negotiate shared meanings within the context of their personalities, their very different families of origin, and any discrepancies in their larger sociocultural contexts. For couple therapists, the risk of ignoring the post-modern perspective involves fostering prescribed and internalized meanings that are irrelevant, demeaning, or inhibiting of a given partner or couple.

Post-modern theory has been applied to the couple's experience of living in an intimate relationship with one another. Examples of culturally prescribed meanings that detract from couple functioning include arguments about right and wrong that arise from dichotomous thinking, a mutual search for and avoidance of fault and blame, and outdated role prescriptions.

Dichotomous thinking leads to arguments about who is right and who is wrong. Given the lack of alternative options, such as both being right for different reasons, the partners' ability to examine the way in which they interact as both the source and potential solution to their distress becomes obscured. Dichotomous thinking also dooms the dichotomous thinker to what systems theorists term first-order change: more of the same or the opposite (Chapter 4). Liz was trapped in an argument about correct or incorrect mothering behavior with her own mother that left her unable to comprehend the third option Martin was suggesting, that she do what was best for her. Instead, she vacillated between being a good mother by her family of origin's definition or doing the opposite and continuing on her career path as it was before she became a mother.

The search for fault and blame similarly dooms partners to becoming stuck in the problem. Not only does the search for fault and blame preclude a focus on solutions by miring partners in a search for individual fault and blame, it also ignores the systemic factors that contribute to the problem and its maintenance. Experience suggests that people are so accustomed to finding fault and ascribing blame that they will argue with their couple therapist about the utility of addressing anything else until the question of fault is resolved and often times an apology tendered.

Outdated role prescriptions limit flexibility and isolate couples who do not fit easily into the dominant cultural model. Dominant culture includes agreed-upon ideas, values, beliefs, knowledge, norms, and customs that reflect the viewpoint of those in power. In the United States at the time of this writing, the dominant cultural view of couples remained white, heterosexual, cis-gendered, married, and monogamous, with each partner being similar in terms of demographics such as age and religion, and the family of procreation able to live on the male's income so that the female could be at home during the couple's childrearing years. While the majority of couples do not fit this prescribed model, those with power to determine cultural norms do (Basirico, Cashion, & Eshleman, 2014). While Liz and Martin fit the dominant cultural model in terms of being married, monogamous, cis-gendered, and of similar age and socioeconomic background, they deviated from it in that Martin was black, Liz was bisexual, and together they were a biracial couple. The impact, in terms of dominant cultural prescriptions and how they might influence Martin and Liz's experiences, as well as the meanings they attach to them, will be discussed in detail in Chapter 9.

Narrative Couple Therapy

Narrative couple therapy is a perspective grounded in post-modern theory. Narrative therapies, whether individual, couple, or family, originated in the work of White and Epston (1990).

Narratives are stories. Cultural narratives are socially constructed and agreed-upon stories that reflect dominant cultural norms and standards. In the second decade of the twenty-first century in the United States, cultural narratives reflect white, male, Christian, heterosexual, cis-gendered, middle-aged, upper-middle and upper income, well-educated discourse. They are not universally applicable, although those who live in the early twenty-first century United States perceive them as such. The result is that those individuals, couples, and groups for whom the dominant cultural narrative does not fit are marginalized and often demeaned.

Cultural narratives influence and limit personal narratives. For example, Liz's cultural narrative about gender roles was antithetical to her personal wishes and as a result her personal narrative about mothering was laden with self-doubt and self-criticism. Martin's personal narrative was also influenced by the cultural narrative about race. As a result, his personal narrative included self-doubt about his professional value apart from being black. Liz and Martin's couple narrative was likely influenced by the dominant discourse about being a good mother, a good provider, and good partners.

Stop and Think:

Be sure to include your responses in your journal.

1. Think about your story about yourself and then write a few paragraphs or pages about it.
2. How has your narrative been influenced by the culture in which you were raised?
3. How has your narrative been impacted by the dominant culture?

There are four premises underlying the narrative couple therapy approach. First, narrative couple therapy presumes that meaning is constructed, or derived, from experience. As a result, narrative couple therapists focus on meaning, rather than the behavior, cognitions, or emotions attending experience.

A second premise of narrative couple therapy is that experience can be interpreted in multiple ways. As a result, individuals and couples can make choices about how they interpret their experience of their relationships. While the partners may not be aware that options exist, the narrative couple therapist can guide them to awareness of alternative interpretations in order to effect change.

A third premise of narrative couple therapy is that language conveys a story. The story is the partners' narrative about themselves as a couple. Narrative couple therapists ask couple clients to make their implicit story explicit and then locate the problem in the narrative, rather than in the partners. For example, from a narrative perspective Liz and Martin's problem was likely to be the meanings they attached to their story about themselves, rather than Liz's faulty mothering, Martin's fear of angering her, or their inability to solve problems effectively.

The fourth premise of narrative couple therapy is that the narrative becomes part of a feedback loop that influences subsequent interpretations and ascriptions of meaning to here-and-now experiences. In other words, the narrative maintains the problem. A narrative couple therapist disrupts the feedback loop by encouraging the couple to change the narrative to a more functional couple story.

Narrative couple therapists create a safe therapeutic space from which to work. After identifying the couple's current narrative, narrative couple therapists ask the partners to view the problem as residing in the narrative, rather than in themselves as individuals or as a couple. At the same time, they are asked to take responsibility for the impact of their narrative upon the identified problem in their relationship. Taking responsibility differs from blame; its purpose is to empower couples with the belief that if they created their narrative they can also change it. Narrative couple therapists then guide couples to develop alternative narratives that result in alternative outcomes. New narratives are dynamic, or changing, rather than mired in the language of a problem.

Narrative couple therapy is not a technique-driven approach. However, Freedman and Combs (2015) have identified overarching techniques of intervention.

Narrative couple therapists assess the couple's current situation, name the problem, and explore the couple's relationship with the problem. Once alternative narratives are constructed, they also assess, with the couple, the usefulness of these narratives.

Throughout the work, narrative couple therapists remain grounded in the here-and-now. They listen to the problem as external to the relationship and deconstruct what the couple presents in order to hear meanings, values, the couple's relationship to the problem, and alternatives that have roots within the current situation. They question the dominant cultural narratives when their impact upon the couple is not useful. They also expose gaps and contradictions in the couple's narrative to facilitate the partners questioning its utility.

Narrative couple therapists facilitate naming both the problem and the desired outcome of changing the couple's narrative. As new narratives emerge, they are told, witnessed, and circulated. What is often not apparent in writings about narrative couple therapy is that the narrative sustains the status quo, which, however unpleasant, is a familiar situation. Change may be perceived as a threat to the equilibrium of the couple system. Unless push-back against changing narratives is addressed, the emergence and consolidation of new narratives may be impeded.

Narrative couple therapists take a collaborative stance with couples, bringing knowledge and skills to the collaboration that the couple may not already possess. They take the position of not knowing, of discovering along with the couple what within a narrative may be useful while using their professional expertise to determine what is not.

Stop and Think:

Be sure to include your answers in your journal.

1. Think about a close relationship with which you are involved. It can be with a partner, good friend, or your parents or grandparents.
2. Now identify the narrative that maintains the relationship the way it is. Even if the narrative is not problematic, describe an alternative narrative about the relationship.

Liz's struggle with balancing her professional and mothering roles, most relevantly in the context of her interactions with Martin around the subject, was amenable to narrative couple therapy. The meanings she and Martin ascribed to mothering, to a woman with children working outside the home, and to partners' roles in one another's decision-making processes all derived from their experiences being raised by women who exemplified the dominant cultural model of mothers remaining at home with children. Liz and Martin also constructed meaning from their experience coming of age at a time when women pursued careers in addition to mothering. Their narratives were likely also affected by racial and gender issues. Whether Liz's bisexuality played a role in the pressure she brought upon them to assume traditional gender-based roles is unknown. Finally, Liz and Martin constructed meaning from their experience interacting with each other around Liz's decision about whether or not to work outside the home.

While there were multiple ways in which they might have interpreted their experiences, they chose the one they presented to their couple therapist. This interpretation was predicated upon Liz's narrative that while there were choices about how to balance mothering and a professional career, she was not free to choose one because of her mother's narrative. Martin's role in helping her resolve her resistance to this culturally prescribed meaning was viewed by both as a partner's job. However, Martin also viewed any opinion from him to mean he was taking over a decision that was not his to make and thus created tension with the dominant cultural role of husbands as authorities.

Liz and Martin's narrative involved an on-going conflict about what Liz "should" do about her career and whether and how Martin would participate in her decision. The word "should" reflects a subjective command that Liz both accepted and struggled to reject. Their couple narrative also included a degree of hopelessness about their relationship as a couple.

Their narrative became a feedback loop. Each time they attempted to talk about Liz's career decision, the meanings they ascribed to this new interaction were influenced by the meanings they had ascribed to prior unsatisfactory interactions around the same topic. Thus, the meaning of Martin's reluctance to influence Liz's decision may have begun for her as an unnecessary caution and then moved to an unwelcome inflexibility on his part and, by the time they presented for couple therapy, to lack of support. For Martin, the initial meaning ascribed to Liz's request for help may have been a consideration for the impact of her decision upon them as a couple and as parents, then moved on to an annoying demand and a refusal on her part to appreciate his wish to stay out of her way so that she could make a decision that was right for her.

COUPLE THERAPIST: So you both think that Martin is not being a supportive partner because he doesn't want to influence your decision, Liz, and hasn't found another way to support you other than saying he'll support whatever decision you make.

LIZ: He's really not being that nice.

MARTIN: I don't know what she wants me to do.

CT: What does it mean to you, Martin, when she asks you what you think?

MARTIN: That she's asking me to make a decision for her that I don't have to live with the consequences of.

LIZ: Yes you do, Martin.

CT: And, Liz, when he says he wants you to make your decision independently of his influence, what does that mean to you?

LIZ: That he doesn't want to deal with me.

CT: OK, so those two meanings are very different. I'm wondering what other meanings each of your experience with the other might have.

MARTIN: I'm not sure what you're asking.

CT: Liz?

LIZ: I don't know, either.

CT: I'm thinking there are already two meanings you might attach to your argument about whether Martin will offer input to your career decision, Liz. One is that he does not want to deal with you and a second is that you are asking him to make the decision for you. I'm thinking there are others, like you have different views of your roles as partners and maybe even about the relative importance of this decision for Liz as an individual and for you as a couple.

Note: The process of identifying alternative meanings brings the meanings that Liz and Martin have already ascribed into awareness for them and thus makes a piece of their implicit narrative explicit.

We will resume the session with a focus on the narrative.

CT: OK, so part of your narrative, or story, is that Liz tries very hard to engage Martin in dialogue about her career decision and Martin consistently refuses because he believes his input would be too influential on a decision that will impact Liz for many years to come. Because you each view his role so differently, you are left feeling that he does not support you, Liz, and confused about what she wants, Martin.

LIZ: Yeah, I guess. Sounds like I should appreciate Martin more than I do, though, and I don't like that view of myself.

CT: Well, the story could be that you disagree about Martin's role in the decision and because of that you have not yet appreciated his position and the caring behind it.

Note the use of the word "yet".

LIZ: I like that better.

CT: Martin?

MARTIN: Yes, I think that's pretty accurate. But I'm not sure what we do about it.

CT: One place to start is to remember when your argument begins, you are falling back onto a narrative that's familiar but not the only one possible. You can choose different meanings, like the one we just talked about, for your experience and re-author your story so that it works better for you.

Stop and Think:

Be sure to include your responses in your journal.

1. What resonated with you about narrative couple therapy?
2. If you were designing an approach to couple therapy based on the theories you have studied, what would you include from narrative couple therapy? Explain your answer. What would you exclude, again explaining your answer?

While space limits the depth into which this excerpt can go, it makes clear that in narrative couple therapy conceptualization and practice, the problem resides in the narrative that arose from meanings ascribed to experience. It does not reflect a problem in either partner or the couple. However, it does influence their interactions. By changing the meanings ascribed to experience and the narratives that arise from them and then feed back upon themselves, narrative couple therapists allow couples to resolve the problem narratives they brought to couple therapy.

Feminist Couple Therapy

Feminist couple therapy is based upon the premise that, as with race, the dominant cultural narrative reflects the male perspective, excludes and demeans the female perspective, and thus impacts couple relationships. The goal of feminist couple therapy is to expand the male perspective to include the female viewpoint and to allow couples to promote their own definitions of gender.

It is important to note the difference between sex and gender. Sex is a biological phenomenon in which the presence of a y-chromosome triggers certain hormonal events early in the gestation period. These events then influence subsequent brain and musculoskeletal development, the development of genitalia, and the development of secondary sex characteristics in puberty. While biological sex varies along a continuum, at least partially accounting for cis-gender, transgender, and non-binary gender identities, the complex relationships between biological sex and gender is beyond the scope of this textbook.

By contrast, gender is a social construct. As such, it is defined differently by different societies and by the same society at different points in time. In other words, the meaning of gender is derived from context and may not be the one-size-fits-all of the dominant cultural model.

Feminist theory, as applied to feminist therapy, suggests resistance and subversion as methods for redefining gender. Brown (1994, p. 25) explained:

> In feminist therapy, resistance means the refusal to merge with dominant cultural norms and to attend to one's own voice and integrity.... Each act of feminist therapy...must have as an implicit goal the uncovering of the presence of the patriarchy as a source of distress so that this influence of the dominant can be named, undermined, resisted, and subverted.... Awareness and transformation mean teaching of resistance, learning the ways in which each of us is damaged by our witting or unwitting participation in dominant norms or by the ways in which such norms have been thrust upon us.

Brown (1994) recommended a less politicized approach to practice, suggesting feminist couple therapists engage their couple clients in a process of questioning the cultural stereotypes that limit options for individuals. Questioning norms, values, roles, and stereotypes that prevent individuals, couples, and families from accessing the full range of options available to them increases options for change, a goal shared by a variety of couple therapies, and is therefore incumbent upon couple therapists, despite its political overtones and potential discomfort for said couple therapists.

Feminist couple therapy grew out of the work of feminist family therapists. Most notable of these were Peggy Papp, Olga Silverstein, Marianne Walters, and Betty Carter. All four were associated with the Women's Project in Family. The feminist family therapy approach held that traditional theories of family therapy perpetuated a model of male power that demeaned women. As an example, structural family therapists described a common triangle in which the mother was over-involved with the symptomatic child and the father disengaged; intervention involved bringing the father closer to the mother so that he could rescue the symptomatic child from her over-involvement. While structural family therapists (Minuchin, 1974) would interpret their work as a description of what they observed, the implications identified by feminist family therapists also apply and underscore the influence of dominant cultural stereotypes on couple therapy theory.

Feminist couple therapists, whether male or female, help couples increase their awareness of gender expectations and evaluate the impact of those upon their relationship. They do not promote a political or philosophical agenda, despite the theoretical literature, because ethical proscriptions prevent imposing the viewpoint of the couple therapist upon couples. Such imposition would risk discounting non-dominant cultural views of gender roles. Rather, feminist couple therapists encourage couple clients to explore options for changing the meaning ascribed to experience to include equal validity of the female perspective. As noted, feminist couple therapists note cultural differences in views of gender roles that may affect a particular couple in order to practice ethically with diverse populations.

Feminist couple therapy is premised upon three principles. First, feminist couple therapists avoid the assumption that individual choices are biologically based. Second, feminist couple therapists remain mindful that each partner's experience is determined at least in part by her or his gender experiences. Finally, feminist couple therapists adhere to the principle that partners may be helped by clarifying their assumptions about how each will fulfill roles, especially those associated with gender.

Knudson-Martin and Mahoney (2009) examined gender power in couples across the life cycle. They concluded that sociocultural barriers create couple distress by impeding efforts toward equal power in gender roles and that equality of gender roles was associated with what they termed relationship success. To the extent that husband stonewalling, or withdrawal from interactions, is a form of gender power inequality, Gottman and Silver's (1999) observation that marriages in which the husbands stonewall and are not responsive to their wives' attempts to engage them are more likely to end in divorce tangentially supports the importance of gender power equality.

Stop and Think:

Be sure to include your responses in your journal.

1. Describe your intellectual and emotional reaction to the politicization of feminist couple therapy theory. What resonated with you? What concerned you? Explain your answers.
2. Describe your beliefs about gender roles in heterosexual relationships. Then describe your beliefs about gender roles in same-sexed relationships. How might these beliefs apply to work with couples in which one or both partners' gender identity or appearance does not match these beliefs?
3. Do you think stonewalling, a phenomenon observed primarily in cis-gendered males, is a form of power? If so, what might alter the power balance? Explain your answers.

Liz's role dilemma and its manifestation in her relationship with Martin might benefit from a feminist couple therapy perspective. In the dominant cultural model, men work outside the home to provide for the financial and status needs of the family, while women care for home, children, and the emotional needs of the family. Although gender roles have become more egalitarian in recent decades, research suggests that even when the woman in a heterosexual couple works outside the home she more often than not assumes an inordinate share of home and child care. Like the writer, Liz's ultimate decision was to work part time while raising her children, thus limiting her career and taking over the majority of the home and child care. Martin wanted to be involved with his children and was an engaged father and husband. However, because of the difference in time each of their jobs consumed, they agreed to an unequal division of household and child care responsibilities.

COUPLE THERAPIST: I'm confused, and so I wonder whether you are, too. You both embrace the changes in the definition of a mother's role, and Martin, it sounds like you want to work it out so that Liz can return to work full time if she wishes or stay home full time or continue to work part time.

MARTIN: Correct.

CT: But it sounds like the old gender roles and your mother's attachment to them make it difficult for you to decide what to do.

LIZ: Absolutely. My mom is so convinced she's right, and of course several of my friends have left their careers because they want to be at home with their children. Makes me feel like there's something wrong with me, or missing in me.

CT: Well, you don't completely fit the cultural stereotype for women. I'm wondering whether that's a bad thing.

LIZ: No. Absolutely not. At least that's what I believe. And I don't want to be like my mother.

CT: And yet sometimes you sound like it's a bad thing, like when you said maybe there was something the matter with you that you didn't want to be home full time.

LIZ: Yeah, I see what you mean. But what about Martin?

CT: Yes. Since your mother also stayed home, Martin, I imagine you are also affected by the cultural stereotypes for women.

Note: The feminist couple therapist used Liz's attempt to shift focus to Martin as an opportunity to talk about the impact of gender role stereotypes and Liz's ambivalence about them on their relationship.

MARTIN: Yeah, but more of my friends' mothers had to work. And mine did, too, from time to time.

CT: Of course. I was thinking that when mothers choose to work outside the home they fly in the face of the dominant cultural model for women, whereas when mothers have to work outside the home it's somehow more acceptable. But maybe not to the mothers themselves? I apologize for not considering the confluence of race and economics in this country.

Note: The therapist, being white and middle class, had the privilege of choice, as did Liz. Whether she had caught herself assuming the privilege was universal or not, Martin likely would have noticed. Given that no couple therapist is perfect, acknowledging her privilege and its impact on her intervention was intended to mitigate its potentially negative impact on her therapeutic relationship with Martin.

MARTIN: It's OK.

CT: [Nods] For the two of you, I think it's important to bear in mind that some of the pressure is external and that that pressure sometimes screams louder than what you want. It's difficult to tease out what you want from what you think you should want, and we can work some more on that, maybe write the story of what you think you should want and then re-author it in the places you'd like to change it. For the two of you as a couple, I think it's very important to examine the impact of cultural expectations on your relationship, so you can get them out of your discussions.

Note: The couple therapist used the post-modern framework common to narrative and feminist couple therapies and borrowed a specific technique from the former to apply to the latter. Like all post-modern theories, feminist couple therapy emphasizes changed meanings as the key to resolving couples' presenting problems.

Solution-Focused Couple Therapy

The term solution in solution-focused couple therapy refers to meanings. Like other post-modern theorists, solution-focused couple therapists intervene to collaboratively change the meaning partners ascribe to their couple experience and then create new meanings. Solution-focused couple therapy adds the specific goal of increasing the frequency with which the problem does not happen. Solution-focused couple therapists also target identification and utilization of the couple's strengths during the therapeutic process. Like most post-modern theories of therapy, solution-focused couple therapy entails a collaboration between the couple and the couple therapist. Unlike narrative and feminist couple therapies, however, solution-focused couple therapy extends beyond theory into the specifics of practice (Hoyt, 2015).

Solution-focused brief therapy, which preceded solution-focused couple therapy, entails a brief intervention on a particular problem. The solution in this older approach emerges from the hypothetical situation in which the problem is miraculously solved. Couple therapists ask the partners what they imagine would be different without the problem and how they would know the problem was resolved. If you are interested in learning more about solution-focused brief therapy, DeShazer's (1988) book is referenced at the end of this chapter.

The earlier brief approach to solution-focused couple therapy, like the brief strategic couple therapy described below, focused solely on the presenting problem. That change would be positive and permanent was not considered. By contrast, solution-focused couple therapy uses language to empower couples to construct useful solutions to their problems and to attach useful meanings to their experiences as couples that will have repercussions throughout their relationship.

Solution-focused couple therapy theory identifies as post-modern, and practitioners are willing to sacrifice brevity for the constructions they advocate. Like narrative couple therapy, solution-focused couple therapy joins the couple where it is, exploring the partners' hopes and aspirations for their relationship. The clients' experience is given primacy, and techniques are client-centered during solution development.

Assessment includes the use of DeShazer's (1988) "miracle question" and questions aimed at learning about the couple's relationship history and their here-and-now experience. Follow-up to the "miracle question" includes asking what each partner would do in response to the other changing in the way he or she would like. Solution-focused couple therapists also ask the couple about the times the problem is not present in their lives.

Stop and Think:

Be sure to include your responses in your journal.

1. People tend to imagine that the outcome of a desired change will be positive, but sometimes there are unintended consequences. Think about a time you wanted something to change and it did. What did you find positive about the change? What, if anything, surprised you by being less than you had hoped?
2. Think about someone to whom you are close. Now think about something that you would like the person to change. Asking yourself DeShazer's miracle question, imagine that you woke up one morning and the person had changed in the way you would want. What might that be like for you? Be sure to include how you think it would help and how it might be less than you imagine.

Solution-focused couple therapists attend to how each partner views the couple's functioning, with strengths and resiliency as resources for change underscored by the couple therapist. If a couple can identify what skills and resources they use when the problem is not present in their here-and-now experience, they can begin to use those resources to address the problem when it occurs.

Solution-focused couple therapists also facilitate each partner's awareness of her or his own power, or agency, in the relationship. Solution-focused couple therapists validate emotional experience and ask how each partner contributes to the couple's strength and resiliency. Partners are asked to assign a numerical value to their hope, motivation, and progress in couple therapy.

Techniques of solution-focused couple therapy include interrupting "problem talk" in order to avoid feedback loops that exacerbate the problem. Strategizing about solutions that will reduce the frequency and impact of the problem is very different than using language that suggests the relationship is problematic. This distinction of meaning is crucial in all post-modern theories of couple therapy.

At some point during each couple therapy session, solution-focused couple therapists leave the room for a brief period to consult with a team, if available, or to organize their thoughts if they are working alone. When the couple therapist returns to the session, he or she first compliments the couple on the work they have done in the session, highlighting the positive contributions of both partners to improving the relationship. He or she then describes the competing views of the solution and goes on to work collaboratively with the partners to negotiate a workable solution for them as a couple. Upon termination, or ending of the clinical work, the solution-focused couple therapist asks the partners specific questions about their satisfaction with the process. These questions are framed in a positive, non-problematic way and at the same time are sufficiently open-ended to allow for areas of dissatisfaction.

We join Liz and Martin about 35 minutes into a couple therapy session with a solution-focused orientation.

LIZ: He just blows me off. He says "do whatever you want" and thinks that's communication.

COUPLE THERAPIST: So when Martin says, "Do whatever you want," you view him as unwilling to talk about it.

LIZ: Yes.

CT: How could he phrase it so that you knew he was willing to talk about it?

LIZ: He'd say [pause], he'd say [pause], I don't know, it doesn't mean anything if he's just parroting what I tell him to do.

CT: It would be helpful to know how he could convey to you a willingness to discuss your decision.

Note: Rather than talking about the problem, which is the meaning Liz attached to Martin's words, CT kept the focus on a possible solution.

LIZ: He could ask me.

CT: Terrific. What would he ask you?

LIZ: Maybe what I want to do, or what I think are the pros and cons of my options.

CT: OK. Martin, she's given you a possible solution. It's fine to rephrase it, to use your own words.

MARTIN: You want me to ask her now?

CT: Sure.

MARTIN: Liz, what are your options? I want to support whatever you decide, and I know that you want to talk it through with me.

LIZ: I don't know. That's the problem.

MARTIN: Is that why you've been asking for my help?

LIZ: Yes, partly. I also think you should have a say in what I do.

MARTIN: But it's your career.

LIZ: But it affects you. And us as a family.

CT: Let's take a break here. I'll leave you two and be back in 5 or 10 minutes. [Exits]

For illustrative purposes, the session occurred in an academic setting with a consulting team of four trainees and a faculty member observing through a one-way mirror. Liz and Martin had given consent and were aware of being observed. During the break, CT and the team shifted their attention back and forth between observing Liz and Martin's conversation about what happened during the session and talking about the team's observations, assessments, and recommendations. Team members were skeptical about how easily Martin responded to Liz's request, hypothesizing that he could have been withholding what Liz wanted in service of a homeostatic mechanism in their relationship and that the burden might now shift to Liz to maintain homeostasis. They speculated about how she might return them to homeostasis, including magical thinking that talking would produce a solution about which she was not ambivalent, whereas the entire dilemma was fraught with ambivalence and therefore no such solution would be found.

CT: The team and I were talking about what just happened in the session, and we all wanted you to know we were impressed with how you asked, Liz, and how you responded, Martin. You did just about everything we've been talking about you both wanting. And you both communicated clearly and the other listened uncritically.

MARTIN: Yeah, something about what you both said made me realize that's what she's wanted all along.

CT: So I'm curious, Liz. If Martin continues to respond this way at home, what will change?

LIZ: Well, we'll talk without fighting.

CT: You won't fight about whether Martin wants to talk about your career decision. But what about what happens when you talk about it?

LIZ: We'll figure it out.

CT: I am confident you will. I continue to wonder about how. You've been wanting this for a long time. Now that you have it, how will it make a difference?

LIZ: I guess we'll see how the conversation unfolds.

CT: OK. I'd like you to think more specifically about what you expect to change. We don't have time to continue today, but let's begin there next time.

Stop and Think:

Be sure to include your answers in your journal.

1. What did you find compelling about the application of solution-focused couple therapy to Liz and Martin's couple dilemma?
2. What were your concerns about the solution-focused couple therapist's approach?

Post-Modern Correlates of Systemic Couple Therapy Theories

Two uniquely systemic family therapy theories arose during the second half of the last century: Minuchin's (1974) structural family therapy and Haley's (Haley, 1963; Madanes, 1981) strategic family therapy. These theories viewed the presenting problem as residing in the family and intervened exclusively on the level of the family system as a whole. Couples were viewed as subsystems from both structural and strategic perspectives, although they received more attention in the former as a critical point of intervention for restructuring the family. These theories were adapted for couple therapy by post-modern theorists.

Structural Couple Therapy

Structural couple therapy focuses on three aspects of the couple system: the boundaries around it, the internal differentiation within it, and the resources available to it. Boundaries reflect couple rules that emerge from repeated interactions and symbolize how partners manage the physical and emotional distance between themselves and between them as a couple and other family and non-family systems (Esposito & Hattem, 2017, pp. 110–111). Most couples arrive at a distance that is comfortable for the couple system, though not necessarily for the partners as individuals, as described in the subsection on distance regulation in Chapter 4.

Boundaries vary along a continuum from diffuse to rigid. Diffuse boundaries are permeable, or easily penetrable. Couples with diffuse boundaries appear unclear as to where one partner stops emotionally and physically and the other begins. Diffuse boundaries result in enmeshed relationships, where partners speak for one another and assume the other does not have needs independent of their own. Partners in enmeshed relationships may appear to be very close to one another and care deeply about each other. However, without recognition of the partner as a separate person with her or his own identity, thoughts, emotions, meanings, and desires; partners in enmeshed relationships are unable to truly view, empathize, or accept each other. By contrast, rigid boundaries are impermeable, or impenetrable, and result in disengaged relationships. Partners both appear and are disconnected emotionally and physically from one another. Structural couple therapists promote clear boundaries—a concept that suggests boundaries that lie somewhere between diffuse and rigid—so that partners are able to connect meaningfully without subsuming their individuality, are associated with healthier couple system functioning.

Internal differentiation refers to each partner's individual development of self and the couple's identity as a functioning system. Internally differentiated partners are able to see, share, empathize, and accept themselves and each other. Couple differentiation involves a stable sense of the couple as a system. Liz and Martin evidenced internal differentiation by shifting their primary allegiance from their families of origin to each other and by creating a stable, if distressed, couple system prior to introducing children into their family.

Resources are monetary, instrumental (task-related), and emotional supports external to the couple. For example, there is no one in Liz and Martin's extended families who is available to provide regular child care. However, Liz and Martin have the financial resources to purchase the child care they need. As described in Chapter 1, they have a sufficient social network for it to be considered a resource.

The practice of structural couple therapy involves assessment and intervention. Structural couple therapists assess the boundaries around and differentiation within the couple system, feedback loops, subsystem rules, and partners' expectations through observing interactions during couple therapy sessions.

The three goals of intervention are (1) to replace those aspects of the structure of the relationship that prevent the changes necessary to resolve the presenting problem; (2) to enact new ways to relate that strengthen boundaries and internal differentiation; and (3) to reframe the presenting problem so that the solution becomes clear to the couple. The three stages of couple therapy include (1) creating a therapeutic alliance; (2) destabilizing the dysfunctional structure; and (3) nurturing positive changes that create a more functional structure. The role of the structural couple therapist is to direct interventions.

Structural couple therapy, like structural family therapy, may appear vague (Simon, 2015) and judgmental (Esposito & Hattem, 2017). As with any theory and resultant approach to couple work, the areas in which it can be critiqued are more than counterbalanced by its demonstrated effectiveness with couples and families.

LIZ: My mother never lets up. And now she's got Barbara calling me saying, "Now that you have two children you really need to stop working. If you don't, you're going to regret it when they're older and it's too late. And you'll have nobody but yourself to blame." She sounds just like my mother. And Martin hates it, because I get really upset and he can't figure out what's going on with me.

COUPLE THERAPIST: It's almost as though your mother becomes part of your marriage when she or Barbara tells you how you and Martin should be raising your children.

Note: Liz spoke for Martin, describing feelings of his that she would have no knowledge of unless he expressed them. This is a sign of enmeshment, and would lead to a structural therapist asking to hear how he feels from Martin. However, CT could not address both boundary issues simultaneously.

LIZ: Yes, it is. [Pause] I never thought about it that way before.

CT: How can the two of you together keep Sally and Barbara out of your marital decision space?

This intervention was aimed at restructuring Liz and Martin's couple system by removing members of her family of origin from it and returning them to their place in the larger family system of which Liz and Martin as a couple were a subsystem, or part. The goal of this restructuring was to strengthen Liz and Martin's couple boundary. The intervention led to an enactment, or practice, as the session unfolded. For reasons of space and repetitiveness, we turn now to the other post-modern systemic theory of couple therapy.

Brief Strategic Couple Therapy

The goal of brief strategic couple therapy, like that of its precursor, brief problem-focused couple therapy, is to resolve the presenting problem as quickly as possible. Prevention of the recurrence of the presenting problem or a new, related problem is not considered. While the brevity is attractive in terms of client commitment and third-party reimbursement, theoretical and ethical concerns about ignoring the potential for relapse of symptoms or development of new ones stop some couple therapists from using this approach.

Brief strategic couple therapists accomplish their goal by disrupting feedback loops, more recently termed ironic processes (Rohrbaugh &

Shohan, 2015). Feedback loops are considered an adaptation to symptoms that paradoxically, or ironically, maintain them. The concept of feedback loops, upon which strategic theory was based, and their role in maintaining the problem were described in Chapter 4. One of Haley's favorite techniques was to prescribe the symptom, in other words ask the couple to do more of the same, based on the assumption that the feedback loop would spiral the system out of equilibrium and the couple would of necessity develop new mechanisms for coping (i.e., second-order change). These new mechanisms were assumed to be more functional than the old, although some couple therapists question the assumption that any change is more functional.

The practice of brief strategic couple therapy begins by defining the problem with as much specificity as possible, including the partners' perspectives about it. The couple and couple therapist then explore additional solutions and identify those situations in which partners do more of the same to create a problem-solution loop. Using the partners' views of themselves and their relationship, brief strategic couple therapists frame interventions aimed at partners doing less of the same. Specific interventions arise from specific complaints, though all are predicated on the concept of disrupting feedback loops and preventing use of established homeostatic mechanisms.

Stop and Think:

Be sure to include your answers in your journal.

1 Is all change, by definition, for the better? Why? Why not?
2 What are the potential risks and benefits of disrupting ironic processes and blocking the use of familiar homeostatic mechanisms and then assuming the couple will discover a more functional homeostatic mechanism?

The role of the brief strategic couple therapist is to persuade the partners to do less of the same through indirect control. The brief strategic couple therapist puts himself or herself in a one-down position from the partners and advises them to go slowly as a paradoxical intervention.

Strategic family therapy was also predicated on the power of the therapist (Haley, 1963).

Like solution-focused couple therapists, strategic family and later strategic couple therapists often worked in teams. In academic or training centers, these teams consisted of trainees and colleagues who observed a portion of the couple therapy session and then, during a break, met with the couple therapist to share their observations and ideas. Partners would also be seen separately, in order to obtain a more complete view of how each viewed himself or herself and their relationship. As mentioned elsewhere, seeing partners individually risks becoming part of a relationship triangle that subverts both trust in the couple therapist and in the process of couple therapy.

Liz and Martin's presenting problem entailed a feedback loop, or ironic process, of escalating tension around who would make Liz's decision about balancing career and mothering and how it would be made. When the tension became sufficiently high to threaten the couple system's equilibrium, they employed the ironic process of ending their interaction without resolution and with an overlay of resentment. Re-engaging in the same argument in the same way exemplified a first-order change, namely doing more of the same.

COUPLE THERAPIST: Martin, I think you should start bringing up Liz's career decision, maybe every night till the two of you get it resolved.

Note: When a couple therapist prescribes the symptom, he or she risks compliance. Ethically, the couple therapist must consider the risks if the couple agrees. CT decided the risks were minimal by comparison to the potential benefits.

MARTIN: What?

CT: I think you should bring up Liz's career every night.

MARTIN: I don't get it.

CT: Well, you two haven't resolved her problem when she's brought it up. So I think you should take a turn and maybe talk about it even more.

MARTIN: I really don't get how that's going to help.

LIZ: I don't, either.

CT: Look, you asked me to help you. I don't know everything, I could be wrong. What I hear is that you want to find a way to resolve this problem and what you're doing isn't working. So I say, do more.

Note: The brief strategic couple therapist assumed that Liz and Martin would either resist or become so exhausted with getting nowhere that they would find an alternative way to resolve their identified problem. In either case, the ironic process, or feedback loop, would be disrupted and change would be presumed to result.

Post-Modern Correlates of Psychodynamic Couple Therapy: Emotionally Focused Couple Therapy

Leslie Greenberg with his colleague and successor Susan Johnson described emotionally focused couple therapy (EFCT) as an integration of psychodynamic, experiential, systems, and narrative approaches to couple therapies. Emotionally focused couple therapy is systemic and post-modern in that it emphasizes the creation and maintenance of emotional experience and associated meaning by the couple system. It is psychodynamic in its use of attachment theory to explain emotional needs and how they are experienced and enacted in couple relationships (Greenberg & Johnson, 1988; Johnson & Greenberg, 1995).

Johnson (2015) pointed out three benefits of emotionally focused couple therapy in the current practice of couple therapy. First, by focusing on a couple's unique experience, emotionally focused couple therapy allows for diversity, whether cultural or individual. Second, emotionally focused couple therapy supports feminist approaches by defining attachment needs as normal, rather than a pathological phenomena found primarily in women. Finally, by defining itself as both integrative and brief, emotionally focused couple therapy fits the current theoretical and managed care environment.

Emotionally focused couple therapy views couple distress as the result of an insecure attachment between partners and their resulting anxiety about the durability of the relationship, also called separation anxiety. It provides an application of Bowlby's attachment theory (Bowlby, 1969; Bowlby & Schore, 1973) to couples. Bowlby and his colleagues described attachment as beginning in infancy, when a primary caretaker was essential to an infant's survival and abandonment by this caretaker tantamount to annihilation. The effects of attachment needs and abandonment fears formulated in infancy on development were also described by these writers. The premise that a secure attachment is essential to a couple's relationship is thus linked to the psychodynamic perspective.

Emotionally focused couple therapists view the needs for connection and importance to another human being as normal and healthy (Greenberg & Johnson, 1988; Johnson, 2015). The dominant cultural narrative frames attachment as, in some way, regressive and unhealthy. "Needy," "dependent," "clingy," "insecure" are all derogatory words applied to emotional responses that tend to occur when attachments feel insecure and thus arise from the insecure attachment, rather than the individual partner(s).

Stop and Think:

Be sure to include your responses in your journal.

1. Describe your reaction to the idea that it is acceptable and even desirable to need a secure attachment to a partner?
2. What negative and positive connotations do you attribute to this notion and your reaction?
3. What is it like for you, or what do you think it might be like for you, to come home to someone who is genuinely happy to see you and cares more than anyone else in the world about how you are?
4. How does or might that knowledge, when secure, help you during the times you are not with your partner? How might that knowledge, when insecure, disrupt you?

Many of us have learned from the cultural narrative to deny or reject the need we have to feel securely connected to another person for one aspect of our sense of well-being and importance. Women and men both tend to judge their need for a secure attachment negatively, irrespective of their self-efficacy outside the relationship. The dominant cultural narrative encourages men to deny their need for a secure attachment, to be independent, and to resist entrapment in a relationship; male dependency is thus marginalized and negatively sanctioned. The dominant cultural narrative also encourages women to hide their need for a secure attachment by being flirtatious, seductive, or otherwise indirect as they attempt to get this need met. Despite attitude shifts in a significant segment of the population, the dominant cultural narrative continues to view real men as seeking as much uncommitted sex with as many women as possible; while women are charged with withholding sex in exchange for commitment, however insecure the attachment may be.

Emotionally focused couple therapy views couple distress and conflict as a "struggle for separateness and connectedness" (Greenberg & Johnson, 1988, p. 19). Adult partners must balance their need for individual identity with their need for security, or continuity, with a significant other in the couple relationship equivalent of Schopenhauer's porcupines (Luepnitz, 2002). As couples create this balance between dependence and independence, both partners must also allow themselves to be vulnerable by revealing who they truly are to the other. Following such revelations, partners must also accept the other for who she or he is. Vulnerability and acceptance are the underpinnings of a durable attachment.

Emotionally focused couple therapists facilitate increased vulnerability by asking what each partner sees in the other, what meaning each ascribes to these observations, and how each is affected emotionally and behaviorally by what she or he sees. Trust, foundational to a secure attachment and freedom from the fear of loss, or abandonment, is associated with each partner ascribing positive meanings to the other's behavior. Emotionally focused couple therapists reframe meanings ascribed by one partner to the other in a more positive light and facilitate enactments that allow partners to experience one another in a more positive way. Note that the post-modern emphasis on meaning is accessed in emotionally focused couple therapy through emotional experiences, thus linking it to the foundational experiential couple therapies.

Emotionally focused couple therapy theory also posits that partners test their core beliefs about themselves in relationship with their partners. While the concept of core belief addresses meaning, its cognitive-behavioral correlate is the concept of schemata. In distressed relationships, beliefs about oneself may be catastrophic, putting pressure on the partner to disconfirm them. For example, Liz believed she was ugly and fat and that wanting to return to her career meant she was a bad mother. She asked Martin repeatedly to disconfirm these catastrophic core beliefs about herself. However, both the manner in which she asked and the way in which he heard her requests left him confused and as a result his attempts to disconfirm her catastrophic thoughts were received by Liz as invalidating and uncaring. Like most people who find their negative core beliefs about themselves discounted, rather than disconfirmed, by their intimate partners, Liz continued to test them. An emotionally focused couple therapist would intervene to coach both partners toward more effective self-revelation as well as disconfirmation of the other's negative core beliefs, by first making self-revelation and disconfirmation of her negative core beliefs explicit and then coaching both Liz's delivery and Martin's response.

The goal of emotionally focused couple therapy practice is to use emotional experience and expression to evoke and create new emotional and interactional experiences and thus change couple dynamics. Emotional experience is also used to assess interpersonal, or relationship dynamics.

The practice of emotionally focused couple therapy is grounded in four principles. First, it is assumed that the past is evoked in the present when the partners' ability to attach and respond to one another becomes blocked. When conflict loomed between Liz and Martin, each was hampered by past experiences and negative core beliefs about appearance and anger. As a result, neither was able to demonstrate a secure attachment to the other through self-revelation and disconfirmation of these negative beliefs and as a result both felt insecure about their bond.

A second principle of emotionally focused couple therapy is that vulnerability and empathetic responses to it, both of which are essential to a secure attachment, are impacted by emotional experience. As a result, emotionally focused couple therapists evoke and assess partners' primary emotional responses to one another.

A third principle of emotionally focused couple therapy involves attending to interactive process, or couple dynamics, rather than the content of the problem. This is the systemic component of emotionally focused couple therapy.

The fourth principle of emotionally focused couple therapy is that emotionally focused couple therapists restructure interactions using evoked emotional experience as a motivator. In this way, they create new attachment experiences for the couple.

Emotionally focused couple therapists begin by creating a safe and collaborative therapeutic environment. They build alliances, assess emotional experience and interaction cycles, and develop a contract regarding the goals of couple therapy collaboratively with the couple. Emotionally focused couple therapists then restructure couple interactions to create new emotional experiences that ensure a secure attachment bond. By amplifying normal fluctuations in emotions and interactions, emotionally focused couple therapists create the new while maintaining coherence, rather than simply disrupting previous dynamics. They coach partners to reveal and respond to one another's vulnerabilities in new ways aimed at increasing attachment security. As is evident, the role of the emotionally focused couple therapy couple therapist is collaborative and empathetic.

Like narrative couple therapists, emotionally focused couple therapists consider the meanings partners ascribe to their own and to the other's behaviors and emotional responses. Throughout the process of intervention, emotionally focused couple therapists target emotions to change meanings ascribed to the other and through these changed meanings alter the couple's dynamics. They identify sequences of behaviors and emotions and then explore the meaning underlying these sequences. They reframe and redefine the problem as involving the emotional bond that the couple has already recognized to be dysfunctional. They thus externalize the problem in the narrative sense.

The following excerpt is, like the others in this chapter, about Liz's career decision. The intervention in this excerpt, however, is based on the principles and practices of emotionally focused couple therapy.

COUPLE THERAPIST: Martin, when Liz asks you to help her decide whether and how much to work outside the home, what happens for you?

MARTIN: I don't know. I just think it's her career and I shouldn't intrude.

CT: And yet she's asking you to intrude.

MARTIN: I disagree.

CT: So you don't agree she's asking you to intrude?

MARTIN: Oh, yeah, she's asking. I don't think I should, just because she's asking.

CT: What's happening inside you right now?

MARTIN: I don't know. I'd really like to leave.

CT: Sounds like you feel trapped. You want to flee, and yet you're here.

MARTIN: I don't want to deal with this.

LIZ: See, I said he didn't want to deal with me.

CT: Liz, tell Martin when he wants to flee, it feels to you that it's you he wants to get away from.

LIZ: Well, don't you?

MARTIN: It's not you. It's this conversation. She's right I feel trapped. You want something, and I want to be a good husband and give you what you want. But I don't want to hurt you. And I don't want you to do something you don't want to do because of something I said.

LIZ: Don't you think I can think for myself? I just want your damn input.

CT: Liz, Martin just told you about a feeling he has. I want to come back to you in a moment, but first I'd like to explore more about what's going on with Martin that he reacts to your question in a way that feels so frustrating.

LIZ: Sure, fine.

CT: Martin, you said in an earlier session that Lynette [Martin's older sister] thinks she's always right, even when she's not, and when you were little if you said or did something she didn't like she'd say you were dumb and hit or pinch you and then call you a crybaby if you cried. And that you felt angry and stupid when that happened. And I wonder whether you feel any of those things when Liz asks you to tell her what you think she should do?

MARTIN: Probably. Yeah. It was so discouraging with Lynette.

CT: And did you want to get away?

MARTIN: Oh, I did.

CT: Liz, can you respond to what Martin just said about himself before we turn to what it does to you?

LIZ: Sure. No, I guess I don't get it.

CT: That when you ask him what he thinks about your career options, he feels some of what he felt growing up, that if he says what you don't want to hear you'll get angry and call him names, maybe even hurt him.

LIZ: Have I ever hurt anybody? Really, Martin.

MARTIN: You can be pretty sure of yourself, Liz, and you've got a lawyer's way with words.

LIZ: That's different.

MARTIN: Yes and no.

CT: Liz, what happened for you when Martin was talking about his sister and how he felt about her?

LIZ: The usual. I wanted to tell her to get over her self-righteousness and bossiness. She can be very sweet and loving, and so controlling and bossy. All at the same time.

CT: But what about her doing it to Martin when he was a child? Tell me about your reaction when Martin described being a child on the receiving end of it.

LIZ: Oh. I wanted to...tell her to back off.

CT: What's the feeling?

LIZ: Anger.

CT: You're angry at her.

LIZ: Yes.

CT: And Martin?

LIZ: I want to hug him.

CT: What's the feeling that comes with the doing?

LIZ: Love, sad for him. I want to tell him it will be OK.

CT: I think it would be helpful if you told him that now.

LIZ: It will be OK.

CT: [To Liz] "Martin, when you were describing Lynette, I felt..."

LIZ: When you were describing Lynette, I felt sad and angry.

MARTIN: [Nods]

CT: When you two skip that step, the step of showing yourselves to one another and empathizing, it just bounces back and forth between your pain. So instead of feeling the connection you're feeling now, you feel the opposite, disconnected and alone even though you're with each other. [Pause] When you feel connected, Liz, it may feel safer to tell Martin what you want from him and about the part of you that's scared of making the "wrong" decision.

LIZ: I want reassurance.

CT: Say more.

LIZ: I want to know you won't be mad at me.

CT: You're afraid he'll be mad at you. I imagine you're also afraid you'll be mad at you.

LIZ: Yeah, that, too.

CT: Sounds like you want him to assure you he won't be mad.

LIZ: Yes.

CT: How can he assure you you don't have to be mad at yourself?

LIZ: [Pause] I guess he can't. But he can tell me he won't make it worse, that he'll love me even if I screw up.

CT: You're afraid he won't love you if you make the wrong decision?

LIZ: [Nods]

CT: Martin?

MARTIN: Of course I'd still love you. I'd be upset for you, but I wouldn't stop loving you.

CT: Upset for her? Not with her?

MARTIN: No, I mean yes, not with her. [Pause. To Liz] Is that really all you want?

LIZ: [Softly] Yes.

MARTIN: Wow, that's not what I thought at all.

CT: Tell Liz what you thought she wanted.

MARTIN: I thought you wanted me to decide for you.

LIZ: [Smiles] Well, that'd be nice, too. But, no, I want to know you won't be mad. And I would still like to know what you think. It would help me because you might think of something I didn't.

Note: This is an example of disconfirmation for a core belief.

CT: Before we go on to that important conversation, I'm curious what you made of Liz wanting you to make her decision for her, Martin, when you thought that's what she wanted.

MARTIN: I thought she was trying to get me to do the heavy lifting for her.

CT: Sounds like you didn't like that.

MARTIN: No. It felt inappropriate, because her career is hers. And like a trap.

CT: Liz?

LIZ: Well, that explains a lot.

CT: Can you elaborate?

LIZ: Yeah. I felt put down the way he refused to talk through my decision with me.

CT: And alone?

LIZ: Yes. Abandoned, as you would say. [Smiles]

CT: When the two of you talk through the decision, it's important that you share what you're feeling and hearing, like you did just now. Because you'll recognize each other's feelings and respond to them anyway, and clarifying them for each other will help avoid misunderstandings that lead to either or both of you feeling dismissed.

LIZ: OK. How do we do that?

CT: We've just done some of it. Why don't you and Martin begin a conversation in the time we have left, and I'll intervene to coach you if I think it'd help.

LIZ: OK. I don't know what to do, Martin.

CT: Liz, when you think of yourself staying home full time with your children, what happens?

LIZ: I think it's a good idea, best for the kids.

CT: And yet when you talk about your mother, you say you don't want to be like her. I suspect when you think about staying home full time some glimmer of her emerges.

LIZ: Well, of course. I don't want to be her.

CT: What do you want?

LIZ: I don't know.

CT: When you think about working full time, what happens?

LIZ: I think I'd be a bad mother.

CT: What about for you? Maybe ask yourself whether you'd enjoy it.

LIZ: Oh. For me? I'd miss my kids. I'd miss so much of what happens, you know, MJ's first steps and his first drawings, Christina's play dates.

CT: And if you weren't working at all, would you miss anything about work?

LIZ: Some things. Yes.

MARTIN: [To CT] Can I say something?

CT: Of course.

MARTIN: I think...

CT: Begin with I feel or I hear.

MARTIN: OK. You love both, Liz. You love being with the kids, and you love your work. And from the time Christina was born, you talked about working part time. It sounds like the best solution to me, you get some of everything you want. It's a way to do both.

LIZ: But my career will never go anywhere. I'll stay an associate forever, never make more money, always be one-down because I chose the mommy track.

CT: I can't tell whether that scares you or infuriates you, or maybe both.

LIZ: Both. Martin, you don't get it, I won't be taken seriously.

MARTIN: No, being a black man I'd never understand not being taken seriously.

LIZ: You're right. I'm sorry.

CT: You both know what it's like to not be taken seriously, either because of your race or your gender. That's something you can empathize with each other about. And then the question becomes, how does it matter to you that your career would not go where you thought it might?

LIZ: Well, I won't make as much money. And I worry that will bother Martin.

CT: Tell him you're worried, then, and ask him to tell you what he thinks.

LIZ: Martin, I'm worried me making less money will put more pressure on you and you'll resent that.

MARTIN: Really, Liz? You think I care? We can live fine on what I make and half your salary, or whatever percent you choose to work.

CT: Martin, it seems like you had an emotional reaction, too, when Liz said she worries her reduced salary potential will bother you. Can you also respond to her worry, tell her how you reacted?

MARTIN: [To CT] You heard I got pissed off.

CT: It was hard to miss. I suspect Liz heard it, too.

LIZ: No kidding.

MARTIN: OK. I felt like you were accusing me of being shallow, only caring about money and not about you or our kids.

LIZ: Really? I didn't intend.... Wait, you think our kids would be better off if I was home?

MARTIN: Not necessarily. But if you think I care about money more than I care about you, then you probably don't think I care about them, either.

CT: Liz, you didn't intend to accuse Martin of caring more about money, and yet that's what he heard. And, Martin, Liz is worried. In some respects, it doesn't matter about what because she needs you to acknowledge her worry.

MARTIN: I don't want you to worry. I feel like I've been supportive every way I know how, but maybe I overlooked something.

LIZ: No, I'm just worried. Like she said earlier, I'm afraid of making the wrong decision.

MARTIN: I know, but I don't think any of your options are wrong. Really, I don't. It's a question of which one you want.

CT: I'm going to stop you here. That exchange sounded very different than your old arguments. Did you sense it, too?

LIZ: Mmhm.

Stop and Think:

Be sure to include your responses in your journal.

1. What do you think the emotionally focused couple therapist was attempting to do in this excerpt from Liz and Martin's couple therapy? Be very specific.
2. What were your reactions as you read the transcript? Again, be very specific.
3. What would you have done differently, had you been the couple therapist? Explain your answer.

Conclusions

In this chapter, you read about six theoretical approaches to couple therapy: narrative couple therapy, feminist couple therapy, solution-focused couple therapy, structural couple therapy, brief strategic couple therapy, and emotionally focused couple therapy. The first three arose directly from post-modern theories of individual, couple, and family therapy. Structural and brief strategic couple therapies applied post-modern thought to foundational theories of family therapy, while emotionally focused couple therapy integrated post-modern thought with psychodynamic and systemic theories.

In the transcripts of couple therapy using each of these six theoretical approaches, note that the couple therapist, Liz, and Martin remained the same people. Only the couple therapist's theoretical approach differed. Note also that, for reasons of brevity and lack of repetition, the excerpts were taken fairly far into the work so that you could see results. Most couple therapists, like individual and family therapists, find that real clients are frequently less compliant than Liz and Martin were in this chapter's transcripts and that success is often not as rapid as it may have appeared.

Stop and Think:

Be sure to include your answers in your journal.

1. Compare and contrast the six transcripts. Think about how they appeared to you, as well as the theoretical models they portrayed.
2. Which theoretical perspective did you find the most compelling?
3. Which theoretical perspective did you find least compelling?
4. Did you read anything that especially impressed or disturbed you? Explain your answer.

Having reviewed theories of couple therapy in this and the previous two chapters, we will turn in the next chapter to additional treatment modalities. While the focus of this textbook is on couple therapy, it is important for couple therapists to be aware of these other modalities. Some couple therapists practice one or more of them, and all couple therapists find the need to refer clients from time to time to those they do not practice.

References

Basirico, L. A., Cashion, B. G., & Eshleman, J. R. (2014). *Introduction to sociology (16th ed.).* Redding CA: BVT.

Bowlby, J. (1969). *Attachment. Attachment and loss.* New York NY: Basic Books.

Bowlby, J. & Schore, A. N. (1973). *Separation. Anxiety and anger.* New York NY: Basic Books.

Brown, L. S. (1994). *Subversive dialogues. Theory in feminist therapy.* New York NY: Basic Books.

DeShazer, S. (1988). Clues. Investigating solutions in brief therapy. New York NY: Norton.

Esposito, J. & Hattem, A. (2017). *Introduction to family counseling. A case study approach.* Los Angeles CA: Sage Press.Gottman, J. M. & Silver, N. (1999). *The seven principles for making marriages work.* New York NY: Random House, Inc.

Greenberg, L. S. & Johnson, S. M. (1988). *Emotionally focused therapy for couples.* New York NY: Guilford.

Haley, J. (1963). *Strategies of psychotherapy*. New York NY: Grune & Stratton.

Hoyt, M. F. (2015). Solution-focused couple therapy. In A. S. Gurman, J. L. Lebow, & D. K. Snyder (Eds.). *Clinical handbook of couple therapy* (5th ed.). New York NY: Guilford Press.

Johnson, S. M. (2004). Practice of emotionally focused couple therapy (2nd ed.). New York NY: Brunner-Rutledge.

Johnson, S. M. (2015). Emotionally focused couple therapy. In A. S. Gurman, J. L. Lebow, & D. K. Snyder (Eds.). *Clinical handbook of couple therapy* (5th ed.). New York NY: Guilford Press

Johnson, S. M. & Greenberg, L. S. (1995). The emotionally focused approach to problems in adult attachment. In A. S. Gurman (Ed.). *Clinical handbook of couple therapy* (4th ed.). New York NY: Guilford Press.

Knudson-Martin, C. & Mahoney, A. R. (Eds.). (2009). *Couples, gender, and power. Creating change in intimate relationships*. New York NY: Springer Publishing Company.

Luepnitz, D. A. (2002). Schopenhauer's porcupines. Intimacy and its dilemmas. New York NY: Basic Books.

Madanes, C. (1981). *Strategic family therapy*. San Francisco CA: Jossey-Bass.

Minuchin, S. (1974). *Families and family therapy*. Cambridge MA: Harvard University Press.

Rohrbaugh, M. J. & Shohan, V. (2015). Brief strategic couple therapy. In A. S. Gurman, J. L. Lebow, & D. K. Snyder (Eds.). *Clinical handbook of couple therapy* (5th ed.). New York NY: Guilford Press.

Simon, G. M. (2015). Structural couple therapy. In A. S. Gurman, J. L. Lebow, & D. K. Snyder (Eds.). *Clinical handbook of couple therapy* (5th ed.). New York NY: Guilford Press.

White, M. & Epston, D. (1990). *Narrative means to therapeutic ends*. New York NY: W. W. Norton.

For Further Study

Brimhall, A. S., Gardner, B. C., & Henline, B. H. (2003). Enhancing narrative couple therapy process with an enactment scaffolding. *Contemporary Family Therapy*, 25 (4), 391–404.

Dulwich Centre. (2015). *What is narrative therapy*? Dulwich Centre Publications Pty Ltd & Dulwich Centre Foundation, Inc. Retrieved from http://dulwichcentre.com.au/what-is-narrative-therapy.

Gottman, J. M. (1991). Predicting the longitudinal course of marriages. *Journal of Marriage and Family Therapy*, 17, 3–7.

Rockquemore, K. A. & Laszloffy, T. A. (2003). Multiple realities. A relationship narrative approach in therapy with black-white mixed-race clients. *Family Relations*, 52 (2), 119–128.

CHAPTER 8

Additional Approaches to Couples

Learning Objectives

1. Identify potential barriers to the decision to commit to a permanent relationship.
2. Describe the three reasons couples go to premarital or pre-commitment counseling.
3. Evaluate the evolution of thinking about sex therapy and the utility of the intersystems approach.
4. Discuss the potential benefits and drawbacks of couples group therapy for couples.
5. Describe the use of couples enrichment groups and their contextual relevance.
6. Identify and evaluate the considerations and how they are managed when couple issues emerge during individual psychotherapy.
7. Describe the various ways in which couple and family therapy intersect.

In this chapter you will read about four methods, or modalities, for delivering couple therapy and its alternatives: premarital or pre-commitment couple therapy; sex therapy; couples therapy groups and couples enrichment groups; and individual and family therapy. None of these was addressed in the previous, theory-based chapters.

Couples present to couple therapists requesting premarital or pre-commitment therapy as a decision-making, stress reducing, and/or preventive measure. Couples seeking premarital or pre-commitment therapy may wish to ensure they have communication and problem-solving skills at their disposal, in an effort to avoid more intractable problems at a later time.

Other couples describe various sexual issues as their presenting problem or request couple therapy specifically for sexual issues in their relationship when initially inquiring about couple therapy. While experience suggests that sexual issues may reflect couple dynamics, sex therapy as a subspecialty of couple therapy is sometimes indicated.

Couple therapy has been offered in groups. Couples enrichment, also known as relationship enrichment (RE), always occurs in a couples group context. Couples group therapy delivers couple therapy to several couples in a group setting, while couple or relationship enrichment groups serve non-distressed couples wishing to improve their relationships in the context of groups of couples. These approaches, as well as the clinical considerations for choosing couples group therapy or relationship enrichment for a particular couple, will be described.

Couple therapy sometimes occurs in the context of individual or family therapy. Napier and Whitaker (1978) described a family that presented for therapy because of the oldest child's acting out behavior. As family therapy progressed, marital issues within the couple subsystem emerged, and the ensuing couple therapy occurred both with and without the children present. A similar situation arose for Liz and Martin when their daughter Christina exhibited symptoms in late adolescence that brought them to family therapy. During the course of family treatment, Liz and Martin's couple issues re-emerged (Esposito & Hattem, 2017). The arguments for and against attempting to do couple therapy in the context of one partner's individual therapy will be addressed in this chapter.

Premarital and Pre-Commitment Counseling

Many clergy members require that couples engage in some form of premarital counseling as a prerequisite to a religious wedding ceremony. Prepare/Enrich is among the best known and widely used (AAMFT, 2017).

Premarital counseling offered in a clerical setting usually addresses how the couple intends to manage finances, how the partners communicate, and their agreed-upon life goals. Clergy help couples resolve differences and make suggestions to smooth their path forward. Unless the clergy member has been trained in pastoral counseling with couples, however, she or he is unlikely to utilize a systemic perspective to either recognize or address the couple's dynamics.

Secular couple therapy with a premarital or pre-commitment focus differs from programs conducted within a religious setting in that religious doctrine is not a part of the work. For example, a secular couple therapist can provide information about birth control and disease prevention that may violate the doctrines of a particular religious denomination. Each couple is free to utilize or ignore the information provided by a secular couple therapist, and a sensitive couple therapist would ask the couple about any religious proscriptions to which the partners adhere with which she or he may be unfamiliar.

Couple therapists are also approached by unmarried couples who are committed to a long-term relationship without the specific goal of marriage. Some couples intend to remain unmarried. Others reside where a marriage license is difficult for them to obtain despite the 2015 Supreme Court decision granting equal access to the rights and privileges of marriage to all couples. And yet other couples are in the process of deciding whether to formalize their commitment and make it public.

More frequently, couples request premarital counseling when they are in the process of planning their wedding ceremony and celebration. Sometimes specific issues between partners or with one or both partners' families of origin arise while planning a wedding. Some couples recognize that issues exist in their relationship that love and marriage will not resolve despite cultural mythology that marriage is tantamount to living happily thereafter. Still other couples are referred by concerned friends, relatives, clergy, health care professionals, or the attorneys involved in prenuptial agreements.

When families are blending following a divorce or death of one or both partners' previous spouses, parents may be wary of their children's reactions to their remarriage. Sensitivity to one's children and age-appropriate communications are important as relationships and family boundaries change. Children, including adult children, find their relationships with a single parent to be different from what they were when both biological parents were together. These relationships change again when a divorced or widowed parent commits to a new life partner. Because many children did not want their parent's relationship with their other biological parent to end, they may be ambivalent about that parent's remarriage.

Couples who are blending their families as well as committing to one another may also experience step-parenting issues that lead them to couple therapy. It is important that the couple negotiate each partner's relationship with the other's biological children as well as with the other living biological parents.

Children may unrealistically believe that if neither parent remarries the family will be reunited. Or they may not wish to share the parent with a new partner. They may also object to the existence of their future step-siblings, if not the step-siblings themselves. As of this writing, a re-mastered DVD of Salvador Minuchin working with a blended family was available through AAMFT (Minuchin, 2007). The mother's sons had returned from their father's house to discover two of her new husband's children were sharing their rooms. Rather than seeking premarital counseling, the couple waited until conflict between the mother, step-father, and her younger son became unbearable to them to seek family therapy.

The other biological parent of one partner's children can also present problems for a new relationship, either by negative comments to the children or direct confrontation with the previous partner or her or his new partner. Partners' unresolved issues from previous relationships can undermine their new one, and while it may be impossible to work with the ex-partners present, couple therapists can help the partner who is in their office manage both the former and present relationships in ways that neither undermine the latter nor harm the children.

The information on premarital or pre-commitment therapy is divided into three broad categories based upon the couple's goals for their couple therapy: to decide whether or not to marry; to address issues that have arisen during the wedding-planning process; and to prevent couple problems from remaining unresolved and therefore worsening over time.

The Decision to Formally Commit

Prior to third-wave feminism, economic options for women whose families were not wealthy were limited to marriage or a relatively low-paying profession such as teaching, nursing, or secretarial work. It is worth noting that the remuneration for work in these professions began to increase after third-wave feminism began and men subsequently entered these fields in significant numbers. Wealthier women may have had more financial options. However, their families continued to encourage them to marry within their socioeconomic group in order to maintain and expand financially and politically beneficial social networks. Men's options were similarly limited by the choices available to and pressures placed upon the women to whom they were attracted. At the same time these options began to increase, birth control became more available to unmarried women. Along with economic options, family planning allowed women and therefore men to couple without marrying.

Unless limited by enculturation, couples currently have the option to partner in long-term relationships without marrying. Some couples choose to remain in long-term relationships without cohabiting or marrying. Others cohabit without a legal marriage or spiritual wedding. And still others find that attempts to block equal access to the benefits of marriage by the jurisdiction in which they reside preclude marriage as an option. A friend of the writer's and his husband traveled to another state to marry because of the laws in the state in which they lived at the time. Not all LGBTQIA couples have the time and money to travel for this purpose.

Couples may request help from a couple therapist while deciding whether or not to formally marry. One partner may wish to marry while the other rejects either the institution of marriage or the commitment entailed in marrying, and the couple may be experiencing conflict as a result. The couple's conflict may arise from the meanings each partner attributes to their different perspectives, how they communicate about these differences, and their difficulties resolving their differences in addition to their divergent wishes while remaining a couple.

A second group of unmarried couples seeks couple therapy while in the process of struggling with the decision about whether or not to move their relationship forward toward increased commitment. They may have been an identified couple for a long enough period of time to have struggled with and even resolved issues of commitment, fidelity in a monogamous relationship, or a mental health or substance abuse problem that is of greater concern to one partner and/or the source of ambivalence about committing to the relationship. Sometimes partners are under pressure from their families of origin or social network to marry. Other times, one or both have anxieties about marriage that leave them hesitant to impose the institution upon their relationship.

Commitment phobia is not a clinical term and, to the writer's knowledge, is not found in the professional literature. However, because it appears in the self-help literature and has become part of the dominant culture's vernacular, it is worth mentioning as a potential source of a couple's struggle with the decision to marry. Commitment phobia appears in many forms, including the inability to find a perfect partner, multiple relationships with the intention of permanence that do not last because of a perceived flaw in the partner, and leaving well-functioning relationships that are moving toward commitment in search of an ideal relationship that does not, in fact, exist. Fear of commitment may also manifest in a number of brief liaisons that end after a few weeks or months. Carter and Sokol (2004) first coined the term commitment phobia in their book about men, although women are not immune to commitment phobia.

By altering the facts of their history only slightly, Liz and Martin could easily fit any of these categories. Because Liz's parents' marriage had been plagued by substance abuse, violence, and unhappiness, she might have worried that marriage would change her relationship with Martin in a negative way or been concerned about feeling as trapped as her mother did. Given the time in which she came of age, she could have easily rejected marriage as an institution, in part a political statement and in part self-protection from finding herself in her mother's position.

Additionally, Liz and Martin said they chose to marry rather than cohabit out of respect for Martin's mother, Roxanne's, religious beliefs. It could as easily have happened that Martin wanted to marry before cohabiting but Liz refused, noting they were young, had not known one another very long, and were in a social network of people who cohabited before or instead of marriage. This difference might have precipitated on-going, unresolved conflict and feelings of rejection and pressure by and from the other.

Finally, Liz and Martin might have broken up over both career conflicts and different time lines for marriage and presented for couple therapy to obtain help deciding whether to marry or go their separate ways. Or Liz, who had avoided sexual intimacy with men and emotional intimacy with women partners from the time she was assaulted until she met Martin, might have continued avoiding emotional intimacy and, as a result, avoided commitment to a man who could potentially hurt or frighten her again.

Legal barriers to marriage exist outside a couple's relationship. Until the 1967 Loving v. Virginia Supreme Court decision, biracial marriage was not considered a civil right, and same-sexed marriage was not considered a civil right until 2015. In addition to legal barriers, ethnic and religious differences between partners may create barriers imposed by a couple's families and social networks and therefore outside the jurisdiction of the courts. Liz's father, Bill's, racist attitude toward Martin at the beginning of their relationship may not have resolved as easily for Martin as for Bill. Conceivably, he could have decided he did not want to be treated as less-than by his wife's family and ended the relationship. One of Liz's college roommates also expressed opposition to her marrying Martin, and as a result their friendship ended. Similarly, had Liz or Martin been Jewish or Muslim or Hindu and the other not, pressure against the marriage may have been exerted by their families and their religious communities. As it was, Liz's commitment to Catholicism was such that their inability to be married as a church sacrament did not trouble her, although her mother disapproved of her attitude and Martin's mother, who was reconciled to the possibility he would marry a white woman, was unhappy about his choice to marry outside their religion.

Stop and Think:

Be sure to include your answers in your journal.

1. Have you experienced legal, racial, ethnic, or religious barriers as you've created a relationship? Has anyone you know?
2. How have you or the person you know handled the situation?
3. Did the relationship survive? If yes, what did the partners do to mitigate the impact of the barriers? If not, identify ways in which the barriers undermined the relationship.

Wedding Planning

Couples present for couple therapy when the stresses they are experiencing overwhelm their resources for coping, in other words, when they lack resiliency. A stressful event, even a positive one, requires a couple to adapt to a new situation. To review, resilience, or the ability to adapt to stress, is determined by the meaning assigned to the stress, as well as by the financial, emotional, and social resources the couple brings to the situation. When stresses are defined as manageable and resources are sufficient, the couple is said to be resilient. Sometimes the stress and/or the meanings attached to it are more than the couple's resources can bear.

Weddings are expensive, and planning is often stressful for both a couple and each set of parents. Some couples may disagree about whether planning the wedding will be shared or the primary responsibility of one partner. Others argue over the myriad details that emerge during the process of planning a wedding. Still other couples argue about the behavior of one or both partners' parents. And finally, couples may argue about how to allocate the resources available for what can be a very expensive event. Bringing the families and the couple's friends together for an event may also involve anticipatory stress.

One or both sets of parents may have different expectations than the couple about their role in planning the wedding, the size of the wedding, and how elaborate the reception will be. Some parents become more anxious and involved than the couple would like. Finances or perceived social obligations may dictate differences in what the couple and one or both sets of parents want. Extended family conflicts may become problematic, for example, when one partner's sibling becomes angry that his or her young children will not be invited to a Saturday evening wedding or a parent says that a relative or family friend who the bride or groom dislikes must be invited even though the result is one less invitation for the couple's friends.

The couple's parents may be displeased by their adult child's choice of partner for a variety of reasons. Some parents may be concerned the partner does not treat their child well. Other parents may be concerned about what they have observed in the couple's relationship that could become problematic, for example one partner being more ambitious or domineering than the other. Parents may be concerned or even outraged that their adult children are marrying outside the family's socioeconomic, ethnic, religious, or racial group or about a same-sexed marriage. Had Sally and Bill or Samuel and Roxanne objected to Liz and Martin's biracial marriage to the extent they refused, for example, to invite family or friends or even attend the wedding themselves, their attitude and behavior could have become a source of tension between Liz and Martin.

Stop and Think:

Be sure to include your responses in your journal.

1 Think about a family or friend's wedding at which you have been a guest. What did you like about it enough to include in your own? What did you find distasteful? If you were close to one of the partners, how did she or he feel about the wedding and how did she or he negotiate it with family?

2 Think about the wedding you would like or the wedding you had. What are the most important aspects of it for you? Are these things your family also values and can afford? If not, what may happen or did happen as a result of attempts to negotiate a wedding that meets or met your needs and theirs?

3 What are or were your family's expectations for your choice of partner? How might you choosing someone who did not fit their expectations influence your relationship with them? How might it influence their attitude toward planning your wedding?

Premarital or Pre-Commitment Counseling as Prevention

As noted earlier in this chapter, premarital and pre-commitment therapy can serve as a preventive mechanism for potential problems in the future. Resolving how the partners will manage finances, careers, and parenting; learning to communicate more effectively about difficult topics, for example, sex; and observing and changing relationship dynamics that may contribute to misunderstandings and conflict can help resolve issues before they are overlaid with the frustration and pain that arise when they remain unresolved over a long period of time.

The literature uses the term "premarital counseling." However, couple therapists including the writer have worked with committed couples who are not married to improve their relationships. Thus, the term pre-commitment therapy may be a better descriptor, although premarital will be used when describing literature that focuses only on premarital work.

The American Association for Marriage and Family Therapy (AAMFT, 2017) described premarital therapy as entailing five to seven sessions during which a couple therapist reviews pencil-and-paper assessment scales already completed by the partners, works toward the goals identified by the couple, facilitates negotiation of potential issues identified by the assessment tools using couple strengths identified by these tools, guides the couple toward improved communication, and provides an experience that demonstrates the potential benefits of couple therapy should problems arise later.

Premarital assessment tools can be found at the AAMFT website and in the professional literature. RELATE locates couples on a 16-point framework of relationship styles. FOCCUS, or Facilitating Open Couple Communication, Understanding, and Study, provides the couple therapist with information about the couple's communication styles and potential pitfalls. PREPARE, or Premarital Preparation and Relationship Enhancement, identifies areas to target during premarital couple therapy. Flowers and Olson (1993) also recommend using their ENRICH marital satisfaction scale in premarital work with couples. This tool identifies 10 domains of marital, or relationship, satisfaction.

Research indicates that assessment-based premarital interventions are more effective in improving communication and relationship satisfaction six months following couple therapy than are either self-directed or therapist-directed programs (Busby, Ivey, Harris, & Ates, 2007). Couples who participated in the study described assessment-based interventions as helpful, in that they provided a mechanism for talking about previously taboo subjects. Couples also reported that their communication improved and that they developed a new perspective on their relationship from working with their couple therapist.

Premarital and pre-commitment therapy can occur in conjoint (i.e., one couple with one therapist) couple therapy or in couples groups. Being in a group can have unintended consequences for distressed couples when they compare their own relationship to those of less distressed couples in the group. Early in a relationship, comparisons are not as stark as they become after years of unresolved conflict. However, individual psychopathology in either partner that meets the criteria for a personality disorder (American Psychiatric Association, 2013) can undermine group functioning and thus group intervention of any kind is contraindicated.

Had Liz and Martin presented for premarital counseling, the couple therapist might have identified some or all of the issues that subsequently led to the problems they brought to couple therapy. He or she would have guided their communication, provided a more empathetic perspective on each of them and their struggle, and explored the impact of Liz's trauma as well as the couple's dynamics on their sexual relationship. Premarital intervention could but might not have prevented the problems they brought to couple therapy several years later.

Stop and Think:

1. Think about your current or previous relationship with a partner or a close friend or relative's relationship. Using it as a model, how might the couple benefit from preventive couple therapy?
2. What might prompt you to seek premarital or pre-commitment couple counseling?
3. Would you consider working with couples early in their relationship to prevent future problems? Explain your answer.

Sex Therapy

Sex therapy can be viewed as either a couple therapy intervention aimed at a specific couple problem or as an independent discipline. Couple and family therapy programs do not always require trainees to learn about human sexuality or couple therapy with clients for whom sexual dysfunction is either a presenting or associated problem. Additionally, some states have independent licensing for sex therapists, and professional encroachment may be discouraged even when a couple therapist is well trained and within his or her professional rights to practice sex therapy. As a result, couple therapists may refer to sex therapists when issues relating to a couple's sexuality arise.

Experience suggests that couples who identify sex as the presenting problem may be describing the symptom that brought them to couple therapy. In that case, addressing the underlying issues that manifest as sexual problems may be essential to fully resolving the sexual dysfunction and to preventing the re-emergence of sexual or other problems following therapy. Liz and Martin's struggles about her career may have spilled over into their sexual relationship, as noted in an earlier chapter, without the sexual problem being the only issue requiring resolution.

Issues in a couple's sexual relationship, when not overlaid with years of hurt feelings or a sense of failure, may be relatively simple to resolve. For example, timing is important in any form of communication, including sexual. If partners have different sleep patterns such as one being a "night owl" and the other being a "morning person," the solution may be as simple as finding a time that works for both such as going to bed together and the partner who is unready for sleep either reading in bed or getting up when the other goes to sleep. Timing sexual encounters during the childrearing years can also be difficult. Lack of opportunity may be interpreted as lack of interest or attractiveness, and such meanings can be talked about and possibly reframed as lack of child-free time, thus decreasing the detrimental impact of the ascribed meaning.

Couples also suffer from lack of information about sex. Variation exists in the effectiveness of coital positions, with some being more comfortable and/or stimulating for a particular individual or couple than others. Couples may not have accurate information about anatomy, the role of foreplay, and myths such as whether or not it is safe to engage in sexual intimacy during menstruation, pregnancy, or following a cardiac event. While couple therapists may need to consult with one partner's physician about her or his specific condition, they can work with couples to help them maximize pleasure and emotional intimacy within any biomedical constraints that exist.

Both the professional literature and experience suggest that, like substance abuse and intimate partner violence, sexual issues frequently remain unspoken unless the couple therapist asks about them. Embarrassment, shame, and guilt may make it difficult for couples to acknowledge sexual difficulties when asked, much less initiate the conversation. Thus, the couple therapist may need to ask at least once about the couple's sexual intimacy when it is not the presenting problem, just as he or she asks about substance use and physical and emotional violence in the relationship.

Stop and Think:

Be sure to include your responses in your journal.

1. How comfortable are you talking about sex with friends or a sibling? What about sex, if anything, are you comfortable discussing? What about sex, if anything, are you uncomfortable discussing and what makes it difficult for you to talk?
2. How comfortable are you talking about sex with a partner? What, if anything, would you add or delete from your answers to Question 1 when answering about a partner and what prompted you to make these changes?
3. What would need to happen for you to become more comfortable talking about sex with a friend or sibling? With a partner?

Masters and Johnson (1966, 1970) were the first writers to identify sexual dysfunctions and treatments. They viewed all sexual disorders as individual problems impacting the client's partner. The partner was used as an informant during sessions and as a sexual surrogate for homework assignments.

Kaplan (1974) added sexual desire as a part of the sexual response cycle that Masters and Johnson (1966, 1970) had overlooked. She placed sexual desire as a prerequisite to arousal and orgasm in the human sexual response cycle.

Like Masters and Johnson, Kaplan (1974) did not hold a systems view of sexual dysfunction. Rather, she relied upon a psychodynamic model of intrapsychic conflict in the absence of biomedical disease or medication side-effects. Homework was behaviorally based, with incremental assignments. Sensate focus was the preferred treatment for erectile dysfunction and inorgasmia. The goal was to remove performance anxiety and fully attend to the pleasurable aspects of sensual and then sexual touching without the expectation of penetration. As may be obvious, her work and that of her colleagues ignored all but heterosexual relationships.

In sequential homework assignments, couples began with affectionate touching all over each other's bodies except for genitals, progressed to genital touching, and only when the couple was comfortable was intercourse prescribed. If behavioral intervention failed, then a psychodynamic approach to treating the emotional disorder thought to underlie the sexual dysfunction was initiated. For example, delayed ejaculation was considered to be a symptom of ambivalence about engaging in sex. This ambivalence may have arisen from a childhood sexual trauma or from family-of-origin taboos or hyper-sexuality. Larger sociocultural issues and the dynamics of the couple's relationship were largely ignored, as were couples whose relationship was not heterosexual.

LoPiccolo and LoPiccolo (1978) recommended assigning partners mutual responsibility for homework assignments. Both partners were instructed to initiate homework assignments at least once or twice during the time between sessions. While overlooking the possibility that the sexual disorder was serving a function in the couple system, this contribution did help remove the onus from the symptomatic partner.

Weeks and a colleague had introduced the idea that the couple is the locus of both the sexual dysfunction and its treatment in 1987 (Weeks & Gambescia, 2015). They viewed the role of the sexual dysfunction as similar to the role of any symptom. As a result, the couple, rather than the symptomatic partner, became the identified patient, and the sexual symptom was viewed as a homeostatic mechanism in the couple's relationship that would only resolve when the homeostatic function of the symptom changed.

Sexual dysfunction may be a form of distance regulation, or maintaining a comfortable emotional space within the couple system. It may also be the battleground of a couple's conflict about responsibility and/or trust.

Some couples develop a rule that one partner will take primary responsibility for initiating sex and then find themselves unable to alter this pattern when it no longer meets their needs. They then present with conflict around changing the initiation rule, blaming one another for not initiating sex and expressing feelings of rejection masked by anger and even accusations of infidelity.

To review, rules are a way of conceptualizing the patterns that emerge from repetitive couple interactions, and they represent how the couple manages various aspects of their relationship. The couple's implicit contract also reflects these rules. When one partner initiates change in the couple's contract and the rules underlying it, the homeostatic function of the rules is disrupted and a feedback loop ensues, often triggering an attempt to restore equilibrium. One partner may wish to restore the previous equilibrium, while the other may not.

A couple who has stopped engaging in sexual activity because of a stand-off regarding whose responsibility it is to initiate sex has lost an important aspect of their intimacy over a dynamic unrelated to their emotional or biomedical health. Sexual intimacy, when not fraught with negative meanings, can be an important source of good will and attachment. Additionally, the meaning of no longer having sex with one's partner may reinforce self-schemata and trigger a negative cycle of self-reproach and disappointed expectations.

Weeks and Gambescia (2015) developed what they have labeled an intersystems approach to treating sexual dysfunction. Their intersystems model examines five system levels: individual biology, individual psychology, the couple system, multi-generational family-of-origin systems, and the sociocultural systems of which the couple is a part, with attention to historical context.

The biopsychosocial model developed for use in primary care medicine offered a similar conceptualization. This model approaches the diagnosis and treatment of both biomedical and psychosocial disorders from three broad levels of human systems: biomedical, psychological, and the couple, family, and increasingly larger community systems in which a patient or client is embedded (Doherty & Baird, 1983). As an example, a physician once referred a client to the writer because she displayed depressive symptoms. All but one of the numerous medications the client was ingesting listed depression as a common side-effect. To ignore the potential impact of a medical condition, a mental illness, or the pharmaceutical treatment of either is as detrimental to treatment as ignoring the impact of trauma, intimate partner violence, substance use, negative schemata, intrapsychic conflict, or the couple and family system of which the client is a part.

On the biomedical level, it is incumbent on sex therapists and couple therapists treating sexual disorders to consider the symptomatic partner's health status, life cycle stage, and lifestyle as potential contributors to the problem. A number of medical conditions and pharmaceutical treatments impact sexual functioning, most notably impaired desire associated with the serotonin re-uptake inhibitors such as Prozac that are often prescribed for mood disorders, specifically depression, and the older medications used to treat high blood pressure. Couple therapists can recommend that the symptomatic partner consult a physician to rule out the presence of biomedical contributors and can seek permission to discuss the patient's health with his or her primary care practitioner.

Life cycle also impacts sexual functioning. For many people, sexual responsiveness declines as they move into their late 40s and beyond. Arousal and orgasm may be slower to occur and formerly relied upon methods of sexual intimacy may no longer be effective. Couple therapists can normalize the changes associated with aging and suggest alternative ways to maintain satisfying sexual intimacy while at the same time recommending the symptomatic partner consult a physician to rule out other biomedical contributors.

Couples also experience transient biomedical and life cycle changes that impact their sexual relationship. These include recovery from illnesses, surgery, or accidents; stress, for example at work or with a child; grief, for example over the death of a family member or friend; sadness and worry that do not meet the diagnostic criteria for a mood or anxiety disorder; pregnancy and menopause; transition to parenthood; sleep loss; and similar situations that, unlike aging or a chronic illness, do resolve. It is especially important that couples avoid attaching more dire meanings than warranted to transitory changes.

Lifestyle factors both impact sexual functioning and are affected by psychosocial factors. Obesity and substance abuse are among the lifestyle factors that diminish sexual functioning. Shift work, especially if both partners are working different shifts, and frequent business travel may reduce the opportunities a couple has to engage in sexual activity. Lifestyle factors that can be changed require intervention, including possible referrals for specialized treatment. Couple therapists can also help couples adapt their sex life in so far as possible to the inalterable realities of their lives.

Psychosocial factors that can impair sexual functioning include a history of trauma for one or both partners, psychological disorders that are beyond the scope of an introductory textbook to describe in one or both partners, each partner's self-esteem and body image, and the security of the couple's attachment. One or both partners' family of origin may have imparted inaccurate information about sex and sexuality, a sense of guilt about sexuality, and inhibitions and taboos against talking about sex that may manifest in difficulties discussing sex with the partner.

Sociocultural contributors include how each partner's religion and culture view sexuality, the values and attitudes conveyed by the culture about sexuality, cultural myths about sexuality, and the meaning of being a sexual adult in relationship with one's partner. All of these vary among cultures and all of these fluctuate over time. Within the current dominant culture in the United States, standards of a sexually attractive weight for women, for example, have shifted from the Marilyn Monroe image of the 1950s and retained that of the Twiggy model of the 1970s (Douglas, 1994).

From a systems perspective (Chapter 4), the couple system is the source the problem, its maintenance, and its solution. When viewed as an individual problem, partners may ascribe meanings to sexual disorders that worsen partners' self-image or their relationship. For example, the meaning of erectile dysfunction may be "he no longer finds me attractive" to the non-symptomatic partner and "I am a sexual failure" to the one bearing the symptom. Alternatively, when viewed as a couple system issue, erectile dysfunction may be a mechanism for maintaining an emotional and physical distance that is comfortable to the partners and that, in the absence of a biomedical challenge, could be maintained in other ways.

Other examples of couple issues impacting sexual functioning include unresolved conflict that manifests in one partner punishing the other by withholding sexual intimacy, and intimate partner violence triggering post-traumatic stress symptoms during sexual interactions. During an argument in the couple therapist's office, Liz accused Martin of withholding sex when she achieved career success.

The movie Annie Hall also provided an example of how different meanings can exacerbate a couple's sexual problem. In a split-screen scene, Woody Allen and Diane Keaton were each in their individual psychotherapist's office describing their dissatisfaction with the frequency of their sexual intimacy. Allen complained that "she never wants sex, only three times a week"; Keaton complained that "he always wants to have sex, three times a week!" For them, the problem resided not in the frequency itself but in the meaning each partner attached to it and in the couple's inability to negotiate a frequency acceptable to both partners. The film provided an example of the ineffectiveness of communicating about and negotiating a solution to a couple problem with an individual psychotherapist, where it became two complaints absent the partner's perspective or an opportunity to work together toward effective change.

Weeks and Gambescia (2015) added impaired sexual satisfaction as a sexual disorder and a source of couple distress. Sexual satisfaction and relationship satisfaction have been demonstrated to correlate with one another and to worsen over time in a negative couple spiral for distressed couples. The relationship between sexual and relationship satisfaction may improve with improved communication about partners' experiences, behaviors, and expectations. Expectations vary across cultures and ages, so the couple therapist works with the couple's expectations rather than her or his own. Cultural variance in expectations may be even more difficult to manage with LGBTQIA couples than with heterosexual couples, as acceptance of dominant culture gender identity and sexuality that is not heterosexual varies across cultures.

In proposing what they deemed the first systems-based approach to sexual dysfunction in couples, Weeks and Gambescia (2015) described three steps for couple therapy with sexual disorders. In many ways their recommendations paralleled those of the theorists about whom you read in previous chapters. Their intersystems approach combines elements of behavioral and psychodynamic thought in a post-modern theory targeting sexual aspects of the couple's relationship.

As with any approach, couple therapists first explore the presenting problem from each partner's perspective. This includes addressing the partners' ability to communicate clearly with one another about sex, how partners express their mutual attraction, any attraction either might have to others, and the partners' commitment to one another.

The second step in Weeks and Gabescia's (2015) treatment strategy is an assessment of influences on the problem from all five system levels. This assessment occurs in a conjoint, or couple session, and is informal. Scheduling individual sessions for the purpose of client comfort about certain topics, such as a sexual trauma that preceded the partner, is left to the couple therapist's discretion. However, if a secret is learned in an individual session and the partner who revealed it refuses to tell his or her partner, the recommendation is to view the couple as unready to address the sexual dysfunction and to suspend or end the couple therapy. Other methods for dealing with secrets will be discussed in Chapter 11.

The final step in the intersystems model is intervention from a couple systems perspective. Intervention is collaborative, begins with the issue that is deemed easiest to address, and includes cognitive, behavioral, and emotional aspects of the problem.

Intervention techniques are borrowed from various theoretical models of couple intervention. Behavioral techniques are used and, when they are insufficient, then psychodynamic interventions are utilized. The role of the therapist is not to be a technician but rather to be a collaborative partner, addressing issues as they emerge.

Specific techniques of intersystems couple therapy for sexual disorders are aimed at reframing their meaning, reducing anxiety associated with sexual intimacy, facilitating communication, providing behavioral homework to reduce anxiety and promote sensuality, changing irrational thoughts, altering unrealistic core beliefs and expectations about sex, psychoeducation regarding sex, and reality testing of cultural and familial mythology regarding sex. You are already familiar with a number of these techniques from reading previous chapters. Addressing both performance and response anxiety, differentiating sensuality from sexuality, and using behavioral techniques to increase awareness of sensuality and sexual pleasure in homework assignments are unique to sex therapy.

Stop and Think:

Be sure to include your responses in your journal.

1. Considering the evolution of sex therapy for couples, which model most resonates with your beliefs about how sexual problems arise? Explain your answer.
2. How comfortable would you be asking people you do not know about their sexual relationship? How comfortable would you be educating them about sexual behaviors that might improve their satisfaction with their sexual relationship? Explain your answers.
3. What are your own family's beliefs and myths about sex? How have these affected you?
4. What are your cultural, including racial, ethnic, and religious beliefs about sex? How have these affected you?
5. Imagine that your family and cultural beliefs were different than they are. How might your views of sexuality be different?

It cannot be overemphasized that couple therapists need to be alert to any embarrassment partners may experience when attempting to discuss their sexual relationship. Clients may not be immediately forthcoming with detailed answers as a result of embarrassment or even shame. The couple therapist's role entails being sensitive to the partners' discomfort, comfortable talking about sex himself or herself, and willing to ask a specific question a second time without judgment if the answer indicates the client previously hid information.

COUPLE THERAPIST: Liz, you mentioned in a session early on that you thought Martin withholds sex when you have a work success. Something else was on the table at the time, and we've never returned to the subject of your sexual relationship. I'm wondering how your conflict shows up in your sex life now.

Note: The couple therapist avoided asking a yes-no question, using a more open-ended one that could still be countered by Liz or Martin.

LIZ: I don't remember that.

CT: OK.

LIZ: I think when he's mad at me.

CT: And Martin, what do you think?

MARTIN: Do we really have to talk about this? I think everything is fine in that department.

CT: I think it's worth talking about your sexual relationship for two reasons. One is Liz's history [of sexual assault], and the other is that because the subject was raised I want to be certain it's not being swept under the rug.

MARTIN: OK, well, I try not to get mad, you see, so I think Liz is just looking for an answer for you.

LIZ: You get mad, Martin. We don't talk when you're mad, and we don't have sex when you're mad.

CT: So talking and sex are related? You two don't communicate in any way, including sexually, when Martin is angry? [Looks at Martin, who shrugs] What about when you're angry, Liz?

LIZ: Well, I try to be a good wife. Probably like my mother taught me.

CT: Can you clarify what you mean for me?

MARTIN: She just lies there like she's doing me a favor.

LIZ: Not always.

MARTIN: Mostly. And it's not a turn-on, Liz. I want you to be happy, too.

LIZ: How can I be happy doing something I think I'm supposed to do?

CT: Let me interrupt this. Liz, when you're going along with Martin initiating sex when you're not into it, what happens for you?

LIZ: I don't know. My mind stops working, my body just goes along.

CT: Sounds like you're describing sex you didn't consent to.

MARTIN: Hey, I wouldn't do that to her.

CT: I know. And I'm sorry that sounded like an accusation. My intent is to find out how Liz experiences those times. It's not about what you do so much as about what she experiences, which has an impact on you.

MARTIN: OK.

CT: When you're in that place, Liz, what would be helpful?

LIZ: To be left alone.

CT: And yet you're complying with Martin's wishes not because you have to but because you want to be a good wife to him the way your mother defines good wife, which is following a stereotype you don't even agree with that leaves Martin feeling like a rapist and you like a victim.

LIZ: My mother?

MARTIN: I'm not sure I'd go that far.

Note: CT intentionally embellished what Liz said to question the assumption underlying her behavior and Martin's response to it.

CT: I'm wondering whether there's a way to resolve your anger before you get close, so that it doesn't feel to either of you like you're participating against your will.

LIZ: I guess he could hold me. Touch me affectionately. Ask me what's up.

MARTIN: I could do that.

CT: It's very important that you not move on to sexual touching at these times or ever, unless you both want to. Liz, the word "want" is important here, that you're not complying because you think Martin wants you to but only when you also want sexual intimacy with him. I'd like you each to comment about what you need and what you perceive the other's message about sex is once during the upcoming week, whether you need to or not, for the practice.

Stop and Think:

Be sure to include your response in your journal.

1 What do you think about CT's choice to shift focus from Martin to Liz in this excerpt?
2 What were CT's alternatives?
3 What would you have done had you been the couple therapist?
4 How could CT have acknowledged the importance of Liz's assault history without ignoring her accusation about Martin's indirect expression of anger in their sexual relationship?
5 Did you identify a homeostatic mechanism at play that successfully returned Liz and Martin to a comfortable subject and blocked the potential for change?

Details about the couple therapist's specific suggestions, such as sensate focus techniques, are beyond the scope of an introductory textbook. The purpose of this section of the chapter was to underscore the importance of including a couple's sexual relationship in their couple therapy work and to introduce you to the professional literature. If you are interested in incorporating sex therapy into your work with couples, you will have opportunities for specific training as you move into specialized coursework and clinical supervision.

Couples Group Therapy and Couples Enrichment Groups

Couples group therapy and couples enrichment groups are distinguished by their goals and the populations best suited to them. A brief introduction to each follows.

Couples Group Therapy

The use of group settings as a modality for individual psychotherapy began in the middle of the last century. Group psychotherapy grew out of the work of Jacob Moreno (1946), Fritz Perls (1992), Irving Yalom (1970; Yalom & Leszcz, 2005), and the encounter group movement of the 1960s. The dynamics of the interpersonal relationships among group members and between each and the therapist facilitator were assumed to reflect other significant relationships in each individual's life. Changing these interpersonal dynamics within the group context was expected to reverberate across each group member's relationships outside the group. This psychodynamic approach had direct implications for working with couples. Additionally, therapy groups became systems of their own, with all the attendant characteristics of human systems, thus generalizing easily to group work with couples and families.

Moreno (1946) developed a method called psychodrama in which group members enacted a scene symbolic of one member's family experience and then re-enacted the same scene in the ideal way it might have occurred. For example, the group member playing the critical parent would convey the same message first in a critical and then in a non-critical way. Perls (1992) also placed one group member on the "hot seat" and then both the therapist facilitator and group members confronted that member on his or her dysfunctional ways of interacting within the group and the impact on group members. Yalom (1970; Yalom & Leszcz, 2005) took a gentler approach than Perls' to identifying ways in which a group member undermined what she or he wanted in relationships with others, using feedback from both himself as the group facilitator and group members. Like Perls, his approach was existential, focusing on the here-and-now. Yalom utilized his own countertransference, or reactions to group members, for information about the impact of relationship dynamics within the group and to guide his interventions.

Group therapy has expanded beyond the psychodynamic model to include behavioral, psychoeducational, and support groups. Group therapy, as noted above, has also been expanded to include groups of couples and families.

Psychoeducational groups focus on specific topics, such as parenting adolescents, and the facilitator provides information about the topic to group members. Both parents need not participate. Groups are of relatively short duration, and any attention to a specific parenting problem brought by one of the members is illustrative only. By contrast, support groups focus on individuals, couples, or families sharing a common life stressor, such as caring for an ill family member or adapting to a life-threatening biomedical diagnosis. Information is imparted, and members support one another with empathy and shared stories. Support groups are especially helpful for couples who are socially isolated by the challenge they face.

Group therapy for couples began to appear as a treatment modality during the second half of the last century, as practitioners recognized the receptiveness of an increasing number of couples to both healing and improving their relationships. During that period of time, the middle class was reasonably affluent and the insurance industry had not yet restricted access to mental health care in order to maximize profits by denying services and restricting available practitioners. The dominant cultural narrative of the time emphasized enhancing personal health and development. As the divorce rate began to climb in this more affluent and self-aware milieu (see Chapter 2), couples were more often both able and willing to invest money and time to enhance the quality of their relationships and thus their quality of life than couples were at the time of this writing. The current climate of funding only what is deemed by the insurance industry to be "medically necessary," denying reimbursement for couple therapy, a diminishing middle class, and a greater emphasis on quantity rather than on quality of life has created an environment in which couples most often present for treatment when the distress in their relationship has threatened to dissolve it.

At the inception of couples group therapy, however, the number of couples seeking couple therapy combined with the newness of the field of couple therapy led to a demand that exceeded the availability of couple therapists. Exploring ways to meet the needs of couples seeking help, couple therapists began experimenting with doing couple therapy in couples groups. Kaslow and Lieberman (1981) noted that a couples group context not only allowed more people access to couple therapy but also reduced the pressure on any one particular couple's relationship that a conjoint session, with its singular focus on only one couple, necessitated.

Zimmerman, Prest, and Wetzel (1997) later adapted solution-focused couple therapy for use in couples groups. They described a structured, theory-based program lasting six weeks and tested it on a sample of 23 couples. Couples groups were comprised of no fewer than three and no more than five couples. These couples were married, predominately white, and lived in a college town. Although the results cannot be generalized beyond the demographics of the sample, couples who participated reported positive changes.

Some couple therapists have recommended that couples participate in both conjoint and couples group sessions throughout treatment (Kilgo, 1975). Others have suggested that the couple therapist work with distressed couples in conjoint couple therapy while each partner participates in a different individual psychotherapy group. While expensive, these protocols allow both partners to address their own relationship issues without their current relationship distress overwhelming them (Feldman & Kahn, 2009; Hendrix & Hunt, 2004).

A consistent observation of those working with couples in therapy as well as enrichment groups is that partners in healthy relationships heal one another through the transference and attachment processes described in Chapter 6. Because the transference relationship may be detrimental to each partner in more distressed couples, participation in couples groups may be similarly detrimental for more distressed couples (Feld, 2004; Hendrix, 1988). Hendrix and Hunt (2004) noted that when partners are unable to listen to one another empathetically, the presence of both partners in a couples therapy group can trigger the fight, flight, or freeze response in either or both partners. In conjoint couple therapy, the couple therapist can monitor and intervene whenever the negative transference between partners appears. By contrast, in couples therapy groups the couple therapist's attention is diluted by the needs of the other couples.

Feld (2004), Hendrix (1988), and Hendrix and Hunt (2004) expressed similar cautions about negative transference between partners in conjoint couple therapy. In the writer's experience and in that of the theorists described in Chapter 6, couple therapy presents an opportunity to disrupt negative transference and create a more secure attachment between partners. The argument likely centers around whether intrapsychic wounds can only be healed in individual psychotherapy. Those practitioners who integrate psychodynamic and systemic theories view the answer differently than those who do not hold a systemic perspective.

It may be instructive to consider the similarities between disrupting negative transference between partners and disrupting feedback loops and homeostatic mechanisms that interfere with the resolution of a couple's distress. In both cases, the role of the couple therapist involves using her or his theoretical knowledge and practice skills to identify what partners cannot observe themselves. Couple therapists then interrupt these psychodynamic and systemic processes, even in the face of partners' push-back, or resistance.

Stop and Think:

Be sure to include your answers in your journal.

1. Given what you know about Martin and Liz, what might be the risks and benefits to them of couples group therapy?
2. Given what you know about Martin and Liz, what might be the risks and benefits to them of conjoint couple therapy and individual therapy groups?
3. Given what you have read, do you think Martin and Liz can heal their relationship without each engaging in their own individual psychotherapy? Explain your answer.

Couples Enrichment Groups

Couples enrichment groups, like couples therapy groups, deliver couple therapy in a group context. The goal of couples enrichment groups is to enhance an already satisfactory and stable relationship by teaching partners new relationship skills. Distressed couples who participate in couples enrichment groups observe happier couples, compare themselves, and then may ascribe even more negative meanings to their own distress.

The term relationship enrichment (RE) originated with the work of Guerney (1970). In its current iteration, couples enrichment groups are part of a structured program grounded in psychodynamic and systems theories. The mutual impact of partners on their relationship and the relationship on each partner is an example of system theory's concept of circular causation. Enrichment occurs through each partner's transference relationship with the other, a psychodynamic conceptualization.

When they originated, couples enrichment groups sometimes involved intensive retreats lasting several days. Couples learned new skills in a couples group and then went off on their own to practice. Current couples enrichment groups entail a pre-determined number of weekly meetings.

Couples enrichment groups begin with assessment. The couple therapist who will facilitate the group meets with each couple in one to three conjoint couple sessions. These allow the couple therapist to assess whether the couple might benefit from a couples enrichment group and, if necessary, to strengthen the couple's relationship prior to inviting them to participate in a couples enrichment group.

Once a group of three to five couples is formed, the couple therapist teaches the couples group five new skills. Members volunteer to demonstrate each skill with the couple therapist and then couples practice on their own in isolation from the other couples in the group. When not delivered in an intensive retreat, practice is directed through homework assignments between group meetings.

Ginsberg (2006) listed three core relationship enhancement skills that comprise the couples enrichment group agenda. These core skills entail (1) being non-judgmental about one's own feelings while expressing them to one's partner; (2) listening empathetically without judging one's partner's feelings or how the partner expresses them; and (3) acknowledging each partner's importance to the other and the importance of the relationship to both of them. These three skills are called owning expresser, empathetic responder, and emotional engagement, respectively. Partners are coached to take turns expressing their feelings. Before each new turn, the partner who will be expressing acknowledges his or her feelings about the other partner's expression and about the relationship's importance.

Once the couples in the couples enrichment group become proficient in these three core skills, sessions move on to generalizing the skills and homework assignments to use in everyday life. The final phase of couples enrichment groups is maintenance of the three skills over time. Couples schedule skills practice sessions with the couple therapist and the group continues meeting monthly for six months. At the conclusion of the maintenance phase, couples review the quality of their relationship.

The role of the couple therapist is to create a safe environment, engage couples who are in conflict despite the partners' emotional arousal, teach relationship enhancement skills, and model these skills. The couple therapist also maintains awareness of the limits of his or her influence on couples and conveys trust in them to heal themselves using their training in relationship enrichment skills.

Stop and Think:

Be sure to include your answers in your journal.

1. What did you see as the differences between couples enrichment group therapy and couples group therapy, as described in the previous section?
2. What are your thoughts about any differences you noticed?
3. Knowing what you do about Liz and Martin, do you think they would be good candidates for a couples enrichment group? Explain your answer.
4. If you were practicing couple therapy, would you want to facilitate either couples groups or couples enrichment groups? Explain your answer.
5. Would you want to facilitate individual psychotherapy groups focusing on relationship issues? Explain your answer.
6. If you were practicing group therapy, especially with couples, would you be more likely to use a psychodynamic or a more structured approach? Explain your answer.

Liz and Martin's couple therapist facilitated women's groups from time to time, and these groups sometimes elected to focus on relationship issues. One of her colleagues facilitated couples enrichment groups. Because of her systemic training, she recommended couple therapy, rather than individual or group therapy, when Liz approached her after she and Martin reconciled. She also thought it unwise to refer them to a couples therapy group or a couples enrichment group at that time.

> LIZ: Amy said you do groups. I think it would help me if I were in a group of other women dealing with relationship problems, so I could see how they manage husbands like Martin.

COUPLE THERAPIST: I don't know Martin, but what I do know about you and about couples leads me to think it'd more helpful for someone to observe how you and Martin interact with each other and then help you make changes in the ways you interact.

LIZ: But I've told you.

CT: Yes. Seeing is different than hearing about and doing couple therapy when something is happening between two people is also very different. And I think both are more effective than one of you working alone without the other, especially at this critical point in your relationship.

LIZ: Yes, but I don't get support from Martin for my career. I was hoping I could get it in a group.

CT: I think a women's group looking at careers might be very helpful. I've also found through the years, as have other therapists, that working on couple issues without the other partner present can be detrimental, rather than helpful, worse than not doing anything at all. So a women's group about careers would focus on career issues and not husband issues.

LIZ: Well, what about a couples group for us? Wouldn't that be less expensive?

CT: If that's all you were doing, then yes, it would be less expensive. Many couples who are in couples groups are also doing individual or couple therapy at the same time.

LIZ: No, I'm sure I've heard about couples groups, like at churches and things.

CT: You may be thinking of relationship enhancement groups.

LIZ: Maybe.

CT: Those are aimed at improving relationships that are already relatively problem free. You may want to join one at some point, but right now being around couples who seem to have it more together could leave you feeling even worse about your own relationship.

LIZ: It sounds like you want to keep us to yourself.

CT: [Smiles] It probably does. But even more, I want you to get what you need so that you and Martin can both be content with what you have together. Then it'd be fine for you to be in a couples enrichment group to make your relationship even better.

Stop and Think:

Be sure to include your answers in your journal.

1. What was your reaction when Liz accused the couple therapist of wanting to "keep us to yourself"?
2. If you'd been the couple therapist, how would you have wanted to respond?
3. What did you think of CT's response? How might she have improved upon it?

Individual and Family Therapy

As previously mentioned, couple issues may emerge during family therapy sessions. Couple issues may also become apparent from the frequency and manner in which one partner talks about the relationship during individual psychotherapy sessions.

In a family system, it is not uncommon for a child to manifest symptoms of the parents' relationship distress. The child, rather than the couple, then bears the symptoms and often the label of sick or problematic family member. Minuchin's (1974; Minuchin, Rosman, & Baker, 1978) concept of triangles exemplifies this phenomenon, and his research with fragile diabetic children whose blood sugar spiked when they observed their parents arguing provided empirical support. Referring a symptomatic partner for individual treatment similarly reinforces the notion that he or she is the sick or problematic one.

Some child and adult psychotherapists, as well as some primary care practitioners notice clues beyond a child or partner's symptoms that suggest couple or family distress. These biomedical and psychosocial practitioners then refer for couple or family therapy. When Christina was 17, her primary care practitioner noticed an unusual weight loss as well as scarring on her arms and legs. Neither could be attributed to an underlying biomedical cause, and the practitioner recommended family therapy because he had also observed similar symptoms in Liz. Liz and Martin's conflict re-emerged during family therapy sessions. Liz and Martin then had the opportunity to revisit their couple issues (Esposito & Hattem, 2017).

When couple issues emerge in a family therapy context, the family therapist has the option to address them with the entire family present or separately with the couple alone in conjoint couple therapy. To the writer's knowledge, guidelines for which context to use are not clearly specified in the couple or family therapy literature. Different theoretical models and different couple and family therapy practitioners have different preferences. However, most have observed that children know far more than their parents suspect about the couple's relationship issues and so theory, logistics, and the couple's comfort level may inform any one couple and family therapist's choice of whether to work on couple issues with or without the children present.

Sometimes it becomes helpful to schedule one or more family therapy sessions as part of couple therapy. The writer has worked with couples whose children have been concerned about their parents' relationship and curious about their couple therapy. At her urging and when appropriate, couples have sometimes reluctantly extended and their children happily accepted an invitation to a family session. During the session, the couple therapist has asked the children to arrange their parents as they would like to see them together and then themselves in relation to their parents. The process of creating and processing a visual and experiential family tableau has been called sculpting. The couple therapist has then talked to the children about their experience doing the sculpting while the parents listened quietly. She has processed the family therapy session with the couple during their next couple therapy session. Partners have sometimes commented that their children had helped them view themselves in a slightly different light.

Couple issues that emerge during individual therapy present in an entirely different way than those that arise during family therapy, as the conversation between Liz and CT in the previous section illustrated. Some couple therapists argue that systems theory posits that individual change occurring for any reason, including one partner's individual therapy, by definition creates changes in the couple's relationship as well as in all of the other relationships of which the individual is a part. Others argue that individual therapy with one partner risks the potentially deleterious effects of talking about the partner without the therapist observing the couple's dynamics.

Stop and Think:

Be sure to record your responses in your journal.

1. Think of a time you talked to one of your friends instead of the person with whom you were upset about something that was bothering you about that person. Also think about a time a friend has talked to you about someone else instead of directly to that person.
2. How did talking to the third person help, hinder, or have no effect upon the situation?
3. What might be the benefits or risks of one partner in a committed relationship talking about the other's perceived flaws to someone outside the relationship?

As has been apparent throughout this textbook, Liz and Martin, like many distressed couples, frequently experienced and ascribed very different meanings to the same events. Additionally, because couple dynamics are often outside partners' awareness, a couple therapist working with only one partner would have no way of discerning those dynamics and thus no effective way to intervene to change them.

The reverse also happens. Individual issues may emerge during couple therapy. Whether these are treated with the partner present or one or both partners referred for individual psychotherapy again depends upon the theoretical orientation of the practitioner and the comfort levels of the partners.

For example, Martin's anxiety about his anger and Liz's about her weight could be addressed with the other present. However, the couple therapist would need to monitor empathy between the partners in order to maintain a safe environment for the one struggling with an individual issue. If a partner's empathy can be accessed while the other is vulnerable, the potential to heal the individuals and the couple's relationship simultaneously is enormous.

Ethical issues generally preclude the same therapist from working with one or both partners in individual therapy and the couple in conjoint couple therapy (see Chapter 11). If either partner's empathy or comfort level is insufficient to do individual work with both partners present, then referrals for one or both partners to different individual psychotherapists are indicated. Permission for the one or two individual psychotherapists and the couple therapist to communicate with one another so that they can ensure they are working as a team is helpful.

Some individual psychotherapists conduct conjoint couple sessions from time to time while working with an individual. This alternative may be useful when an individual's issues have impacted the couple without creating relationship distress. When one partner suffers symptoms of post-traumatic stress, has survived an abusive childhood, or has discovered unfinished issues from a previous relationship, then periodic conjoint sessions with his or her partner to maximize the positive impact of the individual work on the client's relationship and ensure that the individual work is not detrimental to the relationship may prove helpful. If couple issues requiring additional intervention emerge during a conjoint session, the individual psychotherapist would refer the couple to someone else for couple therapy.

As with any treatment modality or problem, a therapist is ethically required to practice only within the boundaries of his or her training, experience, and competency. An individual psychotherapist who has taken a single couple and family therapy class in graduate school needs to refer for couple or family therapy. Similarly, a couple or family therapist who has not been trained to work with certain individual issues must refer even if the partners are willing and able to engage in individual work in the presence of the other. You will read more about these and other ethical issues unique to couple therapy in Chapter 11.

Conclusions

You have read about premarital and pre-commitment counseling, sex therapy, couples group therapies, and the ways both couple and individual issues emerge and are treated in individual, couple, and family therapy contexts. In the three preceding chapters, you were introduced to a number of theories of couple therapy and their application to the couple you are following in this textbook, Liz Manning-Jones and Martin Jones. These theories included the overarching concepts of systems theory, the foundational behavioral and psychodynamic theories of couple therapy, and six post-modern theories of couple therapy.

In the third and final section of this textbook, you will learn more about the practice of couple therapy. Chapters include special topics in couple therapy, the couple therapist's experience doing couple therapy, ethical issues in couple therapy, and additional services to which couple therapists refer. The book concludes with a look into the future for Liz and Martin, their couple therapist, and for you as you complete this introduction to couple therapy.

References

AAMFT. (2017). Marriage preparation. Retrieved from http://www.aamft.org/iMIS15/AAMFT/Content/Consumer_Updates/Marriage_Preparation.aspx.

American Psychiatric Association. (2013). *Diagnostic and statistical manual of mental disorders* (5th ed.). Washington DC: American Psychiatric Publishing.

Busby, D. M., Ivey, D.C., Harris, S. M., & Ates, C. (2007). Self-directed, therapist-directed, and assessment-based interventions for premarital couples. *Family Relations*, 56, 279–290.

Carter, S. & Sokol, J. (2004). *Men who can't love. How to recognize a commitment phobic man before he breaks your heart*. Lanham MD: M Evans and Company.

Doherty, W. J. & Baird, M. A. (1983). *Family therapy and family medicine. Toward the primary care of families*. New York NY: The Guilford Press.

Douglas, S. D. (1994). *Where the girls are. Growing up female with the mass media*. New York NY: Random House.

Esposito, J. & Hattem, A. (2017). *Introduction to family counseling. A case study approach*. Los Angeles CA: Sage Press.

Feld, B. (2004). Using systems thinking to understand attachment in couple and couples group therapy. *Group*, 28, 127–141.

Feldman, D. B. & Kahn, G. B. (2009). The integration of relationship-focused group therapy with couple treatment. *International Journal of Group Psychotherapy*, 39 (1), 109–126.

Flowers, B. J. & Olson, D. H. (1993). ENRICH Marital Satisfaction Scale: A brief research and clinical tool. *Journal of Family Psychology*, 7 (2), 176–185.

Ginsberg, B. G. (2006). Relationship enhancement couple therapy and couple group therapy. *Group*, 30 (2), 5–24.

Guerney, B. G., Jr. (1970). *Relationship enhancement.* San Francisco CA: Jossey-Bass.

Hendrix, H. (1988). *Getting the love you want. A guide for couples.* New York NY: Atria Books.

Hendrix, H. & Hunt, H. (2004). *Receiving love. Transform your relationship by letting yourself be loved.* New York NY: Atria Books.

Kaplan, H. S. (1974). *The new sex therapy.* New York NY: Bruner/Mazel.

Kaslow, F. & Lieberman, E. J. (1981). Couples group therapy: rationale, dynamics, and process. In G. P. Sholevar (Ed.). *The handbook of marriage and marital therapy.* New York NY: Springer.

Kilgo, R. D. (1975). Counseling couples in groups. *The Family Coordinator*, 24 (3), 33–42.

LoPiccolo, J. & LoPiccolo, L. (Eds.). (1978). *Handbook of sex therapy.* New York NY: Plenum Press.

Loving v. Virginia. (1967). Retrieved from https://www.law.cornell.edu/supremecourt/text/388/1.

Masters, W. H. & Johnson, V. E. (1966). *Human sexual response.* Boston MA: Little, Brown.

Masters, W. H. & Johnson, V. E. (1970). *Human sexual inadequacy.* Boston MA: Little, Brown.

Minuchin, S. (1974). *Families and family therapy.* Cambridge MA: Harvard University Press.

Minuchin, S. (2007). Unfolding the laundry. Retrieved from https://www.aamft.org/iMIS15/AAMFT/store/store.aspx?cmd=prod&prod=V001.

Minuchin S., Rosman, B. L., & Baker, L. (1978). *Psychosomatic families. Anorexia nervosa in context.* Cambridge MA: Harvard University Press.

Moreno, J. L. (1946). *Psychodrama volume 1.* Boston MA: Beacon House

Napier, A. Y. & Whitaker, C. A. (1978). *The family crucible.* New York NY: Harper & Row.

Perls, F. S. (1992). *Ego, hunger, and aggression.* Gouldsboro ME: The Gestalt Journal Press.

Weeks, G. R. & Gambescia, N. (2015). Couple therapy and sexual problems. In A. S. Gurman, J. L. Lebow, & D. K. Snyder (Eds.). *Clinical handbook of couple therapy (5th ed.)*. New York NY: Guilford Press.

Yalom, I. (1970). *The theory and practice of group psychotherapy*. New York NY: Basic Books.

Yalom, I. & Leszcz, M. (2005). *The theory and practice of group psychotherapy* (5th *ed.*). New York NY: Basic Books.

Zimmerman, T. S., Prest, L. A., & Wetzel, B. E. (1997). Solution-focused couple therapy groups. An empirical study. *Journal of Marriage and Family Therapy*, 19, 125–144.

For Further Study

Berg, R. C., Landreth, G. L., & Fall, K. A. (2013). *Group counseling. Concepts and procedures*. New York NY: Routledge.

Braithwaite, D., Olson, L., Golish, T., Soukup, C., & Turman, P. (2001). "Becoming a family": Developmental process represented in blended family discourse. *Journal of Applied Communication Research*, 29 (3), 221–247.

Gonzales, J. (2009). Prefamily counseling. Working with blended families. *Journal of Divorce and Remarriage*, 50, 148–157.

Wheeler, G. (1991). *Gestalt reconsidered. A new approach to contact and resistance*. New York NY: Gardner Press.

CHAPTER 9

Special Topics in Couple Therapy

Learning Objectives

1. Paraphrase the difference between diversity and multiculturalism and describe the importance of the distinction to the practice of couple therapy.
2. Describe the steps to developing a culturally competent practice of couple therapy.
3. Discuss the ways in which narrative therapy specifically addresses issues that may arise in couple therapy with bicultural, biracial, and LGBTQIA couples.
4. Describe the distinction between cohabitation, open relationships, and polyamory on the one hand and race, ethnicity, gender identity, and gender preference on the other in regard to their impact on couples.
5. Contrast uncoupling due to the death of a partner with dissolution of the relationship, or divorce.
6. Discuss the similarities and differences of the four transitions across the life cycle addressed in this chapter.
7. Illustrate the goals of couple therapy for couples facing biomedical and mental illness or substance abuse.
8. Discuss the ways in which trust is impacted by extra-relationship affairs, intimate partner violence, and unmet expectations.

When you read the word couple, what is the visual image that first comes to your mind? Our dominant cultural associations with the word couple include youth, physical and mental health, white, middle class, heterosexual, Christian, of western European descent, monogamous, harmonious, and permanently committed to one another legally and spiritually. This dominant cultural model excludes and thus implicitly delegitimizes, marginalizes, and demeans a significant number, likely a majority, of couples. Couple therapists cannot practice ethically or effectively without recognizing the impact of the dominant cultural model upon their assumptions and then stretching themselves to learn about and respect other ways of being. In other words, couple therapists must develop cultural competence and maintain a multicultural approach to our work with couples.

This chapter begins with a brief description of cultural competence. It then addresses a handful of specific forms of coupledom that are outside the dominant cultural model. The scope of this chapter is sufficiently broad that the content will not, of necessity, be treated in depth. The underlying theme will be the ethical imperative to develop and maintain a multicultural perspective and a culturally competent approach to couple therapy, so that couples whose demographics and values do not fit the couple therapist's world view receive sensitive and respectful treatment. Students are encouraged to learn more about these and other topics related to the practice of multicultural couple therapy through individual research, group assignments, and future coursework.

Stop and Think:

Be sure to include your responses in your journal.

1. Describe the image that first occurred to you when you read the word "couple."
2. How does that image fit the dominant cultural model summarized above?
3. What characteristics of yourself and your experience influenced your image?
4. What characteristics of yourself and your experience influenced how well your image fit the dominant cultural model?

Cultural Competence

A full description of culturally competent couple therapy practice is beyond the scope of a single chapter in an introductory textbook. However, there are several terms and concepts that may be helpful to bear in mind as you read the remainder of this chapter.

Diversity refers to changes in numbers. Killian (2013) cited a rapid increase in biracial marriages between 2005 and 2015, and the 2010 census indicated that interracial marriages increased 28 percent, from 7 percent of new marriages in 2000 to 10 percent of new marriages in 2010. This is an increase in diversity that may lead to more biracial couples seeking couple therapy. However, it is critical for couple therapists to remember that the term diversity implies difference and thus conveys an underlying assumption that the dominant cultural norm is the standard by which everyone else is evaluated.

By contrast, multiculturalism is about existing power structures that differentially impact individuals and therefore couples based on gender, sexual orientation, ethnicity, race, religion, age, socioeconomic status, country of origin, and health. Rather than assuming, for example, that heterosexual couples represent the norm while same-sexed couples embody a form of diversity, a multicultural perspective holds that the power structure inherent in any society determined that heterosexuality is normative, leaving same-sexed couples marginalized, demeaned, and with far less power.

Members of disempowered cultural groups must adapt to those with more power in their everyday lives. They thus may find themselves moving back and forth between disparate cultures on a daily basis. Examples include using language differently within and outside a particular community. The term white privilege derives from the phenomenon that white people do not need to think about how they use language, move, appear, or behave because white people have more power than people of color.

Couple therapists hold power because of their role as expert. Additionally, couple therapists from the dominant culture bring the privileges associated with their cultural status. Clients from disempowered groups may interact with their couple therapist as they do with other members of the dominant culture, irrespective of the couple therapist's multicultural competence.

It is essential for couple therapists to be sensitive to power differentials and to acknowledge and minimize the impact of their own privilege on their work. Post-modern theorists acknowledged the importance of multiculturalism and attempted to mitigate its impact with a collaborative client-therapist approach that attended to meanings ascribed by the client. While the couple therapist's multicultural competence is essential, it may not be sufficient for clients who are used to being marginalized by members of the dominant cultural group.

Stop and Think:

Be sure to include your responses in your journal.

1. Discuss the implications of the distinction between the concept of diversity and that of multiculturalism for you as a person and as a professional.
2. Think about a time you have adapted your behavior to fit the wishes of someone in power and describe what you believed you needed to do differently in order to manage the situation.
3. Did you need to adapt because of the situation or because of a characteristic about yourself? If the former, imagine what it would have been like if you had been unable to tell yourself the situation was time and location specific. If the latter, what are the commonalities of the situations in which you must adapt because of that characteristic about yourself?
4. If you identify as a member of the dominant culture, now imagine yourself having to adapt in such a way multiple times each day. Record your thoughts about what that might be like for you.

The first step in developing a culturally competent practice is exploring one's own world view. We view the world through our unique experiences, which include our experiences as members of various cultural groups, or intersectionality, and the values we have acquired as a result.

Liz and Martin's couple therapist was a middle-class, white, cis-gendered, heterosexual female. As such, her world view had been influenced by third-wave feminism and she believed that women who could afford to stop working outside the home were free to choose how to balance work and family. As a white woman, Liz had the power to disregard her suggestion that Liz find a balance that worked for her. Had Martin been a Middle Eastern or Latino man who subscribed to the traditional cultural values associated with those ethnicities, he might have found the couple therapist's suggestions to Liz unhelpful at best and disrespectful at worst. Further, the cultural power imbalance might have discouraged him from disagreeing with her. As it happened, Martin was a black man whose family of origin was immersed in white culture and whose own experience had exposed him to the values Liz and the couple therapist shared. However, upon meeting him, a culturally competent couple therapist would not assume that Martin would feel empowered to disregard her suggestions when they were incompatible with his own world view.

Stop and Think:

Be sure to include your responses in your journal.

1. Re-answer the questions about world view from the Stop and Think at the end of Chapter 3.
    1. What do you know about how the world works and how do you know it?
    2. What do you believe about human nature?
    3. What do you believe about how relationships work?
    4. How do you define a successful outcome of couple therapy?
    5. How do you define couple health?
2. How do your experiences, including your culture, race, and gender, affect your world view?
3. Summarize your world view based on your answers to the six preceding questions.
4. Now review your previous responses to those seven questions.
5. What did you alter now that you have begun to understand the concepts of multiculturalism and cultural competence?

Multiculturalism mandates that couple therapists adhere to the reality that all experience is context-based. If the couple's cultural context differs from that of the couple therapist's, then understanding the couple's dynamics and needs within the partners' cultural context is critical to practicing competently. This context includes not only the meanings a culture ascribes to coupledom but also the ways in which the dominant culture marginalizes and disadvantages members of the client's culture. Subtle demeaning and exclusion are often part of a client's daily experience, as stereotypes and biases are projected by members of the dominant culture onto non-members. And these micro-aggressions impact not only the partners' individual mental health and functioning but also the couple's. The salient point for couple therapists is that defensiveness, withholding information, discomfort expressing feelings, and a variety of behaviors that may be evaluated negatively by a couple therapist of the dominant culture may appear very different when viewed in the context the couple's experiences as members of a disempowered population. The meanings partners ascribe to their behavior and experience also may differ significantly from those the couple therapist ascribes by virtue of the cultural power differential between them even before accounting for individual differences.

Multicultural competency is demonstrated through the recognition, verbal and otherwise, of the oppression and marginalization of women, people of color, immigrants, refugees, and anyone who is not a white, monogamous, heterosexual, cis-gendered, Christian displaying culturally approved gender-specific role behavior. Multicultural competency does not require a couple therapist to already know everything about a couple's culture(s); however, it does require her or him to be open to learning from the couple as well as from workshops and supervision with more culturally competent couple therapists (Lum, 2007; Pope-Davis, Coleman, Liu, & Toporek (2003).

Stop and Think:

Be sure to include your answers in your journal.

1 Do you think Brown's (1994) exhortation to couple therapist's to view feminist therapy as an act of resistance to the dominant cultural narrative (Chapter 7) also applies more generally to multicultural couple therapy?
2 Explain your answer with examples from your experience or from what you have read about Liz and Martin.

Couples Who Do Not Fit the Dominant Cultural Model

Most couple therapy theory and research has been based on the assumption that couples are white, middle class, heterosexual, cis-gendered, and married as young adults. In the post-modern era, theorists have questioned the utility of applying these models and methods to couples who do not fit the dominant cultural stereotype. For example, couple therapists assume that each heterosexual couple is unique while generalizing about same-sexed couples. Multicultural practice necessitates recognizing the uniqueness of all couples while acknowledging the existence and impact of culturally defined world views and the societal constraints upon couples for whom the dominant cultural model cannot be generalized.

When couple therapists from the dominant culture assume, however unconsciously, that race, ethnicity, sexual orientation, gender identity, age, health, or socioeconomic status have no bearing on the presenting problem, they risk overlooking a crucial feature of the couple's experience. Alternatively, when couple therapists from the dominant culture assume, however unconsciously, that one or more of these demographic characteristics is the predominant factor in a couple's problem, they risk overlooking the way the couple defines the presenting problem. Minority stress, relationship status, and obstacles to social support exist and may exacerbate the presenting problem; couple therapists need to recognize these stressors not experienced by members of the dominant culture while simultaneously considering that a couple's demographics may not be central to either the presenting problem or the couple's perception of it.

Bicultural and Biracial Couples

The Supreme Court did not overturn laws banning biracial marriage until 1967, a year after Liz and Martin were born (Loving v. Virginia, 1967). In other words, had they been a generation older and lived in a state that continued to ban interracial marriage, Martin and Liz's marriage would have been considered a criminal act.

Stop and Think:

Be sure to include your responses in your journal.

1. What would be uncomfortable for you about working with a biracial couple like Liz and Martin? Be specific and honest. If you did not password protect your journal or have not been keeping it in a private place, you may do so now. The point is, we are all a product of culture, and the more honest you are with yourself about the impact of your cultural experience the less likely your prejudices will impact your clients in detrimental ways. Note that this statement reflects the writer's experiential world view.
2. React to the following statement: Prior to 1967 for biracial couples and 2015 for same-sexed couples, the dominant culture's discomfort pre-empted people's right to marry.
3. In your world view, where does one person's right to be comfortable limit another's rights? Does your answer differ when the one whose right to comfort is white and the one whose rights are in question is a person of color? What about a situation in which the uncomfortable person is heterosexual and cis-gendered and the one whose rights are being considered is not?

Race and culture are social constructs (Basirico, Cashion, & Eshleman, 2014; Gannon, 2016; Lum, 2007). While most people think of race as a group of physical attributes associated with ancestry in a specific geographic location, that conceptualization of race is itself a socially agreed-upon construct. In other words, an individual's race is part of her or his cultural identity, rather than a list of biological attributes or association with a geographic region.

Culture is a set of norms, rules, beliefs, language, and artifacts that define a group with which members identify (Basirico et al., 2014). When members of a cultural group violate cultural norms, as Liz and Martin did when they married, negative sanctions may ensue.

Liz and Martin may be described as a biracial couple. Liz's family was of eastern European descent, and she grew up in white, middle-class, Catholic culture. Martin's family identified as black, middle class, and Protestant. If Liz had been a Muslim of Middle Eastern descent and Martin a European Jew, they would have been described as a bicultural couple because the Middle East is an arbitrarily drawn geographic region categorized as an ethnic, rather than a racial group, and religion is considered an aspect of ethnicity.

Socialization to one's culture impacts one's world view. As a result, each partner's world view, and thus the meanings he or she ascribes to the behaviors and intentions of the other, are influenced by her or his culture. Even when couples are of similar ethnicity and race, family cultures differ and these, too, influence meaning.

Culturally based misinterpretations of one another may create unique difficulties for biracial and bicultural couples. Killian (2015) suggested that when the partner of a more privileged culture assumes her or his cultural world view is superior to the other's or when either partner devalues the other's world view, the resultant disrespect and resistance between them may become problematic. He suggested couple therapists explore each partner's cultural experience, as well as how they manage differences as a couple. As part of assessment and intervention, he recommended that each partner speak for the other, in order to bring to awareness the meanings they ascribe to one another. The couple therapist can then facilitate the partners co-authoring their identity as a bicultural or biracial couple.

Biracial and bicultural couples, like other couples who do not fit the dominant cultural model, experience what is termed minority stress. Minority stress results from the beliefs and attitudes imposed by the dominant culture, as well as both verbal and physical aggression. Members of groups outside the dominant cultural norm may absorb these demeaning attitudes into their sense of self or project them onto their partner. Couple therapists must remain alert to the impact of such attitudes on partners' mental health and couple dynamics and intervene to externalize the dominant cultural narrative and empower the partners to reject the view of the oppressor.

Members of groups outside the dominant cultural model also suffer from trauma or anticipatory trauma associated with discrimination and hate crimes. Either or both partners may exhibit symptoms of trauma requiring the couple therapist's intervention.

Martin's parents came of age during the civil rights movement, when violence occurred around school desegregation and accessing voting rights. They and their friends were never as comfortable interacting with members of the white community as their children were. Martin had noticed white people's surprise that he was a highly educated professional, grew up in a middle-class family, and was married to a white woman. Such surprise is an example of micro-aggression. These people's white privilege was exemplified by the expectation that they could share similar facts about themselves without even considering anyone would be surprised by them. Perhaps more stereotypically, several of Liz's friends and colleagues had expressed distaste when they learned Martin was black, and a close friend of one of Martin's sisters had been aggravated by his choice to marry a white woman.

Couple therapists find themselves working with partners whose race or ethnicity not only differs from each other's but also from the couple therapist's. It is critical that couple therapists maintain awareness of their own biases and openness to learning about the partners' cultures and the influence of culture upon them. When the couple therapist is of the dominant culture, he or she must be alert to couples acting from an assumed one-down position and intervene to create a more collaborative therapeutic relationship.

Stop and Think:

Be sure to include your responses in your journal.

1. Describe how narrative couple therapy fits the practice of couple therapy with biracial and bicultural couples.
2. What other theoretical approach(es) may be relevant to biracial and bicultural couple therapy? Explain your answer.

LGBTQIA Couples

LGBTQIA couples share the experience of social devaluation and marginalization irrespective of the ethnicity and race of either partner. Both partners have been raised in a culture that assumes the superiority of heterosexuality and cis-gendered identity and both will likely have experienced hostility and aggression individually and as a couple. Heterosexual couples, like white couples, enjoy a privileged position of safety and acceptance that LGBTQIA couples do not.

Stop and Think:

Be sure to include your responses in your journal.

1. If you are heterosexual, imagine what it would be like to be cautious about holding hands in public or kissing good-bye on a date or at the airport. How would you feel? How would you react to those feelings?
2. If you are not heterosexual, how do you feel and what are your reactions to the ways in which heterosexuals have treated you?
3. What were your family's attitudes toward LGBTQIA couples? What were those of the spiritual group with which you identify? How have these attitudes affected you?
4. What would you need to feel comfortable working with heterosexual couples if you are not heterosexual or with LGBTQIA couples if you are not LGBTQIA?

Green and Mitchell (2015) identified three unique challenges faced by LGBTQIA couples. These included decisions about and consequences of "coming out" to family, co-workers, and friends; role ambiguity between partners; and the potential to be denied access to the benefits of marriage. While access to marriage became constitutional law in the same year Green and Mitchell published their chapter, hurdles to marriage for same-sexed couples remain fixed in some jurisdictions and so the third challenge they listed has not disappeared.

Minority stress also applies to LGBTQIA couples. An individual's religious group may label him or her sinful, and the LGBTQIA individual may concur. In addition, the threats of electroshock therapy (euphemistically termed conversion therapy) and denial of employment and other legal rights currently being promoted by those in the public eye influence everyone, albeit in different ways if one is heterosexual than if one is not.

In 2009, Liz's nephew, Paul, went to another state to marry. His husband, Matt, had been dishonorably discharged from the military when someone informed their commanding officer that he was communicating with a male lover during the period euphemistically referred to as don't-ask-don't-tell. That being gay was dishonored took an emotional toll on Matt, given the meaning of dishonor. It also left Matt without the financial benefits of an honorable discharge. That he had been betrayed by someone he had considered a friend and that a dishonorable discharge would appear on background checks and thus affect his earning potential for the rest of his life were not only acts of discrimination but also subtle acts of violence not only against himself but also against his future husband and their children. The sequelae of trauma may include anger, anxiety, depression, feelings of worthlessness and hopelessness, withdrawal, substance abuse, and intimate partner violence.

Family, friends, and co-workers may reject one or both LGBTQIA partners when they learn who the partner is. Bisexual and transgendered individuals have traditionally experienced additional rejection from gay and lesbian communities. LGBTQIA couples may also find themselves in conflict about who to tell, what to tell, and when to tell. Conflict between partners may ensue when one is more uncomfortable revealing his or her sexual orientation than the other or one feels excluded from the other's family, co-workers, and/or friends.

Couple therapists can encourage LGBTQIA clients to become involved in a community of those sharing their experience. However, LGBTQIA communities tend to be predicated on white culture and people of color may be doubly excluded, both from their culture because of their sexuality and from those they would expect to comprehend their sexuality by lack of cultural sensitivity (Green & Mitchell, 2015; Lum, 2007). This phenomenon is similar to the women's movement ignoring the experience of women of color and poor women.

Trust may become an issue if one or both partners has accepted the cultural myth that gay men are promiscuous. For couples in which a partner identifies as bisexual, the myth that monogamy is impossible may also become relevant. Couple therapists must bear in mind that any commitment of monogamy entails foregoing all other relationships, irrespective of the gender of potential partners, and that people are capable of making that commitment irrespective of their sexuality and the myths surrounding it. To assume that a gay man is incapable of monogamy is as demeaning as overlooking the legitimate fears of his partner. Liz, who identified as bisexual, wanted a monogamous relationship and thus chose to limit her future partners to Martin irrespective of her sexuality. Martin trusted her and did not worry that she would betray him with either another man or a woman.

Role ambiguity is a unique challenge for same-sexed couples and for partners who share the same gender identity. Role ambiguity is a sociological term referring to situations in which the expectations attached to a particular role are unclear. For example, traditional gender roles for heterosexual couples prescribe the behaviors necessary to meet role expectations. In the traditional, dichotomized roles of the dominant culture, a husband is expected to earn a living for the family and his wife is expected to care for their home and offspring, only working outside the home when financially necessary. The writer referred to "his wife" in the last sentence to underscore the dominant cultural perspective that excludes same-sexed couples and partners with non-binary gender identification. Liz and Martin were socialized to these dominant cultural roles and had chosen to question them. They had discussed their expectations for one another and agreed to share both income and parenting responsibilities.

Partners in LGBTQIA couples have learned the culturally prescribed behaviors associated with their birth genders. As noted, these roles tend to be dichotomous and complementary. So if there are two wives or two husbands, instead of one of each, observing one's family and childhood friends does not provide clues as to who is primarily responsible for what. Similarly, if one or both partners' gender identity is non-binary, then no role expectation is attached, which also results in role ambiguity. The risk of unclear expectations for any couple is that they will not be met, leading to relationship dissatisfaction and instability, and this risk is compounded for LGBTQIA couples because roles cannot be assumed to be binary gender-based.

After the birth of their first child, Liz found herself questioning her previous commitment to challenging the traditional mother role. As a result, she experienced conflict between her role as a professional and her role as a mother. Both roles were clear to both Liz and Martin. However, for Liz, they appeared incompatible. By contrast, relationship roles cannot be assigned on the basis of gender in same-sexed, same gender-identified, or non-binary gendered couples and thus the role configuration Liz questioned would likely not be clear to either partner.

Until roles are clearly specified, they cannot be negotiated and so when role expectations are ambiguous they also become difficult to discuss. For LGBTQIA couples, each partner's expectations for the other and for the relationship may not become clear until they have been violated and thus role ambiguity may remain unaddressed. Once identified as a source of distress, however, couple therapists can facilitate the exploration of expectations and role preferences for same-sexed and same and non-binary gender-identified partners. Green and Mitchell (2015) suggested that couple therapists can encourage LGB couples to observe and discuss roles within the LGB community. Involvement in the community facilitates creating new social networks and role clarity. As previously noted, this community tends to be less inclusive of transgendered, queer, and intersexed members, leaving the recommendation inapplicable to them.

Couple therapists working with LGBTQIA couples thus explore a variety of issues in addition to relationship dynamics. These include whether the heterosexual model of coupledom fits at all, how the couple defines itself, the impact of being a couple on each partner's other relationships, rules about monogamy and safe sex, how to manage money and tasks, expectations and obligations regarding permanence, availability of health care power of attorney and inheritance and any provisions for these, clarification of the emotional commitment if the couple is unable to marry, resolving previous relationships that did not clearly end in divorce, and how embedded the couple is within a supportive community (Green & Mitchell, 2015).

Exploring an unmarried LGBTQIA couple's intention about whether or not to marry is also an important part of couple therapy. Marriage is a public commitment and as such involves "coming out" legally. Until 2003, federal law did not override state laws criminalizing consensual sex with a same-sexed partner. And not until 2015 did the Supreme Court extend access to the rights and benefits of marriage to same-sexed couples, and an application for a marriage license may require a binary gender identification in most, if not all jurisdictions. The decision to marry is thus fraught with historical oppression, discrimination, and fear, and the couple therapist must acknowledge all of these.

Heterosexual and cis-gendered couple therapists working with LGBTQIA couples need to be aware of their own heterosexual and cis-gender biases and become more familiar with LGBTQIA communities. Many couple therapists have had little personal experience with couples who are not white, Christian, financially comfortable, heterosexual, and cis-gendered. Honesty with oneself, requesting clarification from clients, learning in supervision and workshops, and seeking out members of groups with which the couple therapist is unfamiliar may increase his or her comfort and effectiveness.

Couples Choosing Not to Marry

Because of the laws described in the previous subsections of this chapter, the freedom to choose not to marry has been, until recently, a prerogative only for members of the dominant culture. Additionally, women have been informally barred from the choice to not marry in three ways: restricted ability to own property until 1900, restricted ability to obtain credit until the 1970s, and inability to earn equally as laws guaranteeing equal pay for equal work remain to be passed as of this writing. Many religious groups discourage cohabitation without marriage, further restricting options for delaying or not marrying unless one wishes to be celibate. Some states, like North Carolina, have passed laws restricting cohabitation for heterosexual as well as LGBTQIA couples in an attempt to discriminate against the latter.

Stop and Think:

Be sure to include your responses in your journal.

1. What do you think of the choice to cohabit?
2. Does it make a difference to you if the couple chose to cohabit before, rather than instead of, marrying?

Assuming the option not to marry, remaining single is preferable to being coupled for some. For others, coupling without cohabiting is desirable. Still others wish to cohabit. Some couples cohabit without the intention of permanence. Other couples decide to live together because the partners feel ready to commit to cohabitation yet unready for marriage. Some couples cohabit as a test before marriage. Other couples reject the institution of marriage or do not view public, legal commitments with the intention of permanence as compatible with their personal goals or beliefs.

When a person or couple does not conform to the norm of marriage, social consequences that may affect both the person and the couple are triggered. For example, Liz had wanted to cohabit prior to marriage. Martin was concerned about his mother's reaction because of her strong religious beliefs and involvement in their church community. He thought she would be both embarrassed and disappointed in him. Liz asked whether becoming engaged prior to living together would be easier for his mother, and Martin did not think it would. So they married before sharing an apartment.

Because Liz and Martin shared the goal of marrying and only disagreed about timing, their decision was relatively uncomplicated. When one partner wishes to marry and the other does not, however, a variety of related problems may arise. These include one or both partners acquiescing while hoping the other will change his or her mind; fighting about the meaning each ascribes to marriage or the level of commitment each has to the other; or endless arguments about the correct view of the institution and meaning of marriage. If Liz had had an understandable fear of becoming stuck in a negative situation as her mother had or concern that marriage would impede her career goals, one or more of these couple problems may have ensued. Couple therapists neither make decisions for their clients nor tell them what to do. However, they can facilitate conversations in which each partner is heard and validated by the other, facilitate negotiation between partners, and minimize recrimination if a mutually agreed-upon solution cannot be found.

Experience suggests that arguments about who is right and who is wrong are not only unproductive but also detrimental to couples because the argument is without resolution, and unresolved arguments tend to generate ill will. Strong beliefs and opinions, especially in a situation that is viewed as a dichotomy, are difficult to change. When couples argue about who is right and who is wrong, the most likely outcome is that they will end the argument without resolving it and both will feel frustrated, invalidated, and/or unheard. Had Liz and Martin argued about whether he was right to prioritize his mother's feelings, they would likely have engaged in numerous, unresolved arguments about the correctness of Roxanne's values and Martin's loyalty to her, rather than negotiating a way to resolve their different preferences. Additionally, because white Western culture tends to prioritize the individual while all others tend to prioritize the group (Lum, 2007), Liz and Martin's culturally influenced views regarding how to balance the needs of individuals with those of the group may be different. A culturally competent couple therapist would be attuned to such discrepancies underlying their argument.

Systemic and post-modern perspectives focus the couple therapist on the couple's dynamic and the context and meaning of an argument to each partner, rather than the irresolvable content. The writer has been known to say, "You've been arguing about this topic since before you met me and haven't yet convinced the other you're right. I'm wondering whether it's safe to assume you're never going to agree about this and then figure out a way to make the situation workable for you?"

Open Relationships and Polyamorous Couples

One of the drawbacks of practicing couple therapy is discomfort with one's friends and relatives' prurient fascination with open relationships and polyamory. Couples are unique, whether inside or outside of the dominant cultural model, and it is incumbent upon a couple therapist to become comfortable talking about sexuality and only raise concerns when sexual behavior is not consensual between partners or is unsafe.

Like any other couple that does not fit the dominant cultural model, open relationships and polyamorous couples are not problematic unless external social or internal individual and couple pressures are exerted. If both partners are in agreement, then their choice to reject monogamy will not be a problem between them. However, if one partner wants an open or polyamorous relationship and the other does not, problems may arise around their disagreement and/or the acquiescence and unhappiness of the partner wishing monogamy. As with disagreements about cohabitation, couple therapists can help couples negotiate their differences and avoid unresolvable arguments that lead to more hurt and anger.

The writer has found herself struggling with her own feelings when one partner talks about the need for multiple partners in order to fully realize her or his potential as a human being (Chapter 10) and the other does not. What is relevant here is that, if the couple therapist views one partner's statement as discounting the other partner, then it is possible the partner is feeling discounted. Thus, making the possibly unintended impact of the statement explicit may help a caring partner restate his or her wishes in a more inclusive way.

Partners in open relationships sometimes find themselves becoming more emotionally involved with sexual partners than they had intended, creating problems similar to infidelity for monogamous couples. While this may be less likely in polyamorous relationships because other partners are presumed to be secondary, couple therapists who remain alert to how each partner in the primary relationship talks about secondary partners can detect its presence.

Transitioning Couples

As individuals and couples transition from one stage to the next in their life cycles, challenges arise. As noted in Chapter 3, stage theories of individual and family development presume these challenges occur and posit that their successful resolution is prerequisite to future development. In this section, you will read a brief description of four couple transitions and the issues those transitions create that may bring couples to couple therapy.

Marriage

The decision to marry and the impact of planning a wedding on a couple were touched upon in Chapter 8, as well as in the previous subsection. However, marrying is an important transition and deserves mention here.

Making a public commitment with the intention of permanence alters expectations placed upon partners and the couple. Each partner's expectations change, as do those of members of their social network, cultural group, and the larger society as embodied in statutes and attitudes. While roles and couple dynamics may not change, the meaning attached to being a couple, as well as culturally learned expectations for husbands and wives, do. However, descriptions of these changes are more anecdotal than researched.

Coming together as a committed couple is a transition to intimacy with a peer in the individual life cycle, the first stage of both the couple and family life cycles, and a transition for parents as their children marry and form new families. While these are dominant cultural conceptualizations, most couples and couple therapists subscribe to them to some extent.

Successfully transitioning to marriage involves living intimately with a life partner, negotiating shared goals and expectations, assigning roles, and presenting as a couple rather than an individual to the larger society. Individuals and couples struggle with these transitions, and couple therapists assess and intervene to facilitate successful transitions to marriage that will generalize to negotiating the future changes that the couple will face.

Childbearing Choices

Most cultures expect newly coupled partners to begin bearing children. While many couples choose to procreate, others do not. And although some couples are unable to bear children, this subsection will focus on couples who decline the option to bear or adopt children, while fertility challenges will be addressed later in the chapter.

Not all couples wish to have children. Of those who do, some delay childbearing. Pressures from family and friends can be destabilizing for a newly formed couple choosing not to have children or to delay childbearing. Additionally, attitudes about the age beyond which pregnancy is not an option vary. Highly educated couples may choose to delay childbearing while they establish their careers, yet family and old friends may view them as selfish for not procreating by a specific age. Such pressures and demeaning attitudes may impact one partner more than the other, undermining previous agreements about whether and when to bear children.

While same-sexed couples cannot procreate together, alternatives exist. Some lesbian couples select one partner to become pregnant or each bear a child. Some gay and transgendered couples find a surrogate or female friend to bear a child fathered by one of the partners if possible. Other couples adopt children, although barriers to LGBTQIA adoptions continue to exist in many jurisdictions.

Adoption is a challenging process at best, an insurmountable one at worst. It is expensive, frustrating, and unlike pregnancy does not allow a period of time to adapt to the impending changes a child brings. Attitudes about adopted children vary, opinions about when to tell the child are myriad, and international adoptions present numerous legal, financial, and cultural challenges.

However a child enters a family, couples must then adapt to the presence of another human being whose needs take precedence in their relationship. Family and friends' expectations change, as do partners' expectations for themselves and each other. Partners lose sleep and careers are impacted by the demands and expectations of parenting. Sleep loss leads to grouchiness, dysphoria, and the misperception that one will never sleep again. There are so many new tasks associated with parenting that each partner may believe he or she is doing more than a fair share and the other is not. Another source of distress between partners may be the expense of a new family member. Child care, clothes that are continually being outgrown, doctor visits, toys, and paraphernalia such as diaper bags, car seats, and strollers are all expensive. If the child presents additional challenges, all of these changes are exacerbated. Finally, differing approaches to parenting as well as religious and ethnic differences may become more difficult to negotiate once a child's socialization is at stake.

Research indicates that marital satisfaction declines dramatically after the birth of the first child. Couples who were previously content may find that the stress, sleep loss, and demands of the child challenge their equilibrium and resources for coping. Liz and Martin's first presentation for couple therapy illustrated this phenomenon. Couple therapists are in a unique position to help couples manage these stresses and develop new ways of relating to one another to accommodate the changes.

Aging

Aging is included here because couples' experience as well as the meaning of experience changes when either partner ascribes meaning to a specific birthday, when children become adults and leave home, when partners' parents die, when one or both retires from working outside the home, or when one becomes ill. The meaning attached to these events determines a person or couple's view of aging. Yalom (2008) wrote about the four aspects of meaning in one's life in his book about aging and death.

As noted in Chapter 8, sexuality changes as partners age. Energy, flexibility, stamina, and interest in doing what the partners once did diminish. Priorities change, and couples often consider how they wish to grow old and take care of the other when one of them becomes incapacitated and/or dies. Some couples move to be closer to adult children and grandchildren, forcing partners to rebuild their social network in the new location. Others struggle to adapt to retirement or with one partner becoming debilitated. The likelihood of issues associated with when and how to convince a partner to stop driving, fear of losing the partner, guilt for wishing an ill partner gone, and the physical and emotional toll of caring for a sick or disabled partner increase for couples as age increases.

Liz's parents had retired and her father had died by the time she and Martin returned to couple therapy in 2002. None of Liz and Martin's four parents had considered what they would do when they could no longer live in their single-family dwellings. Liz's father had become unwell although not incapacitated. He then suffered a cardiac event and lived only a few hours afterward. Her mother required constant emotional support from her daughters, even while Liz was caring for school-aged children and working part time. Liz and Martin had to adapt to changes in Liz's availability and the children's upset while she comforted her mother. After several months, Sally became interested in a widower she met at church and her demands on her daughters decreased. However, he later developed Alzheimer's disease and the toll of taking care of him at home began to undermine Sally's health.

Uncoupling

A fourth transition is one all couples face: uncoupling. Every couple uncouples, whether through the death of a partner or the decision by one or both partners to dissolve their couple relationship. Married couples cannot legally dissolve their relationship without divorcing, although some couples remain married and estranged for years.

Death. When one partner dies, the other finds himself or herself uncoupled despite her or his wishes to the contrary and grieving her or his partner. Grief groups may be available, as well as individual therapy for grief. Additionally, some couples present for couple therapy while one partner is dying, either to resolve long-standing issues between them before it becomes impossible or to manage their differing ways of handling illness and death.

When a death is sudden, there is no opportunity for the partners to experience anticipatory mourning or to say good-bye to one another. The bereaved partner may feel confused and guilty that he or she did not notice precursors that might have been treatable, in addition to feeling sad, angry, abandoned, and anxious following the loss of a life partner. The bereaved partner may see her or his own mortality in the loss. She or he may also fear life uncoupled and, having had no opportunity to prepare for it, find herself or himself unprepared for the unfamiliar and anxiety-provoking demands of managing on her or his own.

While a medical team might have warned Liz's father that his prolonged abuse of alcohol and later abuse of prescription medication could create the health problems that resulted in his death, his wife Sally did not anticipate it. They were in their 60s, and both were enjoying retirement. They lived close to children and grandchildren, were able to care for their home of many years, and continued an active social life. Bill had managed the family's finances, and Sally had no idea how to pay the bills that continued to arrive after he died.

Other deaths are prolonged, allowing the bereaved partner time to anticipate her or his loss and to say good-bye. However, the bereaved has also observed her or his beloved's suffering and often been the primary care-giver. Watching someone one loves suffer is emotionally painful. Care-giving, especially as a couple ages, is exhausting and takes both a physical and emotional toll. Additionally, the bereaved may feel some degree of relief that the partner's suffering and her or his own full-time care-taking have ended. Cultural expectations may preclude sharing relief with friends and family members, and the bereaved may feel emotionally isolated and even guilty for having wished her or his beloved to be free of pain.

Two years after Bill's death, Sally married the man she knew from the church she continued to attend. Jim was 12 years older than Sally and developed symptoms of Alzheimer's within a few years of their marriage. Sally refused her daughters' suggestions that she consider alternatives to being his full-time care-giver as his symptoms became increasingly difficult to manage. By the time Jim died, Sally was physically and emotionally exhausted, weakened, and short of breath. She was also relieved not to spend every day at the facility where he was placed during the last few months of his life. However, his adult children from his first marriage were quick to pressure her to move out of the house he had owned when they married.

Following a death, whether expected or not, family and friends may surround the bereaved for a period of culturally prescribed mourning rituals, after which the members of the bereaved's support network return to life as it was while the bereaved cannot. Not understanding the extent to which virtually every aspect of daily life changes for the bereaved, friends and family members may express impatience or concern about her or his grieving process. Although grief therapy is beyond the scope of this textbook, should a bereaved partner return to the couple's couple therapist, it is important to assure the bereaved that everyone grieves differently.

The creators of the latest *Diagnostic and Statistical Manual of Mental Disorders* (American Psychiatric Association, 2013) decided that in order to relieve the symptoms of grief it would be immediately diagnosable as a mental disorder and thus eligible for treatment with anti-depressant medication. In earlier editions, which were based on agreed-upon clinical observations, denial, guilt, perseveration, and malingering were considered symptomatic of unresolved grief, while grief itself was not considered pathological. The inevitable sadness and related symptoms, such as changes in sleep and appetite, were termed uncomplicated bereavement and were not medicated unless they became a biomedical health concern for the patient.

Stop and Think:

Be sure to include your responses in your journal.

1. What is grief? Use what you have learned in classes and observed in yourself and others to guide your answer.
2. What might be the drawbacks of avoiding grief, either through emotional denial or the use of medication to dampen the feelings associated with it?
3. What might the advantages, if any, be?

Partners rarely die simultaneously. However, one's risk of dying increases during the first two years following the death of a partner. The medical community is alert to the health of bereaved patients. Couple therapists working with bereaved clients or their family members can also listen for signs of health consequences and recommend consulting a physician when needed.

Several factors external to both the deceased and bereaved partners may complicate bereavement. These include statutes limiting the rights of unmarried partners, a social network depleted by aging, and the couple having blended their families. Couples who are unable to marry or choose not to legalize their relationship may find statutes that limit inheritance, custody of minor children, and visitation and health care power of attorney rights for the partner of a dying patient. When legal access to marriage was denied and where it remains difficult to obtain, couples have no choice but to forfeit these rights.

Aging may limit access to social support. When couples grow old together, their friends and family members may have predeceased them. Siblings and friends of long duration, as well as parents and grandparents are no longer available to provide support. While the partners continue to support one another with the help of adult children, if any, elderly parents may be reluctant to turn to their children for help and may be increasingly unable to help each other. Then, when one partner dies, the other does not have the social support she or he may have once had. And, as you have learned, social support is essential to adaptation.

Bereavement may also be complicated in blended families. While biological siblings may fight over objects and inheritances, step-siblings may be resentful of one another and of the surviving parent/step-parent. Step-children may resent or even legally oppose a step-parent inheriting anything. Prenuptial agreements and legal statutes may ultimately protect the bereaved partner, but no legal document can prevent step-children from attempts to undermine it that cause the bereaved partner emotional and financial distress. As previously noted, Sally sold her house and moved into her second husband's when she remarried. As he became increasingly demented, Liz and her sister, Barbara, worried not only about their mother's health and safety as his care-giver but also about what would happen to her after he died. As it happened, his children wanted her out of his house as soon as he was institutionalized and challenged the prenuptial agreement and will allowing her to remain in the couple's home and retain their furnishings until her death.

Dissolution and Divorce. Couples sometimes find themselves faced with what is referred to legally as irreconcilable differences between them. The partners no longer derive contentment or feelings of self-worth from their coupledom. Couple dynamics may have led to frequent, hurtful, and unresolved fights; emotional and physical distance may have become a homeostatic mechanism; or verbal or physical abuse may have arisen.

Some couples continue to live together despite loss of warmth, respect, love, or attraction. Others decide to dissolve their relationship. Although one partner may claim she or he was surprised by the other's request to end the relationship, experience as well as a systems perspective suggest that most partners covertly agreed to dissolve their relationship and then designated one partner to initiate the termination of the relationship.

When partners decide to cease cohabiting, they must divide possessions and any blended assets. When they are legally married, they must also legally divorce in order to end their coupledom. Some couples choose to remain separated without divorcing. These partners then remain legally and financially responsible for one another unless a binding separation agreement is in place. If the couple has minor children, divorce agreements include custody and child support arrangements. If the couple has not married, the jurisdiction in which they live may prohibit parental rights for the non-biologial or non-adoptive parent.

The formality of ending a relationship with a divorce decree allows emotional closure. When married couples separate without divorcing, they risk prolonging anger, grief, and the hope of reconciliation for both themselves and their children, if any. So long as financial and custody agreements are not in place, lack of clarity may ignite additional anger, confusion, uncertainty, and insecurity. The formality of divorce provides a ritual of closure similar to that of a funeral or memorial service. Just as a wedding solemnizes the couple's commitment, these ceremonies solemnize the end of that commitment.

Anecdotal observations suggest that emotional recovery from divorce takes longer than from the death of a partner. The possibility of reconciliation always exists when both partners are alive. Additionally, the potential for interactions that remind partners of previous hurt and anger continues. By contrast, there can be no hope of reconciliation and no risk of continuing negative interactions when one partner has died.

When the writer was a graduate student, one of her clinical supervisors pointed out that couples often wait so long to request couple therapy that their relationship has already deteriorated beyond repair. In this vein, he believed some couples seek couple therapy for permission to divorce. They have then attempted everything, nothing has worked, and partners may feel more justified divorcing. It is imperative that the couple therapist not experience these couples as a reflection of his or her competence.

When partners are uncertain about whether they wish to remain together, couple therapists empathize with the dilemma while simultaneously making clear that since the partners have to live with the consequences of their decision only they can make it. The couple therapist can help them explore options, including improving their relationship irrespective of whether they remain together, and facilitate negotiation of an end to their relationship with the least amount of damage possible to the partners' emotional health and that of their children.

Liz and Martin were a reasonably resilient couple. They experienced the stress of culturally different world views, society's disapproval, child-bearing and childrearing, managing two careers, and adapting to each other as individuals as mostly manageable. They had financial resources, social and familial networks, and their couple therapist to facilitate their adaptation to stress. Yet their couple dynamics were such that when Liz's father died in 2002, their relationship difficulties re-emerged and rapidly worsened. Both were discouraged.

When Liz called the couple therapist, she said she was finished with Martin and wanted help with how to tell him and the children they were divorcing. The couple therapist reluctantly agreed to see her alone.

COUPLE THERAPIST: We're getting to the end of the hour, and I've noticed you still talk about Martin in a loving way, despite how angry and hopeless you feel. You sound worried about him, as well as about your children. So I wonder whether it'd be worth it to have a session or two with him.

LIZ: I don't think he'd come. I think he's had it with working on our marriage.

CT: Sounds like you've both had it. But if you're at all uncertain about ending it, then it might be helpful to consider whether there's any way to make it better.

LIZ: I guess. OK. I guess I can ask him, but I doubt he'll come.

When Liz and Martin returned together two weeks later, Martin appeared relieved to be there.

LIZ: [Flat affect] I can't do this anymore, Martin. I came here to find out how to tell you and the kids.

MARTIN: What? Liz... No, don't do this. [To CT] We've been good since we were here, what was it, three years ago? Until lately. After Bill died. And we don't seem to be able to find our way back. [To Liz] We were good. We can do it again.

Liz had answered the "why now?" question during her individual session, and Martin confirmed that their relationship had deteriorated following her father's death. The couple therapist explored what had changed after Bill died and assessed their current relationship dynamics. She also continued to address Liz's hopelessness as it arose and Martin's upset about it. She reminded them about the behaviors, ascribed meanings, and subsequent relationship dynamics that had previously worked more effectively for them. Liz softened during their second session, saying Martin had been much "better" at home, and at the end of the hour she said she thought they were back on track and did not need more sessions. Because this had been their pattern, CT had prepared.

CT: You know, sometimes a refresher session or two does get a couple back on track. My concern is that this is the third or fourth time you've been in for a few sessions, stopped as soon as you've felt better, and then come back the next time there's a big stressor in your lives. Which is fine, except that each time you've come back you've been more hopeless about your relationship and it's been more difficult to get back to where you want to be. I think there's something going on that we've missed and that keeps undermining you when there's external stress. It could be as simple as not staying in therapy long enough to consolidate new ways of relating. And, Liz, as I said during our session alone, your father's death may continue to bring up emotional pain for you for awhile that you need to manage empathetically as a couple. He's the first of your parents to die, so this is new for both of you. And he sounds like the most difficult parent, and that raises all sorts of feelings. The bottom line is that you were ready to end your marriage this time, and I'm not sure your relationship would survive another crisis like this in the future. My recommendation is that you continue therapy as a couple until we've identified and resolved whatever keeps undermining you and consolidate the changes you've made, because the risks of not doing this work now seem so dire.

LIZ: Are you saying you wouldn't work with us again?

CT: I'm saying I'm not sure I could help you. And I'm not sure I'm doing you a favor by putting another bandaid on your marital wound and then waiting for you to come in bleeding even harder. It feels like we'd be pretending this crisis management approach is working when the solution has only been temporary.

MARTIN: Whew, that's a lot to digest. Can we think about it?

CT: Absolutely. Couple therapy is never easy, and it's up to you whether you can and want to do the work now. Shall I reserve this time for you and you can let me know if you decide not to use it?

MARTIN: OK.

LIZ: When do we need to let you know?

Stop and Think:

Be sure to include your answers in your journal.

1. How did you react to the couple therapist in this excerpt?
2. How did you react to Liz?
3. How did you react to Martin?
4. If any of your reactions involved a negative judgment, discuss how the person might react if that judgment were communicated, verbally and/or nonverbally, during the session.
5. If you felt sympathy for either Liz or Martin, but not both, how might they each respond to your inevitable nonverbal and possible verbal communication of it?

Other Couple Challenges

Couple therapists play a role in facilitating adaptation to a variety of challenges, as well as providing referrals for relevant services outside their scope of practice (see Chapter 12). The nature of the challenge and the role of the couple therapist with couples facing several challenges will be briefly described in this section. Every couple therapist brings techniques from her or his theoretical orientation to couples facing these challenges, and you may especially recognize aspects of cognitive-behavioral, emotionally focused, and narrative couple therapies in what follows.

Remarried Couples

Although remarriage and blending families is a transition, these changes present challenges that first marriages and childbearing together do not. These unique challenges will be addressed in this subsection.

Ghosts of Previous Relationships. It is crucial for couple therapists working with remarrying or remarried couples to assess the degree and quality of interactions with previous partner(s). When the relationship has been permanently severed, either by death or a childless divorce, vestiges of unresolved distress may linger nonetheless and impact subsequent relationships.

Liz's brother David and his wife divorced in 2000. Although she remarried and David had no contact with their child, she found herself defensive and angry when her second husband accommodated his first wife in any way. Similarly, when Liz's mother Sally remarried she found herself placating her second husband as though he were drunk, irrational, and about to fly into a rage. Her second husband, by contrast, idolized his late wife and pointed out Sally's faults in comparison.

Step-Parenting Challenges. Partners with children from previous relationships need to decide together what role each will take as a step-parent and how they will manage children's reactions to, for example, being disciplined by a step-parent. Couples often argue about childrearing practices and about how the other has treated "my" child or how "your" child has treated his or her step-parent. It is common for two people to differ in their approaches to childrearing. When loyalties are divided because the children's other parent is not the current partner, these differences become more complex. By anticipating the potential for disagreements, noting the added complexity of step-parenting, and negotiating ways of handling the children, couples may circumvent the potential for parenting step-children to undermine their relationship with one another.

Sally's second husband's children were distressed that he had remarried after their mother's death. They referred to Sally as their father's "companion" even after Sally and Jim married, and they declined to attend family events that included her adult children and grandchildren. Once Jim was diagnosed with Alzheimer's disease, Liz and Barbara worried not only about Sally's health and safety but also about whether his will protected her financially and if so whether his children would challenge it. Similarly, David's son Carl informed his step-father that "you're not really my father and you can't tell me what to do."

Blending Families. Children of parents who were formerly married to their other biological or adoptive parent have already experienced a transition from living with both parents to living with only one. When a parent remarries, yet another transition, this one to the new blended family, occurs. Children have not asked for either of these transitions and may be reluctant or even furious about the prospect of more change. Unresolved issues between former partners may re-emerge when one remarries, thus complicating custody agreements.

Children may be reluctant to give up the special single parent-child bond, feel competitive with the new partner for the parent's attention, and display anger, sadness, and anxiety about changes in the family. When parents have divorced, children may have secretly hoped for a reconciliation, and that hope is dashed when one parent remarries. When a parent has died, children may feel the surviving parent is disloyal or dismissive of the importance of the deceased parent.

The way a parent introduces her or his new partner, approaches the topic of remarriage, and includes her or his children in the wedding are important to their adaptation. While the other parent's attitude and behavior are also important, it is not within the power of the remarrying parent to influence an ex-partner.

These factors hold true despite the ages of the children, although the couple's specific ways of approaching and including children may differ with the children's ages. Liz's sister Barbara was furious with Sally for remarrying two years after her father's death. She accused Sally of never having loved her father and of not caring about her adult children's feelings. It is helpful when partners empathize and work together through struggles with their children from previous relationships.

Extended families must also find ways to blend into a new family. Relatives may be offended by the idea of divorce or remarriage or may feel loyalty to the ex- or late partner that precludes welcoming the new one. Partners may disagree on how to handle extended family members. For example, Sally would have liked Jim to talk to his children about how they treated her, whereas Jim was so concerned about upsetting them that he refused.

Step-Sibling Relationships. Partners may also disagree about how to introduce step-siblings to one another. Creating a plan that respects each partner's parenting style and knowledge of their children while maintaining an attitude that blending families can be a positive experience and respecting children's pacing help the transition. Partners seeking help from a couple or family therapist also convey the message that successful family blending is important to them.

Jim remained anxious about upsetting his adult children as he and Sally blended families. He neither conveyed appreciation for the efforts Sally and her daughters made nor empathy for Sally's feelings about how his children treated her. Because Sally had a history of passively accepting her first husband's behavior, her hurt and anger at Jim were never resolved.

Minuchin's re-mastered master tape demonstrating therapy with a blended family is instructive for how not to blend a family (Minuchin, 2007). The couple failed to prepare their children to meet one another and positioned the step-siblings for conflict with one another.

Fertility Challenges

While some couples choose not to have children, others wish to become parents and find themselves unable either to conceive or to carry a child to term. Many couples seek medical remedies to fertility challenges. Insurance reimbursements for these expensive interventions vary.

Sometimes fertility treatment is successful, and sometimes it is not. Sometimes partners agree about how much fertility treatment they are willing to endure, and sometimes they do not. And some couples agree about whether adoption is an option, while others do not. Adoption as an alternative is a complex and expensive process, fraught with delays, frustrations, evaluations, expenses, and roadblocks.

Couples may turn to couple therapy to help with the decision about the timing and amount of intervention, when to stop, and whether to adopt. They also present for couple therapy after the process of fertility treatment and uncertainty about its outcome have taken a toll on their sexual relationship, their emotional relationship, and their finances. In the writer's experience, female partners in heterosexual couples usually wish to continue fertility treatment longer than their male partners, and male partners often acquiesce to their female partners' wishes. For LGBT couples, fertility is not a couple issue but rather that of the partner attempting to become pregnant or to impregnate. While he or she may experience disappointment and upset about fertility challenges, the other partner already knew that he or she would not be a biological parent of their child. Additionally, there is no risk of LGBT partners blaming one another for their fertility challenges, whereas heterosexual couples of necessity discover where the fertility issue resides.

The toll of fertility treatment on a couple's sexual relationship is a unique challenge for heterosexual couples. When a couple is told when to engage in intercourse, irrespective of their motivation or the side-effects of medications used to enhance fertility, the partners may experience sex as a chore. Medication, uncertainty, the disappointment of once again starting a menstrual cycle despite the couple's best efforts to become pregnant, a sense of personal failure and frustration, the financial pressures of unreimbursed medical expenses, hopelessness, and mutual blame not only affect desire but also may impact each partner's feelings about himself or herself and about the other partner.

Couple therapy does not change the biomedical options available to clients. However, couple therapists can facilitate empathy for what the other is experiencing, empathy for oneself, sharing of feelings without recriminations, managing the impact of each other's moods, resolving conflicts arising from the fertility treatment process, and exploring the alternatives of stopping treatment and either adopting or remaining childless. In other words, a couple therapist can work with the couple to prevent the stress of fertility treatment from undermining the couple's relationship.

Biomedical Challenges

Biomedical illnesses present a variety of challenges for couples. The first involves the nature of the illness. Is it acute and temporary or chronic and incurable? Acute illnesses and surgeries, even when recovery is slow, abate, and the couple can look ahead to a time when illness will not be part of daily life. Chronic illnesses, however, are by definition progressive and involve a series of acute episodes from which the patient does not fully recover. Cancer is an example, with each relapse altering options for future treatment and reducing projected life-span.

Couple therapists also assess the impact of the biomedical challenge on the couple, including the extent to which an acute condition or an individual episode of a chronic condition alters the patient's physical and emotional functioning. Some patients do not have the stamina for a full-time job outside the home, while others continue life as it was before the diagnosis except during acute periods of their chronic illnesses.

As with all stressors, the meaning of the stress to the partners, reflected in their narrative about it, impacts their ability to adapt to it. If partners view a biomedical diagnosis as catastrophic, they will behave as though it is. If they minimize it, the ill partner may not get the treatment or accommodations she or he requires. Sometimes partners ascribe different meanings to the diagnosis and treatment and their impact on the patient and couple, resulting in disagreements about the nature and impact of the illness. One couple with whom the writer worked endorsed her reflection that the wife's chronic illness was tantamount to a third person in their marriage.

Partners cannot be certain about the course of a chronic disease and thus about their future. The meaning attached to this uncertainty may be different for each partner and as a result they may experience difficulty communicating about it.

Co-creating a realistic narrative that includes mutual empathy may mitigate the impact of the disease process on the couple. Couple therapists can also encourage couples to utilize and, if possible, strengthen their resources for coping with biomedical challenges. When roles are inflexible, for example, assigned by gender, partners may be unable to accommodate necessary changes. Additionally, couples may hesitate to call upon or even accept help from family, friends, and the professional community. Partners may need to suspend internalized norms of self-reliance and accept help from members of their social network and referrals for extra care at home, patient and care-giver support groups, and psychotherapy. Couple therapists can challenge the belief that how the couple functioned when both partners were well remains the only desirable way to be and then facilitate the exploration of alternatives.

Couple therapy involves facilitating the alignment of meanings and tasks to the reality of the changes brought about by the illness. Each partner's attitudes and feelings may need to be made explicit in order to prevent nonverbal messages from undermining the relationship. As well, each partner can be guided to listen empathetically to the other's feelings about the diagnosis and its impact, simultaneously listening and managing their own reactions in a way that validates the partners' differing perspectives as well as their very different roles of patient and caregiver.

Mental Disorders and Substance Abuse

Mental disorders can be either acute or chronic, whereas substance abuse is by definition a chronic condition. They differ from biomedical illnesses in that there is a culturally learned presumption that mental health and substance use are within people's control. This assumption may lead to low tolerance for an individual suffering a mental disorder or abusing a substance and to partners and members of the social network treating the patient as though the affliction is a choice. From a couple therapist's perspective, the topics covered in the previous subsection apply to this category of couple challenges.

Violations of Trust

Partners may undermine trust in a variety of intended and unintended ways. Extra-relationship affairs when the partners have agreed to monogamy and intimate partner violence are explicit violations of trust. Unmet expectations and circumstances beyond a partner's control, such as a hospitalization for depressive symptoms, are unintended violations of trust that may affect a partner in much the same way as intended violations do. Alternatively, chronically forgetting events important to the partner in the absence of organic brain disease or deterioration can be presumed to be intended, however subconsciously.

Stop and Think:

Be sure to include your responses in your journal.

1. How do you define a sexual affair?
2. How do you define an emotional affair?
3. How do you view the differences between an emotional and a sexual extra-relationship affair?
4. How do you view their commonalities?
5. What trust does intimate partner violence violate?
6. How might unmet expectations be experienced as a violation of trust?

When monogamy is presumed, both emotional and sexual affairs violate trust. The partner violated the explicit relationship contract concerning monogamy. By not being trustworthy with respect to one aspect of the relationship contract, the partner has also reduced trust in the other agreements and assumptions partners have made about their relationship.

However, as the previous Stop and Think suggests, the definition of an extra-relationship affair may not be as simple as it may at first appear. Is kissing a violation of trust? Is confiding in an attractive colleague? Is texting? Most importantly, where is the line between an innocuous friendship and a violation of the relationship contract when the relationship is presumed to be monogamous?

From a systems perspective, any affair may be the result of both partners tacitly agreeing that one will act out the distress in their relationship in a way that creates a problem the partners consider significant enough to request help addressing. The writer has described this phenomenon to couples not in systemic terms but as a couple suicide gesture, a request for help that for any number of possible reasons could not be asked in any other way. Alternatively, however, an extra-relationship affair may be a suicide attempt, and unfortunately these can be successful and result in the death of the relationship.

The meanings each partner ascribes to an affair and its role in the couple's story are both critical to the outcome for the couple's relationship. If either partner views trust as unrecoverable or if the partner who strayed is dismissive of its impact on the other partner, then it becomes more challenging, if not impossible, for the couple to recover. If both view the affair as a crisis in their relationship and maintain hope that they can recover from it, then couple therapy may be helpful. Couple therapists facilitate exploration of alternative ways for managing distress, integration of the story of the affair into the couple's history, empathetic listening, and methods for talking without recrimination.

Intimate partner violence deserves far more elaboration than an introductory text allows. For purposes of this textbook, it will be addressed only in terms of its violation of trust. The scholarly and governmental literature describing intimate partner violence includes its prevalence and the emotional and physical consequences for the victim and observing children (Office on Women's Health, 2015; World Health Organization, 2017). The governmental websites are included in the references for this chapter, as is a recent and comprehensive book by Augusta-Scott, Scott, and Tutty (2017). It is crucial that anyone intending to practice couple therapy be familiar with the literature. Some jurisdictions, for example, California, require continuing education about intimate partner violence for marriage and family therapy licensure.

Intimate partner violence undermines trust that one is safe with one's partner, whether one is the perpetrator or the victim. Briefly, systems theory holds that violence arises from the relationship dynamics, although individual differences account for why some partners become violent while others do not. Treatment recommendations have varied over time, and couple therapists do not agree about when conjoint couple therapy is appropriate.

Every couple therapist needs to assess for intimate partner violence because it is more prevalent than acknowledged and because violent couples do not often initiate conversation about it. Additionally, couple therapists need to maintain referral information to keep victims and any minor children safe.

Intimate partner violence can be verbal as well as physical. If one partner has been coerced and her or his self-esteem undermined, she or he can be said to be the victim of intimate partner violence. Intimate partner violence can also be sexual, despite a move by some jurisdictions to legitimize marital rape.

A third and far more insidious violation of trust involves unmet expectations. If either partner feels that she or he cannot trust the other to uphold the expectations as well as the agreements of their relationship, trust may become problematic. Extra-relationship affairs and intimate partner violence are, once acknowledged, agreed-upon occurrences. Even when nuanced, such as whether a kiss is a violation of trust, couples either agree, disagree, or agree to disagree about the nature and extent of the violation of trust. Partners have a much more difficult time articulating what it is about an unmet expectation that violates trust.

Stop and Think:

Be sure to include your responses in your journal.

1. Define trust from your perspective.
2. List how people you know have violated your trust and include your reaction to each.
3. What accounts for the differences in your reactions?

Conclusions

This chapter has introduced you to a variety of topics about couple circumstances that impact couple therapy. The specifics of this chapter focused on working with couples who do not fit the dominant cultural model, transitioning couples, and couples experiencing various challenges. While topics were not exhaustive of each category, you were introduced to some of the issues arising when a couple therapist is a member of the dominant culture and the client couple is either a couple of color, biracial, biculturual, or LGBTQIA. Open relationships and polyamory were also addressed, although these are relationships of choice. The transitions affecting couples that were included were the transition to marriage, parenting, aging, and uncoupling. Differences between uncoupling due to death and uncoupling due to dissolution of the relationship were addressed. Couple challenges included remarriage, fertility, biomedical, mental health and substance abuse, and violations of trust. The latter included extra-relationship affairs, intimate partner violence, and unmet expectationst.

All couple therapists need to maintain a multicultural perspective and a culturally competent practice, assess for intimate partner violence and substance abuse, and be familiar with clinical approaches to issues arising during the transitions and crises couples invariably face. Additionally, couple therapists must develop competency or be prepared to refer when a challenge outside their scope of practice arises. Chapter 12 examines the specifics of the services for which couple therapists refer and the referral process.

References

American Psychiatric Association. (2013). *Diagnostic and statistical manual of mental disorders (5th ed.)*. Washington DC: American Psychiatric Publishing.

Augusta-Scott, T., Scott, K., & Tutty, L. M. (2017). *Innovations in interventions to address intimate partner violence. Research and practice*. New York NY: Routledge.

Basirico, L. A., Cashion, B. G., & Eshleman, J. R. (2014). *Introduction to sociology (16th ed.)*. Redding CA: BVT.

Brown, L. S. (1994). *Subversive dialogues. Theory in feminist therapy*. New York NY: Basic Books.

Gannon, M. (2016). Race is a social construct, scientists argue. *Scientific American*. Retrieved from https://www.scientificamerican.com/article/race-is-a-social-construct-scientists-argue/.

Green, R. J. & Mitchell, V. (2015). Gay, lesbian, and bisexual issues in couple therapy. In A. S. Gurman, J. L. Lebow, & D. K. Snyder (Eds.). *Clinical handbook of couple therapy (5th ed.)*. New York NY: Guilford Press.

Killian, K. D. (2013). *Interracial couples, intimacy, and therapy: Crossing racial borders.* New York NY: Columbia University Press.

Killian, K. D. (2015). Couple therapy and intercultural relationships. In A. S. Gurman, J. L. Lebow, & D. K. Snyder (Eds.). *Clinical handbook of couple therapy (5th ed.).* New York NY: Guilford Press.

Loving v. Virginia. (1967). Retrieved from https://www.law.cornell.edu/supremecourt/text/388/1.

Lum, D. (2007). *Culturally competent practice. A framework for understanding diverse groups and justice issues (3rd ed.).* Belmont CA: Brooks/Cole.

Minuchin, S. (2007). *Unfolding the laundry.* Retrieved from https://www.aamft.org/iMIS15/AAMFT/store/store.aspx?cmd=prod&prod=V001.

Office on Women's Health. (2015). Violence Against Women. Retrieved from https://www.womenshealth.gov/violence-against-women/types-of-violence/domestic-intimate-partner-violence.html.

Pope-Davis, D. B., Coleman, H. L. K., Liu, W. M., & Toporek, R. L. (2003). *Handbook of multicultural competencies in counseling and psychology.* Los Angeles CA: Sage.

World Health Organization. (2017). Definition and typology of violence. Retrieved from http://www.who.int/violenceprevention/approach/definition/en/.

Yalom, I. (2008). *Staring at the sun. Overcoming the terror of death.* San Francisco CA: Jossey-Bass.

For Further Study

Carlson, J., Sperry, L., & Lewis, J. A. (2005). *Family therapy techniques. Integrating and tailoring treatment.* New York NY: Routledge.

Diller, J. V. (2007). *Cultural diversity. A primer for the human services (3rd ed.).* Belmont CA: Brooks/Cole.

Doherty, W. J. & Baird, M. A. (1984). *Family therapy and family medicine.* New York NY: Guilford Press.

Fadiman, A. (1997). *The spirit catches you and you fall down. A Hmong child, her American doctors, and the collision of two cultures.* New York NY: Ferrar, Straus and Giroux.

Koch-Hattem, A. (1987). Families and chronic illness. In D. Rosenthal (Ed.). *Family stress.* Rockville MD: Aspen.

Morgan, O. J. & Lizke, C. H. (2012). *Family interventions in substance abuse. Current best practices.* New York NY: Routledge.

Pope, M., Pangelinan, J. S., & Coker, A. D. (2011). *Experiential activities for teaching multicultural competence in counseling.* Alexandria VA: American Counseling Association.

Rockquemore, K. A. & Laszloffy, T. A. (2003). Multiple realities. A relationship narrative approach in therapy with black-white mixed-race clients. *Family Relations,* 52 (2), 119–128.

Walzlawick, P., Beavin, J. H., & Jackson, D. D. (1967). Pragmatics of human communication. New York NY: Norton.

CHAPTER 10

The Couple Therapist's Experience Doing Couple Therapy

Learning Objectives

1. From a systems theory perspective, describe the power differentials between client couples and couple therapists.
2. Illustrate the importance of a couple therapist's self-awareness of the limitations of her or his world view.
3. Describe how a couple therapist's family blueprint for couple relationships may impact her or his practice of couple therapy.
4. Discuss the ways a couple therapist's relationship history may impact her or his practice of couple therapy and what he or she can do to manage this impact.
5. List the various considerations in a couple therapist's comfort talking about sexual intimacy.
6. Illustrate the challenges of managing multiple relationships in couple therapy.
7. Discuss the risks of idealizing a partner or the couple therapist.
8. Describe the processes by which couple therapists identify and manage their own issues so that they do not intrude upon their effectiveness practicing couple therapy.

In this chapter, we will explore the unique challenges that practicing couple therapy presents. In addition to their training and experience, couple therapists bring themselves as human beings to their work. Each couple therapist's experience observing parents and extended family members living in intimate relationships, his or her own relationship history, her or his cultural image of an ideal relationship, and her or his current satisfaction or lack thereof with his or her own relationship status contribute to her or his approach to and experience of any given couple.

Couple therapists bring their temperament, emotions, and history, as well as their knowledge and personal and professional experience, to couple therapy. Couple therapists develop feelings about each partner and each couple with whom they work, the work itself, and the people and events that populate their lives when they are not working.

Dominant cultural norms prohibit sharing intimate relationship details with others. Yet couple therapists must address these proscribed topics with client couples. Additionally, the couple therapist's gender experience often differs from at least one of the partner's, risking feelings of exclusion from a suspected alliance between the couple therapist and the other partner.

The couple therapist must observe, consider, and decide when and how to address the content of the couple's verbal communications, contradictory nonverbal communications, relationship messages and dynamics, attempts to triangle the couple therapist into the relationship, and partner alliances to defend the couple system's equilibrium from the couple therapist's interventions. She or he must observe couple conflict to assess what relationship dynamics prevent resolution and also interrupt the conflict before it becomes destructive.

Couple therapists, being human, may be tempted to view one partner more favorably than the other. They may find themselves induced by the system's dynamics to choose a side, despite efforts to resist. They may also find themselves reminded of their own relationship distress and, just as one or both partners might idealize the couple therapist so the couple therapist may compare her or his own partner unfavorably to the preferred partner in the couple client.

Couple therapists also bring an array of external demands to their work. Couple therapists work with a number of clients. At any given time, the case load may be especially demanding. Add to the demands, expectations, and responsibilities to clients the equally important demands, expectations, and responsibilities to friends and family members, and then imagine the task of focusing on a particular couple in the ways described in previous chapters.

When Liz and Martin returned to couple therapy in 2002, the couple therapist was the mother of young children and her father was dying. During his illness and for about a year after he died, she arose early, exercised, helped her children get ready for school, talked to her husband, maintained a private practice, left work in time to meet the school bus, helped her children with homework and supervised activities and play dates, cooked dinner, with her husband helped the children get ready for bed, returned client calls, and then called her mother to talk for at least an hour. During this period she also dealt with her sadness about her father, frustration with her mother's seemingly endless emotional needs, exhaustion, concern that her children's needs were not being met, concern about friends experiencing difficult times in their lives, concerns about clients, and the impact of all of this on her marriage. When Liz described similar events in her own life, the couple therapist needed to remain alert to her own reactions so that she would not conflate them with Liz's.

Stop and Think:

Be sure to include your answers in your journal.

1. Think about a stressful situation you have experienced.
2. How did the stress affect your concentration, feelings, and relationships?
3. How did you manage the stressful situation's impact on these other aspects of your life?
4. What might you have done to lessen its impact on clients had you been practicing couple therapy at the time?

The Power of the Couple's Dyadic Relationship

In Chapter 4, you read that a couple system is greater than the sum of its parts and that the dynamics, or repetitive interaction patterns, are more powerful than either partner or the couple therapist. You also read about homeostatic mechanisms that return the couple system to equilibrium in the face of change.

From a systems perspective, couple therapy begins with the couple therapist in a disadvantaged position with respect to the couple's dyadic relationship. Behavioral, cognitive-behavioral, and strategic couple therapy theories attempted to level the playing field by re-empowering the couple therapist as an expert authority (Haley, 1963). These theories did not account for the impact of the mostly white, male, cis-gendered, and middle-class socioeconomic status of most couple and family therapists of the time. Despite ethical codes prohibiting the use of dominant culture membership to attain or maintain power, couple therapists who are part of or even perceived by couple clients to be part of the dominant culture invariably derive power as a result and this power invariably impacts the pwer differential with the couple system.

Alternatively, experiential couple therapists viewed the role of the couple therapist as working from a one-down position to build a healing relationship with the partners and empower them (Napier & Whitaker, 1978). Post-modern couple therapies also promote the role of the couple therapist as collaborative (Dulwich Centre, 2015).

In addition to being less powerful than the couple's dyadic relationship, the couple therapist is also a witness to the couple system's efforts to maintain equilibrium. Even when both partners are unhappy with the status quo, they may fear that changing risks destabilization of their relationship, with potentially devastating consequences. Experience suggests that change is sometimes devastating. More often, however, the fear of change is far worse than the consequences of changing.

What is relevant here is that the partners' ambivalence about change is communicated to the couple therapist in contradictory messages. On the one hand, the partners' expressed goal is change, and the couple therapist may measure her or his success in terms of helping them meet that goal. On the other hand, change may be perceived as so threatening that partners avoid, challenge, and otherwise resist the couple therapist's efforts on their behalf. As a result, the couple therapist may experience frustration with one or both partners and a sense of professional failure.

Approaches to couple therapy differ in how, though not whether, ambivalence is addressed. The concept that homeostatic mechanisms impede the very change that may facilitate enhanced couple system functioning provides a theoretical explanation of couple ambivalence. However, homeostatic mechanisms identified by the couple therapist are likely outside the partners' awareness. Normalizing ambivalence as part of the human condition and exploring the specific ambivalences partners bring to couple therapy may allow the partners to access their own ambivalence. Noting that their ambivalence is about change and not about each other may also be helpful. "I am scared of what change will bring" and "I am ambivalent about you" are two very different statements, and it is crucial that partners do not conflate them.

Couple therapists may also need to self-soothe. "I'm failing this couple" and "I don't like working with these people" are very different messages than "I am frustrated that this couple's ambivalence about change is complicating couple therapy and impeding our success." The couple therapist, once freed of responsibility to magically overcome the couple system's homeostatic mechanisms on her or his own, can remind herself or himself that ambivalence does not define the partners and therefore frustration with the system dynamics is not the same as frustration with them as individuals.

In addition to self-soothing, couple therapists must find a way to leave their frustration about the progress of a particular couple at the office. There are a variety of components of self-care, including self-soothing, for example, "I have done all I can do for them today," that will be addressed in Chapter 11.

Liz and Martin's couple therapist found herself increasingly frustrated with them for ending couple therapy whenever their symptoms abated and then returning even more frustrated and hopeless when there was new stress in their lives. While she had suggested each time that they consider remaining in couple therapy long enough to consolidate the changes they had made, they had declined, expressing confidence they could manage on their own and citing limitations of time and money as reasons to do so. The couple therapist liked both Liz and Martin a great deal and found herself wanting them to be happy together. She also realized that her goals for them were irrelevant and might be exacerbating her frustration when she believed Liz and Martin were dismissing her attempts to help them. For all of these reasons, she thought about what she would say if they again wished to end couple therapy prematurely after they returned in 2002.

Liz and Martin decided to remain in couple therapy after the excerpt described in Chapter 9, with the agreement that they and the couple therapist would re-evaluate her recommendation periodically. The couple therapist surprised herself by finding herself ambivalent about their decision. On the one hand, she liked and cared about them and wanted to be part of the healing of their relationship. On the other hand, she knew the work would be difficult and potentially frustrating, and she did not look forward to the latter. She knew that anxiety about change sometimes outweighed a couple's desire to change and that her responsibility was limited to helping partners manage their anxiety about change, exploring how they could move through it, and elaborating the consequences of avoiding it. She knew it was beyond her power to force any couple to opt for change. However, she believed she had gone further than simply pointing out the consequences of not changing, and while she believed she had acted in Liz and Martin's best interest she knew she had also pushed the limits of ethical behavior and felt an added responsibility to ensure a good outcome as a result.

A related challenge for couple therapists involves the consequences of asking about each partner's goal for the outcome of couple therapy. Given the potential that one or both partners will have an unstated agenda, asking during the first or second session what each wants the outcome to be circumvents the possibility of the couple therapist inadvertently colluding with one's goal while ignoring the other's. For example, if one partner is involved in a secret extra-relationship affair and hopes couple therapy will uncover an irreconcilable difference as a rationale for ending the relationship, he or she may unconsciously collude with the couple therapist to identify and embellish problems. Alternatively, he or she may view the couple therapist as colluding with the partner to keep him or her trapped in the relationship.

One of five scenarios is likely for couples entering couple therapy. First, both partners may want to remain together. Second, one or both partners may be unsure of what they want the outcome to be. It is especially important for the couple therapist and both partners to understand disparate goals. Making a decision can be a goal of couple therapy, perhaps based upon whether the partners are able to move past their anger to recover loving and empathetic feelings toward each other. Third, both partners may have decided their relationship is unworkable but because of children or other considerations they would like to either explore the possibility of remaining together or obtain help in ending their relationship. A fourth scenario occurs when one partner wishes to remain in the relationship while the other is finished with it. In such cases, the relationship is irretrievable and the couple therapist can only help the partners end it in the least destructive way possible. A fifth possibility arises when at least one of the partners continues to hide his or her true agenda. While the couple therapist may experience anger or frustration when the truth inevitably emerges or is suspected, she or he is not responsible for either partner's honesty but only for her or his own willingness to honestly address difficult subjects.

Whichever theoretical model best fits your world view as an individual and as a professional couple therapist, it remains important to be attuned to the power of the couple system and to one's own reaction to it. Couple therapists who acknowledge their emotional responses are, as you saw in Section II, more able to effectively intervene to facilitate successful outcomes in couple therapy than those who ignore themselves.

The Couple Therapist's World View: Cultural and Gender Perspective and Values

The concept of intersectionality reminds us that we are not defined by one cultural variable but by many. The writer noticed that she was taken more seriously by clients as she moved from being a young woman in early career to a middle-aged woman in mid-career. Would this have happened sooner had she been male? A colleague said she hated being tall until she became a psychotherapist and realized she was taken more seriously than shorter women, which happened much younger than middle age.

Each couple therapist's world view is defined by experiences like these that are associated with his or her gender, height, age, race, ethnicity, religion, sexual orientation, gender identity, marital or relationship status, parenting status, the region in which he or she was raised, the region in which she or he practices, his or her family-of-origin customs and beliefs, whether she or he has siblings, etc. For example, the writer is identified with a particular racial and ethnic group, gender, sexual orientation, and age cohort. She was born in one region of the country and lived and practiced in a very different one for several decades. She is a mother who has also experienced reproductive loss, partner loss, and the blending of a new family. Her father was a refugee who was fortunate enough to have family already living in this country and willing to sponsor him. Her father suffered several biomedical illnesses, her mother suffered a mental health disorder, and as a result she was partially raised by her mother's parents. All of these factors, together and separately, have influenced her world view and how she has approached client couples. Both her world view and her approach to client couples have been altered by experience, even though her theoretical orientation has remained consistent.

Stop and Think:

Be sure to include your answers in your journal.

1. List all of your cultural characteristics.
2. Describe your experiences growing up in a few sentences.

3. How have these characteristics and experiences influenced how you view the world?
4. How do you and the members of your family characterize people outside your demographic group? For example, what are the attitudes about cohabitation, non-traditional roles for men and women, LGBTQIA couples, racial and ethnic groups other than your own, intergenerational and biracial or bicultural relationships, divorce, remarriage?
5. How comfortable are you when you meet someone whose life experiences have differed from yours because of these and other factors?
6. How might your answers to the previous questions impact your work with couples?

Comfort with a given couple also impacts the couple therapist's experience working with that couple. Couple therapists have blind spots, and completing the Stop and Think exercise above will not identify all of them. Rather, each couple therapist must remain self-aware enough to identify her or his attitudes as they arise and address them in supervision, by attending workshops, and when appropriate with the client couple. While it is not alright to say, "I am uncomfortable with your sexual orientation," it is reasonable to say, "Tell me about how your sexual orientation has affected you growing up, in the world now, and about the non-sexual aspects of your relationship." This approach allows the couple therapist's empathy for all client experiences to emerge, as well as information about the client couple's unique experiences at the intersection of each partner's various identities.

The Couple Therapist's Family Blueprint for Relationships

As a society we do not teach people how to create and sustain a workable couple relationship. We do not ask people to consider what is important to them in a life-partner or in a life-long relationship. We do not teach people how to self-soothe or to use self-soothing to regulate emotional expression. We do not teach people how to manage conflict effectively, especially in emotionally intense relationships. We do not ask people to question the dominant cultural myths that love will fix any problem, that needing to work on a relationship is an indication it is unhealthy, or that anyone lives "happily ever after." With the exception of premarital counseling, we wait for something to go wrong and then send in mental health professionals to treat the symptoms. This approach applies not only to couple therapy, but also to the medical profession and the judicial system. It leaves the professional with a much more difficult task and the clients much more distressed.

In the absence of a psychoeducational or preventive approach to couples, we learn about relationships through observing those close to us. The relationships you have observed closely, especially those between your parents, a parent and any step-parent or other intimate partners, between partners within your extended family, such as grandparents or aunts and uncles, and in your social network, combine with cultural prescriptions and mythology to provide your model for how to be in a relationship. Like an architect's blueprint, your observations and experiences within your family, social group, and various cultural groups guide how you view relationships and what you do within your own intimate partner relationship.

Stop and Think:

Be sure to include your answers in your journal.

1. What does working on a relationship tell you about the partners and the relationship? How has your culture—movies, books, your family, your friends—influenced your thinking?
2. What feelings do you identify as negative? What do you do when you experience them?
3. When you are upset with someone with whom you are close, how do you handle your upset? How would you like to handle your upset?
4. When two people you care about are in conflict with each other, how do you handle the situation? How would you like to handle the situation?
5. Did you identify anger as a negative emotion? What experience(s) have led you to this conclusion?
6. Do you identify conflict as negative? What experience(s) have led you to this conclusion?

This family-of-origin blueprint is what future couple therapists bring to their own relationships as well as to their training. In order to practice effectively, couple therapists need to assess, and some may also need to challenge, their own ingrained notions about couples.

When a client couple recreates the couple dynamics of the couple therapist's family of origin, the couple therapist may quite naturally react as though he or she were once again a child dealing with her or his own parents. Alternatively, the couple therapist may want to protect one or the other partner from the couple's dynamics, much as he or she may have been the peace-maker or couple therapist in her or his parents' marriage. Finally, a couple therapist may view the couple's relationship as more desirable than that of her or his own intimate partnership. Self-awareness, monitoring one's own reactions to client couples, putting those reactions aside during sessions, and addressing them outside of sessions in supervision or the couple therapist's own psychotherapy are all essential. Self-awareness and appropriate action avoids this type of countertransference from intruding upon the couple therapist's clinical judgment and ability to act in the best interest of the client couple.

Many people who are attracted to the field of couple therapy have observed distress in their parents' relationship. Additionally, many couple therapists and future couple therapists were in the role of peace-maker in their families of origin, the one responsible for staying out of the way, protecting siblings, or comforting one of the parents. A psychodynamic couple therapist might even posit that couple therapists put themselves in a position to do what they could not accomplish as children: help distressed couples like their parents find a less destructive way to interact.

Couple therapists, like couple clients, may unconsciously use intimate partnerships to attempt to heal what they experienced as children. Unconsciously, people tend to choose partners believed to be capable of helping heal the pain and frustration of relationships with our parents, including failed attempts to help them. Napier suggested that the divorce peak at seven years has to do with couples giving up on mutual healing and then discovering there is little else holding them together. Additionally, their thwarted efforts may have undermined their relationship. Couple therapists, like couple clients, are not immune to such risks.

Whether you subscribe to these psychodynamic assumptions or not, ethical practice requires couple therapists to remain aware of their personal reactions to their client couples and to prevent these reactions from impeding their clinical judgment. This requires couple therapists to examine their own personal and cultural experiences, assumptions based upon them, ways in which they might impact judgment, and current ways of managing their intimate partnerships. Only through self-awareness can couple therapists discover the options available to them and stop themselves from reacting in ways that undermine, rather than facilitate couple therapy.

Couple conflict provides an example of a potentially challenging situation for a couple therapist. The dominant culture appears to fear anger. As a result, couple therapists and client couples who have been raised under its influence often learn to view anger and conflict in negative ways. If anger and conflict have not been well managed within an individual's family of origin, that person may conclude that conflict is best minimized because when allowed to happen the results can be destructive. As a result, the person may tell himself or herself that he or she is not angry or that anger is destructive. The person then develops ways of avoiding or denying these anxiety-provoking angry feelings. Anger may then manifest inappropriately, as in road rage, depression, self-harming behaviors like cutting, or abuse of people and substances, including food.

Anger is a primary and thus unavoidable emotion. Similarly, conflict, irrespective of whether it is expressed and resolved, is inevitable when two people live together in an emotionally intense and high-stakes relationship. If one's self-esteem is in part connected to loving and being loved and one's way of being in the world defined in part by being one partner in a couple, then partners will likely guard their relationship from perceived threats, including anger and conflict. The unintended consequence is that anger may erupt far more intensely than if the conflict had been acknowledged and resolved sooner, thereby confirming partners' fears about anger. Long-held grievances arising from unresolved conflict create an additional challenge for couples.

You were asked how you view anger and conflict in the Stop and Think at the beginning of this section. Review your answers, asking yourself what they reveal about your comfort with conflict?

As previously discussed, couple therapists need to be sufficiently comfortable with anger to recognize their own and the message it brings them (Lerner, 2014). Couple therapists also need to learn to be comfortable when their couple clients express anger, including indirectly, and are in conflict. Becoming comfortable with other people's anger may be an even greater challenge for some people than being comfortable with their own. You read examples of Liz challenging the couple therapist, as well as of Liz and Martin arguing. Couple therapists need to take responsibility when they have inadvertently precipitated a client's anger. However, when client anger is the result of the couple therapist blocking the couple's homeostatic mechanism from once again leaving the issue unresolved, the couple therapist needs to be mindful that she or he is creating a situation in which the outcome of conflict may be positive for the client couple and avoiding a repetition of the client couple's pattern of leaving anger unresolved. It is the couple therapist's professional task to put aside her or his own need to avoid conflict, become defensive, or be liked in favor of her or his professional judgment concerning what the client couple needs. And this task necessitates the couple therapist becoming more comfortable with anger and conflict, especially when directed at the couple therapist herself or himself.

The Couple Therapist's Relationship History

Each couple is affected by the partners' individual relationship histories as well as the couple's relationship history. Similarly, a couple therapist is affected not only by her or his current relationship situation but also by her or his relationship history.

Stop and Think:

Be sure to include your answers in your journal.

1. Describe your relationship history. What has been positive? What has been distressful to you?
2. How has your experience influenced how you feel about yourself as a current or potential partner?
3. How might your experience and your evaluation of it impact your work with a couple whose dynamics mirrored your experience?
4. How might your experience and your evaluation of it impact your feelings about partners who were similar to your current partner?
5. How might your experience and your evaluation of it impact your feelings about partners who were more similar to your ideal partner than is your current partner?

In 2002, Liz and Martin's couple therapist was in the midst of a contentious divorce. During the deterioration of their marriage, her husband had become increasingly demeaning of her appearance and of her abilities as a mother and professional. His attitude and behavior were similar to her father's toward both her mother and step-mother. Both women had tolerated his behavior to the point that their self-esteem suffered, and the couple therapist had similarly continued relationships with boyfriends and then with her husband long after they became emotionally destructive.

As a result of her history, the couple therapist found herself wondering why Liz did not appreciate Martin's gentleness, modulated anger, and attitude of wanting what was best for her. She believed she would be happy with a man who treated her as Martin treated Liz and wondered what she could do to help Liz appreciate what she had. While mutual appreciation between partners is a reasonable therapeutic goal, the one-sidedness of the couple therapist's thoughts prompted a member of her peer supervision group to suggest that she re-examine her feelings about the couple in light of her personal situation. She acknowledged that she envied Liz for having found a man who treated her as Martin did. She was usually attracted to men who were about her own height and solidly built. Because Martin was tall and slender, she did not think she was sexually attracted to him, despite his emotional attractiveness to her. Her peer supervision group speculated that her relationship situation and history were clouding her ability to think systemically and risked leading her to not only blame Liz for her own distress but also to inadvertently violate a critical ethical boundary with Martin. The couple therapist acknowledged that blaming one partner for relationship distress without examining the role of the couple's dynamics was counterproductive, seductiveness with a client reprehensible, and that allowing her own situation to interfere with her clinical judgment was unethical.

The couple therapist also identified with how Liz expressed her discontent. The couple therapist had avoided bringing parental attention to herself as a child, aligned with her mother during parental conflict, and remained conflict avoidant in her own relationships as an adult. She knew she waited so long to express her concerns or discontent that, like Liz, they flooded her, leaving her unable to express them constructively. She then blamed herself for instigating problems in her intimate relationships when she failed to address her concerns less destructively. She had learned to be comfortable with client couples' conflict during her training and the early years of her career. However, she continued to want to hide any feelings that might lead to conflict with her own intimate partner.

The couple therapist brought her personal issues to her psychotherapist and their impact on her work to her peer supervision group. These were appropriate routes for the couple therapist to take in order to minimize the impact of her relationship history and current relationship distress on her clinical work. Acknowledging and addressing what she as a human being brought to her work as a couple therapist minimized the risk that her own issues would intrude on her couple therapy with Liz and Martin or any other couple with whom she worked.

Talking about Sexual Intimacy

Sexual intimacy is part of any couple's communication. Even couples who identify as asexual, practice celibacy, or who have not been sexually active for many years communicate in some way about their lack of sexual intimacy. Because human sexuality is so much a part of intimate partnerships, many couple therapists include the partners' sexual relationship in their assessment. During the course of couple therapy, partners may share more intimate details about themselves as individuals and about their relationship as they become more comfortable, or the couple therapist may ask about the impact of their distress and any changes in their dynamics on their sexual relationship. Discussing sexual intimacy creates an emotionally intimate bond between the couple therapist and the couple client. As one of the partners in a couple with whom the writer worked once said, "It feels like you're in our bedroom." While that was not a place any of the three of us wanted the writer to be, the statement characterized the emotional intimacy of practicing couple therapy.

Stop and Think:

Be sure to include your answers in your journal.

1. How comfortable were your parents displaying physical affection with you?
2. How did they express affection with each other?
3. How did they talk about other people in terms of sexual attractiveness and/or sexuality?

4. How comfortable were they if and when they explained sex to you? How comfortable were you?
5. How do you communicate with a partner about your sexual intimacy with her or him?
6. What words do you use to describe anatomy and sexuality? Are they euphemisms, clinical terms, or vernacular?
7. When your friends talk about sex, do you participate? How?

Many couple therapists bring socially learned expectations about privacy, and especially about sexual privacy, to their training. As a result, they may be uncomfortable asking probing questions, and this discomfort may be increased when the questions are about sex. Additionally, because of the taboo nature of the subject, couple therapists may be uncomfortable using accurate terminology and may find themselves using the euphemisms families develop to describe anatomy and sexual behavior.

Partners may share the couple therapist's discomfort, and so it is critical that couple therapists learn to model a matter-of-fact attitude about the sexual aspects of a couple's relationship. Word choice and other nonverbal messages can convey information about the couple therapist's comfort or discomfort with both sexual anatomy and sexual behavior. A couple therapist who has become comfortable talking about these important aspects of a couple's relationship conveys a reassuring comfort to clients who may be uncomfortable talking about their sexuality.

It is also important that couple therapists learn to be comfortable with sexual behavior that may be outside their comfort zone. So long as sexual behavior is consensual and safe, the couple therapist's role is to remain focused on what is distressing the client without judgment.

Couple therapists are trained to address relationship dynamics and the meanings partners ascribe to their experiences, irrespective of the content of those experiences. As a result, couple therapists must be comfortable talking about how those dynamics and meanings impact the partners' lives, without expressing or being distracted by their own discomfort regarding content and without communicating judgment or prurient curiosity.

Failure to assess the myriad ways a couple's dynamics and the meanings partners ascribe to their experiences impact the entirety of their lives risks overlooking aspects of the presenting problem the couple may be reluctant to share. Couple therapists must be willing to ask about uncomfortable topics, such as intimate partner violence, substance abuse, and all sources of distress and potential resources for coping, including the dominant culture's socially taboo topics of money and sex. Achieving comfort talking about a client couple's sexuality thus involves overcoming the couple therapist's own socialization.

Clinical supervision, peer supervision, workshops, and one's own psychotherapy all facilitate a couple therapist's ability to unlearn the social conventions that apply outside of couple therapy. Experience suggests that, once a couple therapist gets beyond her or his discomfort about asking probing questions and talking about socially prohibited topics, the freedom to do so in couple therapy facilitates talking about them outside of couple therapy, for example with the couple therapist's own partner. Experience also suggests that those with prurient interests seem to have greater difficulty becoming ethically competent couple therapists than those who have learned to consider probing personal questions about sex inappropriate or rude.

Although Liz accused Martin of withholding sex when she received career recognition, both were reluctant to return to the subject of their sexual intimacy. Because the accusation reflected dynamics that appeared in less fraught aspects of their relationship, the couple therapist concluded that assessing their sexual intimacy was important. She did not ask irrelevant questions, but rather broached the subject of how their struggles about Liz's career manifested in their sexual relationship, listened to what Liz and Martin communicated both verbally and nonverbally, and then asked follow-up questions. One of the first things she addressed was their embarrassment talking about sex. She accomplished this not only in explicit verbal communication but also by nonverbally demonstrating her own comfort talking about it. While neither Martin nor Liz wished to focus on their sexual relationship and neither considered their sexual intimacy to be problematic, they were willing to explore ways to prevent their couple distress from intruding on their satisfaction with their sexual relationship, thus allowing themselves the positive feelings about one another that generally emerge following sexual encounters.

After developing an emotionally intimate relationship with clients, couple therapists must then manage their feelings when couple therapy ends. Couple therapy terminates for a variety of reasons, some of them mutually agreed upon and some of them not. You will read more about termination in Chapter 13. As you have already read, Liz and Martin left couple therapy several times, despite the couple therapist's recommendation that they remain until the work was completed. When they committed to continuing treatment in 2002, they then remained until the work was at a mutually agreed-upon end.

Once couple therapy ends, the couple therapist's relationship with the partners and with the couple also ends. Saying good-bye can be very difficult. Partners may be sad that they will no longer be in contact with the couple therapist and delighted to be finished with the hard work of couple therapy. The couple therapist may derive self-esteem and personal well-being from having helped the couple achieve their objective. Like the couple, he or she may also be sad to say good-bye.

You will read about dual roles as an ethical issue in Chapter 11. Both boundary and ethical violations regarding dual roles occur when a couple therapist attempts to relate to clients in any role other than as their couple therapist. This holds true after couple therapy ends. While some professional codes of ethics allow a non-therapeutic relationship to develop after a waiting period of two or more years, others permanently prohibit any role other than couple therapist. The writer has made a professional practice to decline requests to engage in a social role following the ending of couple or any other form of psychotherapy, despite the ethical codes of the American Association for Marriage and Family Therapy defining a waiting period. In her experience, clients may return after many years, and once a second role has begun it cannot be undone.

As a society, we are not very good at saying good-bye. Think about your high school graduation. While you were very excited to be moving on to further independence, you may also have been sad to say good-bye to friends you had known most of your life. High school graduates often promise to remain in touch. Yet life after high school takes individuals in many directions, and over the years you may have found that you no longer have much to talk about with your high school friends. By denying this possibility, graduating seniors pretend they are not in fact saying good-bye. Part of couple therapy is avoiding such pretenses and talking about the process as well as the clients' and couple therapist's feelings about saying good-bye. Couple therapists may need to talk more about their sadness saying good-bye than is appropriate with the couple and once again peer supervision or the couple therapist's own psychotherapy are appropriate places to explore feelings about clients.

Managing Multiple Relationships

A couple therapy session includes four relationships: each partner's with the couple therapist (2), the partners' relationship with each other (1), and the couple's relationship with the couple therapist (1). Systems theory also examines the couple-couple therapist system. By contrast, individual psychotherapy only encompasses one relationship, that between the individual client and the psychotherapist.

The presence of four relationships during any given session is not the same thing as dual roles, which entail performing more than one role with the same individual or group. Additionally, the prohibition against dual roles applies only to the couple therapist, not to the clients. Thus, the partners play two roles, individual and partnership, while the couple therapist only plays one, couple therapist, despite being in a relationship with each partner and with the couple.

Some couple therapists find attending to the dynamics of four relationships far more challenging than attending to only one. Others find the intensity of individual psychotherapy less rewarding than the challenge of managing multiple relationships simultaneously.

Pressure to Take Sides

Partners in distressed relationships often view the same things very differently and may describe an argument at home as though each was at a different event. Having failed to receive validation of their experience from one another, one or both partners may turn to the couple therapist for both validation and resolution of the argument. In other words, the couple therapist may find herself or himself being asked to take sides in the argument.

Martin believed that wanting the best for Liz was the best way for him to demonstrate support for her. Liz, by contrast, defined support as listening to her think through her decision and providing feedback on her thoughts. When she accused Martin of not being as supportive at home as he claimed, she also turned to the couple therapist for validation.

Empathy and agreement are not the same, as noted earlier in this textbook. The couple therapist was able to empathize with both Martin's desire to support Liz and Liz feeling unsupported. Additionally, a systems perspective allows a couple therapist to detach from the either-or dichotomy that forces one to agree with one partner and disagree with the other. The couple therapist's systemic view led her to suggest that the issue was not who is right and who is wrong but rather lack of clear communication about what each partner meant when using the word support. She thus demonstrated empathy, avoided a coalition with one partner against the other, and redirected their focus to their communication, which could be clarified and used to facilitate resolution of their argument.

Stop and Think:

Be sure to include it in your journal.

1. Think about a time two people about whom you cared were arguing and either wanted you to take sides or were asking someone else to.
2. What was it like for you, either being asked to takes sides or observing someone else being asked?
3. What do you imagine the two people might have wanted from a third person that they were not getting from each other.

When a couple therapist appears to side with one partner against the other, she or he compromises her or his therapeutic relationship with the couple. Couple therapists must thoroughly examine their own feelings when one or both partners asks them to take sides, especially when a couple therapist feels more aligned with one partner than the other. Failing to acknowledge and remain aware of her alignment with Martin's kindness toward Liz would have left their couple therapist vulnerable to communicating nonverbal messages of alignment that belied her messages of neutrality.

Nevertheless, even the most careful couple therapist's communications may be misinterpreted by a partner for whom validation feels more important than resolution. Sometimes, a partner will confront the couple therapist about siding with the other partner. Sometimes, however, one partner decides he or she no longer trusts the couple therapist, and the couple terminates couple therapy as a result. A third possibility is that one partner says to the couple therapist at some point in the future, "Remember when you [sided with me]?" To avoid compromising the therapeutic relationship, couple therapists need to be attentive to any indication that either partner thought he or she had endorsed one partner over the other and encourage partners to express any concerns they have about the work.

The Therapist as Ideal Partner

When partners are unhappy with one another, they may be vulnerable to idealizing the qualities of others and then assuming these others would be better partners than their current one. They may do this with friends, friends' partners, physicians, colleagues, or their couple therapist. Couple therapists may be especially at risk for being idealized because in practicing couple therapy they display their warmth, empathy, caring, knowledge, experience, humor, and intelligence in order to maximize outcomes for couple clients. These qualities foster the trust essential to successful couple therapy. They are also compelling. While assuming that any couple therapist behaves identically in his or her non-therapeutic relationships is a mistake, couple clients do assume that what they see of the couple therapist is all of who she or he is. The writer told her then teenage children that a client had said she was the calmest person the client knew. Her children fell off their chairs laughing, because they had observed her in emotionally charged situations with the most important people in her life and knew she was not always calm.

If a couple therapist is unhappy in her or his own intimate partnership or is single and wishes he or she were partnered, the couple therapist may be at risk of idealizing one of the partners. As noted earlier in this chapter, Liz and Martin's couple therapist found herself idealizing Martin because he treated Liz more respectfully than her estranged husband treated her. While it is appropriate to identify and question a partner's idealization of the couple therapist during a couple session, couple therapists must resolve their idealization of one of the partners outside of couple sessions. A couple therapist assumes responsibility for facilitating couple clients' mental health to the extent possible; the reverse is not true, as full responsibility for the couple therapist's mental health and resulting ethical behavior resides with the couple therapist.

Experiencing Couples

The writer has found couple therapy to be the most exhilarating, as well as the most challenging mode of therapy. Observing and then deciding how to manage each partner and the couple's spoken and unspoken communications, the couple's dynamics, the couple therapist's reactions to each partner and to the couple, and maintaining ethical standards of practice requires intense concentration, rapid decision making, and an ability to prioritize the couple's needs over the couple therapist's and balance the couple's needs with each partner's at all times. Additionally, experience suggests that couple therapy often unfolds mysteriously. It can become frustrating, as the couple system's homeostatic mechanisms and the partners' ambivalence repeatedly undermine the couple therapist's best efforts. It can also seem hopeless, and the couple therapist may find herself or himself questioning his or her ability to be helpful to a client couple. The latter becomes even more difficult if the couple begins to lose hope and turns to the couple therapist for guidance through the hopelessness. To counterbalance all this, experience indicates that partner ambivalence and couple homeostatic mechanisms are overridden suddenly and for no apparent reason, and change ensues. While such change can be explained in hindsight, it cannot be predicted and thus practicing couple therapy requires a couple therapist to tolerate ambiguity and to learn and practice patience.

As a couple therapist's skill and experience increase, it becomes easier to self-soothe with a reminder of how often couple therapy has been productive. This allows the couple therapist increased tolerance for the hopeless, frustrating times.

Couples frequently present for couple therapy after years of unresolved fights have compounded the initial problem with anger and hurt. By the time the couple presents for couple therapy, these processes may have eroded the partners' good will toward each other. The couple therapy then becomes much more difficult than it would have been had the couple sought treatment sooner, and this is an additional source of frustration for the couple therapist. If the couple is able to tolerate couple therapy and willing to work on their relationship, as opposed to passively being fixed by an expert, then there remains hope that their issues can resolve. And when a couple reclaims the mutual caring, respect, friendship, and love that has been masked by conflict and hopelessness, the couple therapist who shares their journey may feel buoyed as well. While it may be wise not to attach one's self-esteem to one's clients' successes or lack thereof, to celebrate a couple's success and one's facilitative role in it is human.

Just as a couple therapist must be alert to unwarranted self-recriminations, he or she can acknowledge her or his facilitative role in successful outcomes. Note the two crucial words in the previous sentence: unwarranted and facilitative. Couple therapists learn from mistakes, most of which require attention but not self-recrimination. And just as a couple therapist's mistake is not going to undo a relationship if for no other reason than that the couple system is more powerful than the couple therapist, so a couple's success resides with the couple. Couple therapists play a facilitative role in a couple's success; however, the couple rather than the couple therapist is responsible for moving their relationship forward.

It also bears mentioning that couple therapists cannot be responsible either for the partners' ability to tolerate the process of couple therapy or for their ability to work on their relationship together. Individual mental health issues may preclude taking responsibility for one's own contribution to the couple dynamics, sharing the couple therapist's attention with the partner, and empathizing with the partner. Alternatively, one or both partners may decide the potential benefits of change do not outweigh the risks for them at a given time, even though the risks of deferring couple therapy may be significant. They may be too overwhelmed with demands outside of their relationship to bring the necessary focus and emotional resources to couple therapy. Or one partner may have already left the relationship emotionally and not wish to return. Yet another possibility is that one or both partners expects the couple therapist or the other partner to fix the relationship or change himself or herself. Finally, a topic perceived as shameful to one of the partners, such as substance abuse or intimate partner violence, may deter his or her willingness to participate in couple therapy.

As noted throughout this chapter, couple therapists bring not only their knowledge and skills but also themselves as human beings to their work. A couple therapist's views are determined by his or her cultural and theoretical world views, experiences being part of one or more intimate partnerships and a child of one or more parental partnerships, what is currently happening in her or his personal and professional life, and his or her temperament. At any one point in time, he or she may be experiencing multiple demands both from other clients and colleagues at work and from her or his family, friends, and volunteer activities outside of work. And this list is likely not exhaustive.

Being aware of the potential for one's feelings and the stresses of one's life to impact one's work as a couple therapist is crucial to both ethical practice and successful client outcomes. Once these have been identified, the couple therapist then uses the tenets of his or her theoretical perspective as well as peer supervision, consultation, and his or her own individual therapy to decide how to manage them in ways that allow for ethical couple therapy practice.

Stop and Think:

Be sure to include your answers in your journal.

1. Imagine yourself as a couple therapist, perhaps working with Liz and Martin.
2. What might it be like to focus on the couple's needs when you are sad, angry, or worried about something that is happening in your own life?

3. What might it be like to focus on the couple's needs when you are distracted by multiple demands in your own life, for example, your partner's job is at risk, one of your parents has just been diagnosed with a serious illness, one of your closest friends needs a lot of attention, or another client appears suicidal?
4. How might your feelings and the multiple demands in your life impact how you practice couple therapy?
5. What would be your concerns about that impact?
6. How might you handle that impact?
7. How might you handle feelings of frustration with partners or the couple with whom you are working at a time of high personal stress?

Practitioners vary in their approaches to revealing personal information. Some adhere to strong boundaries and the withholding of any personal information. Others allow some degree of self-revelation. These couple therapists advocate revealing only what must be revealed, such as potentially helpful countertransference observations or the need to take time off to visit an ailing parent. No school of couple therapy allows for self-revelation in a way that increases the couple therapist's inherent power or burdens the couple client. For example, when a partner with an infant says she is much crankier than she intends to be and the couple therapist says, "I remember how not sleeping when my kids were babies left me incredibly irritable"; the couple therapist is displaying empathy that can be followed by a question about how the client might normalize the consequences of sleep loss and self-soothe that the baby will one day sleep through the night. Alternatively, responding with, "My children slept through the night by the time they were three months old" suggests that the couple therapist is a better parent than the client, while responding with talk about the couple therapist's own sleep loss as a result of her or his worries shifts focus from the client to the couple therapist. In other words, revealing personal information to convey empathy or needed information is very different than revealing personal information to shift focus from the client or to embellish the therapist's already presumed expertise.

Irrespective of intent, a couple therapist's feelings and the distraction of competing demands may leak out in nonverbal communications to which one or both partners may be attuned. Thus, the risk of the couple therapist not acknowledging the existence of distractions is that one or both partners will attempt to care for the couple therapist, perhaps by avoiding difficult conversations that might further stress him or her. If a couple therapist decides to or cannot avoid revealing personal information, it is incumbent on him or her to remain alert to efforts by either partner to care for or meet the needs of the couple therapist with respect to the revelation and assure the couple that he or she is grateful and yet wants to focus on what the couple needs during the session.

An example from the writer's experience may be illustrative. She was pregnant with her second child at the same time that the wife of a male colleague with whom she shared office space was pregnant. Because the writer's appearance changed as the pregnancy progressed, the pregnancy and its impact on her clients had to be addressed well in advance of her parental leave. These impacts included ambivalent feelings triggered in one client struggling with fertility issues and another whose marriage was falling apart as she felt herself aging out of the possibility of having children. Clients were also impacted by the couple therapist's impending absence for a number of weeks. The clients of her colleague, by contrast, observed no physical change in his appearance, and he did not mention his parental leave until a week or two before the baby was expected. Because the baby might have been born earlier than expected, the clients were at risk of not seeing their couple therapist for a number of weeks with little warning. The fact that he, like the writer, was undeniably attached to his family, may have been perceived by some clients as an unwanted shift of attention away from them. Parental leave forces clients to recognize that they are not the sole focus of their couple therapist, a phenomenon that may be ignored under other circumstances. Leaving time to address these issues, if possible, facilitates client coping. Some events, however, like the death of a declining parent, cannot be predicted and the impact on client couples must be deferred until after the couple therapist resumes working.

Several couple therapy theorists have argued that a couple therapist's reaction to a couple can be useful. For example, when a couple therapist becomes frustrated with the partners' ambivalence about change and the strength of the couple's homeostatic mechanisms, it is likely that the partners experience similar frustration. By acknowledging his or her own frustration without placing blame on the client couple and then asking the partners whether they are also frustrated, the couple therapist makes the couple's covert frustration overt and allows a shift in focus to the competing wishes expressed in ambivalence, the risks of not changing, and what the couple, with the couple therapist's help, can do.

Couple therapists may find themselves dreading appointments with particularly difficult, frustrating, or distressed clients. Accessing empathy may help. However, when the couple therapist feels manipulated, disregarded, or frustrated with couple client behavior, these feelings may indicate a process that needs to be addressed. While the couple therapist might choose less pejorative words than manipulated and disregarded, one or both partners' behavior toward the couple therapist may reflect how they treat one another and therefore be a source of distress in their relationship that warrants addressing. For example, a couple client who occasionally cancels appointments because of a work demand and acknowledges the inconvenience has a very different impact on the couple therapist than one who cancels routinely when something comes up one partner would rather do. The question becomes, do the partners view their couple therapist as a collaborative partner in their care or as a servant to use at their discretion? It is important that a couple therapist address such behaviors before he or she becomes too angry at the client couple to be effective. It is also important because the partners may be treating one another with the same disregard and thus their relationship may benefit from addressing such treatment of one another.

Experiencing Liz and Martin

As has become apparent, the couple therapist liked and respected both Liz and Martin. Her impression was that they cared about each other and wanted their relationship to be more than something to be endured until their children left home. The couple therapist also agreed with Liz and Martin's views about working mothers and wondered whether she had nonverbally communicated her wish to defend Liz from Sally's attempts to induce enough guilt and self-doubt that she assumed a more traditional role.

The couple therapist occasionally wanted to defend herself when Liz challenged her. She recognized that, while unsure of herself in many respects, Liz could also be somewhat intimidating in her certainty. The couple therapist personally identified with Liz's ambivalence about how to balance her roles as mother and professional. While the couple therapist's financial options were more limited than Liz's, the way she had balanced her career and mothering left her feeling that she was either ignoring her children or failing her clients most of the time. Her estranged husband's rage that she had not attended to their marriage further exacerbated her own self-doubt.

The couple therapist's concerns about projecting her image of an ideal partner onto Martin were addressed earlier in this chapter. She was also concerned she might, at times, appear insensitive to Martin's experience as a black man. Sometimes Martin's unflappable appearance left her wanting to defend him from Liz's verbal attacks. She knew this had to do with her own experience as a child aligning with one parent against the other and that neither her beliefs nor experiences could be clinical guideposts to her work with Liz and Martin. Finally, she worried that her attempts to assure Martin that she as a white woman was not aligned with his white wife could be perceived by Liz as discounting her perspective.

In terms of Liz and Martin as a couple, the couple therapist had become frustrated with their repeated decisions to discontinue couple therapy prematurely. With only one exception, all of the theories you read about in Section II allowed for a period of consolidating change prior to ending couple therapy. Thus, her frustration was consistent with her clinical opinion that their disinclination to continue through the consolidation phase had negative consequences for their relationship. Chapter 9 included the transcript of how she addressed this frustration with them. The ethics of her intervention will be addressed in Chapter 11.

The following excerpt is from a couple therapy session three or four months after Liz and Martin committed to continuing couple therapy long enough to consolidate the changes they made. The couple therapist noticed that they were not speaking to one another when she greeted them, whereas usually she found them talking and laughing together in her waiting room. They held their bodies rigidly and only nodded in response to her greeting. As soon as they were seated in her office, Liz, who usually asked the couple therapist how she was, began.

LIZ: We had a bad night last night. [Glaring at Martin] You tell her.

MARTIN: [Quietly] I'm fine, Liz. Go ahead.

LIZ: [Frowning, shaking her head, and turning to the couple therapist] It was 9 o'clock at night, I'm on the phone listening to my mom crying about how awful it is to be alone and then asking me—me!—whether she should accept a coffee invitation from some "cute" man she met at church. And in the midst of all this,

MJ gets up and starts running around and calling for us. And Martin's all plugged into his computer and completely ignoring his son. Just expected me to take care of it without even checking to see what I was doing. What if it had been a professional call? [Liz had negotiated a half-time position with her law firm.] So I said to my mother, "Mom, MJ is up and I need to go see what he needs." And she goes, "Now that you're a working girl, I would think that husband of yours might help you" in that disapproving voice of hers. I don't know what was worse: Martin apparently expecting me to do everything or my mom saying I'm a bad mother because I work at the same time she's criticizing him for not sharing parenting. [To Martin, raising her voice] I can't believe your level of disrespect for me.

MARTIN: I told you I was sorry, Liz. I know when one of the kids needs us, I'm as responsible as you are.

LIZ: [To CT] The contrite husband [rolls eyes] as always. [To Martin] But that doesn't cut it, Martin. You need to pay attention to me and the kids, not just keep apologizing because you never do.

MARTIN: I can't go back and undo last night, Liz. And you yelling at me isn't going to change that.

LIZ: Oh, now it's my fault for "yelling"? How about you stop acting like you don't have to be a father just because I don't work full time anymore.

CT: Let me interrupt. I hear how upset you both are.

LIZ: [Sarcastically] That's nice, but he's not. He's never upset. [Quietly] It's always me.

CT: I've noticed how easy it is for you to fall back into old fights about being parents and about Liz's career. And I keep wondering what is getting in the way of you both getting what you want and need.

At this point, there was a pause, after which one of two scenarios occurred.

Scenario 1

MARTIN: I think it's habit. [Liz looks confused] No, Liz, I really do. I think we got in the habit of you being the one to be sure the kids are OK and take care of them when they're not. It made sense to me, because you were around more. But it doesn't work when I'm home.

LIZ: No, it doesn't.

MARTIN: So what do you want me to do when you say, "I've been at work all day today. I'll go take care of it"?

LIZ: Oh. Well... [Pause] I guess I'd like you to follow my lead.

MARTIN: And that means paying attention to what you want, and not to the kids, on a day you've worked?

LIZ: Well, if you'd been paying attention last night, you would have known I was stuck on the phone and that MJ needed one of us.

CT: I'm curious because I wasn't there. How would he have known you were on the phone?

LIZ: Oh. Well, he could have checked when he heard MJ.

CT: Yes. I'm also wondering whether it would help to plan ahead. Like, decide that on Liz's work nights she'll take primary responsibility for the kids and on nights when she's been at home with them Martin will. Or ask each other on a day-by-day basis, although if your kids are like mine were at that age, I think it would help to agree before the evening begins.

Scenario 2

LIZ: You know, I don't think I care what it is. I think I am done fighting about this. I'm sick of being angry.

CT: Yes, and yet what I'm hearing in the anger is how much you still want your marriage to be alright, how much you want Martin to work with you to take care of the kids.

LIZ: I don't think so.

CT: Maybe not. I'm not sure you'd be so angry if you didn't care, though.

LIZ: Really, I don't want to go there. I'm exhausted, and I'm done. I told you when we started that I wanted to find a way to live with Martin until the kids are grown, but maybe he'd be a better father if I weren't there when he was with them.

MARTIN: Liz...

LIZ: You two can continue talking. I'm done. [Gets up and walks toward the door.]

CT: I'd like you to stay and finish the session, whatever you decide now or afterward.

LIZ: Thanks, but no.

Stop and Think:

Be sure to include your answers and observations in your journal.

1. If you had been the couple therapist, how would you have felt at the end of Scenario 1? at the end of Scenario 2?
2. If you had been the couple therapist, what would you have done differently in Scenario 1? in Scenario 2?
3. In groups of six, assign three people to argue why Liz and Martin should remain together and three to argue why there is no point in continuing to work on their relationship. You do not need to believe the perspective assigned to you, although

your argument needs to be consistent with what you know about Liz and Martin. Allow each side 3–5 minutes to present the argument and then group members can discuss what has been presented for 5 or 10 minutes.

The couple therapist in Scenario 1 was exhausted after the session and also felt good about the work she had done. The couple therapist in Scenario 2 was shocked, felt she had failed Liz and Martin, could not shake the feeling that she was responsible for their decision to end their marriage, and wondered whether she was competent to continue practicing couple therapy. She worried that Liz, being an attorney, would conclude that she had behaved unethically and sue her for malpractice and/or report her to her licensing board. What differentiates couple therapists who move beyond such experiences from those who do not is their willingness to examine and take responsibility for mistakes of judgment, as well as the role of negative self-talk in their personal and professional lives. Peer supervision, consultation, and individual psychotherapy all facilitate a couple therapist's recovery and continued work.

Supervision

Couple therapists in training must be supervised by a licensed couple therapist. In some jurisdictions, supervisors must also be certified by their professional organization and/or a state licensure supervisor designation. Clinical supervision involves meeting regularly to examine all aspects of each client case. Different licensure boards and professional organizations require different amounts of supervised practice. These boards and organizations also denote the ratio of practice to supervision hours, and whether and how much of the required supervision can occur in groups.

Couples must give informed consent to treatment by a supervised couple therapist in training. Couple clients are given contact information for the supervisor, in the event they have questions or concerns. Both the couple therapist in training and the clinical supervisor practice under the same legal and ethical mandates to protect client confidentiality and otherwise maintain ethical practice (Chapter 11). If it happens that the supervisor knows the client couple in another context, he or she cannot supervise the case due to the prohibition against dual roles.

Clinicians learn to be supervisors through coursework and supervision of their supervision. Some professional associations, such as the American Association for Marriage and Family Therapy, require both, as well as refresher classes every five years to maintain the designation Approved Supervisor. Some states require that clinical supervisors be certified by their professional organizations or have practiced in the state for a specified number of years. Supervising the supervision of supervisors in training adds yet another level of certification required by some professional organizations.

After licensure, couple therapists continue to face professional challenges and may benefit from colleagues' input. Many clinicians seek peer supervision to fill this need. Peer supervision in group practices, in-patient settings, and agencies may occur during the workday. However, those in small or individual private practices do not have ready access to a group of colleagues and are only paid for their time with clients. As a result, they often form peer supervision groups. Because post-licensure supervision is not mandated, laws governing peer supervision do not exist. However, both legal and ethical protections for clients apply. Clinicians in peer supervision groups must be careful to protect client confidentiality and remain cautious about other legal and ethical violations.

The distinction between supervision and psychotherapy must be maintained in both pre-licensure training supervision and peer supervision following licensure. When a couple therapist seeks help with her or his reactions and feelings about clients, the supervisor or peer supervision group may facilitate recognition that the couple therapist's personal issues impede the couple therapy and may require psychotherapy to resolve. The supervisor or peer supervision group maintains focus on professional clarity and ethical practice, while treatment of the couple therapist's own issues is done by the couple therapist's psychotherapist.

A third form of supervision, consultation, involves meeting briefly with a senior colleague for input to an identified client case or situation. Some professional organizations, such as the American Association for Marriage and Family Therapy, require members to be certified to practice consultation.

Liz and Martin's couple therapist sought consultation with a senior couple therapist with expertise in multicultural practice. Additionally, she sought input from her peer supervision group and talked to her individual psychotherapist, as described earlier in this chapter.

Conclusions

This chapter explored the experience of practicing couple therapy, using Liz and Martin's couple therapist as an example. You read about the power of the couple's dyadic relationship and the impacts of the couple therapist's world view, including his or her ethnicity, race, religion, gender identification, and age on her or his couple therapy practice. You also learned about how the couple therapist's family of origin and relationship history may impact her or his practice of couple therapy.

This chapter also reviewed the couple therapist's comfort in talking about sexual intimacy and the difficulty in managing the multiple relationships inherent in couple therapy. You learned about the couple therapist's need to resist taking sides in couple disputes and about the risks of idealizing either a partner or the couple therapist. More general comments on the experience of practicing couple therapy and their application to the couple therapist's experience working with Liz and Martin were included.

Finally, the roles of supervision, consultation, and the couple therapist's individual psychotherapy in managing the experience of practicing couple therapy were explored. While legal and ethical subjects were touched upon throughout the chapter, you will examine legal and ethical considerations in the practice of couple therapy more fully in the next chapter.

References

Dulwich Centre. (2015). *What is narrative therapy?* Dulwich Centre Publications Pty Ltd & Dulwich Centre Foundation, Inc. Retrieved from http://dulwichcentre.com.au/what-is-narrative-therapy.

Haley, J. (1963). *Strategies of psychotherapy*. New York NY: Grune & Stratton.

Lerner, H. (2014). *The dance of anger*. New York: Harper/Collins.

Napier, A. Y. & Whitaker, C. A. (1978). *The family crucible*. New York NY: Harper and Row, Publishers.

For Further Study

Napier, A. Y. (1988). *The fragile bond. In search of an equal, intimate and enduring marriage*. New York NY: Harper Collins.

Perls, F. S. (1977). *In and out of the garbage pail*. New York NY: Bantam Books.

Whitaker, C. (1989). *Midnight musings of a family therapist*. New York NY: W. W. Norton & Company.

Yalom, I. D. (2000). *Momma and the meaning of life. Tales of psychotherapy*. New York NY: Harper Perennial.

CHAPTER 11

Ethics of Couple Counseling

Learning Objectives

1. List the specifics of who is protected by licensure statutes and ethical codes.
2. Describe the importance of protecting client rights.
3. Explain the relationship between the couple therapist's power and the couple client's boundaries.
4. Describe the ethical considerations arising from dual roles, bartering, and scope of practice violations.
5. Evaluate the ethical arguments about secrets in couple therapy.
6. Discuss the ways in which self-awareness and self-care are interrelated.
7. Illustrate the relationship between cultural competence and ethical practice.
8. Apply five ethical considerations to Liz and Martin's couple therapy.

Many of the challenges couple therapists face have legal and ethical implications, and this chapter will introduce you to these aspects of couple therapy practice. The explicit purpose of all laws and codes of ethics, such as licensure laws, is to protect the public. Licensing laws protect the public from a practitioner's false claims of knowledge and skills and also provide a gate-keeping mechanism for the profession. Similarly, legal statutes and professional codes regarding ethics protect the public from illegal and unethical practice on the part of the couple therapist. Statutes and codes pertaining to ethics also protect clients and those with whom they come in contact from themselves when necessary.

Adherence to both legal and ethical codes is mandatory for licensees and for couple therapists in training. Violation of legal statutes carries specific civil and sometimes even criminal penalties. Violations of ethical codes can lead to suspension or revocation of a couple therapist's license to practice. Some violations, such as revealing confidential information and sexual interactions with a client or former client, violate both legal statutes and ethical codes and carry civil, criminal, and licensure penalties.

Laws governing the practice of couple therapy are enacted by state legislatures and are enforced by the state in which the couple therapist is licensed to practice. Laws are clear and precise statements delineating illegal behavior and its consequences. Some legal statutes, such as those governing the reporting of abuse of dependents, are relatively consistent across all 50 states. Others vary from state to state.

Additionally, couple therapists are required to adhere to professional codes of ethics. Some are included in state licensing laws, while others are attached to the national professional organization(s) of which the couple therapist is a member. Violating ethical codes can lead to suspension or revocation of licensure. Some situations entail violation of both legal and ethical codes, for example, sex with clients and violation of confidentiality except when the latter is required by either a court or reporting laws.

Ethical codes define the parameters for making judgments in situations that are not clearly specified by law. Ethical codes may not be updated as quickly as new situations arise, however. For example, the ability to connect with clients using mobile phones, internet therapy, and social media has developed faster than ethical codes can be created and enacted, and thus ethical codes do not cover every eventuality faced by a couple therapist.

In the absence of clear ethical guidelines, couple therapists must make ethical decisions. Models of ethical decision making are available. Licensing laws require continuing education in ethics, and professional meetings, peer supervision groups, consultation, and workshops allow couple therapists to learn about and discuss the ethical implications of various situations in which they find themselves.

The remainder of this chapter will describe specific legal and ethical mandates within the two broad categories of respecting clients' rights and respecting clients' boundaries. Legal and ethical issues surrounding scope of practice, abandonment, secrets, triangulation, and hugging will also be discussed. Ethical decision-making models and considerations are addressed in a fourth section of this chapter. Finally, self-awareness and self-care as methods for ensuring ethical practice will be discussed.

Respecting Clients' Rights

Protecting clients entails both knowing and respecting their legal rights. These rights are specified in the statutes governing licensure in every state and in the ethical codes of every mental health professional organization.

The fundamental right of all couples is to receive ethical treatment by a couple therapist who has met the criteria to practice in her or his jurisdiction. Specifics surrounding this right are far more complex than may be apparent. The legal challenges couple therapists most frequently face involve confidentiality, compliance with federal law, and reporting both abuse and client danger to self or others, which includes the duty to warn intended victims. This section provides you with an introduction to these three areas of concern.

Confidentiality

All client couples have the right to privacy in all aspects of their work with a couple therapist. This means that couple therapists cannot reveal any information, including acknowledging they know either partner, to anyone, unless they have obtained written consent from both partners. The writer has been asked more than once why she ignored a client she had seen in a public setting. The answer is that she cannot acknowledge recognition of the client unless the client initiates contact first. If a client smiles or says, "Hello," then the couple therapist can reciprocate. The point is that if someone were to ask how the client and couple therapist knew each other, it is the client's information to reveal, not the couple therapist's, and therefore the client's right to choose whether to take the risk of revelation by acknowledging the couple therapist. By contrast, the couple therapist's responsibility is to protect the client's privacy by not initiating behavior that could lead to revelation.

Clients can waive their right to confidentiality in particular situations. For example, if one or both partners is also in individual psychotherapy or taking psychotropic medication, it may be helpful for the mental health practitioners to exchange information with one another. Clients can withdraw permission to reveal information at any time, although they cannot do so retroactively. All clients who wish to file claims with a health insurer must allow the couple therapist to communicate confidential information to the insurance company, such as diagnosis and dates and type of treatment.

Two exceptions to the client's right to confidentiality exist. First, if the couple therapist suspects, based on her or his professional knowledge and experience or on information revealed by the client, that either partner is a danger to herself or himself or to another person, the couple therapist is required by law to report his or her suspicions to the appropriate agency. Reporting laws, duty-to-warn laws, and the impact of both on couple therapists will be described in more detail later in this chapter.

A second exception to the legal requirement to protect client confidentiality occurs when a couple therapist is ordered by a court or government agency to reveal confidential information. Couple therapists are not immune from being charged with contempt of court if they refuse, and this threat overrides restrictions on protecting confidentiality. Legal statutes also protect couple therapists from being successfully sued for violating client confidentiality when a court order or reasonable suspicion of danger to self or others is in effect.

Health Insurance Portability and Accountability Act

The Health Insurance Portability and Accountability Act (HIPAA) is a 1996 federal statute specifying clients' rights to their health information and the responsibilities of all medical and allied health practitioners, including mental health professionals, to protect these rights. The details of HIPAA and the regulations surrounding it are complex and beyond the scope of this chapter. Relevant to the present discussion, HIPAA specifies that patients, or in the case of couple therapy, clients, own their personal health information. This allows them to ask for their medical records at any time (U.S. Department of Health and Human Services, n.d.).

Two potential challenges arise for couple therapists as a result of this client right. First, like all practitioners of psychotherapy, couple therapists are required to include diagnoses and treatment plans written in medicalized clinical language. While a couple therapist would share her or his assessment of what impedes a couple's change, she or he would use verbal and nonverbal language aimed at conveying empathy and hope while side-stepping potential client defensiveness. Medical records contain very different language and no nonverbal messages and thus may be upsetting or even destabilizing for clients to read.

Second, when the couple is the client, both partners own the medical records. In other words, the couple is the client. Yet, the couple is an entity that cannot request its own medical records, so requests may be initiated by one or the other partner. When, for example, one partner requests the records for use in divorce proceedings, the couple therapist is faced with an ethical dilemma but not a legal one. It bears noting that the writer was once advised by counsel to redact any reference to the spouse when one partner's attorney subpoenaeded records for divorce proceedings a number of years after the couple terminated couple therapy in order to comply with the legal requirement of the subpoena without violating the other partner's confidentiality.

Reporting Laws

Couple therapists are required to report certain suspicions to the agency specified by the laws of the jurisdiction in which they practice and in a timely manner as specified by these same laws of the jurisdiction, despite the fact that such reporting is a violation of client confidentiality. Reporting laws are designed to protect clients, their dependents, and the public.

State laws allow for the involuntary hospitalization of clients who are a danger to themselves or to others or who are unable to care for themselves. Since couple therapists do not have hospital privileges unless they are also licensed physicians, they must call the local 9-1-1 phone number. In some jurisdictions, an ambulance is sent; in others, the police apprehend the client. If a couple therapist is in a position to reasonably suspect that a client is a danger to self or others or unable to care for himself or herself, fails to call 9-1-1, and a bad outcome occurs, the couple therapist is liable in terms of the outcome.

Couple therapists are also legally required to report suspicion of abuse of a dependent, including minor children, the elderly, and the disabled. These dependents are assumed to be unable to protect themselves and therefore require the professionals with whom they or their suspected abuser comes into contact to alert the appropriate agency on their behalf. Failure to report suspected abuse of a dependent can lead to charges of co-conspiring in the abuse.

Some individual psychotherapists, couple therapists, and family therapists have argued that reporting laws, by requiring them to breach confidentiality, destroy trust and any possibility that the therapeutic relationship could be beneficial to the client. While this may be true, those who have written and who are charged with enforcing reporting statutes have prioritized protecting the public over healing the client. Irrespective of whether any given couple therapist agrees or disagrees with that prioritization, it remains legally enforceable.

The key word in the reporting laws is that the couple therapist need only suspect that the client is a danger to self or others. Couple therapists are expected to use their professional training and experience to determine whether it is reasonable to suspect either danger to self or others, inability to care for self, or abuse of a dependent. The wording exempts the couple therapist from responsibility to verify what he or she suspects. Investigations are the responsibility of the agency to which the couple therapist reports. In other words, a couple therapist does not need to prove abuse has occurred, but rather to suspect in his or her best professional judgment that it may have. The same is true of danger to self or others.

The wording of reporting laws also protects couple therapists from being successfully sued for violation of client confidentiality when reporting suspected danger to self or others or abuse of a dependent. Clients are not prevented from suing. However, as long as the couple therapist has documented what led him or her to reasonably suspect what led to the reporting, adhering to legal statutes takes precedence in these cases and the couple therapist is protected from being successfully sued.

Stop and Think:

Consider four hypothetical scenarios with which couple therapists may be faced. What would you do if you were the couple therapist in each? Be sure to include your answers in your journal.

1. A distressed couple has been fighting about each partner's parenting skills when one accuses the other of having slapped their child hard enough to knock her or him to the floor. The accused partner responds, "Now you've gone too far trying to prove your point." While it appears that the accusation might be part of escalating anger between the partners, the couple therapist has also noticed that the accused partner uses physically violent language and his or her nonverbal communication of rage consistently exceeds what one would expect based upon the provocation.

2 During a couple therapy session, one of the partners, who is also in individual psychotherapy for depression, says he or she does not know how he or she can "go on." After doing a suicide assessment, the couple therapist determines that the partner is at immediate risk (suicidal ideation and a plan that includes a time and accessible method). Both partners agree that they do not want the suicidal partner hospitalized, and the other partner claims that he or she can keep the suicidal partner safe at home. However, one of the partners had mentioned that the non-suicidal partner kept a loaded hand gun in their home for protection. When asked, he or she declined to remove the bullets from the gun and store them where the suicidal partner could not access them while that partner was at risk.

3 A couple is talking about how to manage an elderly parent who is living in their home and whose dementia includes combative behavior. During the discussion, one of the partners guiltily confesses that the stress led him or her to push the elderly dependent. As a result, the elderly parent fell and broke a bone. The emergency room physician was only told the parent fell.

4 During a couple therapy session, the couple therapist learns that intimate partner violence has occurred during the week. The couple therapist has experience and training working with intimate partner violence. What considerations might lead the couple therapist to report the violence?

Duty to Warn

The courts have set a legal precedent, codified into law in many jurisdictions, that couple therapists have the responsibility to warn the intended victim(s) when a client threatens violence. The precedent was set in the 1970s, following an incident in 1969 on the University of California at Berkeley campus (Tarasoff v. Regents of the University of California, 1976).

As required by law, the student's individual psychotherapist informed the police when the client threatened violence against a fellow student. The authorities acted upon the psychotherapist's report, apprehended and questioned the client, and then released him. He later killed his intended victim. Her family sued, and an appeals court subsequently upheld the lower court's decision that it was incumbent upon the psychotherapist to inform not only the police but also to warn the intended victim (Tarasoff v. Regents of the University of California, 1976).

This duty-to-warn precedent suggests the need for couple therapists to violate client confidentiality when a specific threat has been made. In jurisdictions in which the duty to warn has been codified in legal statutes, couple therapists must treat their duty to warn in the same way they treat reporting laws. In jurisdictions in which it is not codified into law, the couple therapist would rely on legal precedent if sued for violating confidentiality by warning the intended victim.

While client confidentiality is violated when both reporting laws and duty to warn need to be invoked, the results of the latter are even more complex than the former. Both reporting danger to self or others to the police or a social service agency, whichever the jurisdiction specifies, and warning an intended victim may undermine the confidentiality and therefore trust of the therapeutic relationship. In addition, however, warning an intended victim also disrupts any relationship the intended victim and the client may have had.

Couple therapists learn how to report suspicion that a client is a danger to self or others or is perpetrating the abuse of a dependent in graduate school, post-degree supervision, and while studying for licensing examinations. Finding an intended victim may be a much greater challenge. The couple therapist may not know enough about the intended victim to find her or him. And even if last name and either city of residence or workplace is known, finding the intended victim may require extra delicacy to avoid violating confidentiality unnecessarily to uninvolved third parties. The couple therapist must make a reasonable effort to warn. Reasonable is a vague term, and deciding when a reasonable effort has been made may require legal consultation. Fortunately, professional liability insurers make staff attorneys available to insured mental health professionals for this kind of consultation.

While couple therapists must protect themselves, their practice, the agency for which they work, and their families from the legal ramifications of failing to report or warn, they must also be cognizant and prepared for the ramifications of complying with the relevant legal statutes and precedents. When faced with a duty to warn, peer supervision as well as consultation with an attorney may be advisable.

Respecting Clients' Boundaries

Ethical practice requires couple therapists to respect the couple client's emotional and physical boundaries. When these boundaries are violated, clients may feel uncomfortable, mistrustful, and even unsafe, all of which undermine trust in the therapeutic relationship and, as a result, the effectiveness of treatment. Additionally, boundary violations increase the power imbalance between the couple therapist as expert and the client couple in need of help. Hence, they risk or even embody an abuse of power.

Questions of boundary violation arise around issues including touching, the couple therapist initiating contact between sessions, inserting the couple therapist's needs into the couple therapy and thereby increaseing the inherently unequal power, dual roles, and bartering. A couple therapist who respects client couple boundaries simultaneously respects the client couple, the therapeutic alliance, and the risks of abusing his or her inherent power in the relationship

Touching

Liz was a sexual assault survivor. At the most fundamental level, physical abuse and sexual assault involve a violation of physical space with unwanted touching. Like many survivors, Liz became anxious if not fearful when anyone other than Martin or her children initiated physical touching of any kind with her. She said that sometimes she even flinched when one of them touched her. Clients who have not experienced abuse or assault may also be sensitive to being touched or may mistake what the couple therapist intended to be a supportive touch for a sexual advance. For these reasons, couple therapists refrain from initiating touch, even when they use touch to convey caring in non-clinical situations.

LIZ: I'm so confused. I want to do the right thing, and I'm not sure what it is.

COUPLE THERAPIST: What would feel right to you, Liz?

LIZ: I don't know.

CT: If you knew, what would it be?

LIZ: Both. I love my work, and I want to be with my children, too.

CT: Then it sounds like you know what you want.

LIZ: To work part time?

CT: That's a way to do both. And it sounds like you already know you could make it happen, if it's worth the professional trade-off.

LIZ: But my mother says... [Pause] I really just said that, didn't I? But what if she's right? What if I hurt my kids?

CT: I suspect you know best what's right for you and your family. And I think you deserve to listen to your own voice about how you balance being a mother and being a professional.

Stop and Think:

Be sure to include your responses in your journal.

The couple therapist, who often used supportive touch in her personal life, was tempted to touch Liz's arm to underscore her empathy for Liz at the beginning of the excerpt.

1. Did you share her temptation?
2. What do you think the benefits and drawbacks of the couple therapist's decision to refrain from supportive touch might have been for Liz?

Contacting Clients between Sessions

Initiating contact with clients between sessions for any reason other than scheduling is a boundary violation. Couple clients agree to a specific time, place, duration, and frequency of contact with the couple therapist. If the couple therapist initiates contact outside these agreed-upon limits, she or he is violating the client couple's personal and temporal space.

Scheduling issues are excluded from boundary violations, because the realities of a couple therapist's life may require him or her to occasionally reschedule sessions at the last minute. Couple therapist initiated scheduling changes are best kept to a minimum so that the couple can trust the couple therapist's reliability. Informing clients in advance and during a regularly-scheduled session of the couple therapist's need to reschedule is preferable whenever possible.

It is not uncommon for couple therapists, who cannot address everything at once, to decide while writing a case note that an overlooked topic would have been helpful to address during the session. In an early session, Liz brought up a sexual issue that the couple therapist did not address at the time because she believed Liz and Martin changed the subject of their disagreements as a homeostatic mechanism that then interfered with resolving any of these disagreements. She chose to avoid reinforcing this homeostatic mechanism and so chose to remain focused on the topic at hand and return to the sexual issue at a later session. When she reconsidered the advisability of her decision after the session, she refrained from contacting Liz and Martin about it and chose instead to defer exploration of their sexual relationship to an agreed-upon couple therapy session time.

Inserting the Couple Therapist's Needs

Couple therapy is for and about the client couple. It is incumbent on the couple therapist to manage her or his own problems and issues outside of sessions with client couples. Bringing the couple therapist's issues to the client couple violates the agreed-upon boundary separating the couple therapist's role of practitioner and the client couple's role of client. While clients may wish to care for their couple therapists as they feel cared for by them, switching roles creates dual roles (see below) and shifts the attention away from the client couple and their couple therapy work.

Liz and Martin's couple therapist refrained from telling Liz how fortunate she was to be married to Martin, in contrast to the couple therapist's own marital problems. The comparison would have not only violated the boundary between the client couple and couple therapist but also, because of the couple therapist's power, changed the focus to her own pain.

Unequal Power

As repeatedly noted, couple therapists are in a more powerful position than are couple clients. The couple therapist is the educated, experienced expert to whom the couple client has turned for help at an especially difficult time in the relationship. The partners are suffering, vulnerable, and in need of what they hope the couple therapist can offer. In this state, clients may be willing to accept whatever a confident and seemingly reasonable couple therapist presents to them.

In an individual psychotherapy class the writer once taught, undergraduate students conducted a mock psychotherapy session with acting students playing the client. In a debrief at the end of the semester, several acting students commented that the psychotherapy students' words had remained in their minds long after the mock sessions ended. If a student who knows she or he is acting is influenced to this extent by another student he or she knows is only beginning training, imagine the extent to which real clients can be influenced by their individual, couple, family, and group therapists. Being an expert imbues the couple therapist with the powers of knowledge, experience, authority with all its attendant meanings, and clinical wisdom as described by Siegel (2013).

As discussed in Chapter 9, the power of a couple therapist is increased when he or she is a member of the dominant culture, while the client couple's power is diminished if they do not share this membership. Some male clients have difficulty with women in positions of authority and may use male privilege in an attempt to intimidate a female therapist. Martin, being black, was more vulnerable to being intimidated by both his white female couple therapist and his white wife. Ethical practice required the couple therapist to attend to these and similar power differentials, as well as to how partners attempt to balance power and manage their more powerful couple therapist.

Ethical practice requires that couple therapists remain mindful of the risks of abusing unequal power. It may be tempting, especially when partners ask for the couple therapist's opinion about what they should do, to tell them. However, whatever the couple therapist says may be interpreted by the partners through the screen of the couple therapist's expertise. If a physician you trust diagnoses you with strep throat and prescribes penicillin, you assume he or she has knowledge and experience that you do not, and you comply with the treatment. The same is true for client couples and their couple therapists.

A couple therapist can only imagine what she or he would do if she or he were in the partners' situation. What she or he thinks would work for herself or himself may not be a good fit for the client couple. Furthermore, it is the couple, not the couple therapist, who must live with the consequences of their decisions and subsequent actions.

Consider these alternative responses from Liz and Martin's couple therapist:

Scenario 1:

LIZ: So you think my mother is wrong and I should ignore her?

CT: I do.

Scenario 2:

LIZ: So you think my mother is wrong and I should ignore her?

CT: You are a far greater expert than I on what your mother knows and the consequences for you of ignoring her. I'm simply suggesting you might feel less confused if you give your own voice the credence it deserves.

Scenario 3:

LIZ: So you think my mother is wrong and I should ignore her?

CT: Martin, you've been part of Liz and her mother's life for a long time now, and I'm curious whether you'd like to weigh in.

Scenario 4:

LIZ: So you think my mother is wrong and I should ignore her?

CT: Oh no, I think you should listen to your mother.

Stop and Think:

Be sure to include your answers in your journal.

1 What were your reactions to each of the four scenarios?
2 What do you think Liz and Martin's reactions to each of the four scenarios would have been?

3 What else might the couple therapist have done?
4 What would you have done had you been Liz and Martin's couple therapist?

Dual Roles

Ethical practice prohibits couple therapists from engaging in dual roles with a client couple or with either partner. The concept of dual roles refers to any situation in which a couple therapist assumes more than one relationship role with the client couple or with either partner. Thus, a couple therapist cannot engage in a therapeutic relationship with his or her student or a couple therapist in training who she or he supervises, a colleague, friend, family member, or anyone else he or she knows socially, professionally, or in any capacity unrelated to being in a couple therapist-couple client relationship.

The reason that engaging in dual roles is a violation of professional ethics has to do with protecting the boundaries around the couple therapist-couple client relationship. Specifically, dual roles risks contamination of the therapeutic relationship. As you have learned from reading transcripts of Liz and Martin's couple therapy, couple therapists often ask or say what is not socially appropriate in other settings. Because dual roles entails multiple settings, it may be confusing if not impossible to violate socially prescribed rules of interaction in one context and not the other with the same person.

Stop and Think:

Be sure to include your answers in your journal.

1 Think about a time when a friend or relative has complained to you about a significant other who made that person unhappy. How much of what you were thinking were you willing to tell the person? Explain your answer.
2 Would you say something to a friend, colleague, or family member that you were reasonably certain would infuriate or

hurt the person because you believed saying it was critical to the person's mental health? Explain your answer.

3 Imagine that Liz and Martin had known about the couple therapist's situation with her estranged husband, as they would have had they also known her in an additional role. Do you think they would have trusted her with their own marriage? Explain your answer.

Although she only knew Liz and Martin in her professional role, the question of dual roles arose for Liz and Martin's couple therapist because she had previously served as Liz's individual therapist. She was careful to address the potential problems arising from these dual roles at the beginning of couple therapy. While two of her colleagues in her peer supervision group were critical of her decision to work with Liz and Martin in couple therapy, her ethical decision-making process led her to determine that they were capable of deciding for themselves whether to work with her or accept a referral. She decided that her ethical responsibility entailed fully describing the risks to Liz and Martin so that they could make an informed decision and offering them a referral to another couple therapist.

There are also risks of doing individual psychotherapy with one or both partners simultaneously with conjoint couple therapy. As you saw, some theories of couple therapy include individual sessions with each partner during the assessment process. Individual psychotherapy with one partner is viewed as distinct from a single individual assessment session with each partner.

Beyond the question of dual roles, the risk of even a single individual assessment session by a couple therapist is that a secret between partners would be revealed to the couple therapist. In the dual role as both individual and couple therapist, ethical decision making about how to handle a secret becomes complex. If the couple therapist believes that one or both partners would benefit from individual psychotherapy while simultaneously engaging in conjoint couple therapy, the couple therapist also engaging in individual psychotherapy with one or both partners would create an on-going situation of multiple roles. A referral, or two referrals if both partners wish individual therapy, is advisable.

Individual psychotherapists are focused on and advocates for the needs of their clients. As you have seen, a couple therapist must focus on both partners and the couple's dynamics and advocate for the couple system. Attempting to engage in both the role of individual psychotherapist and the role of conjoint couple therapist inevitably creates competing demands from each role, with the attendant risk of contaminating both the individual and the couple therapy and thus reducing the effectiveness of both.

Sometimes couples finish couple therapy and one partner requests individual sessions with the couple therapist. Agreeing to this dual role risks two negative outcomes. First, the couple therapist's view of both partners has been influenced by the couple therapy work. Second, engaging in individual psychotherapy with one partner precludes the ability of the couple therapist to engage in future couple therapy sessions with the client couple without violating the ethical prohibition against dual roles.

Some dual roles are even more fraught. Consider the situation in which a clinician in training seeks couple therapy with her or his supervising couple therapist. What would happen if the student or partner decided the couple therapy was not helpful or their relationship dissolved and the student blamed the couple therapist who was also her or his clinical supervisor? A couple therapist in training is dependent on her or his supervisors to document the number of training hours the student has completed and to recommend to the licensing board when the student is prepared to practice independently. With her or his future in the balance, how comfortable might a couple therapist in training be with telling the couple therapist and supervisor that he or she is dissatisfied? Being dependent upon the couple therapist's future good will to recommend the trainee for full licensure might result in the couple therapist in training feeling trapped in ineffective couple therapy were the couple therapist also his or her clinical supervisor.

These risks are attendant on all dual roles. Friends, relatives, colleagues, and other people a couple therapist knows outside his or her role as a couple therapist likely cannot be approached from a neutral, non-judgmental, and clinically objective perspective. Additionally, a friend or relative may expect the couple therapist to side with her or him against his or her partner, as he or she has done during casual conversations. Or the friend or relative may discount the couple therapist's interventions, knowing the couple therapist's life is also imperfect.

Dual roles also present risks to confidentiality. If a couple therapist knows a partner in more than one context, how does he or she remember what has been said in confidence and what has not? And how would she or he handle a question or comment from a third person about the person with whom the couple therapist has engaged in dual roles?

Stop and Think:

Consider the following three scenarios.

1. Both partners are in individual as well as conjoint couple therapy with the same therapist. One partner complains about the other's alcohol consumption and angry outbursts during an individual psychotherapy session.
2. A couple invites the couple therapist they worked with in premarital counseling to their wedding. During the reception, a relative of one of the partners asks the couple therapist how he or she knows the couple.
3. A former client who was in graduate school at the time the couple therapist worked with her and her partner now requests clinical supervision from the couple therapist. After the former client consents that he or she understands he or she cannot return to couple therapy with the couple therapist if she or he agrees to supervision, the couple therapist agrees to supervise him or her.

For each of these three scenarios, respond to the following questions. Be sure to include your answers in your journal.

1. What would be the temptation to engage in each situation?
2. What are the ethical risks that might arise?
3. How would you handle the risks and situations?

Bartering

Couple therapists are prohibited from bartering for services for reasons similar to those described in the subsection about dual roles. Bartering, by definition, creates a second role for the couple therapist in relationship to the client couple. Additionally, bartering risks abuse of the power inherent in the couple therapist's role.

Stop and Think:

Be sure to include your responses in your journal.

A couple therapist was working with a client couple who did not have sufficient financial resources to commit to the lengthy treatment they appeared to need. One partner owned a small landscaping service and suggested she take care of the couple therapist's yard in exchange for couple therapy. They agreed to meet every other week for couple therapy and in exchange she would mow and trim the couple therapist's lawn, weed the flower beds every other week, and prune and mulch the shrubbery twice each year. When she arrived at the couple therapist's home and discovered that it was on an acre of land with multiple flower and vegetable gardens as well as a variety of vegetation near the house, she realized that what she had agreed to do would take many more hours than she had anticipated. She believed the bartering was weighted against her and in favor of the couple therapist and that the couple therapist had withheld information from her that might have changed her willingness to agree to the barter. She also realized that if she did not complete the agreed-upon work, she risked angering the couple therapist and worried she and her partner would not receive the treatment they needed.

1. Describe the impact of the power differential upon the bartering relationship with the client.
2. The couple therapist noted the shock on the client's face and subsequent subdued behavior and affect. How might he or she have handled the situation, given that the decision to ignore the ethical prohibition against bartering had already occurred and produced negative results?

Additional Ethical Considerations in Couple Therapy Practice

In this section of the chapter, you will explore five additional ethical issues: scope of practice, abandonment, secrets, triangulation, and hugging. While only secrets and triangulation of the couple therapist are unique to couple therapy, all five of these ethical considerations have unique applications to couple therapy.

Scope of Practice

Scope of practice refers to the modalities and specific issues in which the couple therapist's training and experience have sufficiently prepared her or him to practice. The introductory class in which you are now enrolled, whether on the undergraduate or graduate level, is insufficient to prepare you to practice couple therapy. To include couple therapy in your domain of practice, you will also be required to learn more about these and other topics, be supervised by a couple therapist credentialed to practice supervision, and pass a licensing examination in couple and family therapy or another mental health discipline. Then and only then can you include couple therapy as a treatment mode in which you have competence without violating licensing laws and the ethical prohibition against practicing outside one's scope of practice.

Specific issues couples bring to couple therapy must also be within the couple therapist's scope of practice. If one of the partners presents with a significant psychiatric disorder, such as a personality disorder, a dissociative disorder, or bipolar disorder, only a couple therapist who has had specific training and supervised practice working with people who present with the specific mental disorder can see the couple without referring the diagnosed partner for individual psychotherapy with someone competent to treat her or his disorder. Similarly, a couple therapist without specific training in a particular couple issue, such as intimate partner violence, must be willing to refer the couple.

Abandonment

The subject of referring clients to other mental health professionals is closely aligned with the legal and ethical proscription against abandoning clients. While it is legally and ethically imperative to refer rather than treat outside one's scope of practice, it is also legally and ethically imperative not to refuse or curtail treatment except in the client's best interest. A couple therapist who continues to work with the couple while referring one of the partners for specialized treatment outside his or her scope of practice has not abandoned the client couple with whom she or he had agreed to work. Nor has a couple therapist who explains to the client couple that they would be better served working with a couple therapist with more expertise in intimate partner violence once the couple therapist becomes aware of it. However, clients may feel rejected, and it is critical to underscore the difference between not wanting to work with them and the domain of practice consideration.

Couple therapists occasionally must terminate therapeutic relationships with client couples before the couples are finished with the work. Couple therapists move, retire, go on extended parental or disability or family medical leaves, and sometimes die during the course of treatment. While the difficulties such situations create for clients must be addressed, when all the clients who are in treatment with a couple therapist are in the same situation with respect to his or her lack of availability and the couple therapist has done everything possible to mitigate the transition, the situation does not meet the legal definition of abandonment.

Some situations are not as easy to determine and thus create ethical dilemmas. You will learn about ethical decision making in a subsequent section of this chapter.

Stop and Think:

Be sure to include your answers in your journal.

1. A couple therapist realizes during the second session with a new client that the client is talking mostly about his relationship. After suggesting couple therapy might be more appropriate, the client agrees to bring his partner to the next session. The couple therapist, who believes that same-sexed relationships are sinful, is surprised to discover that the client's partner is male. What are the legal and ethical considerations for the couple therapist?
2. If you discovered something about a couple, such as polyamory or intimate partner violence, that made you uncomfortable and had already agreed to work with the couple, what ethical considerations would be part of your decision about how to proceed?
3. How would the ethical considerations differ if the hypothetical couple therapist had never worked with an LGBTQIA couple or had no training in working with polyamorous couples or with intimate partner violence?

Secrets

The subject of secrets revisits the question regarding who the client in couple therapy is. If the couple is the client, then is information provided by either partner in the absence of the other confidential from the other? In other words, if the couple therapist chooses to meet with the partners separately, either during assessment or in response to the couple's request, or if one partner leaves information on a voice mail or transmits it electronically, is anything said or transmitted subject to legal statutes and ethical codes regarding confidentiality from the other partner?

Partners in a relationship generally do not tell one another everything. Some unshared information is irrelevant to the other partner or involves a specific, time-limited situation. Other information may have been shared in confidence by someone outside the relationship with one partner. Secrets only become problematic when knowledge of one partner's secret would negatively impact the other partner.

Liz might keep several kinds of secrets. She never told Martin about gifts she bought him until she gave them to him, nor did she tell him confidential information about her clients. Before her nephew came out to his father, Liz's sister Barbara spoke to her in confidence about her concern that her son did not trust her husband, and Liz did not talk to Martin about the conversation at the time. Martin also surprised Liz from time to time, was unable to share protected professional information with her, and kept confidences of friends and relatives.

Discovering any of these secrets would not have changed how Martin and Liz viewed one another or behaved toward one another or their marriage. However, had either been having a secret extramarital affair, one could assume knowledge of the affair would negatively impact the other and also might change how they viewed and behaved toward one another.

If one partner reveals a secret that might be detrimental to the relationship or that the partner needs to know, for example, an extramarital affair, a gambling addiction that has risked the financial security of the family, a cancer diagnosis, or the intent to leave the relationship, to the couple therapist in the absence of the other partner and requests that the information be kept confidential, the couple therapist then faces an ethical dilemma. If the couple therapist reveals the secret to the partner, she or he assumes agency for the secret bearer, which is a violation of the ethical tenet to protect his or her autonomy. The couple therapist also risks violating trust and thus undermining the therapeutic relationship with one or the other partner, irrespective of how he or she chooses to handle the confidential information. If the couple therapist does not reveal the secret, it nevertheless impacts the couple therapist's interventions, and if later the confidence is revealed by the bearer, the other partner's trust in the couple therapist is impacted negatively.

Couple therapists can attempt to circumvent the risk of a secret by clearly specifying that anything said by either partner is a potential topic for couple therapy and obtaining informed consent to that stipulation. However, despite a couple therapist's thorough efforts, one partner may share a secret in an attempt to force the couple therapist to reveal it to her or his partner. While a couple therapist can offer to facilitate revelation of a secret, she or he can decline to reveal it herself or himself. If the couple therapist also refuses to continue couple therapy in the absence of a revelation by the partner who shared the secret, because couple therapy would be unhelpful at best and counterproductive to the unenlightened partner at worst, ethical issues of abandonment arise.

Triangulation

The risk that a couple therapist will be inducted as a third party into the dynamics of the couple's relationship system has been addressed several times in this textbook. Asking the couple therapist to take sides in a disagreement, explain to the partner how she or he is mistaken, or share a secret are all efforts to create a negative coalition, or triangle, with the couple therapist against the other partner. The result, if successful, would marginalize the other partner and further disrupt the couple's relationship. Therefore, it is ethically, as well as clinically, imperative that couple therapists avoid triangulation.

Hugging

Students often ask about hugging. Legal statutes in all 50 states and the ethical codes of every mental health profession prohibit sexual contact between clients and practitioners. Sexual contact between clients and practitioners violates the principle of beneficence and is a violation of multiple tenets of ethical behavior, including boundary violations, abuse of power, and dual roles. Violation of these statutes and ethical codes may result in both criminal and civil punishments and loss of license. Non-sexual contact, including hugging, is not prohibited as long as a couple therapist is careful to avoid full body contact and thus any genital contact and/or hint of sexuality.

Irrespective of the couple therapist's intent, the outcome of a hug may include a client assuming it was sexual. The clinical judgment involved in determining the risk that a client would misinterpret non-sexual touching as a sexual advance requires careful ethical considerations, discussion with clinical or peer supervisors, and experience. The couple therapist's own ethical imperatives must preclude using one's power in sexual transactions. The couple therapist's awareness of client tendencies to idealize the couple therapist, whether termed transference or conceptualized in another way, is also imperative.

The ethical questions arising from hugs are especially complex in couple therapy, because one partner may initiate a hug with the couple therapist, while hugging would not be welcomed by the other. This places the other partner in a potentially awkward situation. Similarly, the couple therapist may wish to avoid appearing to favor one partner while also avoiding making the other uncomfortable.

The safest route for a couple therapist is to refrain from initiating hugs. The decision to accept a client-initiated hug evolves from theory, ethical codes, and the couple therapist's critical evaluation of her or his intuitive response. The answer may be different for different couples and for different couple therapists.

This paragraph was intended to exemplify, rather than prescribe, an approach to hugging. The writer has chosen to accept hugs clients initiate at the end of the final couple therapy session. Occasionally when a session has been unusually powerful and the client appears to be expressing gratitude and connection, she has accepted a hug. When one partner initiates hugging, she avoids initiating or expecting a hug from the other but carefully monitors and responds, sometimes nonverbally, to the other partner's reaction. She has received hugs from partners who were clearly uncomfortable, and has allowed them to be as brief and disconnected as the client wishes. She has never initiated a hug, even when she has wanted to at the end of treatment or a powerful session, and while following the client's lead has also kept the hug affectionate and relatively brief. On the rare occasions when she has felt the professional need to minimize client-initiated hugs to avoid misunderstandings about client-couple therapist boundaries, she has brought the issue to the client couple as a clinical topic during a couple therapy session.

Ethical Codes and Considerations

All ethical behavior is predicated on the foundational principle of beneficence. Beneficence means prioritizing the avoidance of harm over all other considerations. If a couple therapist can also promote healing, beneficence does not preclude it. However, the minimum a couple therapist must do ethically is avoid harming the couple.

Since most people enter the field of couple therapy intending to be helpful, the ethical requirement of beneficence may seem odd. Yet practicing couple therapists encounter couples who they cannot help. One or both partners may have intractable mental health problems that preclude the ability to benefit from couple therapy, or the couple may have requested couple therapy beyond the point when positive feelings and mutual good will were retrievable. In cases in which couple therapy cannot help, couple therapists are ethically enjoined to be certain it does not harm the couple. If a couple therapist consistently hears hopelessness from both partners and they are consistently not following through on agreed-upon homework suggestions, then asking whether their hearts are in couple therapy may prevent the emotional and financial harm of continuing. Hopefully, the couple therapist's intervention would alert the couple to the need to engage in couple therapy if they wish to improve their relationship, but if they determine they cannot or will not then avoidance of harm entails acknowledging their reality.

Couple therapists can avoid doing harm by respecting client boundaries, refraining from abusing the power of their position, and recognizing the impact of culture on their world view. They can also avoid harming client couples by fostering trust through their reliability, acceptance of the person of each partner, and caring for the partners and the couple. They can further avoid doing harm by remaining self-aware, practicing self-care, and seeking peer supervision or consultation and individual psychotherapy when needed. Finally, they can avoid doing harm by following the legal statutes and ethical codes pertaining to their practice.

Not all aspects of couple therapy practice are clearly defined. When situations arise that have not been codified in law or ethics, couple therapists base their ethical decisions on first avoiding harm and then utilizing ethical decision-making techniques.

Stop and Think:

Be sure to include your answers in your journal.

During a couple therapy session, one partner begins to emotionally decompensate. In order to allow that partner to regain stability and the couple therapist to further assess that partner's fragility prior to moving forward, the couple therapist shifts the focus to what is happening for that partner. The other partner, however, is desperate for resolution of the presenting problem, and the couple therapist is unsure whether that partner can tolerate a delay.

1. Identify the competing demands upon the couple therapist and the potential harm of moving forward with couple work.
2. Identify the potential harm of slowing down to re-stabilize the decompensated partner.
3. What might you do if you were the couple therapist? Explain your reasoning.

Models of Ethical Decision Making

Models of ethical decision making focus on intention and outcome. A couple therapist may intend to avoid harming either partner or the couple and otherwise handle himself or herself in an ethical and professionally competent manner, and yet the outcome of the couple therapy may be unintentionally harmful. Because one cannot predict outcome with complete accuracy when making ethical decisions, couple therapists often rely on intended outcome. Unfortunately, the legality and ethics of their decisions may be judged upon actual outcome.

Stop and Think:

Be sure to include your answers in your journal.

A couple therapist who has taken a continuing education workshop about intimate partner violence to fulfill a requirement by his or her licensing board but otherwise has had no training or supervision in intimate partner violence and who is personally uncomfortable working with perpetrators could argue that discovering on-going intimate partner violence placed a couple outside her or his domain of practice. He or she might then argue that the disruption of referring the couple to a colleague who identifies intimate partner violence as an area of specialization would be less harmful, despite the risk of abandonment, than attempting to help them with a problem that was outside her or his scope of practice. The couple therapist then handles the referral process in ways most likely to be successful, and the couple agrees to see the colleague. However, after ending their therapeutic relationship with the first couple therapist, they decide the new couple therapist is not a good fit and, rather than requesting another referral, stop treatment. Subsequently, the perpetrator maims his or her partner.

1. What were the ethical issues in the couple therapist's dilemma?
2. What would you have done had you been the couple therapist?
3. What would have been the risks of a different ethical decision?
4. How might the couple therapist have felt upon learning the outcome? How might he or she have felt had he or she continued to work with the couple and the partner had been maimed nevertheless?

Bersoff's (1996, Bersoff & Koeppl, 1993) model of ethical decision making has been widely used in the fields of mental health, business, and law. His model proposes four components of ethical decision making for couple therapists to rely upon when confronted by situations not fully addressed by law or ethical codes: understanding ethical principles, familiarizing oneself with one's profession's code of ethics, understanding how ethical decisions are made, and then behaving ethically.

A couple therapist's ethical principles are derived from her or his clinical training and are influenced by her or his world view and theoretical approach to couple therapy. They include beneficence, fostering client autonomy, respecting partners and the couple, justice, privacy, avoiding ethnocentricity, and avoiding isms such as sexism and racism. For example, giving advice, even when requested by one or both partners, presumes that the couple therapist knows better than the client what is good for the client. Giving advice thus uses the couple therapist's power as an expert in a way that flies in the face of beneficence, autonomy, respect, justice, and avoiding ethnocentrism. Instead of responding with advice, an ethical couple therapist relies on her or his theoretical approach to decide how best to empower the partners to recognize and respect their own inner knowledge and to facilitate their work together to determine how to use it.

Each mental health discipline has its own ethical code. These professional codes of ethics provide guidelines for ethical behavior. State licensing statutes also include ethical codes. Licensure requires familiarity and compliance with these codes, as well as on-going continuing education in ethical practice. The state in which the writer practices also requires on-going continuing education in multiculturalism and culturally competent practice (see Chapter 9).

Ethical codes are continually being revised as new situations arise. As recently as 25 years ago, couple therapists and their clients did not have access to electronic mail (email), mobile phones, texting, social media, or remote (internet) therapy as methods for communicating with one another. Clients were unable to use search engines like Google to learn about their couple therapists, and couple therapists were likewise unable to "Google" their clients. Ethical codes from the 1990s and early 2000s therefore did not deal with the many ethical issues arising from the use of cellular phones, texting, social media, search engines, or remote therapy. Given the pace of changes in technology and culture, new ethical challenges will likely continue to outstrip the updating of ethical codes. Thus, although couple therapists can utilize their theoretically derived understanding of ethical principles and their familiarity with their profession's code of ethics when making ethical decisions, guidelines pertaining to every specific situation a couple therapist encounters may not be available.

To understand ethical decision making, Bersoff (1996; Bersoff & Koeppl, 1993) suggested clinicians remain aware of their own intuitive imperatives. As much as a couple therapist may wish to be free of judgment, people learn to differentiate correct or appropriate from incorrect or inappropriate behavior as defined by the culture into which they were socialized. To illustrate, listen for the use of the word, "should." Liz said, "I should really get back to the weight I was before Christina was born," indicating that that weight is the correct one. The couple therapist was also socialized to view thinness as a virtue. Being aware of her intuitive response alerted her to what she and Liz believed to be a moral and therefore ethical imperative, and allowed her to evaluate her own response in light of what was best for Liz and Martin.

Once identified, Bersoff (1996; Bersoff & Koeppl, 1993) recommended submitting the couple therapist's intuitive ethical responses to critical evaluation. Critical evaluation includes viewing the intuitive in light of theory and existing ethical codes. Liz and Martin's couple therapist found herself thinking that Liz "should" not interrupt and demean Martin. Critical evaluation of this moral and ethical imperative suggested that the behavior in question was not helpful to resolving Liz and Martin's relationship issues, because Martin appeared to withdraw or argue in response and thus attempts at resolving an argument were derailed. Additionally, the couple therapist noted that the way Liz spoke to Martin disturbed her because of her own marital situation (see Chapter 10) and because of her own moral imperative to be especially alert to her impact upon clients of color. Neither legal statutes nor the couple therapist's professional code of ethics addressed the specifics of this situation. However, critical evaluation led her to recognize that acting from her own discomfort violated several ethical precepts, including respecting client boundaries by failing to distinguish their situation from her own, refraining from using her power to impose her values, fostering Martin and Liz's agency about how they treated one another, and beneficence.

The fourth aspect of ethical decision making follows logically from the first three and involves ethical behavior. Theory, the principles and rules embodied in ethical codes, and critical evaluation of the couple therapist's intuitive moral imperatives help her or him determine what actions are within the bounds of ethical behavior.

Since ethical decision making and its behavioral outcome happen quickly during a couple therapy session, Bersoff (1996; Bersoff & Koeppl, 1993) suggested the couple therapist's intuition be grounded in her or his familiarity with all aspects of ethical decision making. Liz and Martin's couple therapist chose to closely monitor her impulse to suggest that Liz speak differently to Martin. Instead, she used her reaction to Liz to alert her to the need to focus on the couple's dynamics and interrupt the homeostatic mechanisms that prevented resolution and change.

Culture and Ethics in the Practice of Couple Counseling

Couple therapists' values impact their ethical thinking through their intuition and their moral imperatives. The profession of couple therapy and the theoretical models it utilizes also reflect cultural values. While studying Section II, you may have noted that the theoretical masters of the field were, with few exceptions, white males of western European descent, suggesting a bias toward maintaining the dominant culture and its values in the theories underlying couple therapy. White men also predominate in the state legislatures that pass statutes pertaining to the practice of couple therapy. Finally, the field of couple therapy, like graduate training in other mental health professions, has been difficult to penetrate by students of color (Kiser, 2015).

The relevant conclusion is that the majority of couple therapists bring the values and world view of the dominant culture to their practice. Yet, at the same time, data cited in previous chapters suggest that couple therapists are increasingly seeing couples who do not fit the dominant cultural model and whose values therefore may differ. Because couple therapists are ethically prohibited from imposing their values on clients, ethical practice, as codified in current ethical codes, requires a multicultural perspective with attention and receptiveness to the norms and values of the cultural contexts in which client couples function.

Stop and Think:

Be sure to include your answers in your journal.

1. Is it possible to be value neutral?
2. If so, how can one be value neutral?
3. If not, how does one reconcile one's values when the client couple's values differ?
4. How can a couple therapist prevent the inherent bias of theory and the dominant culture it represents from influencing her or his work with client couples whose culture and world view do not wholly conform to the dominant cultural model?
5. How did your responses to these four questions exemplify ethical decision making?

The Stop and Think contained complex questions with no simple answers. Yet ethical practice requires a couple therapist to be mindful of the fact that her or his world view is neither universally shared nor superior to other world views and is further biased by his or her cultural experiences.

Ethical Considerations Working with Liz and Martin

The couple therapist presented her willingness to resume couple therapy with Liz and Martin in the future only if they agreed to continue beyond reduction of symptoms as her professional opinion that another premature termination of couple therapy could damage their relationship beyond repair. Her professional judgment was that another premature termination of couple therapy would do more harm than good, and her behavior was thus based on the principle of beneficence. Despite that judgment, it was an abandonment threat, a potential abuse of power, and a usurpation of the couple's agency to condition further treatment. As such, she placed herself at the margins of ethical behavior, if not beyond them.

The couple therapist had considered the ethical risks of her approach. She had also considered seeking consultation or bringing her intention to her peer supervision group before acting. She was certain her peer supervision group or a one-on-one consultation with a senior colleague would confirm what she already knew, that expressing a professional opinion without exerting pressure on a couple to behave in a particular way complied with the overarching principles of beneficence and client agency, while exerting pressure in the form of an ultimatum regarding further treatment did not.

The couple therapist then assessed the risk that Liz and Martin would become sufficiently frustrated and hopeless about the benefits of couple therapy and about their marriage that they would dissolve their marriage if their issues once again re-emerged at some point following the end of treatment. She observed that their frustration and hopelessness had increased each time they had returned to couple therapy and concluded that the only way for them to avoid this risk was to commit to couple therapy beyond cessation of the immediate pain that led them to request help. And so she decided that making additional couple therapy contingent upon an agreement to complete the work was ethical because it involved a lesser risk of harm. Nevertheless, the couple therapist's behavior potentially violated the ethical principles of beneficence, respecting client boundaries and autonomy, and risked abandonment and the misuse of power.

Stop and Think:

Be sure to include your answers in your journal.

1. How might the couple therapist have violated the principle of beneficence?
2. How might the couple therapist have violated Liz and Martin's boundaries?
3. How might the couple therapist have assumed responsibility for making Liz and Martin's decisions?
4. How might the couple therapist have abandoned Liz and Martin?

Liz attempted to align with the couple therapist against Martin several times in excerpts cited throughout this textbook. Additionally, the couple therapist needed to resist her inclination to align with Martin against Liz. The couple therapist viewed couple-initiated attempts at triangulation as a homeostatic mechanism employed to stop an interaction that threatened to change the couple system's equilibrium. She resisted these attempts, in part by refocusing Liz and Martin on how their couple dynamics were playing out in the moment. She viewed her own inclination to form a coalition with Martin against Liz as countertransference that would be unproductive to couple therapy, potentially harm the couple, and therefore a violation of the ethical principle of beneficence.

Self-Awareness and Self-Care to Ensure Ethical Practice

Self-awareness and self-care are essential to ethical practice because they combine to strengthen the couple therapist's boundaries and thus protect couple clients from the couple therapist conflating her or his own problems, history, exhaustion, and competing demands with the couple's situation and goals for change. Self-awareness takes place during sessions, while writing and reviewing case notes, and in supervision and the couple therapist's own psychotherapy. With the exception of self-soothing and the decision to defer dealing with a personal issue the client couple has raised, self-care only occurs outside couple therapy.

Self-awareness allows the couple therapist to identify and manage difficulties he or she is having with a particular partner or couple client. Self-awareness also alerts a couple therapist to the need for increased self-care. Self-awareness combined with supervision allows the couple therapist to recognize where her or his blind spots about a couple client are before they become problematic.

Several of the theories described in Chapters 6 and 7 rely on the couple therapist recognizing the parallels between how partners interact with one another and with the couple therapist for both assessment and intervention. Self-awareness allows a couple therapist to recognize the couple client's impact on her or him and to manage her or his reactions, or countertransference. Awareness of her or his thoughts and feelings allows couple therapists to use them as guides to what is happening with the client couple and a reflection of how the partners treat one another and their couple therapist.

Self-awareness also functions to alert a couple therapist when the risk of using the client couple to meet her or his own needs arises and when burn-out is occurring. When Liz challenged the couple therapist, she used self-awareness and self-soothing to respond to Liz without becoming defensive. She also used self-awareness when she recognized her temptation, based on her own relationship dissolution, to tell Liz to appreciate the way Martin treated her.

Self-awareness involves the couple therapist observing his or her thoughts, feelings, and the meanings he or she attributes to the experience of being with a particular couple. In other words, while observing and interacting with the partners and the couple system, couple therapists simultaneously observe themselves. A couple therapist's self-awareness also involves remaining alert to how her or his own thoughts, feelings, and the meanings he or she ascribes to experience may be impacting her or his work with the couple.

Working with distressed clients can traumatize or re-traumatize a couple therapist. Couple clients may struggle with issues similar to the couple therapist's. Liz and Martin's couple therapist felt demeaned by her estranged husband, and although she reacted differently than Martin did, she was triggered when she believed Liz was demeaning Martin. Couple therapists also contain clients' pain, as described in Chapter 6. Unless a couple therapist remains aware of the impact of the clients' pain upon herself or himself and practices self-care to soothe it outside couple therapy sessions, the clients' pain may overwhelm the couple therapist.

Self-care, like self-awareness, is essential for ethical practice because self-care allows a couple therapist to release the impact of what happens in couple therapy upon the couple therapist. The first step in self-care is self-awareness, in this case recognizing the effect of practicing couple therapy on the couple therapist.

Self-care entails a couple therapist caring for and treating herself or himself as she or he treats clients. Couple therapists are empathetic, soothing advocates for their clients, and effective self-care includes empathy, soothing, and advocacy for oneself.

The dominant culture often fails to distinguish self-care from selfishness. Self-care involves placing oneself on an equal footing with others. By contrast, selfishness occurs at the expense of others. Telling clients to call 9-1-1 for overnight emergencies that cannot wait until the morning is a form of self-care, aimed at the couple therapist having time for himself or herself and getting enough uninterrupted sleep.

There are five ways to practice self-care. First, identify and utilize sources of support. For example, if a client has been verbally combative or has reminded the couple therapist of his or her own pain, calling an empathetic and caring friend to talk and laugh about something else or vent about having had a difficult day may help.

Second, create cognitive and emotional boundaries between professional activities and personal ones. These include establishing ways of letting go of what has happened during the workday. Some couple therapists employ rituals, such as burning a candle or sipping a cup of tea between finishing the workday and returning to their personal lives. Others exercise, either before the workday begins or after leaving work before returning home. Still other couple therapists practice meditation, yoga, or tai chi.

A third method of self-care entails participating in a peer supervision group. Peer supervision allows couple therapists to discuss their countertransference issues and seek guidance from colleagues without revealing confidential information about a client couple or either partner. Additionally, self-care may include the couple therapist's own individual psychotherapy to address personal issues raised while practicing couple therapy.

Fourth, couple therapists need to allow themselves periodic breaks. Without breaks, one risks the loss of perspective and empathy, or burnout. Time away need not involve expensive vacations or activities. The point is a break from the intellectual and emotional intensity of practicing couple therapy.

Finally, self-care includes finding a work-life balance that is effective for the couple therapist when she or he is not on vacation. Without this balance, self-care cannot be effective, because lack of balance is likely to become a constant source of stress.

Self-awareness and self-care are fundamental to ethical practice. For example, Liz challenged her couple therapist, leaving the couple therapist feeling uncertain about her competence. Had she failed to recognize and self-soothe, she would have been more likely to respond defensively or submissively to Liz or to have withdrawn, thereby recreating Martin's way of coping. None of these responses would have conformed to the tenets of ethical practice, because they would have been about the couple therapist and not about what the client couple needed. Had the couple therapist not practiced self-awareness and self-care, she also would have been at risk of responding to Liz's challenges by acting out inappropriately through sarcasm, being late or forgetting appointments, and other passive-aggressive behaviors that did not directly address her reaction to Liz and that could harm the therapeutic relationship.

An additional ethical risk of failing to use self-awareness and self-care also bears examining. Had the couple therapist been sexually attracted to Martin, she might have become flirtatious or seductive, especially in light of her own relationship distress. Given the risk, she would have relied on self-awareness and self-care to avoid communicating her attraction to Martin. As it was, she was emotionally attracted to him and needed to use both self-awareness and self-care to avoid communicating her attraction to the way he treated Liz. Communicating sexual or emotional attraction to a client and responding in any way that does not set firm limits when a client is flirtatious or seductive violates both legal and ethical codes. In addition to being prohibited behavior, it violates boundaries and the principle of beneficence.

Conclusions

In this chapter, you learned about the legal statutes and ethical codes governing the practice of couple therapy. These were categorized into two broad categories: respecting client rights, including confidentiality, HIPAA compliance, reporting laws, and duty to warn; and respecting client boundaries, including touching, initiating contact with clients between sessions, inserting the couple therapist's needs into the couple therapy, considerations of inherent unequal power, dual roles, and bartering. Five additional ethical considerations relevant to the practice of couple therapy were discussed: scope of practice, abandonment, secrets, triangulation, and hugging. You also learned about the process of ethical decision making when legal statutes and ethical codes do not address a specific situation you might encounter in the practice of couple therapy. Finally, you learned about the interrelated roles of self-awareness and self-care in ethical practice.

This chapter was not intended to be exhaustive. Additionally, as both statutes and ethical codes evolve, the knowledge required of couple therapists changes. Couple therapists are therefore required by licensing laws to remain current in legal and ethical practice.

References

Bersoff, D. N. (1996). The virtue of principle ethics. *The Counseling Psychologist*, 24, 86–91.

Bersoff, D. N. & Koeppl, P.(1993). The relation between ethical codes and moral principles. *Ethics & Behavior*, 3, 345–357.

Kiser, P. M. (2015). *The human service internship* (4th ed.). Boston MA: Cengage Learning.

Siegel, R. (2013). Wisdom in psychotherapy. *Psychotherapy Networker*, 37 (2), 18–25.

Tarasoff v. Regents of the University of California. (1976). 17 Cal. 3d 425, 551 P.2d 334, 131 Cal. Rptr. 14.

U.S. Department of Health and Human Services. (n.d.). Understanding health information privacy. Retrieved from http://www.hhs.gov/ocr/privacy/hipaa/understanding/index.html.

For Further Study

Backer, A., Goodnough, G., Levitt, D. H., & Moorhead, H. H. (2013). Boundary issues. In D. H. Levitt & H. H. Moorhead (Eds.). *Values and ethics in counseling. Real-life ethical decision making*. New York NY: Routledge/Taylor & Francis Group.

Bradley, N., Whisenhunt, J., Adamson, N., & Kress, V. E. (2013). Creative approaches for promoting counselor self-care. *Journal of Creativity in Mental Health*, 8 (4), 456–469.

Cottonne, R. R. & Claus, R. E. (2000). Ethical decision models. A review of the literature. *Journal of Counseling and Development*, 78 (3), 275–283.

Fadiman, A. (1997). *The spirit catches you and you fall down. A Hmong child, her American doctors, and the collision of two cultures.* New York NY: Ferrar, Straus and Giroux.

Herlihy, B. & Corey, G. (2015). *Boundary issues in counseling. Multiple roles and responsibilities (3rd ed.).* Alexandria VA: American Counseling Association.

Pieterse, A. L., Lee, M., Ritmeister, A., & Collins, N. M. (2013). Towards a model of self-awareness development for counseling and psychotherapy training. *Counseling Psychology Quarterly, 26* (2), 190–207.

Pope, K. S. (2010). *Ethics in psychotherapy and counseling. A practical guide (4th ed.).* New York NY: Wiley.

Roth, H. & Meisel, A. (1997). Dangerousness, confidentiality, and the duty to warn. *The American Journal of Psychiatry, 134* (5), 508–511.

Werth, J. L. Jr., Welfel, E. R., & Benjamin, G. A. H. (Eds.). (2009). *Facing dangerous situations. Increasing clarity about the duty to protect. A review of the duty to protect. Legal, ethical, and professional considerations for mental health professionals.* Washington DC: American Psychological Association.

Wilcoxon, A., Remley, T. Jr., & Gladding, S. (Eds.). (2013). *Ethical, legal and professional issues in the practice of marriage and family therapy* (5th ed.). New York NY: Pearson.

Zur, O. (2007). *Boundaries in psychotherapy. Ethical and clinical explorations.* Washington DC: American Psychological Association.

Mental Health Professional Organizations' Codes of Ethics

American Association for Marriage and Family Therapy Code of Ethics—https://www.aamft.org/iMIS15/AAMT/Content/Legal_Ethics/code_of_ethics.aspx.

American Counseling Association Code of Ethics—http://www.counseling.org/resources/aca-code-of-ethics.pdf.

National Association of Social Workers Code of Ethics—http://www.socialworkers.org/pubs/code/default.asp.

National Organization for Human Services Code of Ethics—http://www.nationalhumanservices.org/ethical-standards-for-hs-professionals.

CHAPTER 12

Couples Requiring Services in Addition to Couple Therapy

Learning Objectives

1. Discuss the contraindications for couple therapy.
2. Enumerate and evaluate the considerations in the decision to treat child symptoms in individual or family therapy.
3. Illustrate the pros and cons of working individually or in groups with partners undergoing the life transitions of illness, death, or divorce.
4. Describe the legal services couples may need.
5. Describe the reasons for referring a couple for public health or social services.
6. Discuss the process of making a referral to another professional or to an agency.
7. Describe the considerations in reporting suspected abuse or danger to self or others.

For some couples, conjoint couple therapy presents challenges that one or both partners are incapable of undertaking. While there is no way to predict in advance whether or not any modality of intervention will benefit any one couple, a couple therapist can learn to recognize indications that couple therapy may be more problematic than helpful for a given couple.

Referring to another couple therapist when problems are outside the couple therapist's scope of practice was addressed in Chapter 11. Couple therapists may also discover a partner or client couple requires services that are not only outside her or his scope of practice but also outside the scope of couple therapy. These include but are not limited to grief counseling, support groups, child therapy, individual psychotherapy, family therapy, spiritual counseling, and various legal, medical, and social services.

This chapter begins with a description of the contraindications for couple therapy. You will then read about other services to which couple therapists refer couple clients and the process of both referring and, when necessary, reporting. These services include mental health related services, legal services, medical services, rehabilitation and adult day care, public health, and social services. As will become evident, careers that include working with couples in contexts other than couple therapy exist, and you may find that one appeals to you more than the practice of couple therapy.

When Couple Therapy Is Contraindicated

Couple therapy is contraindicated when it undermines the ethical principle of beneficence. When one of the partners' behavior or mental health consistently sabotages couple therapy, the potential exists for at least one of the partners to be harmed by continuing to engage in couple therapy. If one of the partners is acting or working toward a relationship goal that is unknown to the other and that would likely change the other partner's behavior or goals for the relationship, that partner's behavior will likely undermine any potential benefit of couple therapy and thus harm the partner whose behavior or goals would change if she or he had access to the hidden information. Examples include a secret gambling addiction and a long-term extra-relationship affair as distinct from an agreement of polyamory. Similarly, if one partner's mental health is unstable, he or she may be harmed by the challenges of conjoint couple therapy.

Partners may present for couple therapy with divergent goals for themselves as individuals and for themselves as a couple. When these goals are shared during the assessment phase of couple therapy, they can be woven into the agreed-upon goals and treatment plan. However, if one partner withholds information about her or his goals, engages in secretive behavior, or otherwise hides information that would influence the course of couple therapy, the withholding of information as well as the information withheld potentially undermines the efficacy of couple therapy and thus harms the other partner.

Consider the situation in which partners have agreed that their relationship will be monogamous. If one partner then engages in an extra-relationship sexual and/or emotional affair, successfully hides the extra-relationship affair from her or his partner, and agrees to couple therapy without intending to end that affair, he or she is unlikely to be fully engaged in the process of couple therapy or to share the goal of preserving the relationship despite having verbally or nonverbally agreed to that goal. Additionally, both the existence of the secretive activity and the content of it being an extra-relationship affair could change the other partner's feelings about and goals for the relationship if it were known to him or her.

If the couple therapist knows of the affair, he or she can condition couple therapy work upon revealing the secret, with consideration of the ethical cautions described in the previous chapter, if the secret-holding partner declines to share the secret. If the couple therapist does not know, he or she is not complicit until he or she begins to suspect disengagement on the part of the partner who is continuing the affair. Once the couple therapist notices signs that one partner is disengaged, he or she would be wise to address them irrespective of what information is revealed as a result.

Stop and Think:

Be sure to include your responses in your journal.

Several months into work with a couple, one of the partners says that he or she has discovered evidence the other is engaged in an extra-relationship affair. The accused partner initially disavows the evidence and accuses her or his partner of being mistrustful. In the course of a subsequent session, he or she acknowledges on-going emotional and sexual involvement with a colleague.

1. What would you do if you were the couple therapist?
2. How might you feel about the partner having withheld information that would have changed what you did as a couple therapist?
3. How might you manage your feelings so that the focus remained on the partner who had been betrayed?

Trust can be regained between partners following extra-relationship affairs. However, it cannot be regained if the betrayal remains a secret or the partner declines to end the extra-relationship affair.

A similar contraindication for couple therapy occurs any time one partner is secretly finished with the relationship, irrespective of the reason, when the other wishes it to continue. In other words, when one partner is unaware that the other partner does not share her or his goals for couple therapy, either both partners' goals must be brought into alignment or couple therapy becomes contraindicated. Thus, if one partner is emotionally finished with the relationship and has no interest in re-attaching to it and the other wishes to remain a couple, couple therapy with the goal of improving the relationship would be at best a waste of time and money and at worst harmful to the partner wishing to continue the relationship.

Liz did not hide her hopelessness about her marriage from Martin or from the couple therapist. Thus, Martin was not harmed nor did the couple therapist continue couple therapy under a false presumption of agreed-upon goals. Had Liz told the couple therapist but not Martin that she was hopeless about the relationship but was willing to continue couple therapy until Martin agreed it was time to end the marriage, her hidden agenda would contraindicate continuing couple therapy. If the couple therapist then agreed to continue therapy, she would be violating the ethical principle of beneficence.

This distinction between one partner's hidden agenda and a shared struggle to determine whether the relationship is viable is critical. Partners may present for couple therapy with one or both uncertain about whether their relationship is salvageable and even whether or not they wish to continue it. So long as they are working together toward the goal of addressing their uncertainties, couple therapy is warranted.

Sometimes, it becomes apparent that one partner would be happier if the relationship ended. It is not the couple therapist's job to decide how to balance individual satisfaction with couple health and to attempt to do so would violate the ethical principle of client autonomy, or agency. Partners remain together for many and varied reasons, some incomprehensible to observers of their relationship. Thus, the couple therapist's role does not include making decisions that affect other people's lives but rather it entails guiding the partners as they make decisions for themselves and their relationship.

A second source of contraindication for couple therapy occurs when one partner's mental health is such that the risks of engaging in couple therapy for that partner not only undermine its potential benefits but are also greater than those potential benefits. Couple therapy requires the couple therapist to listen empathetically to each partner and to mediate interactions between them. If one partner's mental health is sufficiently fragile, sharing attention or being asked to consider the other can be destabilizing. While detailed examples are beyond the scope of an introductory couple therapy textbook, when a couple therapist recognizes that couple therapy consistently leads to one partner decompensating during sessions, or acting out or acting in during or after sessions and the couple reports greater frequency since couple therapy began, the couple therapist may question whether couple therapy is indicated prior to the partner attaining more stable mental health.

This situation is different than one in which partners simply do not understand how couple therapy works and require the couple therapist to explain his or her rationale for intervening as she or he does. When Liz requested couple therapy from the same therapist she had seen for individual work, the therapist explained to Liz that she became a couple advocate in her role as couple therapist with the attendant risk that the contrast between individual and couple therapy might leave Liz feeling that she was no longer her advocate. Liz's mental health was sufficiently stable that the couple therapist was confident she understood the explanation and was able to tolerate, with only minor push-back when frustrated, the couple therapist's attention and empathy toward Martin as well as her advocacy of the relationship.

Consider a brief snippet of transcript from an early couple therapy session with Liz and Martin.

MARTIN: She's always mad at me. [Looks at Liz, who is rolling her eyes] Like that.

COUPLE THERAPIST: So Liz's anger at you is the problem?

LIZ: [Sarcastically] Yep, it's all me.

CT: Liz, I hear you don't agree. And I also want to hear how you view the problem, after Martin finishes.

Although Liz grumbled, she waited. Now consider a similar situation in which one partner's mental health was more fragile.

PARTNER 1: She's always yelling at me. I don't know what's the matter with her.

CT: So her anger upsets you.

PARTNER 1: It's not right. I think she needs to learn anger management.

PARTNER 2: [Expletive]

PARTNER 1: Yell, yell, yell.

CT: [To Partner 2] I want to hear how you view the problem, too, after Partner 1 finishes.

PARTNER 2: [Sarcastically] Yes, of course. It's always about him.

CT: [To Partner 1] You've told me what you think about Partner 2's yelling. I'd like to hear what it's like for you.

PARTNER 1: What do you think it's like for me?

CT: I'm more interested in hearing your words about what it's like for you.

PARTNER 1: [Voice rising] My words. I don't know what you mean. I… I… I…. How can you ask me what it's like? [Pause] You think yelling's OK? You think I should like it? Is that what you think?

PARTNER 2: You notice he's the one yelling now.

CT: Tell me about what you do when she yells at you.

PARTNER 1: Ask her. She's the one doing the yelling. What's she do? What's it like for her? It's her problem. Why are you accusing me of her problem?

Stop and Think:

Be sure to include your answers in your journal.

1. Compare and contrast the transcript of Liz and Martin with the transcript of Partner 1 and Partner 2.
2. What would you do if you were the couple therapist for Partner 1 and Partner 2?
3. How would you feel if you were the couple therapist in each transcript?

Even if the couple therapist in the second transcript had the training and skill to address Partner 1's mental health challenges, doing so in the context of conjoint couple therapy might still be contraindicated. Note that not only did the focus on Partner 1's behavior as a partner destabilize him but also that Partner 2 was unable to empathize with him. It is possible that Partner 2 was an empathetic person who had reached a point at which she could no longer empathize with Partner 1. Alternatively, Partner 2 might have had her own challenges with empathy.

When partners are unable to empathize with each other's experience, couple therapy is contraindicated. Empathy, as noted elsewhere, is the ability to imagine what another person is experiencing. For example, when Liz told the couple therapist that her father had died, the couple therapist was able to empathize with Liz, even though her own father was still alive. The couple therapist was able to listen to Liz's verbal and nonverbal ways of telling her. Based on what Liz expressed and her own personal and professional knowledge and experience of loss, the couple therapist was able to imagine the array of feelings Liz might be experiencing in the process of mourning her father. Despite her empathy, the couple therapist recognized that what she imagined may not have been completely accurate and so she asked Liz probing questions about her reactions to her father's death. Empathy is effective because the recipient feels heard and understood, rather than because the person empathizing has surmised exactly what he or she is experiencing.

When partners do not exhibit empathy with each other and are unable to learn empathy in the context of couple therapy, the challenges of couple therapy for them may be insurmountable. A partner who cannot empathize also cannot comprehend that the other has a thought, feeling, or experience or ascribes meaning that differs from his or her own. When a partner cannot or will not empathize, defensiveness replaces listening between partners. As a result, both the couple therapist and her or his therapeutic interventions become fodder for more couple conflict.

Most people learn empathy by the end of their preschool years. This learning occurs by observing empathetic parents interacting with them and with others. When parents lack empathy, or are too impaired to display it, it becomes more difficult for children to learn empathy.

Empathy can be learned later in life. A couple therapist can demonstrate empathy and guide partners in the mechanics of listening and responding empathetically to one another. Emotionally focused couple therapy (Chapter 7), as well as the foundational psychodynamic couple therapies (Chapter 6), attend to facilitating the development and reclaiming of empathy between partners.

It is only when mental health challenges interfere with partners' ability to learn empathy that couple therapy is contraindicated. If one or both partners' mental health challenges preclude learning empathy in the context of couple therapy, a referral for individual psychotherapy is indicated. A referral is essential because, even if treating the mental disorder is within the scope of the couple therapist's practice, he or she would be assuming a dual role with the partner. Couple therapy is similarly contraindicated if either partner is disengaged from the other to the extent that he or she refuses to empathize with the other, unless that partner expresses a desire to reclaim empathy in the relationship.

Stop and Think:

Be sure to include your responses in your journal.

1. When and how did you learn empathy? If you do not remember, think about the people who were important to you growing up and the extent to which they displayed empathy for you and for one another.

2. How might the couple therapist's probing questions about Liz's experience after her father's death convey empathy?
3. Referring back to the transcript of the hypothetical couple (Partners 1 and 2) above, can you imagine how Partner 1 heard Partner 2 and CT? Can you imagine how Partner 2 heard Partner 1 and CT? Explain your answer.

You will now read about a variety of services to which partners are referred by couple therapists. Individual psychotherapy has been included because couple therapy is sometimes contraindicated. Additionally, partners may wish to work on individual issues with separate psychotherapists at the same time they are working on their relationship in couple therapy. Other services may be instead of or in addition to couple therapy and address aspects of the couple's lives that couple therapy cannot.

Mental Health Related Services

Most couple therapists' scope of practice extends beyond couple therapy. Couple therapists are often trained as couple and family therapists and many graduate programs include individual psychotherapy training. A couple therapist may choose to pursue training in areas of practice that extend beyond couple therapy, for example, eating disorders, mood disorders, and chronic biomedical illnesses. All impact an individual psychotherapy client's relationships. And many couple therapists also enjoy working with individual clients. Identifying an area of specialization does not preclude sufficient training and experience to practice competently in other areas. For example, a couple and family therapist might identify a specialization working with LGBT couples. However, he or she might be competent and also work with heterosexual, cis-gendered couples and presenting problems having nothing to do with sexual orientation or gender identity.

Despite most couple therapists having a wide range of competencies, it is unrealistic to expect that even the best trained and most experienced couple therapist will be competent to deliver the entire range of individual, couple, family, and group therapies that partners and couples may need. Additionally, couple therapists are generally not licensed to practice the entire range of services partners may need. For example, unless a couple therapist is also a physician or a psychologist in the few states that license psychologists to prescribe medication, he or she cannot practice medication assessment and management. As a result, couple therapists refer to other mental health professionals for these services. In this section, you will read about various mental health supports to which couple therapists refer.

Stop and Think:

Be sure to include your responses in your journal.

Many people find it difficult to say no. Think about a time when you had to say no to someone you did not know well. Now think about a time when you knew and cared about the person.

1. What, if anything, about the each situation made it easy to say no?
2. What, if anything, about each situation make it difficult to say no?
3. Now imagine yourself telling a couple with whom you have been working that you cannot help them with an issue they have raised. What would that be like for you?

Divorce Support and Recovery Groups

While divorce support and recovery groups are not for couples, couples sometimes decide to dissolve their relationship during the course of couple therapy. Some couple therapists have obtained training in group therapy and offer group therapy as part of their range of services. If that is not the case or the couple therapist is not currently offering a divorce support group, then being familiar with local divorce support groups allows the couple therapist to offer information about them to the partners.

The dissolution of a relationship involves each partner mourning her or his hopes and dreams for her or his own life as part of the couple and for the relationship. It also involves partners experiencing anger and sadness at themselves and each other and authoring a new personal narrative as not only a single but also as a divorced person. Since the dominant culture brands divorce as a failure, partners must reframe the temptation to label themselves as defective.

Sometimes one or both partners will have done anticipatory grieving to the extent that he or she does not appear to be mourning the death of the relationship. Appearances can be deceptive, and a couple therapist who is working with a couple during their decision-making process will reflect what he or she hears about the partners' feelings.

Anger is also a predictable response to the demise of a relationship. While anger at oneself occurs, it is unhelpful because the past cannot be changed. However, examining one's past behavior and especially those aspects of it that contributed to the demise of the relationship may be helpful in changing how one chooses to behave in the future.

Anger at one's partner is likely the most pervasive feeling expressed after a relationship ends. Anger can help one identify what was unacceptable and thus to be avoided in future relationships. Acknowledging anger allows partners to move on from the dissolution. When anger becomes a source of comfort or self-justification, it likely is no longer helpful.

The presence of biological or adopted children forces separating couples to continue to interact with one another so that children can maintain their relationships with both parents. Couple therapy can help ensure that both partners attend to managing contact in a way that excludes the children from any on-going anger between them. Establishing rules such as talking about changes in schedules directly to one another, rather than using a child as intermediary, and saving angry responses for a time when children are not present can facilitate this goal.

When grief and sadness undermine self-esteem or when anger turns to bitterness, they are no longer helpful emotions. Couple therapists can facilitate the partners acknowledging that each played a role in creating and sustaining the relationship dynamics that eventually undermined it.

Many partners are unable to resolve all their feelings about themselves, their former partner, and the dissolution of their relationship by the time couple therapy ends. Divorce adjustment and recovery groups allow each partner to engage with others undergoing similar transitions and with the guidance of a group facilitator, neither of which the couple therapist can provide unless he or she is trained and experienced in group therapy and happens to be facilitating a divorce group. As with couple therapy, when a partner's emotional challenges preclude effective group participation, a referral for individual therapy may be more appropriate.

Grief Counseling and Grief Groups

Couple therapists sometimes work with partners when one is dying. They also may be working with partners when one of their parents dies. Occasionally and horrifically, a couple presents for couple therapy because the loss or impending loss of a child has overwhelmed the partners' ability to cope. Some couple therapists also practice grief counseling, while others need to refer to a practitioner who does. Sometimes a referral to a grief group is desirable. The couple therapist can help assess which may best serve the client partner or couple.

Grief groups provide the additional support of other people who are grieving similar losses. Medical clinics where terminally ill patients receive care sometimes offer grief groups for patients' survivors. Grief work with an individual psychotherapist or the couple therapist if grief work is within his or her scope of practice may be preferable to a grief group, especially for those who feel unready for a group setting, who are embarrassed about the extent of their grief, or who might be disruptive in a group context. For some clients, the comfort of continuing to work with a therapist with whom they are familiar exceeds the benefits of a group, although this consideration does not negate the ethical requirement that the couple therapist be trained to do grief work.

Although Kubler-Ross' (1969) seminal work on the stages of grief has been challenged by subsequent researchers, many of the phenomena she identified in her five-stage model of grief continue to manifest in bereaved partners. These aspects of grieving do not occur in any particular order, and grief may involve shifting back and forth among the various stages or aspects of grief.

Most people suffering the loss of a partner or parent experience some level of denial.

LIZ: My mom keeps saying this can't have happened, he can't have died.

COUPLE THERAPIST: That's so hard.

LIZ: I know. I wake up some mornings and then a few minutes later remember Dad is dead. [Tearful] It feels like it's happening all over again.

It is also common to feel anger at the person who has died, even when the grieving survivor knows the deceased would prefer to be alive.

LIZ: I don't understand why my mom isn't angry at him. He didn't take care of himself, he drank, he doctor shopped [for multiple prescriptions for pain medication, not as easily done in this time of electronic medical records as it was when Liz's father was alive]. How could he do that to her? To me? To the grandkids? How could he leave us?

MARTIN: It's OK, Liz. He didn't want to leave you.

LIZ: I know. It's nuts. But I am so angry at him sometimes.

CT: I don't think it's nuts, Liz. I imagine you're right that he might be alive had he taken better care of himself. I also don't think the fact that he didn't was about you or your kids.

And, of course, sadness is a component of grief.

LIZ: Sometimes I'm so sad, mostly about what will never be. You know, him watching the kids grow up, being at holidays. Though he was a real [expletive] most holidays, and I don't know why I want that back. [Pause] Anyway, I think it's worse for my mother. And I'm worried about her. She sounds like she's blaming herself for not taking the booze and the pills away from him. That's not good, is it? Because it's not her fault; he would have found a way no matter what she did.

CT: I can't tell you what role his substance abuse played in their relationship dynamic because I never met them. But if your mom is feeling badly about herself, it's more than grief, and I wonder whether she'd benefit from a grief group.

LIZ: Oh, she'd never go to a group.

CT: Would she work with someone individually? For grief counseling.

The fourth stage of grief is bargaining, which even Kubler-Ross acknowledged did not always happen.

> LIZ: My mom said, "If he'd just be alive, I wouldn't grumble anymore about cleaning and cooking." Apparently, she was fine with it until he retired, and then it infuriated her that she had to keep working while he sat around all the time.

Finally, people come to accept the reality of what has happened. Acceptance is not the same as liking the situation; however, it is an acknowledgement of what is.

> LIZ: I think I get it that he's dead, that he's not coming back. I wish it were different, but nothing I think or do will bring him back. I wish my mom saw that, although she seems to be dating this man at her church.

Individual Psychotherapy

It is not uncommon for one partner to seek individual psychotherapy, during which it becomes obvious that her or his problem is in fact a couple problem. Other times, one partner alerts his or her primary care physician to the presence of relationship distress during a routine health maintenance visit. Still other times, there is so much couple stress that an attorney working with one partner or the couple may suggest couple therapy. Liz exemplified the first phenomenon. Since not all individual therapists are trained to do couple therapy, primary care physicians rarely have the training and never the time to do couple therapy, and attorneys have neither the training nor the time, any or all of these professionals may refer to a couple therapist while continuing their work with one or both partners.

By contrast, most couple therapists are trained to practice individual psychotherapy, as was the couple therapist you have been following throughout this textbook. When an individual client devotes a significant portion of more than one session to talking about the partner, couple therapy may be indicated.

Another example of couple therapy interfacing with individual psychotherapy involves a situation in which one partner's mental disorder or mental health history is such that individual issues and the way they are being handled overwhelm that partner's ability to engage in couple therapy. Sometimes these issues can be explored with one partner during conjoint couple therapy sessions. Liz's post-traumatic stress symptoms resulting from having been sexually assaulted could be addressed, when relevant to the couple therapy, with Martin present. Had her symptom picture been more severe (e.g., dissociative symptoms), it might have alarmed Martin to the point that it would require her to work on her PTSD separately with a different therapist.

Other times, as previously noted, the nature of a mental disorder precludes couple work. A partner who is unable to share the couple therapist's attention, who lacks insight and empathy, and who begins to decompensate when challenged to shift perspective or change behavior cannot participate effectively in conjoint couple therapy sessions. He or she would be better served with a referral for individual psychotherapy followed by couple therapy if the partner can tolerate waiting. As described in Chapter 4, individual psychopathology can serve a function in a couple's relationship, and thus the relationship may not survive either a significant change by the partner engaged in individual psychotherapy or the delay of couple therapy necessary to treat the individual psychopathology.

When one or both partners is/are participating in both individual and couple therapy simultaneously, both the individual(s) and the couple can be best served if the couple therapist and the individual psychotherapist(s) exchange information. It is important that the therapy team avoid working at cross-purposes and that each professional shares information that might be helpful with the other(s). However, information can only be exchanged when partners' informed consent has been obtained.

Child Therapy

Couples sometimes bring parenting issues to couple therapy. Because the writer also holds an advanced degree in child development and has worked with parents and children throughout her career, she has been able to work with couples on parenting issues as they arise. When a couple therapist does not have sufficient training and experience, he or she must decide whether to refer for child or family therapy.

One consideration is whether the child's symptoms may be serving as a homeostatic mechanism in her or his parents' relationship dynamics. Children also may have their own challenges, such as learning differences and their sequelae, that require individual intervention. Since many couple therapists are also trained in family therapy, they may wish to schedule a family session in order to assess whether the child would be best served by child therapy, family therapy, or both.

When Liz and Martin's daughter, Christina, developed an eating disorder in late adolescence, their primary care physician referred them to a family therapist (Esposito and Hattem, 2017). Although Christina exhibited symptoms of an eating disorder and was at an age when she would soon live independently of her family of origin, the primary care physician had seen evidence of Liz's restrictive eating and excessive exercise, knew the family's history, and determined that family therapy was the preferred modality for assessing whether Christina would best be served by individual and/or family therapy.

It is especially important to differentiate child behavior problems from homeostatic mechanisms that keep the couple and therefore the family intact. While a child benefits from resolution of a behavior problem, the family dynamic may preclude a successful outcome if only child therapy is undertaken. Additionally, labeling a child with a mental disorder when he or she might not exhibit one outside the family context can be detrimental to the child's self-image while maintaining a dysfunctional family dynamic. As such, diagnosing and treating the child is not always consistent with beneficence. Alternatively, ignoring the child's own challenges apart from her or his role in the family dynamics similarly risks violation of the ethical principle to do no harm.

Family Therapy

The tenets of systems theory you studied in Chapter 4 apply to family as well as couple systems. Thus, depending upon the circumstances, family therapy may be appropriate, especially at the onset of couple therapy (Napier & Whitaker, 1978).

Liz's sister, Barbara, and her husband, Peter, exemplified the phenomenon that a child's behavior problem can maintain equilibrium in the parents' relationship and thus the family. In 2000, their then 16-year-old daughter began exhibiting symptoms of an eating disorder. Sally's vigilance and criticism had affected Barbara, as well as Liz, and Barbara had also struggled with body image and her relationship with food throughout her adolescence and adulthood.

When Barbara's daughter, Patricia, began evidencing symptoms of binging and purging, Barbara and Peter were sleeping in separate bedrooms. There had been unresolved conflict in their marriage for a number of years, Peter had had an extramarital affair, and they had decided to defer separating until their twins left for college. Because their son, Paul, was hiding information about his sexual preference, it was Patricia's evident eating disordcr and their concern for her health that provided a common focus and goal for Peter and Barbara. They avoided mutual blame and instead came together to obtain outside help for her.

Patricia's child psychologist suggested they also consult with a family therapist. The family therapist asked about the history of Patricia's eating disorder and quickly learned that Barbara and Peter's relationship had improved around their mutual concern for Patricia. The child psychologist and family therapist agreed that Patricia would be at risk for intractable symptoms unless the dynamics between her parents changed. Neither therapist suggested the parents needed to remain together. Rather, both agreed that they needed to either resolve their on-going conflict or separate, so that Patricia would not need to remain symptomatic in order to keep them together. From a systems perspective, it is interesting to observe that after Patricia's eating disorder resolved and Paul came out to his parents, Barbara developed breast cancer, which again brought her and Peter closer together.

Family therapy referrals also arise from couple therapy work when children become a focus of attention. Couple therapists can either refer to another family therapist or move between couple and family therapy modalities with the couple, depending upon training and experience with family therapy and the specific characteristics of the situation. Because both couple and family therapy interventions occur at the system level, rather than the individual level, the ethical challenge involving dual roles when working with the larger family as well as the couple are very different than that of the same therapist working with partners individually and the couple together.

Stop and Think:

Be sure to include your responses in your journal.

1. Describe your reaction to the idea that child problems may be better treated in family therapy than in individual child psychotherapy.
2. What issues might arise for you if you were told your problem resided in the family rather than in yourself?

3 What issues might arise for you if you were told your problem was your own and your family had nothing to do with it?
4 What issues might arise for you if you were told you needed to go to individual psychotherapy before engaging in couple therapy?
5 Given the likelihood that neither parents, children, nor partners wish to hear any of these, how might you approach delivering the message? What would make you uncomfortable? What would help soothe you?

Spiritual Counseling

During couple therapy, spiritual topics may arise. For example, partners may discover that their views about end-of-life decisions, burial, and after-life are so divergent that they cannot make decisions together as they age. While a couple therapist can guide the decision-making process and identify impediments to resolution, he or she cannot advise a couple about their spiritual beliefs and practices unless he or she also holds a degree in pastoral counseling. Referring the couple to their clergy person to discuss the spiritual aspects of their decision making while concurrently engaging in couple therapy to resolve couple dynamics around decisions may be indicated.

At the time of this writing, it was neither legal nor ethical for a couple therapist working in a secular setting to guide couples based on religious tenets. Rather, couple therapists in secular settings were ethically bound to follow professional tenets and refrain from imposing their own values, including religious ones, on client couples. A couple seeking, for example, Christian counseling could turn to a practice that identified as Christian with clinical training. Some congregations even maintained lists of congregants for referrals, although the ethical prohibition against dual roles applies if the couple therapist knows the couple from both being members of the same congregation.

Pastoral counseling is a field in which individual, couple, and family counselors are trained in both secular practice and the tenets of their religion. Pastoral counselors are then licensed by the state in which they practice and are able to identify as providing the full range of pastoral counseling services. Seeking couple therapy from a clergy person who has not been trained in pastoral counseling can be problematic, although some couples do so. Without training and supervised practice in couple therapy, system dynamics are virtually impossible for anyone, including clergy, to identify and thus treat.

Patient and Caretaker Support Groups

When a patient is diagnosed with a chronic or life-threatening illness, his or her world view shifts. While everyone is aware of their mortality on some level, prior to being confronted with it most people devise ways to ignore it. Becker (1973) wrote a seminal work in which he expanded Freud's concept of sublimation by positing that it is the mechanism by which we deny our on-going fears both of living fully and of dying. Consider any Woody Allen movie as an example. His anxiety about dying, as well as his anxiety about fully living, was an underlying theme for every character he has written for himself as an actor. The creative processes of writing roles for himself and then acting functioned to sublimate these anxieties (Creativity and Madness, 2007). Becker (1973) had suggested that societal accomplishments have arisen from that sublimation of individual anxiety about living and dying, rather than recognizing the reality that death will happen.

Grief was described earlier in this chapter. When a partner is diagnosed with a life-changing or life-threatening illness, both partners grieve the loss of their lives as they were and of their future together as they envisioned it prior to the diagnosis. They also experience anticipatory grief about the impending death. There is a great difference between knowing that you will die at some unspecified and presumably remote time and knowing that that time is no longer remote.

Clinics in which patients with life-changing and life-threatening diagnoses are treated may offer patient support groups or may refer to support groups in the community. It is also advisable for couple therapists to be aware of patient support groups within the community in which they practice. While participating in a group full of patients whose illnesses are advanced and/or who lack social support outside the group may be contraindicated, that consideration is beyond the scope of an introductory textbook.

Caretakers also may benefit from caretaker support groups. The writer once facilitated a Parkinson's disease group. Several of the participants were couples, with the diagnosed partner and his or her caretaker both attending. Others were caretakers whose partner was too debilitated to participate in the group. All appeared to benefit from sharing stories and suggestions and from knowing they had a place to talk with people who were not afraid to listen to their stories and emotions. They felt safe to express their feelings about the emotional and physical exhaustion of the caretaker role and its impact on the patient, who often felt guilty about what he or she was doing to his or her partner.

The physical and emotional toll of being a partner caretaker cannot be overstated. Unfortunately, it is often overlooked in favor of the patient's seemingly more pressing needs. As Sally's second husband became increasingly debilitated, her blood pressure began to spike, yet she believed caring for her own health could be deferred. A couple therapist working with a couple facing a debilitating and/or life-threatening illness can encourage the care-giving partner to explore joining a caretaker support group, provide her or him with the contact information for one, encourage him or her to consult a physician about any biomedical symptoms, and refer for medication assessment if deemed appropriate.

Stop and Think:

Be sure to include your responses in your journal.

1. You have read about couples groups, divorce groups, grief groups, and caretaker support groups. Given what you have read, what do you find compelling about doing group work?
2. What about group work would be difficult for you?

Hospice

Hospice is a nation-wide organization with affiliates in most localities. Hospice provides palliative care for terminally ill or injured patients and emotional support for their partners and families. Hospice care may be available at free-standing hospice centers, in hospital settings, and at the patient's home.

Hospice does not care for patients who are receiving treatment for their illness or injury. Rather, hospice provides palliative medical care after the physician has informed the patient that all forms of treatment have failed to stop the progress of the disease or the patient has decided the negative aspects of treatment outweigh the decreasingly possible benefits. Palliative care entails keeping the patient physically and emotionally comfortable during the dying process. Hospice personnel work with physicians and communicate with and support the patient and her or his family members as the patient moves through the process of dying and immediately following the death.

Stop and Think:

Be sure to include your responses in your journal.

1. You have read about working with seriously ill, injured, and dying patients. Given what you have read, what do you find compelling about working with dying people and their partners?
2. What about working with dying patients and their partners would be difficult for you?

Medication Evaluation and Management

With few exceptions, states do not license mental health practitioners to prescribe medications. Effective medication management involves understanding the client's medical and family history, other biomedical diagnoses and their management, and how any other medication(s) interact(s) with any psychotropic medications that might be prescribed. Psychiatrists are physicians who have completed residencies in psychiatry and have a more thorough knowledge of mental disorders and available medications than, for example, primary care practitioners; in some jurisdictions, psychiatric nurse practitioners and physicians assistants can also prescribe. Experience and scholarly articles suggest that primary care practitioners also diagnose some mental disorders, such as depression, and prescribe medication. Unfortunately, they often have neither the training nor the time to do a full psychiatric assessment. For these reasons, if the first medication does not work, either because it is not a good fit for the client's physiology or because the disorder is more complex, many primary care practitioners then refer the patient to a psychiatrist for assessment and management.

Couple therapists usually maintain referral relationships with several psychiatrists or other prescribing health care practitioners. As part of the referral, a couple therapist will list three names and explain her or his reasons for recommending each. She or he will also explain her or his reasons for recommending a medication evaluation. Many clients are hesitant about taking medication, and it may be helpful to assure them that the referral is for information and that the client is not required to accept a recommendation for medication even if that is the outcome.

After a couple therapist has referred a partner for a psychiatric evaluation and the partner has followed through on the referral, the psychiatrist reviews the partner's symptoms, her or his medical and family history, and asks about other medications that have been prescribed for her or him. The psychiatrist then determines what, if any, psychotropic medication to prescribe. If the psychiatrist determines that medication might be helpful, he or she then determines the potential for other medications that have been prescribed for the patient to interact with the various appropriate psychotropic medications and what medications have or have not worked for family members with similar mental health diagnoses. Once medication has been prescribed, a follow-up appointment is scheduled approximately a month later. Unless the medication is changed, subsequent follow-up appointments occur at less frequent intervals, generally prior to the psychiatrist renewing the prescription. The initial appointment may be 60 to 90 minutes in duration. Follow-up appointments are brief, usually no more than 20 minutes in duration.

Some mental disorders do not respond to medication, and different patients respond differently to the various available medications. When there is no medication for a specific disorder, medication may be prescribed for the secondary symptoms of the disorder. For example, a partner with a personality disorder may exhibit depressive symptoms arising from the impact of that personality disorder upon her or his life. While no medication for personality disorders currently exists, and therefore some insurers consider treatment of them to be not medically necessary (i.e., eligible for insurance payments), there are medications for the secondary depressive symptoms that may arise from the impact of a personality disorder on a person's life.

A collaborative relationship between a psychiatrist and a couple therapist involves the two professionals exchanging information after receiving informed consent from the partner who is in treatment with the psychiatrist. Exchanging information allows both professionals to work together toward the best possible outcome for the partner and thus for the client couple.

Because a couple therapist cannot prescribe medication unless she or he has medical training and licensure, she or he relies on the psychiatrist to prescribe and manage medication. However, the couple therapist has the opportunity to observe the patient more frequently, as couple therapy appointments usually occur every week or two and the duration of each is 45 to 60 minutes. The psychiatrist may rely upon the couple therapist to monitor changes in the patient's behavior and to alert the psychiatrist if the patient experiences unpleasant side-effects that diminish his or her resolve to continue using the medication. The couple therapist can also encourage the patient to contact the psychiatrist about her or his concerns about the medication.

Some psychiatrists and psychiatric nurse practitioners, as well as others licensed to prescribe in some jurisdictions, practice both medication evaluation and management and psychotherapy. If you are interested in pursuing mental health care from a biomedical perspective and also wish to practice psychotherapy with individuals, couples, families, and/or groups, be certain the training programs to which you apply offer coursework and clinical supervision in both.

Stop and Think:

Be sure to include your responses in your journal.

1. Medication evaluation and management is very different from couple therapy. What do you find compelling about the biomedical aspects of mental health?
2. What do you find compelling about the psychotherapy aspects of mental health?

Legal Services for Couples

Couple therapists who have not been to law school and passed the bar examination in the state in which they practice cannot advise their clients about legal matters. However, couple therapists can note the potential need for legal services, recommend a legal consultation, and provide partners or a client couple with referrals to attorneys. When a referral has been made and an attorney contacted, the attorney will then assume responsibility for determining the need for as well as the type of legal services the client may require.

Experience suggests that a legal consultation can be helpful to one or both partners if one is threatening to leave the relationship. A legal consultation involves an attorney explaining the client's legal rights based upon the answers to questions about his or her situation and the process of dissolving a marriage or domestic partnership. Knowing one's rights is critical to protecting oneself. Knowing what the process of divorce entails, as well as the limits of one's legal rights, can disabuse a partner of the notion that it might be easier to dissolve the relationship than to repair it. It is helpful for the couple therapist to explain that the referral is for information only and neither the couple therapist nor the attorney expects the client to act in any particular way upon the information or any recommendations arising from the consultation.

When one partner has left the relationship or fails to abide by a separation agreement, irrespective of promises of fairness and care, it is imperative that a couple therapist urge the other partner to consult with an attorney and provide her or him with a referral. However, some clients decline referrals for legal and other services. Couple therapists can only recommend; they cannot coerce clients into pursuing a referral. While the writer has worked with several clients who later regretted their decisions to avoid consulting an attorney, she also recognizes that there are limits to her persuasiveness and that ethical codes require her to respect the client's agency even when she is concerned about the client's decision-making process.

When a couple therapist makes a referral to one or more specific attorneys, it is incumbent upon the couple therapist to be familiar with their legal work. Convention dictates three options when making any referral, so that the client can assess who, if any, is the best fit.

It is helpful for the couple therapist to explain his or her reasons for making the referral and to describe her or his reasons for including three professionals on the referral list. While a couple therapist cannot predict what will happen during a legal consultation, he or she can provide general information about the purpose and scope of a consultation. The couple therapist can inform the client that the attorney will ask questions about the client's specific situation and offer legal options for handling it, including the estimated cost of each. The couple therapist can also explain in a sentence or two why he or she included each of the three attorneys on the referral list.

Couple therapists most commonly refer to attorneys for four categories of legal issues: (1) prenuptial agreements; (2) wills, trusts, durable and health care powers of attorney, and advance directives; (3) separation agreements, divorce decrees, and financial and child custody agreements; and (4) competency, usually with respect to an aging partner or a parent of one of the partners. Prenuptial agreements and both wills and trusts generally pertain to affluent clients. Those struggling to make ends meet do not have assets that could be contested at a later time. Irrespective of a couple's socioeconomic status, laws involving separation, divorce, custody, health care power of attorney, and competency apply.

Prenuptial Agreements

A prenuptial agreement is signed by both partners and specifies how their assets and liabilities will be divided after the marriage ends. As noted in Chapter 9, all marriages end, whether through one partner's death or through the dissolution of the relationship. And while wills and trusts may also specify distributions after a death, in remarriages or when there are significant assets, it is sometimes advisable to create both documents.

Some attorneys advise that prenuptial agreements be signed well in advance of a marriage in order to avoid the impression of coercion of either partner to sign. However, a prenuptial agreement can be signed as a postnuptial agreement after the marriage, as well.

An internet search of the topic of prenuptial agreements yields information primarily about anticipating what a marrying couple wishes their divorce settlement to accomplish. High profile cases of people in the public eye exemplify this purpose. The message is, in essence, you can marry me but not for my money.

Prenuptial agreements can also be used to protect the inheritance of children from previous marriages. In many states, property acquired during a marriage is considered community property. Even when assets have been acquired prior to the marriage or inherited, placing them in certain joint assets may render them joint property in some jurisdictions. Partners can agree, in a prenuptial agreement, to circumvent these laws. Partners can also specify an alternative method of distributing assets when the marriage ends in either death or dissolution.

Because prenuptial agreements are created at a time of great hope and happiness yet are focused on a time of anticipated loss and distress, the process of drafting a prenuptial agreement can become contentious and thus challenging for the relationship. While both partners may agree on the need for a prenuptial agreement to, for example, protect children from previous relationships, the process may feel as though loving and committing to a life together are secondary to preserving these assets.

The intent of couple therapy is to facilitate relationship health, rather than relationship dissolution. If a couple's relationship appears fraught, a couple therapist might suggest the partners work on resolving what could become intractable issues. No couple therapist would recommend a couple anticipate how they wanted to handle their divorce as part of premarital counseling or couple therapy but rather only if a couple requested divorce counseling.

Nevertheless, couple therapists sometimes suggest that marrying couples consult an attorney for advice about whether they would benefit from drafting a prenuptial agreement. Presumably such recommendations arise from the partners' desire to protect themselves and their children from previous relationships, rather than because the couple appears on the verge of dissolution. Although it had not yet occurred when Liz and Martin worked with the couple therapist, Liz's mother Sally and her second husband, Jim, sought legal consultation before they married and, as recommended by the attorney, signed a prenuptial agreement. This agreement preserved Jim's considerably greater assets, and especially any increase in his wealth during the marriage, for his biological children and grandchildren. It, like his will, also protected Sally by specifying that she could live in their home for the remainder of her life if he predeceased her, even though he had owned it when they met and his adult children would inherit it upon Sally's death. When his adult children told her to move out of the house after Jim was institutionalized and challenged his will after he died, Sally found the prenuptial agreement helpful.

To summarize, if a couple therapist hears a level of distress severe enough to compromise the relationship, he or she is ethically required to address his or her concerns with the couple. When one or both partners entertains the possibility of divorce, the couple therapist can recommend and provide a referral for legal consultation. Additionally, if a marrying couple talks about unequal assets and concerns for themselves or their children, a couple therapist can also recommend a legal consultation about the advisability of a prenuptial agreement.

Wills, Trusts, and Powers of Attorney

When someone dies, the distribution of their belongings is overseen by the state in which they resided unless a legal document expressing the deceased's wishes exists. The legal document is most commonly known as a will. Wealthier individuals and those who are responsible for someone who may be unable to manage his or her own resources may create trusts for the management of what others inherit from them. Wills and trusts also specify who will be responsible for any minor children at the time of death, unless the children's other biological or adoptive parent is living and has legal rights to custody.

Young couples rarely prioritize creating a will. Their lives are over-full with the busyness of working, raising children, caring for their home, creating a social life for themselves and their children, and maintaining relationships with extended family members. Young couples rarely expect to die. Even Liz, who was herself an attorney with minor children, had not made time to consult with a colleague and create a will. While she declined a referral from the couple therapist when the subject arose during a couple therapy session, the couple therapist was prepared to offer the couples with whom she worked referrals to attorneys specializing in wills and trusts.

As noted in Chapter 9, partners who are unable to marry or who choose not to marry do not have rights to inheritance. Only a will specifying what is to be inherited by the other partner can protect that person from losing not only assets but custody of children in the event the other dies. In some jurisdictions, even a signed document may not override laws intended to disadvantage unmarried couples and discriminate against those in same-sexed relationships and those who are not cis-gendered. As of this writing, a presidential directive has been signed legalizing discrimination against LGBTQIA individuals and couples with respect to adoption, custody, employment, and other rights.

Other related documents having to do with the death or incapacitation of one or both partners include durable power of attorney, health care power of attorney, and advance directives. The first two documents specify a person's wishes in situations in which he or she cannot make decisions for herself or himself, such as paying bills, and allow the partner access to protected health information when she or he must make health-related decisions for the other. Couples generally assign these powers of attorney to each other, with back-up if the other is also too debilitated to serve or has died.

Advance directives specify an individual's wishes regarding end-of-life decisions. These include such questions as whether to initiate or continue life support measures in specified situations and any desired palliative care when death is imminent.

In some jurisdictions, partners may also specify what they wish to be done with their remains following their death. When one or both partners were widowed prior to marrying, such decisions can be fraught for both partners and the children from their previous relationships.

Attorneys can help individuals and couples think through their wishes with regards to all of these legal documents. Both attorneys and couple therapists can facilitate couple discussions around divergent wishes with which the other may not be comfortable.

Separation and Divorce

Couples who remain unmarried, either by choice or necessity, have no rights to one another's property or children should they decide to dissolve their relationship. If the partners wished to protect each other's rights in the event of dissolution, rather than death, they would need to consult an attorney to determine whether a mechanism exists in their jurisdiction.

Most states require some period of separation before a divorce decree can be requested. The length of separation prior to divorce varies by state. In some jurisdictions, it is advisable to file a separation agreement that specifies the date and terms of separation, including allowing partners to function financially and socially as though they are no longer married, and remains in effect until the divorce is final. Financial and custody agreements specified in a separation agreement can also become part of the divorce settlement without being renegotiated. However, they need not be completed prior to a separation or a divorce decree being finalized. Attorneys may recommend specifying temporary provisions regarding finances and custody until a final agreement can be reached.

Couple therapists are not expected to be familiar with all the laws of their jurisdiction nor to remain up to date on changes to various laws pertaining to couple relationships. However, it is reasonable for a couple therapist to advise that, for self-protection, each partner consult an attorney if a couple with whom the couple therapist is working decides to separate.

Collaborative divorce is a process whereby the couple works collaboratively with each partner's attorney, a financial planner, and a couple therapist with the goal of arriving at the best outcome possible given the circumstances of marital dissolution. When professionals from all three disciplines work collaboratively with the client couple, acrimony and prolonged court battles are less likely to occur. However, many partners are so hurt and angry they are unable to participate together in a collaborative divorce.

For a number of years, the writer practiced in a state that required a one-year separation period prior to finalizing a divorce. In order to avoid charges of abandonment and resultant financial and child custody penalties, attorneys usually advised couples to sign a separation agreement. Even in the absence of punitive consequences, a legal document acknowledging a joint decision to separate, granting each partner the right to live as an independent person, and specifying at least temporary child custody and visitation and child and/or spousal support payments may be helpful in minimizing contention around these topics.

The process of negotiating child custody and financial agreements may trigger unresolved partner and couple issues. When there is nothing else left to fight about, money and children become the only options in an ongoing struggle to resolve or change what has happened to the couple. One partner may be furious about the other's infidelity. Yet after a separation, the only available option for expressing that anger to the partner is to fight about money and children.

When partners have decided to end their relationship, they may seek guidance from their couple therapist about how to tell their children about the impending separation. Couple therapists trained and experienced in addressing children's emotional needs at various stages of their development can facilitate the couple's decisions about parenting. Couple therapists, like family therapists, encourage divorcing parents to avoid triangulation of their children into their continuing relationship disputes.

Competency

Competency has to do with whether or not a person is too impaired by biomedical or mental illness, brain trauma, or infirmity or dementia to manage her or his own life. It is a legal term, and couples struggling with competency issues with either one partner or a partner's aging parent would be advised to seek legal consultation.

Stop and Think:

Be sure to include your responses in your journal.

1. What do you see as the advantages of working with couples as an attorney, without the need to intervene with their emotional and relationship dynamics?
2. What do you see as the disadvantages of working with couples as an attorney, without the agreement to intervene with their emotional and relationship dynamics?

Medical Services

Unless a couple therapist is licensed to practice medicine, he or she cannot offer medical advice to his or her clients. However, a couple therapist can recommend that one or both partners consult with a physician and provide the by-now familiar list of three referrals.

Issues for which a medical evaluation is advisable arise in the process of practicing couple therapy. For example, one partner's sexual dysfunction, depressive symptoms, or abdominal pain when stressed may develop and/or be sustained by a couple's dynamics. Each of these and many other symptoms may also indicate a biomedical problem for which treatment other than or in addition to couple therapy is essential. Couple therapists may suggest a routine physical examination or consultation about a particular problem to rule out the possibility of an underlying biomedical problem. Couple therapists can offer a referral if the client partner is not in the care of a physician.

As previously suggested, couple therapists also diagnose mental disorders for which medication may be indicated. For example, if one partner exhibits symptoms of bipolar disorder, referral to a physician for a medication evaluation is indicated. The subject of psychiatric referrals for evaluation and medication management was more thoroughly discussed earlier in this chapter.

Beneficence mandates that a couple therapist recommend a medical consultation if she or he suspects the presence of a biomedical problem. If a problem is discovered and/or medication prescribed, biomedical treatment can facilitate couple therapy. If no problem is discovered or medication is not indicated for the diagnosis, then couple therapy can proceed without concern that a biomedical problem that has been overlooked will either worsen or impede the success of couple therapy.

Rehabilitation and Adult Day Care

Accidents, surgeries, acute illnesses such as cardiac and neurological events, and chronic illnesses including cancer, heart disease, diabetes, schizophrenia, and dementia may require temporary or long-term out-patient treatment. Cardiac rehabilitation, physical therapy, occupational therapy, and speech therapy all follow debilitating or potentially debilitating events, accidents, and some surgeries. Patients with schizophrenia and dementia may require day treatment because they are unsafe alone. Couple therapists are not trained to provide these services, and the partner's physician usually makes a referral. However, couple therapists can work with couples who are struggling with such challenges, with a focus on the impact of the challenge upon the partner and the relationship.

Couple therapy when a partner has been stricken with a life-changing illness or disability cannot alter the facts of the diagnosis and its prognosis. However, couples need to integrate each partner's thoughts, feelings, and the meanings associated with the diagnosis and treatment into their couple dynamics and coping structure. Couple therapists can facilitate identification of thoughts that are helpful and suggest reframing those that are not. They can also facilitate the partners' journey through the various stages and challenges of grief with the goal of adapting to life's reality while allowing and validating sadness, anger, anxiety, and other intense and sometimes contradictory feelings about the situation and each other. Couple therapists can facilitate identification of the meanings partners ascribe to what has occurred. And although they cannot change the facts, they can guide couples in the process of re-authoring the couple's story about those facts. Finally, couple therapists can observe and intervene to foster effective couple dynamics and challenge ineffective ones, disrupting homeostatic mechanisms that impede adaptation to the couple's new reality.

The theories you studied in Section II provide guidance for approaching these tasks. Couple therapists can also seek information from the health care professionals working with the partners, with signed consent to exchange information. The partners are learning new information about the disease or accident and its attendant disability. A couple therapist's curiosity and willingness to listen may be healing for the client couple, and the information obtained may be helpful to the couple therapist in tailoring interventions to fit the limitations of the couple's situation.

Sally's second husband, Bill, sustained a closed head injury while serving in Korea in the 1950s. After they married, he developed symptoms of dementia and was diagnosed with Alzheimer's disease. As he both recognized and resisted the diagnosis, his neurologist suggested they consult with a couple therapist on staff to manage changes and make decisions together about how to manage their future.

Public Health

Public health services may be appropriate when either partner has had sexual contact outside the couple's relationship and the couple cannot afford to receive screening and care from a primary care physician. Public health services maintain records of communicable diseases such as human immunodeficiency virus (HIV), although reporting requirements are the purview of physicians rather than psychotherapists. Public health care is available through the same county agencies that provide mental health and social services to low-income residents of the county.

Social Services

Couple therapists refer client couples with limited resources for social services, including but not limited to public health. Available services vary widely from state to state and sometimes among counties within a particular state. As of this writing, programs like the Affordable Health Care marketplace, Medicaid, SCHIP, food stamps, school lunch programs, unemployment insurance, financial counseling, legal aid, and county health and mental health services remained available.

Couple therapists familiarize themselves with the resources that are available where they practice. They maintain a list of contact information for social service agencies and, if possible, for professionals at these agencies with whom they have previously worked. Relevant information from such a list can then be shared with client couples who might be eligible to benefit from social services. Couple therapists do not need to determine eligibility for services. Thus, it may be advisable to clarify to clients that the referral is for determination of eligibility for services.

Couple therapists also keep contact information for the social service or law enforcement agency to which they must report suspected abuse or neglect of a dependent. Students often ask about whether intimate partner violence is also reportable. It is not, unless the partner against whom the violence is perpetrated is disabled, elderly, or otherwise unable to care for himself or herself. However, couple therapists can provide partners who feel unsafe or about whose safety the couple therapist is concerned with the telephone number of the local women's shelter.

Women's shelters provide a safe and private space for women who are the victims of intimate partner violence and for their children. The address is not made public and anyone wishing protection must contact the shelter by phone. Some of you may have noted the adjective, "women's." Although statistical data suggest that intimate partner violence is most often perpetrated against a female partner, men are also victims of intimate partner violence. However, men are less likely to acknowledge that they have been abused because of the stereotypical expectations for men shared by a number of cultural groups. Additionally, institutionalized sexism has kept women more dependent than men, leaving the presumption that men can more easily escape an abusive situation.

Referring and Reporting

At this point, it may be helpful to review specifics about the process of referring to an agency or to another professional. Similarly, the process of reporting suspected abuse or neglect is also relevant.

Referring

The goal of a referral is that the partners contact the professional or agency to whom the couple therapist has referred them. Presenting a referral as the best resource for meeting an identified need and as a potential addition to and not replacement for couple therapy is critical to its success.

A couple therapist must remain sensitive to any discrepancies between her or his own and the client couple's ethnicity and socioeconomic status when making referrals. Couple therapists must also be sensitive to the possibility that partners may presume the referral means the couple therapist no longer wishes to work with them.

Another important aspect of making a successful referral involves ascertaining that the partners have bought into the need for the referral and are comfortable initiating contact. When the writer practiced in a medical setting, clinic employees scheduled her initial appointments with new clients. The remainder of her experience has been in settings where potential clients initiated contact directly with her prior to the first appointment. Her experience suggests that clients are more likely to honor appointments when they have had direct contact with her. Her belief is that even a brief conversation or email exchange provides potential clients with a sense of who she is as a human being and an attendant budding trust in her ability to be of use to them.

If the couple therapist agrees to initiate the initial contact with a referral on behalf of the client, she or he removes agency from the partners, as the medical clinic protocol did. Alternatively, the couple therapist can alert an agency or professional to whom he or she has referred that the client may contact that agency or professional, so long as he or she does not reveal confidential information about the client.

Finally, couple therapists are advised to follow up with couple clients to determine whether partners have initiated contact with the professional or agency and what services, if any, they have scheduled or received. If the agency or practitioner to whom a couple therapist has referred subsequently initiates contact with the couple therapist to exchange information about the client couple, the couple therapist would respond contingent upon partners signing an informed consent form granting permission to exchange information.

When a couple therapist must report suspected abuse or neglect of a dependent or that a client is a danger to self or to others and when a couple therapist is confronted with a duty to warn a client's intended victim, the couple therapist need not obtain consent to release confidential information about the client. These laws override client confidentiality laws, as noted in Chapter 11.

Reporting

Several aspects of reporting are essential for a couple therapist to know. First, a couple therapist must be familiar with procedures governing the reporting of suspected abuse or neglect and of suspected danger to self or others in the jurisdiction in which he or she practices. These procedures may not be the same. For example, a couple therapist may be required to report suspected abuse or neglect to a social services agency, while suspected danger to self or others must be reported directly to law enforcement.

States also vary in the time allowed between a couple therapist's reasonable suspicion and reporting the suspicion. The time may vary depending on whether the report is of suspected abuse or neglect or of suspected danger to self or others. Some jurisdictions also require a written report within a specified time following the verbal report.

To reiterate, a couple therapist must report suspected abuse or neglect of a dependent. The perpetrator need not reside with the victim but must have power and/or care-taking responsibilities for the victim. A perpetrator may be a parent or step-parent, a neighbor whose child the victim visits, a teacher or coach, a clergy person or religious school teacher, or an extended family member only visited on holidays. Occasionally this means that when a couple therapist reports suspected abuse, he or she may not be able to identify the suspected perpetrator by name and location. The couple therapist is not responsible for researching the suspected perpetrator but only for reporting the known facts of the suspected abuse. As long as the child is a minor at the time the suspected abuse occurred, a report must be made.

Although a couple therapist must report suspected abuse or neglect in a timely manner, she or he may present partners with several options about how to report it. One or both partners may report the suspected abuse from the couple therapist's office with the couple therapist present; one or both partners and the couple therapist may report in a conference call with the representative of the agency to which the abuse must be reported; or the couple therapist can make the report without either partner present. By allowing the client to decide which way the suspected abuse will be reported while denying her or him the option of not reporting, the couple therapist provides the client with as much agency as possible under the circumstances.

Note that the option of the client reporting without the couple therapist present was not available on the list in the previous paragraph. If the couple therapist offered a client couple that option and then the client couple did not follow through on the promise to report, the couple therapist would be vulnerable to criminal and civil charges. Thus, couple therapists are advised to protect themselves by being present for the reporting, irrespective of who is presenting the information to the relevant agency.

When a couple therapist determines that a partner is a danger to himself or herself, the couple therapist has similar options about reporting. One of the partners can call the local emergency number from the couple therapist's office or the couple therapist can place the call with the vulnerable partner in the room. If the partner leaves the room, the couple therapist must report immediately and include the information that the client has left.

If the client is a suspected danger to others, the couple therapist need not offer the client the option of participating in reporting unless the couple therapist feels safe himself or herself. If the couple therapist does not feel safe, she or he can report her or his suspicions immediately after the client has left the session and without informing the client of her or his intention. If the client meets the criteria of suspected danger to self or others in a telephone conversation or other communication that is not face-to-face, the couple therapist will be asked whether he or she knows where the client is, even though the couple therapist is not responsible for obtaining accurate information about either a perpetrator or victim's location. The writer once asked in a phone conversation where the client was. The client immediately disconnected the call and did not answer when she called back. Law enforcement was not optimistic about finding the client; however, the report was made and a search of the general area ensued.

While a discussion of suicide is beyond the scope of this textbook, it is important for every aspiring couple therapist to remember that his or her first duty is to keep herself or himself safe. Couple therapists do not go to the home of a couple client when they receive a call that one partner is suicidal or perpetrating violence. Rather, couple therapists call the appropriate agency or 9-1-1. While the couple therapist must act in a timely manner to ensure the safety of others, she or he has the right and responsibility to protect himself or herself and can in fact make the situation worse by not doing so.

It is also important to remember that when a client is determined to harm herself or himself and does not want to be rescued, there is nothing a couple therapist can do to prevent the harm. Clients sometimes go to great lengths to hide their intentions and plans. It is neither reasonable nor anticipated that a couple therapist read the client's mind, however much the couple therapist and those who survive the client may wish it had been possible.

Stop and Think:

Be sure to include your responses in your journal.

1. How might your life experiences predispose you to be comfortable working with abuse perpetrators?
2. How might your life experiences predispose you to be comfortable working with abuse victims?
3. What about your life experience would require you to remain self-aware about its impact on your work with either perpetrators or victims?
4. When you read about working with suicidal clients, what was your first reaction? What meaning do you ascribe to it?

Conclusions

In this chapter, you read about when couple therapy is contraindicated. You also read about how to make referrals for services other than couple therapy both in addition to and occasionally instead of couple therapy. You also learned about when these services would be indicated. Some of the services to which couple therapists refer are for one or both partners separately.

Others are for the couple. Working as part of a team to maximize the benefits of a variety of services for the couple was also addressed.

A wide variety of referral needs was described. These included referrals to other mental health professionals for divorce support and recovery, grief work, individual psychotherapy, child psychotherapy, family psychotherapy, spiritual counseling, patient-caretaker support groups, hospice, and medication evaluation and management. Referrals also included legal services, medical services, rehabilitation and adult day care, public health, and social services. Specifics of referring and reporting were detailed and examples from Liz and Martin's extended family were included.

References

Becker, E. (1973). *The denial of death*. New York NY: Simon and Schuster.

Creativity and Madness Conference. (Summer 2007).

Esposito, J. & Hattem, A. (2017). *Introduction to family counseling. A case study approach*. Los Angeles CA: Sage.

Kubler-Ross, E. (1969). *On death and dying. What the dying have to teach doctors, nurses, clergy and their own families*. New York NY: Scribner.

Napier, A. Y. & Whitaker, C. (1978). *The family crucible*. New York: Harper & Row.

CHAPTER 13

What's Next for Liz and Martin, the Couple Therapist, and You?

Learning Objectives

1. Describe several possibilities for how a couple's issues might resolve.
2. Discuss the impact of each of these possibilities on the couple and their couple therapist.
3. Illustrate the components of termination.
4. Review and reflect upon your journal assignments.
5. Review and reflect upon your world view.
6. Review and reflect upon your impressions of Liz and Martin and their couple therapist.
7. Describe the possibilities for Liz and Martin's couple therapist.
8. Explore what is next for you as a student.

In this concluding chapter, you will examine the various possibilities for how Liz and Martin's couple therapy ended. You will also learn about the process of ending couple therapy, also known as termination. A third section of this chapter revisits the experience of being their couple therapist in order to exemplify the impact of the ending of couple therapy upon couple therapists.

As your introductory class about couple therapy draws to a close, you will also draw conclusions about your own future working with couples from what you have learned and thought about while reading this textbook and completing the suggested exercises. Finally, you will read the writer's reflections on couple therapy, not as facts but as a glimpse into the thoughts of one couple therapist after many years of working with couples.

What's Next for Liz and Martin?

We left Liz, Martin, and their couple therapist during an emotionally difficult session with several possible outcomes, two of which were described. The transcript from Chapter 10 is included here for review.

LIZ: We had a bad night last night. [Glaring at Martin] You tell her.

MARTIN: [Quietly] I'm fine, Liz. Go ahead.

LIZ: [Frowning, shaking her head, and turning to the couple therapist] It was 9 o'clock at night, I'm on the phone listening to my mom crying about how awful it is to be alone and then asking me—me!—whether she should accept a coffee invitation from some "cute" man she met at church. And in the midst of all this, MJ gets up and starts running around and calling for us. And Martin's all plugged into his computer and completely ignoring his son. Just expected me to take care of it without even checking to see what I was doing. What if it had been a professional call? [Liz had negotiated a half-time position with her law firm.] So I said to my mother, "Mom, MJ is up and I need to go see what he needs." And she goes, "Now that you're a working girl, I would think that husband of yours might help you" in that disapproving voice of hers. I don't know what was worse: Martin apparently expecting me to do everything or my mom saying I'm a bad mother because I work at the same time she's criticizing him for not sharing parenting. [To Martin, raising her voice] I can't believe your level of disrespect for me.

MARTIN: I told you I was sorry, Liz. I know when one of the kids needs us, I'm as responsible as you are.

LIZ: [To CT] The contrite husband [rolls eyes] as always. [To Martin] But that doesn't cut it, Martin. You need to pay attention to me and the kids, not just keep apologizing because you never do.

MARTIN: I can't go back and undo last night, Liz. And you yelling at me isn't going to change that.

LIZ: Oh, now it's my fault for "yelling"? How about you stop acting like you don't have to be a father just because I don't work full time anymore.

CT: Let me interrupt. I hear how upset you both are.

LIZ: [Sarcastically] That's nice, but he's not. He's never upset. [Quietly] It's always me.

CT: I've noticed how easy it is for you to fall back into old fights about being parents and about Liz's career. And I keep wondering what is getting in the way of you both getting what you want and need.

MARTIN: I think it's habit. [Liz looks confused] No, Liz, I really do. I think we got in the habit of you being the one to be sure the kids are OK and take care of them when they're not. It made sense to me, because you were around more. But it doesn't work when I'm home.

This session could have continued in several ways. We will explore the two addressed in Chapter 10, as well as other possible outcomes for Liz and Martin's couple therapy in the next three subsections of this chapter.

Couple Issues Resolve

The following transcript continues the session and defines what is next for Liz and Martin. The last two statements from the transcript above are repeated for coherence.

CT: I've noticed how easy it is for you to fall back into old fights about being parents and about Liz's career. And I keep wondering what is getting in the way of you both getting what you want and need.

MARTIN: I think it's habit. [Liz looks confused] No, Liz, I really do. I think we got in the habit of you being the one to be sure the kids are OK and take care of them when they're not. It made sense to me, because you were around more. But it doesn't work when I'm home.

LIZ: No, it doesn't.

MARTIN: So what do you want me to do when you say, "I've been at work all day today. I'll go take care of it"?

LIZ: Oh. Well... [Pause] I guess I'd like you to follow my lead.

MARTIN: And that means paying attention to what you want, and not to the kids, on a day you've worked?

LIZ: Well, if you'd been paying attention last night, you would have known I was stuck on the phone and that MJ needed one of us.

CT: Were you two in the same room?

LIZ: No.

CT: Then I'm curious how he would have known you were on the phone?

LIZ: Oh. Well, he could have checked when he heard MJ.

MARTIN: Sure, Liz. I could have scooped up MJ and put him back in bed, and then you would have been furious because you'd been at work all day and wanted to do it yourself.

CT: Yes, and listening to the two of you I'm wondering whether it would help to plan ahead. Like, decide that on Liz's work nights she'll take responsibility for the kids and on nights after she's been at home with them, Martin, you will. Or ask each other on a day-by-day basis. Or something, anything, where you would each know who was going to attend to MJ and Christina so neither of you would have to guess.

This transcript segment began with the couple therapist posing a question about Liz and Martin's couple dynamics, specifically by her asking what they thought prevented them from resolving their issues about Liz's work and their parenting responsibilities. It then segued into a strategic discussion, as the couple therapist guided Liz and Martin toward negotiating a way to prevent the conflict that had occurred the previous evening from recurring in the future. The couple therapist encouraged them to attempt what they did in the session on their own at home in order to generalize their listening and negotiating skills.

Stop and Think:

Be sure to include your responses in your journal.

1. What theoretical model(s) was the couple therapist using?
2. What might you have done differently had you been the couple therapist? Explain your answer in terms of the theoretical model(s) that best fits your approach.

After Liz and Martin agreed that they wanted to continue strategizing on their own, the couple therapist asked them to determine a time to do so before the next session, allowing them to experiment and learn whether they were ready to negotiate on their own. If they were unable to strategize without devolving into their repetitive argument, she believed it in their best interest to return to the question of what interfered and find a way to circumvent the obstacles to resolution as quickly as possible.

The couple therapist's intervention in this transcript segment created a context in which Liz and Martin could think through how they wished to simultaneously manage parenting their children and meeting each other's needs. Strategizing alone is unlikely to resolve the larger issue of repeated conflict around the same issues, and failure to resolve recurring conflict often increases feelings of frustration and hopelessness about the relationship for couples, as it had for Liz and Martin. Therefore, the couple therapist revisited the important question of what prevented Liz and Martin from resolving their conflict around careers and parenting after they agreed on a time to practice their negotiating skills at home.

CT: I think it's important to return to the question of what stops each of you from getting what you want from the other. It seems especially important for you to find a way to get what you need from each other about parenting and about Liz's career, because those are the two issues that consistently trigger unresolved arguments.

LIZ: I'm sorry. I lost what you were asking.

CT: I'm wondering what gets in the way and stops each of you from getting what you want from the other. It's not that you don't both want to give it; it's that something prevents the giving from happening.

MARTIN: That's a tough question.

CT: I know, but it's almost as though something compels you to argue instead of change. I see how hard you work here and your good intentions when you leave. And then something like the events of last night happen and you're set back. I think we need to figure out what stops you from using the tools you have and your motivation to change when you're in those kid/career situations.

LIZ: I get so angry I can't even think at those times. I don't know why.

CT: Connect the dots for me. MJ is running around, you're on the phone comforting your mother and also feeling frustrated with her demands, and Martin is getting to do his thing. Something about that triggers your anger.

LIZ: It's that he's not paying attention.

CT: I get the sense that's later. You were listening to your mother and frustrated with her neediness and it sounded like upset that she's asking your opinion about dating before MJ started running around. What's happening then, for you as you're listening to your mother?

LIZ: [Snorts] I want to reach through the phone and strangle her. I mean, really, she has to talk to me about this [expletive]?!

CT: So you're already angry at your mother, and very reasonably so. Yet you don't tell her.

LIZ: Let's not go there, OK? That would trigger a whole range of [expletive] about what a bad daughter I am.

CT: I agree. The point isn't Sally. It's that you were already angry at someone when you heard MJ calling for his parents. What happened then, when you first heard him?

LIZ: [Closes eyes, sighs] I wanted to tell my mother to shut up, my son needed me. I wanted to tell her to shut up before that, but the pressure got much worse when I heard him.

CT: Tell her.

LIZ: I can't. She's...

CT: If you could, if there were no consequences, what would you say?

LIZ: [Pleading] I want to take care of my son.

CT: Sounds like you're begging her.

LIZ: What?

CT: Sounds like you're saying, "Please let me go take care of my son" and not, "Shut up, Mom, MJ needs me" or, "Shut up, Mom" even before MJ started running around.

LIZ: Oh.

CT: Tell her to shut up.

LIZ: [Softly] Shut up, Mom.

CT: Not convincing.

LIZ: Shut the [expletive] up! My kid needs me. You know, you're not the only person in the world who's lost a husband. Go to church and find widows instead of men. Talk to Barbara. [Sarcastically] Oh, I forgot, she's sick of listening to you. Well, I'm sick of hearing about it, too!

MARTIN: Liz…

CT: [To Martin] Let her. It's important.

LIZ: She's lived here all her life, and if I'm the only person she can talk to, that's pretty pathetic. [Sighs] But she needs someone.

CT: And you can't be that person for her, not the only person, because in addition to being a good daughter you have a husband and two children and a career to think about, and being a good wife and mother and lawyer are all important to you, too.

LIZ: No, I can't be her only person. But I can't say those things.

CT: That's a different subject, and an important one. What I'm wondering right now is whether that anger you think you can't show your mother boiled over at Martin when MJ was running around calling for one of you.

LIZ: [Pause] Like I want him to save me from having to do anything about my mother and get mad 'cause he doesn't?

CT: I suspect you know the answer to that excellent question.

LIZ: I hate to admit it, but yes.

CT: OK, so that's one thing that gets in the way of you both getting what you want. Your mother is pressuring you, you want to take care of MJ, and Martin can protect you from having to tell your mother to shut the [expletive] up by intercepting MJ. Is that what you want him to do?

Note: The couple therapist mirrored Liz's use of strong language in order to communicate empathy and validation for Liz's anger at her mother.

LIZ: Yes. [Frowns] No, I want to take care of my son. I mean, I want his help. But if MJ is running around, I'm happy to catch him and settle him back in bed.

CT: [Nods] Martin, I noticed you wanted to stop Liz's anger at her mom, even though it eventually came back on you.

MARTIN: I don't think I realized that it came back at me. But, yeah, her anger makes me uncomfortable.

CT: What was happening for you when you interrupted her and I stopped you.

MARTIN: Discomfort.

CT: About?

MARTIN: Disrespecting her mother. Sally's a mess, and I think Liz is right that she's isolated herself and is now too dependent on Liz. Barbara would probably tell her to shut the, excuse me, [expletive] up, and she knows that and also knows Liz won't. I wish I didn't have to say this, but I think Sally takes advantage of Liz's goodness.

Note: Martin also mirrored Liz and CT's strong language, yet his apology suggested he was less comfortable with it than either Liz or CT was.

CT: And because she's her mother, you'd rather Liz was angry at you than at Sally?

MARTIN: What? No. [Pause] Maybe. Yes, I guess her anger at her mother makes me more uncomfortable than her anger at me.

CT: You can take her anger and Sally can't?

MARTIN: No, Sally's tough. But she's her mother.

CT: And that's sacred?

MARTIN: Yes.

CT: It sounds like being her mother gives Sally permission to treat Liz any way she wants, to ignore her needs and the other demands on her life, including you and your children.

MARTIN: Well, no, Sally should be respectful, too. But I guess it's on Liz if she isn't, yes.

CT: I think that's another impediment to the two of you getting what you want. Liz wants to tell Sally to shut up and let her parent her son, Liz holds in her anger at Sally, and Martin thinks it would be disrespectful of Sally if she didn't. So Liz's anger is right there when MJ gets up and given the choice of turning it on Sally or Martin, you both agree it's better if she directs her anger at Martin. I wonder whether that's what you're fighting about, that you're both hesitant for different reasons to turn the anger where it belongs and so it undermines you getting what you need from the other.

Note: The couple therapist described the result of Martin's value while not challenging the value itself.

LIZ: So then since neither of us wants me to tell Sally to shut up, he needs to pay attention to the kids while I'm babysitting her, right? But you know what, that isn't what I really want. I want to take care of MJ myself.

CT: Tell Martin you'd rather take care of MJ than listen to your mother.

LIZ: My mom says the same things over and over again, and MJ will only be little once. I want to take care of him.

MARTIN: [Thoughtful] OK. That makes sense. Yeah, OK.

CT: I suspect there are other situations that come up that include demands, like work, that compete with caring for and being with your children, Liz. What I heard you say was that MJ and Christina will only be little for awhile. And instead of Martin taking care of them for you, you want your mother to find other people to turn to so you can be with them when you're not at work. I wonder how these things that get in the way of getting what you want from each other about parenting also apply about your career.

Stop and Think:

Be sure to include your responses in your journal.

1 What theoretical model(s) did the couple therapist use to guide her interventions?

2. What were your reactions as you read the transcript?
3. Were you comfortable with the couple client's use of the implied expletives? Explain your answer.
4. Were you comfortable with the couple therapist's use of the implied expletives? Explain your answer.
5. What might the couple therapist have done differently about Liz's anger? What would you have done differently?
6. What might the couple therapist have done differently about Martin's anger? What would you have done differently?
7. What might the couple therapist have done differently about Liz and Martin's couple dynamics? What would you have done differently?

The couple therapist set the stage for Liz and Martin to work on the issues that repeatedly brought them to couple therapy: how Liz balances career with family and what each needs from the other in order for Liz to make her choice about balancing family and career for them as a couple and a family. She also addressed not only the fact but also an example of how resolution of their disagreements can be undermined by extraneous factors both inside and outside their relationship. She hypothesized that once they were able to prevent extraneous factors and their anxiety about them from undermining resolution of their disagreements, they would begin the process of terminating couple therapy.

A couple therapist rarely knows what happens to a couple after couple therapy ends. They may live happily together into old age or regress in the face of new challenges and dissolve their relationship. Myriad other possibilities for remaining together or decoupling exist. Part of the ambiguity of practicing couple therapy involves rarely knowing long-term outcomes for couple clients.

Stop and Think:

Be sure to include your responses in your journal.

1. List your reactions to not knowing the long-term outcome of your couple therapy work with couple clients. If anything on the list leaves you feeling uncomfortable, note it and think about what you might do to feel more comfortable.

2 Revisit your first journal entry, made as you read the introduction to this textbook. What were the similarities and differences between what you wrote in that assignment and your response to Prompt 1 above?

Couple Issues Become Irreconcilable Differences

Sometimes, the issue that brought the couple to couple therapy undermines the relationship before it can be resolved. The relationship may have been irretrievable even before the couple presented for couple therapy. Couples may present for couple therapy with so much anger and hopelessness that the relationship is no longer salvageable. These couples may be seeking an expert's corroboration or reassuring themselves they did everything possible to save the relationship.

Other times, couples may appear to make progress only to discover their differences are irreconcilable, in the opinion of both or at least one of the partners. The following transcript repeats Scenario 2, found in Chapter 10 to refresh your memory and then describes what might have followed.

CT: I've noticed how easy it is for you to fall back into old fights about being parents and about Liz's career. And I keep wondering, what is getting in the way of you both getting what you want and need?

MARTIN: I think it's habit. [Liz looks confused] No, Liz, I really do. I think we got in the habit of you being the one to be sure the kids are OK and take care of them when they're not. It made sense to me, because you were around more. But it doesn't work when I'm home.

LIZ: You know, I don't think I care what it is. I think I am done fighting about this. I'm sick of being angry.

CT: Yes, and yet what I'm hearing in the anger is how much you still want your marriage to be alright, how much you want Martin to work with you to take care of the kids.

LIZ: I don't think so.

CT: Maybe not. I'm not sure you'd be so angry if you didn't care, though.

LIZ: Really, I don't want to go there. I'm exhausted, and I'm done. I told you when we started that I wanted to find a way to live with Martin until the kids are grown, but maybe he'd be a better father if I weren't there when he was with them.

MARTIN: Liz...

LIZ: You two can continue talking. I'm done. [Gets up and walks toward the door.]

CT: I'd like you to stay and finish the session, whatever you decide now or afterward.

LIZ: Thanks, but no.

MARTIN: Liz, please.

[LIZ EXITED.]

Stop and Think:

Be sure to include your responses in your journal.

1. Do you think Liz and Martin stopped couple therapy after this session? Explain your answer.
2. Do you think Liz and Martin separated and divorced after this session? Explain your answer.
3. If you think Liz and Martin continued their marriage, do you think they did it with or without additional couple therapy? Explain your answer.

Before he left the couple therapy session, Martin told the couple therapist they would let her know whether they wanted their next appointment time. Martin left a message a few days later cancelling the appointment. Two weeks after that, the couple therapist received an email from Liz requesting one more session with the goal being to obtain the couple therapist's advice about how to tell their children they were separating.

COUPLE THERAPIST: Please fill me in on what's happened in the last couple of weeks.

LIZ: [To Martin] You tell her.

MARTIN: We decided, well, mostly Liz...

LIZ: Right, blame me.

MARTIN: OK, we both decided that it isn't working, between us. We've tried, we wanted to be a family for our kids, but we just can't keep banging our heads against the wall like this.

CT: So that decision is made, and you're both comfortable, if not happy, about it?

MARTIN: [Tearful] No, I'm not comfortable. But Liz thinks it'll be best for everyone in the long term, and I can't change her mind. If we are going to do it, then sooner rather than later would be good.

CT: Has either of you moved out?

MARTIN: No. We wanted your advice about how to tell the kids first. They're so young, I hate to do this to them. And I'm worried about them.

CT: Before we get to telling the children, I need to offer you both referrals for attorneys.

LIZ: [Snorts] No offense, but I've got colleagues.

CT: Yes, of course. Martin?

MARTIN: I really don't care.

CT: I think you will look back and be happy you had a consultation. Whether or not you and Liz complete the process and divorce, you need to understand the process, your rights, and what you need to do for yourself and your future.

MARTIN: I don't see much future.

CT: I know, not right now. But you will again, and it'd be nice not to regret how you'd handled things now.

MARTIN: OK.

CT: [Hands him a list of three attorneys and their contact information]

MARTIN: I hate this.

CT: I know. There are also support groups for separating couples, sometimes called divorce care, and people usually go before they're divorced. There's one at [name] and another at [name].

MARTIN: [Writing the names on the attorney referral list] I don't think I like the idea of being in a group.

CT: I can also give either or both of you the names of therapists for individual work. It's not a bad idea after a separation.

MARTIN: Not now.

CT: OK. I've already bombarded you with a lot of information. The attorney is the most important. Let me know if you want a referral to an individual psychotherapist. There's one more thing, though, before we talk about the kids.

LIZ: But that's the only reason why we're here.

CT: I know. And I think seeing your physicians, if you haven't recently, is probably a good idea, just to be sure the stress isn't doing anything to you. Attorneys first, MD appointments second, then support group or individual therapy. I know this is a lot to take in, but it's not clear I'm going to see you again so I need to say it all now.

Note: The couple therapist had observed a change in Martin's affect suggesting depressive symptoms and additional weight loss in Liz. Rather than taking couple therapy time when their stated objective was to discuss telling their children they were going to separate, the couple therapist decided to refer them to their physicians for further diagnosis. She decided she would only refer to her specific concerns about either Liz or Martin if they again became relevant during the session.

LIZ: Can we get on with it now?

CT: Liz, I'm wondering whether we need to get your feelings about me out in the open.

LIZ: Look, it's not you. [To Martin] I'm not happy this is happening, either. But if I don't hold the line with both of you, we'll go back to that dysfunctional mess we had, and I really don't want that.

CT: I might be angry at me if I were in your situation.

LIZ: No. I came to you thinking this marriage was impossible. And we all tried. But it turned out I was right, that it's impossible.

MARTIN: Always important to be right, Liz.

LIZ: Shut up, Martin!

CT: It looks like you've lost weight, Liz, and it's only been two and a half weeks.

LIZ: And he's depressed [nods toward Martin]. I don't want to go there.

CT: OK, but both of you, think about seeing your physicians and/or doing some individual therapy.

MARTIN: [Nods]

CT: Now, about the kids: I'd like to begin with your thoughts about what to tell the kids, so I get a sense of what you want to convey, and then we can talk about age-appropriate ways to say it.

LIZ: That Mommy and Daddy fight a lot, which they already know, and we know everyone would be happier if we didn't. And we tried to stop, but we couldn't. So we're going to try living apart and see if that makes things better.

CT: Martin?

MARTIN: I don't know. That sounds good.

CT: I think so, too. I think they can understand it. And it conveys your conclusion that your differences are irreconcilable without blame, which is great.

LIZ: Did you mean *our* conclusion? Or did you mean mine?

CT: Yours, Liz. What bothers you about that?

LIZ: I assumed you'd agree we're hopeless. [Smiles] After all, you've seen us in action.

Note: At this point CT thought, Oh no, Liz. I have a whole other transcript in my head where you two work it out and live reasonably contentedly forever after!

CT: Honestly, I think any relationship becomes hopeless when one partner decides it is.

LIZ: You think I gave up?

CT: I'm still not clear what sounds so bad to you about me saying you decided it was hopeless.

LIZ: Because I'm a hard worker. I'm successful. I don't give up on things.

CT: And you heard me say you gave up on your marriage. Tell me how you view what happened.

LIZ: I decided the fight wasn't worth it anymore, that it wasn't getting us anywhere and the pain was too awful.

CT: So the cost-benefit balance shifted for you.

LIZ: Yes.

CT: And so your options were to continue to work on shifting the cost-benefit or...?

LIZ: Decide it wasn't going to change no matter what we did. Or not soon enough.

MARTIN: Soon enough for what, Liz?

LIZ: Soon enough for me. OK? [To CT] You're always telling me to say what I want. And I said it. I want to stop this useless fighting.

CT: OK.

LIZ: [Nods] OK.

CT: Children sometimes blame themselves, even when their parents haven't been fighting about them.

LIZ: But we were.

CT: Then that's what it sounded like to them. I think you were really fighting about something else, something between you two that has nothing to do with Christina and MJ.

LIZ: Like?

CT: Whether or not you could each get what you want and need from the other. But that's too complicated for young children. And sometimes taking blame is a way for children and adults to feel in control of a situation they aren't in control of, like if I had only done something differently—be a better kid, be a better partner—I could have made everything alright. But it's not one person. And, again, your children are too young to understand that. So you might ask them questions and also assure them that you both love them and will be there to take care of them, just not together. And that it's not their fault, it's one of those things between grown-ups that's difficult to explain. And you might have to explain all this—why you aren't together, that it's not their fault, and that you both love them and will take care of them—over and over again.

LIZ: Do you think we're going to mess up our kids?

CT: Are you worried you will?

LIZ: I wasn't.

MARTIN: I was.

CT: Children, it turns out, are usually pretty resilient. When separating parents listen to their children, even when it hurts, and are there for them, they often do fine, even if there's a rough patch first. If you ever have concerns, though, I'll be happy to give you a referral to someone who works with children and their families.

MARTIN: What do you mean, "When it hurts"?

CT: They may ask you questions about your fighting. And it may be tempting to blame yourself or each other because you're both going to hurt for awhile and that while will be the time your kids are most likely to ask questions. It's important for the kids that they're never in the middle. It's fine for them to see your sadness and know you were very angry at each other. But for kids to hear bad things about their other parent or feel they need to take sides is very hard on them.

MARTIN: I think I see.

LIZ: Thank you. This is helpful.

CT: You're very welcome. I wish I could have done more, that it had turned out differently for the two of you and your children. I also know that separation and divorce are painful events, and it takes awhile for people to heal. It's important for you take care of yourselves, so you can heal. And I think it's important to examine your own roles in what went wrong, so you're less likely to repeat them.

MARTIN: [Tearful] I'm not going to be in another relationship. Liz is the love of my life.

LIZ: [Tearful] I'm sorry, Martin. I think this is for the best, for all of us. And I wish I didn't think that, really, but I do.

Stop and Think:

Be sure to include your responses in your journal.

1. If you had been the couple therapist, how would you have felt during this last session?
2. If you had been the couple therapist, what might you have done differently during this session?
3. Remembering that the couple therapist was going through her own marital dissolution, how might she have been feeling during the session?

This transcript from Liz and Martin's final session with the couple therapist, while painful, did not preclude their reconciling, either before or after a separation or even after a divorce. They had separated and reconciled in the past, before they became parents, and it remained possible they would do so again.

However, Liz, Martin, and the couple therapist could not assume a happy ending for them as a couple. Nor could they predict what life would hold for Liz or Martin following a separation or divorce. Unknowns included whether or not they would fully grieve the dissolution of their relationship so that they could move forward and whether or not one or both would regret the decision and find the other had moved beyond the point of wishing to reconcile. It is not uncommon for the partner who initiated a separation to later wish to reconcile and to discover the other partner, initially so devastated, is no longer interested in reconciling.

Other unknowns involve how Liz and Martin would work together to parent their children and whether each would examine his or her own role in the dissolution of the relationship with an eye toward individual change and avoiding a repetition with someone else of what they had experienced together. Finally, their future, with or without new partners, remained unknown.

Alternative Outcomes of Couple Issues

Western thought tends to dichotomize experience, even though multiple possibilities usually exist. Liz and Martin could have resolved their differences, remained together, and lived happily ever after. Or they could have separated and divorced. Between those extreme outcomes lies a continuum of possibilities, including finding a way to live together contentedly without fully resolving their differences, finding a way to remain together "for the sake of the children" even though anecdotally that can be more difficult for children than parents who divorce, living together reasonably peaceably and at some point reclaiming their joy in being together, continuing to discuss separating without doing it, and continuing to separate and reconcile over the course of many years. Space precludes as detailed a description of each of these possibilities as was given in the two previous subsections.

Stop and Think:

Be sure to include your responses in your journal.

1. Can you think of additional possibilities?
2. Do you think that Liz and Martin were ambivalent about the outcomes of Scenario 1 when they reconciled their differences and remained together? Explain your answer.
3. Even Liz was not ambivalence free as Scenario 2 drew to a close. What are the possibilities in terms of how she handles her sadness and regret that the marriage was ending?

The human condition involves a great deal of ambivalence, despite either-or dichotomies conveying the impression of simplicity. Most people are like Liz and Martin, both loving and angry, wanting and not wanting, and wishing to have their needs met while at the same time hesitant about such satisfaction. Some couples have multiple and conflicting feelings about whether they want to remain together as a couple or go their separate ways, and either or both partners may be internally conflicted about it. The choice is ultimately the couple's; in this respect, the couple therapist is an observer without a voice.

That Liz had lost weight and the couple therapist observed symptoms of depression in Martin might be indications that both were ambivalent about separating. Liz implied ambivalence when she expressed feeling the need to remain firm in her resolve to avoid being swayed by her feelings. Conversely, their ambivalence may have been indicative of their grief for their marriage. Whatever their ambivalence indicated, Liz and Martin did not exhibit the relief that couple therapists sometimes see when the agony of making a decision about a relationship resolves in a decision.

Termination of Couple Therapy

How couple therapy ends becomes relevant as your introduction to couple therapy and this portion of Liz and Martin's story draw to a close.[1] Saying good-bye is part of every human relationship, and the dominant culture

1 Liz and Martin's couple therapy is a prequel to their 2010 family therapy, described by Esposito and Hattem (2017).

is not very good at it. Termination, the clinically relevant term, is thus an important aspect of couple therapy. It is an opportunity to review, reinforce, and enhance the impact of the couple therapy and to reflect on what has happened during couple therapy.

Sometimes, as demonstrated happily when Liz and Martin completed couple therapy and unhappily when they separated, both the couple and the couple therapist agree that they have arrived at an appropriate point at which to end the therapeutic relationship. Other times, a client couple wishing to remain together may not be finished with couple therapy and yet decides to terminate anyway, as Liz and Martin did several times prior to 2002 (see Chapters 1 and 9). In other situations, couple therapists initiate termination of couple therapy, either because of a job change, move, retirement, extended parental or family medical leave, illness, or death.

When the couple therapy work is completed, saying good-bye may be a source of ambivalence for both the client couple and the couple therapist. There are positive feelings associated with the successful completion of couple therapy, sadness and anger when couple therapy ends in the dissolution of the relationship, and sadness about saying good-bye. Because of the prohibition against dual relationships (see Chapter 11), partners and their couple therapists cannot continue relating in any other way when the work of couple therapy is finished.

Termination may be impeded by the client couple's reluctance to experience the discomfort and sadness of saying good-bye. The couple therapist may also experience sadness, which both self-awareness and self-care will help her or him manage. The couple therapist might also validate the sadness and difficulty of saying good-bye, both for the partners and for himself or herself, by acknowledging them verbally during one of the final couple therapy sessions.

Couple clients and their couple therapist sometimes avoid termination with a couple client's flight into illness. A flight into illness involves producing symptoms of distress or ascribing meaning to the symptoms that leads to the belief that they are worse than they are. A flight into illness is a subconscious mechanism for prolonging couple therapy and avoiding saying good-bye to the couple therapist. For example, as couple therapy draws to a close, one partner may raise an entirely new issue. If the couple therapist suspects a flight into illness, for example, because one partner has raised new material more than once as couple therapy has begun to terminate, she or he can address the process directly. Couple therapists can also assure client couples that they may return if need be to get back on track should problems re-emerge.

Sometimes one partner announces at the end of a couple therapy session that the couple has agreed that the time has come to stop sessions. It is reasonable for a couple therapist to request another session with the goal of exploring the decision to terminate and to engage in the process of saying good-bye. If termination is appropriate, validating the partners' experience and framing termination as an opportunity for reflection remain important.

Couples may decide to stop couple therapy even when they acknowledge that work remains to be done to ensure that any positive changes will be maintained. When this happens, the couple therapist may address her or his concerns about stopping couple therapy and her or his assessment of the work to be done. The couple's options for addressing these concerns include continuing couple therapy, terminating anyway, or taking a break and resuming if and when the couple wishes.

When couples agree to begin the termination process, couple therapists move forward with eight components of termination. Although these components do not need to be addressed in any particular order, they cluster in three broad categories: review, maintenance plan, and ending the therapeutic relationship between the couple and the couple therapist, as well as those between each partner and the couple therapist.

The first two components of termination entail review. The couple therapist reviews the couple's initial goals and those added during the process of couple therapy. He or she also reviews what the couple has accomplished and requests input from the partners about their own assessment of where they began and where they currently are as a couple. These components of termination generally do not occur when couples decide to separate.

The next four components of termination involve how the couple can maintain the changes they have made in the face of future stresses or complacency. First, couple therapists ask couple clients to articulate what the partners need to do to maintain the changes they have accomplished. Second, couple therapists ask how the partners might recognize any cues that they are regressing to the previous dynamics that threatened to undermine their relationship. Third, the couple therapist asks the client couple to articulate how partners will manage any regression. The couple therapist can suggest that partners use the techniques they have identified as soon as they notice their previous relationship dynamics emerging. Finally, the couple therapist can suggest the couple client return for further sessions if needed. It may be important to note that getting back on track is far easier than making the changes they have already made. The therapist may also want to suggest that the number of sessions upon return is usually much fewer when a couple seeks help as soon as the partners recognize they cannot accomplish what they wish on their own. If the couple therapist believes either partner would view a return as a failure, she or he can address that concern as part of termination. If a couple has decided to separate, any agreements they made about how to treat each other post-separation can be reviewed.

The last two components of terminating couple therapy focus on the therapeutic relationship and saying good-bye. The couple therapist initiates a conversation about the meaning of the therapeutic relationship to the couple therapist. The couple therapist also allows both partners time to express those feelings that arise for them as they say good-bye to their couple therapist. A couple therapist can also address the couple client's ambivalence about saying good-bye after such an intense and important experience as couple therapy and note his or her own. When couples have decided to separate, these components of termination may be abbreviated.

The following Stop and Think exercise asks you to review and reflect upon this textbook, the class for which you have read it, and your time with Liz and Martin. Because the questions used in termination do not always fit the end of a class, review and reflection are emphasized.

Stop and Think:

Be sure to include your responses in your journal.

1. Review your journal, noting what you would change about what you have written.
2. Reflect on the meaning of the changes you would have made and note your thoughts.
3. How did your increasing knowledge of Liz and Martin enhance the content of what you read? How was it either not helpful or irrelevant?

Students sometimes ask about crying. Saying good-bye at the end of the final session can be an emotionally charged experience for both the partners and the couple therapist. It is not unusual for one or both partners to become tearful. It is also alright for the couple therapist to be tearful, so long as she or he avoids deflecting either partner from his or her own sadness about saying good-bye. This caution is true throughout couple therapy. Partners sometimes reveal information that is emotionally powerful. For the couple therapist to share their sadness, for example at the loss of a beloved pet, or their joy, for example at breaking through a difficult impasse, is appropriate. In the writer's opinion, couple therapists are not automatons and need not behave as though they are. However, expressing emotion must be tempered by care not to distract partners from their own pain or allow couple clients to care for the couple therapist.

The subject of hugging as part of saying good-bye was addressed in Chapter 11. The salient points involve the couple therapist waiting for one of the partners to initiate a hug, respecting that both partners may not wish to hug the couple therapist, and managing the hug in a way most likely to avoid confusing affection with sexuality.

The transcripts in this chapter portrayed some but not all of the aspects of terminating a therapeutic relationship. The couple therapist emphasized different aspects of the couple therapy process and experience and the tone around saying good-bye was different when Liz and Martin completed their couple therapy work and when Liz and Martin decided to separate and ended couple therapy.

In Scenario 1, the couple therapist emphasized Liz and Martin's accomplishments and helped them identify potential triggers and signs of regression, as well as ways to manage a recurrence of symptoms. She offered further sessions on an as-needed basis. She also told Liz and Martin that she had enjoyed working with them, because the feelings were genuine. Had she been at all relieved to see them go, she would have refrained from saying she had enjoyed working with them. The writer has often said to client couples that she has been honored to have earned their trust, to have been part of their journey, and has enjoyed working with them. Again, such positive feelings can be expressed as couple therapy concludes only when they are genuine.

One can imagine that saying good-bye might elicit sadness in all three participants, even as they felt good about their work together and its outcome. One can also imagine Liz initiating a hug to express her affection and appreciation to the couple therapist and Martin only reluctantly following her lead.

Had Liz and Martin separated, termination would, of necessity, have been very different. In Scenario 2, the couple therapist told Liz and Martin that she appreciated how hard they had worked, enjoyed working with them, and wished couple therapy had produced a happier ending. She said these three things because all of them were true and thus could be said genuinely. She did not celebrate joy in a job well done. However, she assured them that from her perspective they worked as hard as they could have and thus recrimination was not warranted.

One concern for separating partners is the potential for both regret and self-recrimination. While some partners do enter couple therapy so that they can assure themselves they have tried everything possible to save their relationship prior to ending it, that was not the case for Liz and Martin. From the couple therapist's perspective, they had done what they could, and even though she believed they could make changes it was not her right to impose that belief upon them after they had decided it was time to end their marriage.

The couple therapist wondered whether, if she had pushed Martin and Liz to engage in individual psychotherapy prior to or concurrently with couple therapy, they could have overcome the hurdles that eventually undermined their relationship. Speculation of this sort undermines a couple therapist's self-esteem. When the couple therapist expressed these sentiments to her peer supervision group, her colleagues reminded her that she, too, had done the best job she could, given the individual and couple issues Liz and Martin had brought to couple therapy.

The couple therapist did not address future signs of regression and how to manage any future regression. Nor did she address achieving goals because neither Liz nor Martin presented with the goal of deciding whether or not to remain together. However, she offered future couple therapy sessions if they found themselves unable to manage a co-parenting relationship sufficiently free of acrimony to avoid damage to their children and each other.

What's Next for the Couple Therapist?

Stop and Think:

Be sure to include your responses in your journal.

1. How do you imagine you would have felt if you had been Liz and Martin's couple therapist saying good-bye to Liz and Martin after the completion of their work together?

2 How do you imagine you would have felt if you had been their couple therapist saying good-bye to Liz and Martin after they decided to separate?
3 What might have left you feeling ambivalent when they left after completion of couple therapy?
4 What might have left you feeling ambivalent when they left after separating?

As noted in the introduction to this textbook, couple therapists must tolerate the ambiguity of the couple therapy process, its outcome, and the couple client's unknown and unknowable future. Couple therapists must also learn to tolerate partners' ambivalence about the work of couple therapy and about their couple therapist.

In the writer's experience, one cannot predict the outcome of couple therapy from outside the couple system. Partners are drawn to one another for many reasons, some cognitively logical and others emotionally logical only when one fully understands the partners and the couple. The writer has worked with partners who seemed to genuinely like and appreciate one another and who decided to separate. She has also worked with partners whose only apparent shared goal and interest was proving that the other was "wrong" and yet who remained together. Ultimately, the decision belongs to the partners and is neither the right nor the responsibility of the couple therapist. The couple therapist is involved as what the writer has termed "tour guide" through the partners' ambivalence and uncertainty as they move toward their shared goal of creating a well-functioning relationship. The couple therapist has no role in the partners' determination of whether the achieved relationship meets both their needs. In other words, the couple therapist uses her or his professional knowledge and skills to guide partners, and then leaves it to them to determine how to use her or him. While the couple therapist may advocate for continued hope and express her or his own, if genuine, she or he cannot prevent one or both partners from basing a decision on their belief that the relationship is hopeless.

Liz and Martin's couple therapist found herself feeling vindicated that her marital difficulties were not entirely her fault when Liz and Martin worked together to complete couple therapy. She believed that her contribution to Liz and Martin's success was a testament to her ability to understand what partners need to do for one another and for their relationship to change their couple dynamics. She had worried that the demise of her marriage indicated that she was not a good partner and concluded that a good couple therapist must have the potential to be a good partner. Her individual psychotherapist suggested that being a successful partner also entailed enacting what she had learned about couples and about herself as a couple therapist.

In the scenario in which Liz and Martin separated, the couple therapist found herself questioning her ability to practice couple therapy. She reviewed her personal and professional failures with her individual psychotherapist and also talked about what she could have done differently with her peer supervision group. As noted earlier in the chapter, her peer supervision group reminded her that she, like Liz and Martin, had done everything she could and that their decision to separate was beyond her power to control.

During couple therapy with Liz and Martin, the couple therapist practiced a variety of forms of self-awareness and self-care. She remained in touch with her own defensiveness, her desire to prod them forward, and her tendency to contrast Martin's treatment of Liz with how her estranged husband treated her. She noted when she recoiled at seeing their names on her calendar and when she became frustrated with them. She engaged in positive self-talk during sessions and outside of sessions she exercised, journaled, talked to friends about difficult workdays, talked about her reactions in peer supervision, and continued her own individual psychotherapy throughout the time she worked with them.

What's Next for You as a Couple Therapist?

How does the process of terminating couple therapy relate to completing your introduction to couple therapy? Like couple therapy, the end of a book or a class is a time to reflect on where one began and what one has accomplished.

The following suggestions for reflection, discussion, and writing will take you through a more detailed process than the previous termination review and reflection did. The prompts are more extensive in nature, because in this part of the chapter you are contemplating what is next for you regarding couple therapy, rather than what occurred during a single term in a single class. These prompts explore knowledge, skills, preferences, self-awareness, and self-care. In the process, you will review your journal in more depth and hopefully summarize and draw conclusions from your experience of reading this textbook.

The first set of prompts reviews the questions you were previously asked about your world view and asks you to reflect upon how the class you are completing and its required textbook may have changed your world view.

Stop and Think:

Self-Reflection:

Using your journal and any new reflections that arise, think, discuss, and/or write about your current world view.

1. How does the world work (predictable, random, pre-determined)?
2. Are choices dichotomous?
3. What roles do fairness and order play in how the world works?
4. Are you most comfortable with people who are rational, intuitive, emotive, or?
5. How do you resolve contradictions and conflict (win/lose, accommodate, compromise, collaborate, negotiate, problem solve, ignore)?
6. What is mental health (balance, absence of symptoms)? What is mental illness?
7. How do people best learn?
8. Do you trust your intuitive responses?
9. Do you trust other people?
10. How much responsibility do individuals have for their lives?
11. How much control do individuals have over their lives?
12. How do you negotiate relationships?

The following set of prompts asks you to review and reflect about the various topics covered in this textbook.

Stop and Think

Self-Reflection:

Using your journal and any new reflections that arise, think, discuss, and/or write about the following prompts.

1. Review your initial views of coupling, including how partners come together and live intimately together over time. Summarize what you have learned that you will take with you into your own life about coupling and maintaining an intimate partnership.
2. List at least three factors that contribute to couple distress and that may be susceptible of change in couple therapy.
3. Did you find yourself noticing new things about couples you know or observe as you read the book and participated in class? Describe what you noticed.
4. To which theory were you most drawn? What was attractive to you about that theory?
5. Which other theories were also compelling for you? What drew you to them?
6. How might you integrate these theories into a cohesive approach to couple therapy?
7. How do your theoretical preferences reflect how you view the world? How do they reflect your intersectional identity?
8. To which special topics in couple therapy were you drawn? What did you find interesting or exciting about them?
9. Describe at least three reactions you have had to what you have learned and what you have surmised from your readings about the experience of doing couple therapy.
10. What aspects of the experience of doing couple therapy did you find fascinating?
11. What aspects of the experience of doing couple therapy did you find interesting?
12. What aspects of the experience of doing couple therapy did you find uninteresting?
13. What aspects of the experience of doing couple therapy did you find horrifying?

14 Think about the range of professionals to whom couple therapists refer. Would any of these be a better fit for you than becoming a couple therapist? Explain your answer.
15 What did you notice when you practiced self-awareness? Is it a practice you continued? If so, what if any benefits have you found?
16 Did you practice self-care prior to reading this textbook? How?
17 Did you begin a self-care practice as you read this textbook? If yes, how has it impacted your sense of well-being? If no, what stopped you?
18 If you were going to practice couple therapy, what do you imagine would be your most and least favorite aspects of the job? Explain your conclusions.

Any professional who works with people, whether individually or in couple, family, or other one-on-one or group contexts will encounter people who evoke positive and negative, as well as ambivalent, feelings. The following group of six reflection prompts addresses your responses to the couple client and couple therapist with whom you have become familiar while reading this book.

Stop and Think:

Using your journal and any new reflections that arise, think, discuss, and/or write about the following prompts. You might prefer to cite specifics as you respond to this prompt or reflect on your general impressions of comfort and discomfort.

1 What did you like and/or dislike about Liz Manning-Jones?
2 What did you like and/or dislike about Martin Jones?
3 What did you like and/or dislike about Liz and Martin as a couple?
4 What did you like and/or dislike about the couple therapist (CT)?
5 What made you uncomfortable as you read the transcripts?
6 What did you learn about managing ambivalence and ambiguity as you read about Liz, Martin, and their couple therapist?

At this point, you may have a good idea of whether couple therapy or working with couples in another professional capacity is a good fit for your preferences and career goals. A final group of six reflection prompts addresses your conclusions about whether you wish to consider working with couples, either as a couple therapist or in another professional capacity.

Stop and Think:

Using your journal and any new reflections that arise, think, discuss, and/or write about the following prompts. You might prefer to cite specifics as you respond to this prompt or reflect on your general impressions of comfort and discomfort.

1. As you read the transcripts, when did you think, "I'd like to do this"?
2. As you read the transcripts, when did you think, "I don't know how I could possibly do this"?
3. As you read the transcripts, when did you think, "This is not what I want to do"?
4. Based on what you have learned in this textbook and the class for which it was assigned and from classes and texts about individual psychotherapy, what do you see as the advantages of individual psychotherapy over couple therapy?
5. Based on what you have learned in this textbook and the class for which it was assigned and from classes and texts about individual psychotherapy, what do you see as the advantages of couple therapy over individual psychotherapy?
6. Reflecting upon your own temperament, history, and style of relating to people, would you prefer to practice individual psychotherapy, couple therapy, or some of each? Explain your response.

These three groups of prompts, as well as the class and textbook you are completing may have elucidated for you whether or not you wish to continue your studies of couple therapy with the goal of one day practicing. Ruling out options that may have appeared to be career possibilities is as important an aspect of your education as is arriving at a career decision.

If you have determined that you do not wish to work with couples in any capacity after the work you have put into reading this textbook and the class for which it was assigned, you can now focus on exploring other career options that are a better fit for you.

If you are an undergraduate student interested in practicing couple therapy, continued study would involve exploring master's or doctoral level training programs in what continues to be called marriage and family therapy. These programs may be found in departments of counselor education and of human development and family studies. These departments, in turn, are housed in schools of education and of human ecology. While clinical psychology, social work, and counselor education programs often include coursework about couple and family therapy, graduates of these programs must complete a set of specified courses and seek internships and post-degree supervision by licensed marriage and family therapists in order to qualify for marriage and family licensure. Mental health professionals who have been trained to work with couples can list couple therapy as a specialty, but only those with marriage and family therapy licenses can call themselves couple therapists.

If you are a graduate student, you already know about professional distinctions and gate-keeping. Your choice is whether to pursue additional training in couple therapy if you are not already in a marriage and family therapy program.

If you are either an undergraduate or graduate student interested in working with couples in a capacity other than couple therapy, you can explore graduate and professional training programs in your chosen field that include training in working with couples. For example, if you are interested in medicine, you can explore medical schools and residencies where the faculty includes at least one member who shares your interest in couples. The same applies to nursing schools, law schools, social work programs, schools of business, schools of public health, law enforcement training, and any additional training you may need to work in social services.

Author Reflections about Couple Therapy

Perhaps the best way to close this textbook is to return to the themes first mentioned in the introduction chapter. These involve the concept of Schopenhauer's porcupines, the ambivalence about intimacy that couples bring to couple therapy, and the intensity of guiding couples through their own strong emotions to a relationship that feels safe and comfortable to both partners. You have learned about how couple dynamics may impede relationship goals and about ways to intervene. You have learned about the impact of the work on the client couple and on the couple therapist, who brings her or his own ambivalence about coupledom to the work. You have learned about the ethical, as well as emotional challenges of practicing couple therapy and the need for self-awareness and self-care.

Couple therapy is a complex phenomenon. Couple relationships include not only two unique individuals but also their dynamics, the history of their relationship, and their sociocultural and temporal context. The partners' relationship with each other is complex, intense, and of utmost importance to them. It underlies each one's self-esteem. And through the processes of second-order cybernetics and induction, the couple therapist inevitably becomes part of the complexity and, more importantly, the intensity of the couple's relationship.

In all honesty, the writer has had a love-hate relationship with couple therapy throughout her career. It can be intensely painful and discouraging, as the couple therapist's work with Liz and Martin exemplified. Alternatively, couple therapy can quite suddenly and for no apparent reason shift from the couple being stuck and the couple therapist barely able to convey hope in the face of their hopelessness to both partners experiencing an a-ha moment that alters the dynamics of their relationship. At these times, practicing couple therapy is an incredibly exhilarating experience. Even after years of practice, it is impossible for the writer to predict if and when such a shift will occur, and thus beginning couple therapy with a new couple client always entails willingness to engage in an uncertain, or ambiguous, adventure.

While Chapter 10 attempted to explain the experience of being a couple therapist, actually sharing partners' experience as they progress through couple therapy is, in many ways, indescribable. While the writer has loved moments of client couple revelation and change, the more hopeless times have been, quite literally, horrible. The ups and downs of the couple's progress and decisions have at times challenged the writer's confidence in her professional abilities and motivation to continue practicing.

The writer finds the puzzle of whether or when a couple will move from stuck to unstuck and the elusive manner in which that seems to happen challenging and therefore compelling. She finds the social constructs around mating, people's ambivalence about the intimacy inherent in being part of a couple, and the phenomenon of what partners do together being so much more than the two people involved all fascinating. She prefers the practice of couple therapy to family therapy and the practice of individual psychotherapy to couple therapy because she has found that the fewer people there are in the room the more intense the relationships are. Additionally, the work of many sessions rarely seems to fall apart over the course of a week with individual psychotherapy clients, as it does with some frequency with couple clients. Her practice has usually included about one-third couples and two-thirds individuals.

The writer has found that the intensity of a couple client's pain, when present in a session, is more emotionally difficult and exhausting for their couple therapist than the pain of an individual psychotherapy client. By contrast, families tend to diffuse the pain of a particular member. To practice any therapy modality effectively, the writer believes a psychotherapist must be willing to experience clients' pain while with them during sessions. However, it is equally essential that he or she leave that pain at the office so that it does not follow the psychotherapist into other aspects of her or his life. It is crucial to leave behind the intense emotional experience of practicing couple therapy, even when a session has ended happily. A psychotherapist needs boundaries between his or her life as a couple therapist and his or her life away from work to avoid burn-out. Maintaining these boundaries requires self-awareness and is an important part of self-care.

This book would not have been written if the rewards of practicing couple therapy did not exceed the challenges for the writer. For readers who choose to move forward in their couple therapy training, know that this is the beginning of an incredible journey.

Conclusions

This chapter has explored several possible outcomes of couple therapy for couples and specifically for Liz and Martin. Ambivalence and ambiguity, two concepts with which you were first acquainted in the introduction to this textbook, were revisited.

As your reading has drawn to a close, you have also learned about the process of terminating couple therapy. The process of terminating couple therapy and its parallels at the conclusion of the class for which you were assigned this book were also described.

You have reflected upon your learning experience while reading this textbook and the transcripts of Liz and Martin's couple therapy. You have also examined ambiguity surrounding Liz and Martin's and the couple therapist's futures.

Finally, you have examined your own conclusions about your interest in practicing couple therapy or a related field involving working with couples in another capacity. While you may find your interests changing over the course of a career or find yourself making a career shift in mid-career, you have identified and reflected upon where your interest now lies, what if any aspects of working with couples resonated with you, and how to explore what is next for you.

INDEX

D

I

L

M

N

O

P

R

S

T

U

W

Y

CPSIA information can be obtained
at www.ICGtesting.com
Printed in the USA
FSHW022042120121
77648FS